The violent friend

Books by Margaret Mackay

Non-fiction
The Violent Friend: The story of Mrs Robert Louis Stevenson
Angry Island

Novels
The Little General
The Wine Princes
The Four Fates
Summer at the Spa
Give Him My Love
Sharon
Mrs Dale of Peking
Homeward the Heart
For All Men Born
Valiant Dust
Lady with Jade
Like Water Flowing

Travel
I Live in a Suitcase

Children's Fiction
Dolphin Boy
The Poetic Parrot
The Flowered Donkey

The violent friend

The story of Mrs Robert Louis Stevenson 1840–1914

By Margaret Mackay

J M Dent and Sons Limited

Made in Great Britain at the
Aldine Press, Letchworth, Hertfordshire
for J M Dent & Sons Limited
Aldine House, Bedford Street, London

First published in this edition 1969
© Abridged edition Margaret Mackay, 1969
This edition is an abridgment of the edition published
in the United States by Doubleday & Co. Inc., 1968

SBN 460 03880 x

Dedication

May one dedicate this adventurous life story to the memory of Fanny's favourite in the Robert Louis Stevenson circle – her compatriot, Henry James, the only one with whom she never quarrelled?

He was fascinated by the phenomenon of the controversial marriage, and must often have thought of using this tiny pioneer, brave and strange – 'tiger and tiger lily', her husband called her – in his portraits of brash American heroines seeking their fortunes abroad.

'They are a romantic lot,' he wrote of the Stevensons, 'and I delight in them.'

> '. . . A violent friend, a brimstone
> enemy. . . . Is always either loathed or
> slavishly adored; indifference impossible. . . .'

– From Stevenson's description of his wife in a letter to James Barrie.

Contents

List of illustrations

Acknowledgments

The author is warmly grateful to the following for information, answers to inquiries, and published or unpublished data:

To Mr Alan Osbourne of Washington, D.C., executor of the Robert Louis Stevenson estate, for gracious permission to publish much family material; to Mrs Lou Osbourne and Mrs Louis Sanchez of Oakland, California.

To the Misses Margaret and J. Renny Catton of Kaneohe, Hawaii, for the valued privilege of access to the Collection of Stevensoniana made by their late father, Mr Robert Catton; to Miss Janet E. Bell, Curator of the Hawaiian and Pacific Collection, for kind arrangements at the Gregg M. Sinclair Library at the University of Hawaii in Honolulu; to Miss Clare G. Murdoch of the Hawaii and the Pacific Section, Library of Hawaii, Honolulu.

To the Society of Authors, London, until recently the literary representatives of the R. L. Stevenson estate in Great Britain.

To Mrs Anne Roller Issler, ex-Curator of the R. L. Stevenson House in Monterey, California, for generous help in many ways; to Mr Robert W. Reese, State Park Historian I in Monterey, for making available the facilities of Stevenson House.

To Dr David N. Druhe of Berkeley, California, for aid in research; to Mr John Barr Tompkins, Head of Public Services in the Bancroft Library at the University of California at Berkeley.

To Mr George A. Young, Superintendent of City Museums, Edinburgh, for many illustrations from the Stevenson Collection in Lady Stair's House; to Miss Elspeth Yeo, Assistant Keeper in the Department of Manuscripts, National Library of Scotland, Edinburgh.

To Miss Marjorie G. Wynne, Research Librarian of the Beinecke Rare Book and Manuscript Library in the Yale University Library, New Haven, Connecticut, for much important material; and for permission granted by Mr David R. Watkins, Chief Reference Librarian at Yale, and the Graduate Department and Library.

To Mr Ernest J. Mehew of London, for reading the manuscript with many expert corrections, suggestions and data.

To the staff of the British Museum Reading Room, London, for several years of assistance; to various borough library staffs in London; to the Information Librarians, United States Embassy, London.

To Mr Michael L. G. Balfour of London, for interesting reminiscences and permission to quote from his writings about his late father, Sir Graham Balfour.

To Mrs Harry Scherman of New York, for sending research material and for kindly reading the manuscript; to Mrs Demaree Bess of Asheville, North Carolina, for unusual data; to Mr J. C. Furnas, admired biographer of R.L.S.

To Miss Lettice Cooper, author and president of the R. L. Stevenson Club of London, and other members, for interest and encouragement.

To Professor Bradford A. Booth, Stevenson expert, of the Department of English at the University of California at Los Angeles.

To Mrs Marjorie Hancock, Deputy Librarian of the Mitchell Library, Sydney, Australia, for useful items.

To Miss Irene Mischler, Head of the Social Sciences Division in the Indianapolis Public Library, Indiana; to Mrs Elvira Foster, Reference Division, Santa Barbara Public Library, California; to Miss Lois M. Jones, Librarian, Literature and Philology Department, Los Angeles Public Library; to Mr Lee L. Burtis, Iconography Department, California Historical Society, San Francisco; to Mr William L. Ramirez, Principal Librarian, Department of Rare Books and Special Collections, San Francisco Public Library.

To Mr H. E. Radford, F.L.A., Borough Librarian at the Central Library, Bournemouth, Hampshire; to Mrs Anne E. Porritt, formerly of Fairfield, Chiddington, Surrey; and to many other friends and colleagues for helpful interest and suggestions.

Part I

An American tomboy from the Wild West 1840 - 75

Chapter I
Prairie child

A dark and unladylike child, Fanny Vandegrift once wistfully asked her parents if she could change her name to Lily.

'You're a little tiger lily!' her mother told her, and the tiger lily became her emblem for the rest of her life.

Fanny was the eldest and prettiest of six surviving children with only one boy – a seniority which may have helped to form one of her essential traits: an ardent and protective bossiness. All were strong-minded except the boy.

She was born on 10th March 1840 in Indianapolis, Indiana, in a little redbrick house. When she was two years old she was baptized into the Presbyterian Church in the White River before several thousand spectators. She was named Frances Matilda, but she was always called Fanny, and as a young woman in France she resumed the original and more aristocratic spelling of Van de Grift.

Her ancestors on both sides, the Swedish Kyns (later Keens) and the Dutch Van de Grifts, were seventeenth-century settlers near Philadelphia. Her maternal great-grandmother was the daughter of James Cook, an English sea captain who was said to be a close relative of *the* Captain Cook.

She liked to attribute her independence and resourcefulness to her early American pioneer blood and background in a mid-western frontier town of three thousand inhabitants. Though Indianapolis was only twenty years old it was the state capital, set on the National Road to what was then the farthest western frontier, Illinois. The Indian tribes had been driven west, but Fanny thought it romantic to see the occasional blanketed bands wandering past, and to await the fortnightly 'mud wagon' with mail and freight and a few passengers from the wide world.

Her father, Jacob Vandegrift, had run away as a youth from his Philadelphia home to escape a cruel stepfather, and settled in Indianapolis. Farming was replacing cattle-grazing on the flat prairies along the prettily wooded but ague-ridden White River and the nearby branch of the Erie Canal. Jacob started a lumber and real estate business, held a purchasing job on the railroad, bought a farm, and alternately made, spent and lost money. Meanwhile he had met and married Esther Keen who – also by chance a Philadel-phian – was visiting her married sister in the town.

'I can remember', wrote Fanny, quoted in her sister Nellie's biography,[1] 'when . . . I would sit on the fence and watch him ride and perform circus tricks on horseback, riding around in a circle.' Without discipline, he was adored by his son and daughters. Probably his slack rein on her childhood helped to make Fanny impatient and assertive. He had the strikingly keen eyes 'which seemed to pin you to the wall when he looked at you' – eyes which Fanny was to have, along with his large shoulders and chest and his small hands and feet.

Esther Vandegrift was a tiny dark beauty, curly-haired, gentle but vivacious. Fanny resembled her in appearance, in nimbleness, in domestic ingenuity, in fortitude and fearlessness, though hardly in her reputation for never a cross word. Once, to protect her children, she captured a mad dog and held its mouth shut with her hands until help arrived.

In time the paternal grandmother left her cruel second husband and came to live with her son's family. Sometimes, after prayers about hell and damnation, Grandma shared her bed with little Fan. 'The bedstead, a big mahogany four-poster, had to be mounted like an omnibus.' Snug in the featherbed, the old lady was 'the best teller of stories I ever heard . . . [She] told every incident as dramatically as though she had participated in it herself, relating appalling stories about witches, death, apparitions, and the Inquisition . . .'.

[1] *The Life of Mrs Robert Louis Stevenson*, by Nellie Van de Grift Sanchez.

Fanny, too, sitting outside on the slanting cellar door after supper, used to tell ghost stories to her playmates – who, as the shadows darkened, huddled together so fearfully that sometimes the little ones slid off into a heap. From these tales grew her adult flair for Gothic melodrama – and perhaps her claims to clairvoyance.

The lively child learned to read when she was very small, and devoured the classics. But she did not care for school, except for composition, drawing and painting. She was said to be 'brilliant but not industrious'.

Being clever with her little brown hands, she helped at home with the pioneer crafts, such as making rag rugs, boiling maple sugar, brewing soft soap and concocting herbal remedies. She sewed beautifully, raised unfamiliar vegetables, and squeezed wild grapes into a calabash for what she poetically liked to miscall 'the blood-red wine'.

Fanny's swarthy gipsy beauty was not admired in the 1850s, though her sister Nellie has described her 'clear-cut cameo profile' and her 'colour like old ivory'. Grandma tried in vain to lighten her olive skin with strong soap, and sewed her sunbonnet onto her hair every day. Given up with the resigned dictum that 'God made her ugly', Fanny grimaced defiantly and turned tomboy. In pantalettes and long braided hair she darted about like a wren. She loved staying at the family farm, and learned to ride horses with her father's dash and daring. She roamed the woods and cornfields, the pastures and willowy river banks, with her cousin Tom and a dark handsome boy named George Marshall. Close companions, he and Fan were annoyed when her younger sister Josephine kept tagging after them. With adolescence their attraction seemed to continue and folk began to predict a match.

Despite her unfashionable colouring, Fanny grew up with plenty of admirers. 'So wide was the circle of her fascination,' recorded Nellie, 'that there was scarcely a tree in the place that did not bear somewhere the name or initials of Fanny Vandegrift.'

Aged sixteen, she was stumping about the yard on stilts when she was introduced to a caller: young Lieutenant Samuel Osbourne, who had recently arrived as a member of the state governor's staff.

'You can have George Marshall,' she is reputed to have told Josephine after his visit, 'I'm going to marry Lieutenant Osbourne.'

Chapter II
First marriage and two mining camps

Sam Osbourne was a Kentuckian of an old plantation family, descended from the sister of the coonskin-capped Daniel Boone. A law graduate from what is now De Pauw University, he was employed as private secretary to Governor Willard of Indiana. He was blond and handsome, gallant and able, but by no means so firm a character as his young wife. His daughter was to picture him in her memoirs: 'He was six feet tall, with a good figure, always dressed well, and had a gay likable way with him that made friends everywhere . . . ' In the prevailing fashion he had a neat golden Vandyke beard.

'They looked like two children', said a guest at the wedding on 5th December 1857. Fanny was seventeen and Sam not quite twenty.

Fanny adored her new husband with all the passion of her youth and her nature – a hot blood which in time was to lend itself, with reason, to jealousy. Sam must have been an ardent and romantic bridegroom, for his children have written of his affection and tenderness. Isobel – Belle – was born about nine months later, dark, sturdy, small and lively like her mother.

'You were a honeymoon child,' her father told her when she was grown up. 'That's why you have such high spirits and such joy in life.'

Fanny was so little and young that an old gentleman in a train asked, 'Sissy, where is the baby's mother?'

Osbourne's sister Cynthia in Kentucky was to remember Fanny more acidly: 'Very pretty, regular features and pretty black eyes, but she was cold and undemonstrative.'

Nellie admitted of her sister that people were sometimes 'repelled by what they considered her cold and distant manner', but maintained that even her family had been slow to realize that 'this apparent detachment and sphinxlike immobility covered a real and childlike shyness . . . the stillness of a frightened wild creature that has never been tamed'.

As for Sam, with all his buoyancy, he occasionally had wayward moods of depression. The broad sunny reef of his nature dropped off abruptly into strange deep waters, causing him to make some reckless change which affected the course of his life and sometimes his family's. Thus, in 1861 he went off to the Civil War in an Indiana regiment, and like many amateur soldiers he was never the same again. He was commissioned a captain, but he resigned after half a year to join the Indiana Legion, or home guard, though the war was nearing its climax. His unheroic withdrawal was not from cowardice, since he was to prove later that he did not mind risking adventure and hardship, but from a growing disinclination to stick to anything or anyone for long.

George Marshall, Fanny's old sweetheart, served bravely until he had to drop out with tuberculosis. He had become Sam's great friend – and then his brother-in-law, having duly married Josephine.

Indiana was far enough north to fare lightly in the war. But occasionally Morgan's raiders made forays into enemy territory, and the tiny Belle was afraid to go out to the gate for fear they might catch her. 'I was reminded of this,' she wrote, 'when I received my first proposal at the age of sixteen from a man who served under Morgan.'

At the end of 1863 Osbourne saw fit, with a quixotic choice of loyalties, to leave his wife and child in order to escort the consumptive George Marshall on the long circuitous route to milder California. The patient died midway at Panama. But Sam went on, without excuse or apology, to the coast, where he decided to try his luck at prospecting in a silver-mining camp in Nevada.

As soon as he was settled he sent for his family. Thus Fanny packed up and embarked on the first of her many long and hazardous travels. She was always game. It was perhaps her least disputable virtue.

'All my life I have taken care of others', Fanny was to write to the American publisher Charles Scribner in the year before her death, 'and yet I have always wanted to be taken care of, for naturally I belong to the clinging vine sort of woman.'

Clinging vine or no clinging vine, for a crinolined girl from the tamed cornfields of the Middle West, with a four-year-old child, it was an imposing journey out to California before the railroad had been built across the west. First she and Belle had to double back eastward, half way across the American continent to New York. Boarding a ship, they sailed south to Panama and crossed the isthmus by the crooked railroad, staring out of the train window at a lush jungle flickering with monkeys and parrots. In the small alien cemetery Fanny paused to weep at George Marshall's grave.

Only fifteen years after the Gold Rush, the beautiful landlocked port of San Francisco was still a jumping-off place from which men set out to seek their fortunes. Sam met his family and took them to a hotel with a wide corridor of velvety red carpet. There was exciting talk of gold and mines, and they were shown pieces of quartz and little bags of gold dust, surprisingly heavy.

Soon they were off to Nevada in a vast, jolting, crowded stagecoach. Any crag might have concealed a hostile Indian or bandit. The Austin camp was a small cluster of log cabins on the rocky heights over the Reese River, with mines above and below. The place was primitive among its peaked scenery, sunk deep in the winter snow. The Osbournes' cabin had a stove, a table, bunks and a few chairs; no carpet or curtains. Like an Indian woman, Fanny did the family washing in water drawn from the river.

She found only six women among the many men working in the mines where they hoped to strike it rich. The men looked rough with their beards and flannel shirts, but most were college educated.

On her arrival a party was about to be held at another camp some miles away, and all the local ladies came jingling up to invite her, squeezed in a sleigh made of a large packing-box on runners. She dressed quickly in the best of her pretty home-made clothes. There was no mirror in Austin, so one of the women held up a shining tin pan to reflect her primping.

Fanny was the belle of the ball, with seven women to fifty men. She never polkaed or square-danced twice with the same partner.

Her vaunted pioneer blood was put to the test with the makeshifts and dangers. Vegetables were very scarce, and there was not much to eat except meat. Already gifted at improvising, she found fifteen different ways of cooking beef, and devised mock honey for griddle-cakes by boiling sugar with a lump of alum.

Once she taught a young Welshman named John Lloyd how to boil a plum pudding in a muslin bag, for Queen Victoria's birthday, but the string broke and the pudding had to be served in soup plates.

One miner, an escaped murderer, left small offerings on her doorstep. He baked dogs and cats of sweetened dough for Belle, dug her a tiny mine 'salted' with coins, and tearfully gave her as a farewell present a coloured linen picture book of *Beauty and the Beast*.

Here Fanny mastered the masculine arts of rolling and smoking cigarettes – a lifelong habit – and of firing a heavy revolver. This precaution was necessary because there were continual scares about Indians in those years of the Apache wars. While she was doing her housework, their faces, even darker than her own, often stared through the cabin windows. She did not dare to pull the blinds for fear of offending them, and placated them with cups of coffee.

Though the Indians' lowering presence was disturbing, it was even more frightening when they vanished for a time, because the community could not know what they might be up to. Once they were not seen for several days, and sudden signal fires flared alarmingly from the mountain tops. The white men stood guard with their guns while the women and children were herded together, lying on the floor of one cabin. Belle's shrill questions were slapped into silence, and soon even the babies obeyed the instinct to keep still.

Osbourne's mine did not pan out at all well, and he lost most of his money. So the family moved to Virginia City, Nevada, the rip-snortin' silver-mining town made famous by Mark Twain. The mountains were gaunt and grey, but they widened to a crystal panorama of snow peaks visible as far as a hundred and eighty miles away. Here were a few more respectable women, as well as the gaudy prostitutes in the saloons. The Osbournes rented a crude shack which Fanny made cheerful with bright blankets and calico. Sam bought a mine, and meanwhile earned their daily bread as clerk of the local court – though the law was scarce in those rantin', roarin' parts.

Presently Fanny found that her attractive husband was sleeping with other women – or probably the spangled beauties in the bars. Virtuous, dogged and courageous in her hard life, she was as much outraged as jealous. However, soon after this discovery Osbourne caught the mining fever again and gave up his job to go off with a close friend, Sam Orr, prospecting in the wilds of Montana. As a memento for his knapsack Belle gave him her treasured copy of

Beauty and the Beast. He trekked so far into the high Rockies that he was out of reach of the mails for a long time, and the alarming months of silence made his wife and friends fear that he was dead.

Meanwhile the Nevada silver boom was waning. Men and women were packing up their few battered belongings and stage-coaching off, downhearted and 'broke', to San Francisco. Fanny joined some friends in the exodus.

San Francisco in 1866 was outgrowing its youth as a Gold Rush port of call and was becoming a settled, pleasant, even comfortable town, scenically packed into the valleys among the steep hills and quays between bay and ocean. It was an odd mixture of wooden sidewalks and marble-fronted façades, of horse-cars and tall-masted ships, of saloons, theatres, plushy hotels, Chinese or Mexican shanties, Italian restaurants, fishy-smelling wharves, seagulls, date palms and fogs.

Fanny stayed in a modest hotel until her money was nearly gone. Then one day someone came to break the news: there was well-founded evidence that Sam and his friend had been killed by Indians. Stoically she made herself an outfit of widow's weeds, and rented a small room in a cheap boarding-house in a poor street near the old shot tower. The place was recommended by a fellow boarder, John Lloyd, the curly-haired rosy-cheeked young Welshman from the Reese River camp. He also had lost his stake in the mines and was now an ill-paid bank clerk, studying law at night with books from the public library.

Fanny found work in a dressmaking shop where, olive-skinned and foreign-looking and deft with her needle, she passed herself off as French. Luckily she met no one who could speak to her in that language. At night in the dingy bedroom she did fancy-work – crocheting baby socks, jackets and bootees, embroidering pin-cushions, sachets and pillow-cases, which she sold through the Women's Exchange.

On Belle's birthday, Fanny and John Lloyd gave her a party. 'My mother,' recollected Belle, '(at the cost of I dare not think how many stitches) bought the head of a china doll and made the body herself, stuffing it with rags.' She also made a wardrobe of dainty clothes from bright silk scraps in her sewing-basket. John Lloyd, from his small pay, bought a set of toy tin dishes, and carpentered a table and two chairs from cigar boxes. At the party the birthday cake was a cup cake which Belle cut with John's penknife. 'My mother, in her black dress, did her best to smile, and when I asked her age she said that . . . she [was] a quarter of a century old.'

Underneath there were currents which the child could not know. The young Welshman seemed to have been rather in love with Fanny – though with reluctance. He was low-paid, ambitious and upright, with a banker's conservatism. He could hardly approve of the fascination he felt for the too-striking little 'widow'. As for Fanny, in her loneliness she was probably not unresponsive to the reliable young man at her side. Aware of her own sex appeal – and her virtue – she had an arch Victorian way with her admirers.

Then one day, when Belle was on the stairs of the boarding-house, the bell rang and at the front door stood a tall handsome man in a wide hat and high boots.

'My little girl!' he cried, and she flew down into his arms.

Osbourne was alive only because he and Sam Orr had strayed away from the rest of their party, who were later massacred by Indians. He had been lost, hungry, half dead from thirst, penniless, exhausted and often endangered in his long tramp over the glaring sand and alkali of the desert. To lighten his pack he had thrown away many things which he needed, but he still had the little cloth picture book of *Beauty and the Beast*.

Chapter III
Roses and rows beside San Francisco bay

Osbourne had come back on borrowed money. Moved by his charm and her relief, his wife welcomed him home to her arms. The old ardent adoration was revived. He settled down – so far as he was able – to take a well-paid job as court stenographer and to speculate in mining stocks. He installed his family in a pleasant little cottage on Fifth Street, and young John Lloyd often came to Sunday dinner.

John's devotion was saluted in April 1868 when a fair-haired, blue-eyed son was born to the Osbournes and named Samuel Lloyd. The boy was called Sam until the mid 1880s when, following the changes in his mother's marital situation, he gradually became known as Lloyd. (For clarity, he will be called Lloyd throughout this book.)

Soon after the baby's birth Fanny found out that her husband was again unfaithful to her, and in July she left with the children for the shelter of her parents' Indiana farm.

'It was a nice big jolly house full of friendly people,' Belle remembered. Mr Vandegrift declared that when he came home he could hear the clatter of voices a mile across the prairie. There was a wide shady porch where everyone gathered in the summer days, the elders in rocking chairs. Belle did not lack a playmate, for her Aunt Nellie was not much older.

In the spring Fanny gave way to Sam's pleas and promises. Bringing along her nearly grown sister Cora, she returned to California.

Sam bought a pretty little white cottage with a peaked roof and a large garden in the outskirts of East Oakland, across the bay from San Francisco. It looked out on the estuary where the ferry-boats crossed towards the mud flats, sometimes grounding. It was one of the old early wooden houses whose thin boards had been brought around Cape Horn in the hold of a ship – snug but flimsy. It had gables and a rose-hung veranda along the front, and flowered wallpaper inside. 'My mother fell on the place with joy . . .' recollected Belle, 'and of all the lovely gardens she left in her trail through life, I think the one at East Oakland was the most gorgeous.' As Fanny herself said, 'My Dutch blood began to come out.' It was her first chance to develop her extraordinarily green fingers. She grew roses galore – and tiger lilies.

For a time she and Sam were drawn closer together in the creation of their new home. She now had a servant, but on the maid's day off she established her reputation as a wonderful cook. She was 'busy with a dozen different things', recorded Belle, 'painting flowers, shooting with a rifle at a mark, grafting roses, stuffing spiced cantaloupes for pickling, or making designs in clay'. She taught her daughter to mix bread and to model a bas-relief. Once they baked the two at the same time, and rocked with laughter at the cook's horror when she opened the oven door and found a strange clay face among the loaves.

Fanny's sewing-machine was often whirring for Belle and herself. 'She was entirely feminine in her love of pretty clothes,' wrote her sister Nellie, 'and . . . always seemed to be dressed more attractively than other people.' Perhaps, however, not everyone agreed with her increasingly picturesque taste. She was described by Nellie at this period as 'a young and slender woman, wearing her hair in two long braids down her back'. Her hands were most unusual – prettier by Victorian fashion than by later standards. They were very small and short, and the fingertips tapered abruptly into rounded points and bent slightly back. They were supple but compact, sensual yet capable, and busy-looking even in repose. Her clear profile was 'Napoleonic' and her mouth was bow-shaped.

Apparently she was satisfied with her own level voice, for when Belle's higher tones rose sharply, she corrected the girl with 'a downward wave of the hand and the repeated quotation, "A low sweet voice in woman"'.

It was now Belle's turn to feel ashamed of her dark gipsy colouring. But Fanny, reacting against the humiliation of her own childhood, told her to consider her flaws a beauty as Sarah Bernhardt did; and she dressed her in yellow or pale blue to make her look darker still.

Meanwhile the cottage blossomed with courtship. A visit to a married sister was a time-honoured way of matchmaking, and Fanny's sister Cora met and married Samuel Orr, Sam's partner in the escape from massacre. The young couple settled down to live in Alameda, across the estuary from Oakland.

In 1871 a second son, Hervey was born to the Osbournes. He was a beautiful, ethereal, sweet-natured child with large dark eyes and golden hair which his mother trained into long golden curls. Not long after the elder Mrs Osbourne travelled out from Kentucky to pay the family a long visit. Stiff and straight in widow's black, she wore her drab hair parted and smoothed over her ears as in a daguerreotype. She was the opposite of her casual, insouciant, free-thinking son. At college, in revolt against her too-strict Methodism, he had become an atheist, and she told her relations that this sin had continued after his marriage because 'Fanny cared little for spiritual things'. Moreover she felt that the young wife was hard-hearted about Sam's flirtations.

'Fanny's temper drove him to most of what he did,' she later maintained.

As for Belle, she wrote years later: 'I cannot remember ever hearing a cross word from my father. If he would ask me to sew on a button, or darn some socks, and it wasn't done, instead of scolding, like most fathers, he'd stick a notice on my mirror: "Miss Handsome's attention is directed to her Papa's socks" or "Miss Osbourne's Papa is now buttonless." Once he asked me to shut the door and I, sitting reading, paid no attention. Suddenly he shouted in his army tone of command: "Leave that door open! I *will* be obeyed!" Naturally I ran to shut it, giving him a hug in passing.'

'Learn to enjoy the moment. Yesterday is gone, tomorrow hasn't come yet', he counselled his daughter – and took his own advice, leaving tomorrow for Fanny to worry about.

One far-reaching day Belle was with a schoolgirl friend on the ferry-boat, bound across the bay to San Francisco for a matinée. Though her dark bronze hair still hung down her back, she was wearing her first tight-fitting dress with darts and whalebones, and her skirt had been lengthened to the tops of her buttoned boots.

While the seagulls wheeled and a string trio played on deck, the two girls noticed a couple of young men eyeing them. One was making a sketch of Belle. Just before the ferry docked, a schoolboy friend appeared, and the girls ventured to send him over to ask if they could see the sketch. The young artist brought it across with a bow; it was dashingly signed 'Jos. D. Strong, Jr.'. They smiled their thanks demurely, the young men lifted their hats, and they parted.

But when the girls had taken their seats at the matinée, a voice said, 'Good day'. Somehow their new admirers had contrived to sit behind them. They learned that the artist, though a Californian, was the descendant of early missionaries in Hawaii. He had just painted a portrait of the Mayor of Oakland with such success that a group of business men had made up a fund to send him to Munich to study. His companion Reggie Birch, also an artist, was going too.

Soon a charming lame gentleman, a friend's friend named Mr Birch, called on Fanny. He asked if he might come again with his son Reggie and Joe Strong. Mr and Mrs Osbourne were interested; they had seen the mayor's portrait and admired it.

A few days later the guests were received on the lawn under the trees. Belle blushed, but no mention was made of any previous meeting, though her father cocked a quizzical eyebrow. To her astonishment her mother let her go to the two young men's studio in Oakland, where Joe painted a small portrait of her while Reggie made a pen-and-ink drawing. (It was he who was later to illustrate *Little Lord Fauntleroy*.) Not long after, the two artists went off to Munich, and the Osbournes did not see either of them again for four years.

At school the incorrigible Belle drew caricatures in the margins of her half-filled examination papers. These amused and impressed her teacher so much that he asked to keep them. Gratified, her mother took her out of high school and, to her joy, sent her three days a week to the School of Design in San Francisco.

Moreover, Fanny herself decided to enrol as a student, engaging a governess called Miss Kate to take care of the two little boys. Fanny had done some painting in the mid Victorian manner: morning glories on a black panel, pansies on a plaque.

It was Fanny who won the silver medal, first prize for the term, with her crayon drawing of the Venus de Milo. (Its plaster cast had been a present to young San Francisco from old Paris. When it was unpacked and the Venus was found to be without arms, the Chamber of Commerce had sued the express company and was awarded damages.)

Like a stage-struck girl, Fanny fell in love with the way of life in the 'artistic' set. The director of the school was Virgil Williams, a recognized artist and a highly educated man who had been trained abroad. His painter wife, Dora Norton, was a student in the school. She soon became perhaps the closest of Fanny's lifelong friends. Belle described her: ' . . . a slim, straight-backed, decisive Yankee woman who prided herself on a frankness that was sometimes rather appalling. She wore heavy silks and velvets, unbecoming hats, fairly rattled with necklaces and bangles, and carried, fastened to her belt, an assortment of silver articles – mesh purse, pencil-case, knife, button-hook – that dangled on the ends of little chains.'

While Fanny and Belle went back and forth to San Francisco by horse-car and ferry, the daughter noticed the attention which her mother attracted. 'I realized how very pretty she was with her pale face, her regular features cut like a delicate cameo, and her lovely eyes "of gold and bramble dew"' – as Stevenson was to describe their glittering lights. 'Her figure was slender, with the hourglass effect slightly accented; and with her nicely shod little feet and dainty gloves she well repaid the many glances cast her way.'

Meanwhile, more education was being pommelled into all three children by Miss Kate. She was an efficient, buxom young woman who adored Fanny and tenderly cosseted the delicate baby Hervey. She forced Belle to learn and practise piano-playing, and to memorize French verbs and converse about the pencil of the shoemaker. 'These studies, insisted on by my mother,' recorded Belle, 'should have prepared me for the great change that was coming in my life.'

'They were not happy together, my father and mother,' wrote Belle. 'When he was away (he often went off on business trips) home was a pleasant place. . . . When I was alone with my father he was always gay and companionable, but when my mother joined us there was often a tension, an atmosphere of suppressed feelings that chilled me.' The couple had bitter quarrels which they tried to hide from Belle and the little boys. Fanny glowered; Sam sulked. But they never told the children why they disagreed.

One day the family were in the sitting-room, Fanny sewing, Belle curled up on the floor against her father's knee while he read aloud from Thackeray's *Vanity Fair*. He had reached the scene where Amelia discovers that her husband, Captain George Osborne, has betrayed her with Becky Sharp. Suddenly Fanny interrupted in an icy voice, 'I wonder that you dare read your own story, *Captain Osbourne!*'

'God Almighty, woman!' groaned Sam. 'Can't you ever forget?'

And their daughter was sent out of the room.

Another time Fanny and Belle were sitting in the parlour when they heard the picket gate click and saw a young woman walking up the path. She was flashy and overdressed, with a come-hither hat perched on a huge chignon. As she stepped up to the porch, nodding and smiling, Fanny rose with frozen fury.

'Why do you come here?'

The visitor hesitated, then tossed her head and said boldly, 'I came to make a friendly call. There's no reason why I shouldn't.'

'There is a very good reason why you should not come to my house', said Fanny.

The girl turned and marched off down the path, her bustle wagging huffily.

East Oakland was still a village. Sam Osbourne's 'lady friends' were a subject of jokes and gossip, and his wife suffered more and more, though she kept a proud silence.

Month by month Fanny was growing farther away from Sam and nearer her new highbrow group of friends, especially Mr and Mrs Williams and a young Irish-American lawyer, Timothy Rearden, who was head of the Mercantile Library in San Francisco, a scholar in Low German, and a colleague of Bret Harte on the *Overland Monthly*. He encouraged her flickering urge to write, criticized her manuscripts, and was as much responsible as anyone for her literary dabbling.

Her long coquettish correspondence with Rearden, then a bachelor, began primly enough in 1874 with an exchange of notes about finding an illustrator for his work through her contacts at Williams's art school. The tempo accelerated. Soon Fanny was writing 'My sister . . . arrived . . . and would be pleased to have you come over and call upon her. . . .' Before long the personal tone became more lively. After asking about the size of the pictures, Fanny added, 'I believe you are cross with me. . . . Let this be a lesson to you. When you marry allow your wife to act according to her own notions of propriety. Come to think of it – I suppose writing this note is another impropriety. Do you suppose Mrs Grundy went to Heaven when she died? If so let me go to – the other place. FANNY M. O.'

Soon the acquaintance had become a flirtation, with rendezvous on suitable pretexts – at the art school, the library, at home. 'Dear Mr Rearden, Things are on such an amicable footing now that I think you may venture in at any time [at the school]. . . . Your concluding remark does not tease me a particle. Amuse yourself that way with John [Lloyd]. . . .' 'Dear Mr Rearden, I dare not let you come in today, if you have anything to say, send a note, you might come the latter part of the week or the first of the next.' Or again, '. . . If you will walk past the school at some given hour not too near noon, I will meet you and give [some specimen drawings] to you with fitting explanation.'

'I send you all I have done. Capitals and punctuations are thrown together in the most promiscuous manner. . . . Since you are so cruel as to throw the question of the propriety of the thing upon my poor little shoulders, I feel compelled to say no more correspondence except upon rare and important questions. . . . The rest of your letter is the usual thing men say to women they consider silly and vain – I haven't lived twenty years without gaining a little knowledge of men and their ways – I am going to have a new pony Saturday. When you choose you may come over and I will take you driving. Your art criticism I scorn. FMO.'

John Lloyd (now a member of the Bar) was also a friend of Rearden's and apparently to some extent a rather frowning confidant.

'Dear Mr Rearden,' wrote Fanny. 'Many thanks for the information and intended service . . . J.L. is coming over to see us one evening this week. Come with him. FMO.' And again on 24th September, 'I have just been hearing the other side of that bouquet business. I'm afraid they're right, you seem dangerous. Consequently you begin to interest me. Now carry this immediately to your mentor [John Lloyd?] as you have every other word I have from you, that he may see whether I have done anything very wrong. . . . Perhaps I shall attempt those stories if you are of the same mind. I was in the library the other day but you were not there. F.' . . . 'Dear Mr Rearden, Much obliged for the book. So awfully sorry about the German; could just as well have done it as not. I suppose it wasn't "proper". Come and see me at home or here. Late in the afternoon is not so dangerous – say half past three. FMO.'

It is very unlikely that this flirtation ever went further than a few thrilling squeezes of the hand. But her letters at that early period – bold, naïve, come-hither, even coarse – open up a different view of Fanny from her later image of the loyal, wronged wife whose eyes and senses were never diverted from the struggle of her marriage until she reluctantly succumbed to her historic love for Stevenson.

By the time the angelic Hervey was four years old, Fanny felt that the neglect and humiliation of her life with Sam had become more than she could bear. Divorce seemed too shocking a step in 1875. But at last she decided on something only a little less *outré* and precarious for a respectable youngish American matron. In the summer she made up her mind to go with her three children to Europe – to Antwerp, where she and Belle would study art. (Decent American or British women could not, of course, go abroad alone unless they made the motions of studying something.)

Before she left she had a long private talk with Mrs McGrew, the carriage-maker's wife, her friendly neighbour in the big white house up the hill which overlooked the cottage. She asked her to keep a sharp eye on Sam, and report on his conduct.

Even the packing was done before she broke the news of the journey to her incredulous daughter. Miss Kate was to shut up the cottage and travel with the family, via Indiana, as far as New York, where she had relatives; Fanny could not afford to take her to Europe. Sam would live in San Francisco and send his wife a small allowance.

Thus Fanny was a kind of Henry James heroine, if she could have realized it.

Part 2

France
La Vie de Bohème 1875-78

Chapter I
A *femme seule* on the continent

Fellow passengers on the steamer from New York admired the pretty petite Mrs Osbourne and her three children – though they mistook Belle for her sister. Fanny was thirty-five and seemed ten years younger. 'When in any difficulty', recalled Belle, 'she only had to look helpless and bewildered, and gallant strangers leaped to her assistance.'

On the second day at sea the Osbournes could hardly believe their eyes when there appeared on deck the faithful Miss Kate. She had taken passage in the steerage. Waving her hands in a tearful scene, she swore that she would go with them whether they wanted her or not. She proved invaluable as chaperone, governess and factotum.

They met a tall Kentuckian who as a youth had been one of Morgan's raiders in the Civil War. In traditional Southern style he asked Mrs Osbourne for her daughter's hand, presenting his credentials, which showed that he was a wealthy owner of cotton plantations. Fanny told him that the girl was too young – she was not yet seventeen. Belle did not realize that he was in love with her; in his early thirties, he seemed like a kindly uncle. Fanny, secretive as usual, did not tell her of the proposal until later – when she reminded her of how as a tiny girl she had been afraid to go out to the gate for fear that Morgan's men might catch her. He chivalrously helped the little family to disembark at Antwerp.

They stayed at the simple Hôtel du Bien Être. At the door Papa Geerhart, big and bald in a white apron, was touched by the frightened little woman with her brood, gesticulating in a foreign language. He led them straight through to the kitchen, and his motherly wife and ten children welcomed them in Flemish. They were to spend many hours drinking coffee in the host's sitting-room.

'Lloyd', wrote his sister, 'showing a trait in his character that lasted through life, chose the prettiest one of the family, Marie, a little girl of ten, and devoted himself exclusively to her.'

Though a *jolie Américaine* without visible husband was likely to be 'misunderstood' on the Continent in the 1870s, Fanny was too poor and too busy caring for her party of five to get into mischief. She liked to say afterwards that she made ends meet in Europe by writing magazine articles. But in fact she was to sell only one fairy tale, as text for an artist friend's illustrations, to *St Nicholas*, the American magazine for children. (It was called 'Too Many Birthdays' and published in July 1878.) Her sole fitful means came dribbling in from Sam, who, though generous, was as careless of his money as of his morals.

Fanny found that Antwerp was not an easy place for a woman to study art. The Academy did not accept females. The American consul finally sent her and Belle to call at the studio of a Rubens-like dignitary in a black velvet robe. He politely advised them to go to Paris, or else to take private lessons from a man he recommended.

But then little Hervey fell ill with a fever. The Belgian doctor was baffled and advised Fanny to take him to a children's specialist in Paris. They packed and left at once.

In Paris Fanny found a small sunny apartment in the quiet Rue de Naples, a little street in Montmartre on the highest ground in the city, near the white dome and panoramas of Sacré Cœur. The fine old houses had been heavily scarred during the Franco-Prussian war of 1870.

Under the specialist's care Hervey's health improved rapidly – for a while. Lloyd was sent to a French school with its uniform of black smock and beret. Only five years after the Siege of Paris, his school-mates insulted his foreign blondness by calling him 'Prussian'. He was sensitive and imaginative, and the jeer hurt.

Fanny always contrived to make even a temporary abode cosy and colourful, if rather untidy. Furnishing was a problem when she had so little money that she had to count every *sou*, every postage stamp. '. . . You never have put on enough', she scolded Rearden on 31st October, 'and I have had to pay the postage all over again, and a fine besides. . . .'

One of his recent letters, she took pains to inform him, 'I read in the presence of my surgical friend who was reminding me very much of you by imploring me to go out and get something to eat. No one considers me safe unless I have been recently fed. I'm not an anaconda, am I? . . . He's an awful swell, the surgeon, but a charming little cherub of a fellow at the same time, and has been just too good to me for words. It was very funny when we were buying the furniture for my rooms. We would hunt out a modest looking shop, look at their cheapest things, talk about half an hour about whether I had better get thirty or forty cent chairs, decide upon the cheapest, and that off our minds, [we] would jump into his elegant carriage with liveried coachmen, and drive off with great magnificence to take a dinner costing ten or twenty dollars. . . .' She even teased Rearden by enclosing a letter to her from Mr Hendricks, the 'surgical friend'.

'I read your letter through a second time,' she went on to Rearden, 'curious to find out in what the gush consisted . . . a faint intimation that you rather liked me, and when reminded of it, sometimes thought of me. . . . Come, don't quarrel with me. I feel lonely and dreary enough without that . . . I have been quite ill, I didn't have those symptoms you so well understand for nothing. And then I have been so anxious and distressed about my sweet pretty baby. . . .

'You ask if I write to John [John Lloyd in San Francisco]. Of course I do. And receive the kindest and best of letters in return. . . .

'I believe that Sam does miss us very much indeed. I had no idea that he would. I thought it would be sort of weight off his mind to have us gone once more. His letter quite touched my heart and I wish you could cheer him up a bit. Somehow I didn't seem to succeed and yet I have tried very hard. I don't like to be selfish, and it makes me feel so if I thought he is unhappy at our absence. I didn't know I should miss him as I do. It was very pitiful to hear my little Hervey in his delirium calling and calling for his father; it made me feel as if I had no right to have him so far away. I will add only one more bit, and that is this: please don't write cross letters to me. If you do I shall cry. . . .'

Apparently the provocative lawyer remained in the foreground, even in Paris. How much did Sam know of this sparring intimacy? A good deal, probably. But before his family had been long away Mrs McGrew reported that he had installed a companion in the rose-bowered cottage.

On 14th December Fanny wrote to Rearden: 'I believe in women's rights in a general sense, so much despised by the "strong-minded" when they deservedly call the "clinging vine". I do not want to be the oak and stand alone; it makes me loathsome to think of the oak with no shelter, no support except what it provides for itself. . . .'

It was an exciting time to be studying art in Paris. The very term Impressionism had been coined only the year before, at an exhibition in which a canvas of Monet's called *Impression: Sunrise* gave a start to that derisive name.

They found that Julien's Atelier des Dames, in a passage off the Boulevard des Italiens, was willing to take women students if they could pay the fees. Dark stairs led to a large north room, stuffy and crowded with easels and stools. The mother and daughter entered the life classes, shocked only at the end of the sessions when the models put on their clothes. Seeing that Mlle Osbourne was a beginner, M. Fleury, the master, asked her neighbour to help her. This lady was a New Englander, and Belle was thrilled when she learned that she was Louisa M. Alcott's sister – the Amy of *Little Women*.

In time Fanny's drawings were praised for a pleasing simplicity. She was rather a puzzle to her neighbours in her dual role of art student and *mère de famille*. The household lived very plainly, often making a meal of smoked herring and black bread. But most of their fellow students were hard up too. Now and then she invited several of them to eat Dutch-American dishes which she concocted with cheap ingredients and few utensils.

Then Hervey fell ill again. For several months he wasted away with the ugly and excruciating malady of scrofulous tuberculosis. His mother described the gruelling details in her letters home while she tended him with passionate care, aided by Miss Kate.

Meanwhile Belle continued at the atelier alone. It did not occur to Fanny that it was improper for a young girl to walk about Paris without a chaperone, or at least a maid. The sparkling Belle had many adventures. One rainy morning in the omnibus a young man kept volubly teasing her. She pulled the bell-rope once, as the signal for dismounting. When the horses stopped, he hopped off and opened his umbrella to escort her. She pulled the rope twice, as a sign to go on, and he was left standing in the rain. The other men cheered.

All winter the evenings in the tiny front room were dead quiet and lonely. Fanny still sometimes wrote to 'Dear Mr Rearden', as she always formally saluted him.

'I am glad you find my letter amusing,' she assured him under postmark of 2nd February, 1876. 'It is more than I can say for yours. My days are stupid and my evenings are so tiresome, that I am glad of letters of any kind. . . .

'If I am spiteful and need to have my claws cut, it is at least a feminine weakness and not an astounding one under the circumstances. . . . When claws are cut more than mine will fall. How do you sharpen yours, on your friend's backs? . . .'

Despite the apparent levity of Fanny's correspondence with Rearden, in fact her whole time and attention were given to the suffering Hervey. Now and then he showed will-o'-the-wisps of recovery. But 'for weeks he lay dying', Lloyd wrote many years later, in a Preface to Stevenson's *Works*, 'while my mother pawned her trinkets to buy him delicacies and toys . . .' He described 'the wasted baby hands, the burning eyes, the untouched hothouse grapes lying on the counterpane'. The expense of his illness forced her to stint the other children to pay the doctor's bills and buy medicines.

'We were miserably poor', wrote Lloyd. 'It seems to me that I was always hungry. I can remember yet how I used to glue myself to the baker's windows. . . .'

Long after everyone else had given up hope, Fanny fought for her child's life. With her strong will she tried to inspire him with a miraculous urge to live. In the first waking of the Parisian spring, with its poplar buds along the sunlit Seine, the child again begged for Papa. She sent for Sam. His business affairs were not doing well but, always a loving parent, he sailed at once. When he disembarked at

Liverpool a telegram was awaiting him: 'STILL LIVING. FANNY.'
He reached Paris in time to see his son alive.

'My dear Tim,' he wrote to Rearden on 5th April. 'I saw a letter
in your handwriting brought into the room by the concierge the
other day, and Mrs Osbourne read it at the bedside of a sick little
boy. Something it contained, I am afraid, gave her some offence.'

Then he stated simply that Hervey had died at five o'clock that
morning.

'. . . we followed him', recalled Lloyd, 'to Père Lachaise, where
we could only afford one of those temporary French graves, surely
the cruellest in the world, from which the bones are flung into the
catacombs at the expiration of five years.'

Sam stayed on in the subdued little family group for several weeks
but he and his wife did not succeed in drawing nearer over their
shared loss, though both must have tried and been distressed by their
failure. In Fanny's obsession of grief she was not really 'responsible'.
When she began to go back and forth with Belle to the atelier, the
observant artists were quick to notice her great-eyed sorrow, and she
found herself in demand as a model for tragic subjects. 'She grew
paler and paler, seldom spoke, and it was like being with a ghost',
recalled her daughter. Worn out from sleepless nights of nursing, she
was weak, had giddy spells, sometimes suffered blackouts of memory,
and had hallucinations.

At the time it was considered loyal and fine to grieve as long as
possible; and she was genuinely 'heart-broken'. She never regained
her full pioneer hardiness. To the Victorians, being 'out of one's
mind' with sorrow was as much a sentimental as a psychological
definition. It was also a prelude to what her critics were later to
deplore as an absorption with illness and cures, amounting to hypochondria.

Lloyd too, was run down from the long winter of strain and under-
nourishment. 'Madame,' the doctor told Fanny, 'it is essential that
you should take this child to the country. . . .'

Naturally, having lost one son, she was terrified at the threat to the
other.

She asked the advice of a bearded young American sculptor named
Pardessus. He recommended the simple little Hôtel Chevillon at

Grez, a small out-of-the-way village on the River Loing, some fifty or sixty miles from Paris.

Grez was in the Fontainebleau forest on the opposite side from Barbizon, the more sophisticated 'capital' of the villages where the painters from the Latin Quarter summered with an entourage of models and *grisettes*. Other females – and virtuous family parties – were almost unknown and certainly unwelcome. Fanny was doubtful. However, Pardessus told her that she would find Grez quiet and respectable enough, especially so early in the season. Fanny was further reassured by the information that the inn was frequented largely by British and American painters, with a sprinkling of French and other Continentals. Pardessus mentioned several names: the Americans Low and Bloomer, the Irishman O'Meara, the brilliantly amusing Scots cousins, Bob and Louis Stevenson. . . .

So the Osbournes put their few bits of furniture in storage and gave up their apartment. Lloyd remembered them all standing forlornly in the rain on a farewell visit to Hervey's small grave. Then – with Sam – they travelled by train and diligence to the Hôtel Chevillon.

The gentle drowsy charm of the Grez region and the Loing valley have been described in many works, including the paintings of Sisley, the music of Delius (who eventually lived at Grez), and the prose and verse of Robert Louis Stevenson. The previous summer he had pictured the scene in a letter to his mother: 'A low bridge, with many arches choked with sedge; green fields of white and yellow water-lilies; poplars and willows innumerable. . . .'

Fanny, like countless other art students, was soon to paint the medieval stone bridge.[1] Smocked shepherds with crooks drove their flocks along the straggling cobbled street past a Norman church, an old mill, and austere stone houses with pointed roofs.

The inn, reached by a long avenue lined with poplars, was later used by Stevenson as a setting in 'The Treasure of Franchard'. It had a stone archway which led through a square court into the garden. The dining-room panels had been painted by artist guests. M. and Mme Chevillon presided with an amiable tolerance of their eccentric clientele. But in fact the Osbournes arrived in May when there was

---

[1] Her canvas is now in the Stevenson Collection at Lady Stair's House, Edinburgh.

only one other guest, a young American art student painting in the long leafy garden which sloped down to the river.

Their presence thus a *fait accompli*, the newcomers were in a position to meet and face the young male bohemians who gradually turned up – including the cousins Stevenson.

Chapter II
'A queer, lank lad in a velvet coat'

On 13th November 1850 – when Fanny Vandegrift was romping on the raw midwestern prairies as a tomboy of ten years and eight months – an infant named Robert Lewis Balfour Stevenson was born to pious upper middle class parents in a dignified old house in Edinburgh.

His mother's father was a Presbyterian minister of gentle birth, while his paternal grandfather, father and uncle were engineers distinguished in building lighthouses – including the still-famous Bell Rock and Skerryvore. It was hoped that the tradition would be carried on by little Robert Lewis, known as 'Smout'. The nickname, meaning young salmon or small fry, lasted until its owner's adolescence, when he levied a penny fine on anyone who used it. There was already a cousin Bob Stevenson, so his family called him Lew. As a Francophile of eighteen – and because he and his father detested someone of the same name – he changed Lewis to Louis, though the pronunciation was unchanged.

An only child, delicate and lonely, he was much in the fond care of two women. One was his mother, Margaret Stevenson, *née* Balfour. At twenty-one she was eleven years younger than her husband, whom she adored. She was tall, slim, fair, serene, practical and humorous, her long face reflected in her son's.

The other woman was his nurse, Alison Cunningham – Cummy. She was cosy and merry during the day, but at his bedtime prayers she so alarmed her charge (like Fanny's grandmother) with the threat of hell fire that he could not go to sleep. His parents were strictly devout, with grace at table and family prayers on the knees; but except on the Sabbath they played whist, and he was made to pray with Cummy that they might be spared from perdition. 'I can never again take so much interest in anything', he recollected, 'as I took, in childhood, in doing . . . what I believed to be sinful.'

The devoted cosseting of his mother and nurse has been linked with the fact that when Smout grew up the several women to whom he was most deeply drawn were all matrons and mothers, many years older than himself.

From his father he received a strong if often dour affection. Thomas Stevenson was stocky, with mutton-chop whiskers, stern, chivalrous and upright, melancholy at home but amusing in company. For all his puritanical grimness his son was to call him in retrospect 'my dear, wild, noble father'. As a lighthouse engineer and inventor, to this day he has saved uncounted thousands of lives by devising the intermittent or revolving light. Louis was always proud of the fact that he had refused to patent it, making the world a gift of the invention which would have made him rich. Queen Victoria presented him with a set of table linen with lighthouses interwoven in the damask.

Smout was always drawing, not from models but from imagination. Once he came to his mother saying, 'Mama, I have drawed a man's body; shall I draw his soul now?'

When he was seven, his brilliant cousin Bob Stevenson, then aged ten, stayed for a winter in the tall grey stone house at 17 Heriot Row. Bob and his sister Katharine were Louis's favourite cousins; they must both have been extremely attractive. As he wrote in 'Memories of Himself', Smout worshipped Bob. 'We lived together in a purely visionary state. We had countries . . . where we ruled and made wars and inventions, and . . . maps. . . . We were never weary of dressing up. . . .'

Within a few years their father Alan Stevenson took Bob and Katharine away to live in France and be educated on the Continent. Smout – a big-eyed, weak-chested, eccentric boy – was left to amuse himself with dreams and books and animals. He cherished his chief companion, a Skye terrier named Coolin, and prayed fervently for Grandfather Balfour's horse.

Louis often stayed with his grandfather at Colinton Manse, near

Edinburgh. He liked 'the deodar upon the lawn . . . the river, the church bell . . .'. The Rev. Dr Lewis Balfour had the 'strong Scots accent of the mind' which his grandson inherited. A widower, 'he had no idea of spoiling children, leaving all that to my aunt' – Miss Jane Balfour, known as 'Auntie', and 'all were born a second time from Aunt Jane's tenderness'.

He had fifty-odd first cousins (forty were Balfours), but as a child he was too 'different' to be popular. He preferred dramatic hide-and-seek games to sports, pretending – like Fanny – that he was ambushing Red Indians. He later said that he had been an Ugly Duckling. As he grew older, however, his puckish spirit began to attract more friends.

Far from outstanding at his lessons in the eminent Edinburgh Academy and elsewhere, he was continually kept at home with colds and illnesses. He had an unhappy term at boarding-school in the suburbs of London, remembering best 'the benevolent cat' which befriended him as he sat and wept on a doorstep. His father mercifully rescued him and took him on the first of several exciting trips to inspect lighthouses along the coast. This gave him a permanent zest for the dash and rhythm of the sea.

In her early married life Margaret Stevenson suffered from the weak chest which Smout inherited. In the winters of 1862–3 and 1863–4 she was ordered to the French Riviera. Her husband and son accompanied her to Menton, where the boy loved his first experience of the palms and cypresses and blue coastline of the south. He acquired from a tutor a fluent and idiomatic (if not grammatical) command of the French language and a permanent taste for things French.

In 1865 Bob and Katharine joined the family for the summer in Peebles in the hilly valley of the Tweed. 'That part of the earth', Louis recalled in his essay, 'was made a heaven to me by many things now lost, by . . . the delights of comradeship and those (surely the prettiest and simplest) of a boy and girl romance.' Evidently the girl was the charming Katharine, who seems to have been a sort of clever nymph. She recollected the days 'when my brother Bob, Louis and I used to ride together. Bob had a black pony, and Louis called it "Hell"; his own was brown, and was called "Purgatory"; while mine was named "Heaven". Once the two boys galloped

right through the Tweed . . . and I had to follow in fear of my
life. . . .'

At sixteen Louis dutifully entered the University of Edinburgh as
an engineering student, but he soon rebelled against the 'icy winds
and conventions' of classic Edinburgh and its polite professional
society. In reaction to the over-strict Calvinism of his childhood he
swung to the point of atheism and for several years he had bitter and
exhausting arguments with his father. Even his optimistic mother
feared the worst would come of his beliefs and conduct. Conservative people disapproved of his excited talk of ideas, in his light
resonant voice with its Scots accent. He made wide waving gestures
and wandered about the room as he spoke. The young people thought
him a *poseur*. 'I did not like him then,' admitted his childhood friend
Flora Masson.

From Bob he picked up the continental habit of wearing a velvet
jacket and wide-awake hat; and being prone to colds, he kept his hair
shoulder-length for warmth. Street urchins hooted at him and he
hooted back. Flora Masson remembered him as a 'queer, lank lad in a
velvet coat', with long spidery limbs of such leanness that his joints
made sharp corners under his clothes. He was five foot ten, with
incredibly fine bones. His hands were long and sensitive. Like
Fanny, he had well-shaped feet about which he too was vain: however
shabby, he was always well shod. His face was oval, with high cheek-
bones, an aquiline nose like his mother's, a deceptively ruddy colour,
fair hair that darkened with the years, an eloquent mouth 'a little
tricksy and mocking', and great brown eyes of a penetrating brilliance,
set exceptionally far apart. His extraordinary glittering eyes, like
Fanny's, were mentioned by all observers.

One grey afternoon in 1868, in her candlelit drawing-room, Mrs
Stevenson was serving tea to Mrs Fleeming Jenkin, the wife of
Louis's favourite professor. She was a very attractive, cultured
woman of strong personality, in her mid-thirties. Though not
beautiful, she had an expressive face and a grand manner; her
family nicknamed her 'Madam'. Before Anne Jenkin realized that
anyone had come into the room, a vibrant young male voice joined the
talk from a chair in the deep shadows. Not until he escorted her to the
door did she have a good look at the thin youth whom she was the
first to discern as one of the most potentially brilliant talkers of his

time. He in turn was charmed. Her encouragement civilized the young rebel. She was the earliest of the four mature women who were to interest him more than any girls.

At length Louis realized that he could not endure an engineering career. All he wanted was to write, which he did constantly. Everything interesting which he saw, read, knew or thought, he expressed in his quick running hand. His vocation was already as inseparable from him as his shadow.

His father was grimly upset at this rejection of his long cherished plans for another lighthouse engineer. Authorship was suitable as a gentleman's hobby, but, as a profession, writing was a frivolous alternative to the family firm. Thomas finally compromised by insisting that his son should take a law degree as an economic insurance. The lad consented, but he remained far from studious.

He was forced to assume conventional evening clothes and manners when he was elected a member of the famous 'Spec.', the Speculative Society of highbrow students. But more and more he took to hanging about low pubs and cheap brothels, where his innate sense of honour and kindliness made him better regarded than in his own sphere – perhaps because in his youth he showed these traits more to the poor than to the bourgeoisie.

In 1870 Cousin Bob returned with a Cambridge degree and became a gifted student of painting at the Edinburgh College of Art. 'The mere return of Bob changed at once and for ever the course of my life', Louis recalled in 'Memories of Himself'. ' . . . I was at last able to breathe.'

Tall, dark and febrile, a dazzling conversationalist on life and the arts, over-stimulating to his cousin, Bob was described by Louis as 'the man likest and most unlike to me that I have ever met. . . . Our likeness was one of tastes and passions . . . almost identity. . . . Laughter was at that time our principal affair, and I doubt if we could have had a better.' They often went home singing, dancing and capering in the moonlight, not with drink but from sheer high spirits.

Charles Baxter was another of Louis's highly articulate companions in levity at the university. He was described by Richard Le Gallienne as 'a preposterously vital and imaginative talker, ample of frame, with a voice like a column of cavalry'. He was loyal, polished and witty, but he led Louis to drink rather too much in their 'pub-crawling'.

Two other friends dominated the scene of Stevenson's youth in Edinburgh. One was the talented but temperamental James Walter Ferrier, who died young. The other was Sir Walter Simpson, shy, respectable and reliable – son of Sir James, who gave chloroform to the world. It was an era of fervent friendships and warm devotion voiced without embarrassment.

In mid Victorian Edinburgh it was tacitly ignored as inevitable that young men of good family should sow their wild oats in the city's shadowy underworld. Stevenson scattered his share and more, for he was passionate, sensual and infinitely curious about life and people. He was known by the nickname of Velvet Coat in the dives which he liked to frequent. He never denied his youthful indulgences in whoring, though he was neither as licentious nor as virtuous as some biographers made out. For one thing, he was too poor for much active 'sin'; his father kept him down to an allowance of only ten shillings, later a pound, a month until he was twenty-three, though he received an occasional tip from his mother. None the less his experience of the underworld was to provide material for many of his darker works, notably *Dr Jekyll and Mr Hyde*.

It was said that his first love was a girl in one of the brothels, who was scolded and even beaten for wasting so much time on an un-profitable client. This cruel injustice reputedly made him want to marry her, hardly a feasible plan for a young student dependent upon stern Calvinist parents for an allowance of six pounds a year.

A derisive quatrain survives from that period:

> O fine religious, decent folk,
>   In Virtue's flaunting gold and scarlet,
> I sneer between two puffs of smoke –
>   Give me the publican and harlot.

This conflict with the puritanical ignoring of sex in his home circle has been widely presumed to underlie the fact that in his early books there are no women characters except as background figures.

Actually his best male friends were in his own social class, and his parents invited 'nice girls' to young dinner parties in Heriot Row. He was by no means unaware of their charms. One of his early love poems speaks of the thrill of sharing a hymn-book in a pew with a pretty girl – perhaps his cousin Katharine. She or another stirred his emotions while they skated together. And later he wrote to Bob that he had very nearly been caught in matrimony by a most eligible young lady.

Nevertheless the great sublimating love of Stevenson's life was his writing. As he said, he 'lived with words', and, like Keats, copied out passages from the masters as lessons in style. To this practice, outgrown with maturity, he himself gave in an essay the title of 'The Sedulous Ape' – a phrase which was to boomerang unfairly against him. 'The artist who says, "*It will do*," ' he wrote, in *Virginibus Puerisque*, 'is on the downward path.'

A cousin made mischief on his deathbed by warning Thomas Stevenson against Bob's corruption of Louis. Thomas met Bob in the street, accused him, and vowed that he hoped never to see him again; Mrs Stevenson had hysterics in the night. Louis denied that he was a 'horrible atheist'; he was merely a questioner. But, '. . . What a *damned* curse I am to my parents!' he wrote to his friend Charles Baxter. Some of his poems and his letters to Bob and Katharine even revealed a mood of suicide.

Then, as if in answer to the young unbeliever's prayers, in the summer of 1873 a beautiful, charming, sympathetic Anglo-Irish-woman named Mrs Sitwell was lying on a sofa beside a window at Cockfield Rectory in Suffolk. She was staying with the clergyman's wife, Maude Babington (*née* Balfour), who was expecting a visit from her young cousin Louis Stevenson. Mrs Sitwell looked out and saw a slim youth walking up the avenue of trees. He was dressed in a black velvet jacket and a straw wide-awake hat, and he had a knapsack on his back.

'Here is your cousin', she called to her hostess.

By coincidence Mrs Sitwell's name was Fanny, and she was also a brunette with small hands and feet. Lush as a houri, but elegant and witty, she slightly resembled the Mona Lisa. She was nearly twelve years older than Stevenson, who was not yet twenty-three. She had lived in Ireland, Germany, Australia, India and England.

Like Fanny Vandegrift she had been married at seventeen – to an Irish clergyman of the Church of England (a distant relation of the literary Sitwells). Like the other Fanny too she was separated from her husband, who had some carefully unmentioned but intolerable failing; probably he 'drank'. Friends helped her to find genteel little jobs – as translator, reviewer and secretary to a daringly co-educational college in London. Like her unknown namesake, she had had two small sons, of whom the younger had died, leaving her weak and unwell.

The elder boy, Bertie, was charmed by Stevenson, who played with him in his gay and fanciful way. As for the mother, she was so enchanted with his scintillating imagination that she wrote to her great friend, Mr (later Sir) Sidney Colvin, a Slade Professor of Fine Art at Cambridge, critic and essayist, and urged him to come and meet this 'fine young spirit', even 'genius' – a command which he obeyed. He was as impressed as she. Between them they formed a major influence in Stevenson's life and career.

'For nearly three years after this', she recorded, 'Louis wrote me long letters almost daily, pouring out in them all the many difficulties and troubles of that time of his life.'

Mrs Sitwell was becoming a legend in London's intellectual life, greatly admired by Henry James, Joseph Conrad and other eminent persons. It was a time when lovely women were put upon pedestals, and Louis passionately adored her as a wishful combination of potential mistress (he only half dared to hope), sainted 'Madonna' and inspiring confidante.

Sidney Colvin was the person who really discovered Stevenson as a writer and guided him into London literary circles. Correct and honourable, he closed his eyes to Louis's fervour for the woman he himself stoically loved. 'He had not only the poet's mind,' he wrote of Louis, 'but the poet's senses.'

No one knows what Mrs Sitwell finally said, after many months, to check Stevenson's mounting ardour when it began to flare out of hand. As Colvin himself remarked, she had a rare gift for staving off youthful desire and turning it into lifelong friendship.

Gradually, too, Louis had to accept the fact that her heart belonged to Colvin, with the permanent sort of platonic devotion conceivable in those days when divorce was an unthinkable disaster in Britain, the more so for a clergyman's wife. Physically chaste according to the ideal of the times, the couple were to love each other all the rest of their lives.

After her gentle rebuff Louis was ashamed, apologetic and deeply depressed for a while. But then he began to change the image of worship and to address the beloved as his Madonna. Here was the need which drew him – and continued to draw him – towards older women. 'What I want is a mother, and I have one now, have I not?' he wrote to Mrs Sitwell. His own mother's coddling has been blamed for this craving; but because Mrs Stevenson was not a 'clever' woman he could never really talk to her as to her maternal successors. He further told his new Madonna, 'I do not know if you are aware how much you help me in my work; it is not only that I have a strong motive; it is that I have always a woman to think of: and that is for so much.'

Meanwhile in the autumn of 1873 Louis was overtaken by the threat of tuberculosis – exhausted, some said, by his dissipations, and possibly by his arguments with his parents. ('O dear, dear, I just hold on to your hand very tight and shut my eyes', he wrote to Mrs Sitwell.) The London specialist ordered him to the Riviera. So he set off for several months in the sun at Menton. There, recovering, he practised his writing, and began to publish a few essays in *Cornhill* (under the initials *R.L.S.*) and in other magazines. Colvin joined him twice for short holidays. The two young men often sat at opposite sides of a hotel table, both writing to Mrs Sitwell.

Andrew Lang, the Scots folklorist, met him at Menton, and was not at first impressed. 'Clad in a wide blue cloak, he looked nothing less than English, except Scotch.'

There also he met two aristocratic Russian sisters in their thirties, each with a little girl. Like characters in Chekhov, the women were vivacious, temperamental and unblushingly outspoken. They told fortunes by palmistry, sang and danced in the Russian style, and served tea from a samovar. The younger was the third in the quartet of mature married women who were the main objects of his part-romantic, part-filial attachments: Mrs Jenkin, Mrs Sitwell, Mme Garsehine and – in a few years – Mrs Osbourne.

One of the small Russian girls was 'a little polyglot button' not yet three, but chattering in six languages. Colvin noted of Louis 'the intensely, quite exceptionally observing and loving interest he took in young children'. This was the first very small child Louis had ever got to know well, and he had a premature spasm of that parental longing which is more often experienced by young girls than by youths. He told Mrs Sitwell, 'I sometimes hate the children I see in the street – you know what I mean by hate – wish they were somewhere else and not there to mock me; and sometimes again, I don't know how to go by them for the love of them, especially the very wee ones.' To his mother he wrote, 'Kids are what is the matter with me.'

Here was the beginning of the delicate and incalculable effect of Stevenson's childlessness on his life, his work – and his marriage.

In April Louis joined Bob, among the studios and cafés of Paris, until he caught a heavy cold. He went home to Edinburgh to find his parents relieved at the return of the black sheep. They advanced his allowance to seven pounds a month and turned the old nursery into a study. He went on with his desultory law apprenticeship – and his writing. Someone gave him a ticket to a concert, from which he discovered that he had a passion for music.

He went to London as often as he could because of the literary life and company. Through Colvin he was elected a member of the Savile Club, a new seat of the intelligentsia. In the words of his eminent fellow member, the poet, critic and editor, Mr (later Sir) Edmund Gosse, 'he was of all men the most clubbable'.

In the early winter of 1874 Leslie Stephen, editor of *Cornhill* (and father of Virginia Woolf), was lecturing in Edinburgh. He took Louis, his new contributor, to the infirmary to call on a poor young poet and critic who had come from London to be a patient of Lister. He had one foot amputated and the other lame from tuberculosis of the bone. This was the burly, red-bearded, loud-talking, hard-drinking William Ernest Henley. He was brilliant and tetchy, gossipy, loving and lovable. A self-made man, he had a permanent chip on his shoulder against those whose help he accepted. But Stevenson was still an underdog and a kindred spirit. 'The poor fellow sat up in his bed with his hair and beard all tangled, and talked as cheerfully as if he had been in a king's palace', reported Louis.

He went constantly to the infirmary and, lacking cab fare, once carried an armchair on his head all the way from Heriot Row. When the patient was better he introduced him, still little known, into his own useful circle – Colvin, Baxter and the rest. Henley was to become one of his greatest friends and colleagues.

Katharine Stevenson caused a crisis by insisting on marrying a Cambridge man named Sydney de Mattos, who was said to be an atheist, a terrible shock to her family. Louis became involved by defending her, partly from affectionate chivalry and partly to uphold his principle of religious and moral freedom. 'I am always bad with [my parents],' he wrote Mrs Sitwell, 'because they always seem to expect me to be not very good.'

His spirits, like his father's, swung up and down between sunny sweetness and a temper which made him call himself 'The Old Man Virulent!' Especially in the winter, chilled and coughing, as he put it, 'the black dog was on my back'.

In July 1875 he actually passed his final examination and was called to the Scottish Bar. The new lawyer bolted off to sail among the Hebrides and to holiday with Bob in France. But in late September his brass name-plate was affixed by Scottish custom to the door of his home, and he made faint gestures of practising. His briefs numbered four in all, and his total fees never reached two figures.

Still, he *was* an advocate. His father had had his way thus far, but no further. For Louis was committed headlong to writing as to a secret vice. The initials *R.L.S.* were beginning to be noticed in *Cornhill* magazine, though at low rates; he did not yet earn more than fifty pounds a year.

After he had 'passed advocate' his parents gave him a thousand pounds – riches indeed – in addition to his raised allowance of twelve pounds a month. The thousand was to last only a few years, partly because he was recklessly generous to friends even poorer than himself. Some of the money he spent in travelling rough about the Continent and Britain, gathering the material for charming essays and his first books.

Bob had given him an entrée into the art colony of Montparnasse in Paris and its summer equivalent in the forest of Fontainebleau. The cousins liked to stay at the little Hôtel Chevillon at Grez-sur-Loing. They had become great friends of the American painter

Will Low, who had recently married a French girl and taken a cottage along the river beyond Grez.

In the summer of 1876 the artists who frequented Grez were shocked when they heard that two women painters had invaded the forest colony – where hitherto the only females, other than their own imported models and *grisettes*, had been peasants and chamber-maids. Worse yet, the newcomers were respectable women, and Americans.

Louis had been on a summer visit to his parents at Swanston Cottage, their white farmhouse in the Pentland Hills, and did not learn of the threat to the Hôtel Chevillon until he returned to Paris and found Will Low painting in his studio there.

'I recall his start of surprise and alarm,' wrote Low. . . .

' "It's the beginning of the end", he averred.'

Bob meanwhile had gone to Grez to freeze out the two women with a cold-shouldering which had been successful with other undesirables. But he did not return to Paris as planned, even being quoted as saying that these women were 'of the right sort'.

Amused, annoyed and inquisitive, Louis decided to go to Grez himself, rescue his cousin and scare away the intruders.

Chapter III

Grez: The fateful meeting

Meanwhile at the Hôtel Chevillon the Osbournes were spending a restful summer among willows, hammocks, easels, good talk, crusty loaves and red wine. Listless in the early days, Fanny wanted only to be quiet, to enjoy nature and to paint. At first she and Belle were gingerly tolerated at the long table in the *salle-à-manger*, where they sat at the English-speaking end. They kept their place, entering into some of the common activities and tactfully forgoing others. Fanny wore deep mourning. The *habitués* melted into compassion when they learned of her lost child, and they vied with one another to be kind and attentive.

Sam Osbourne was there for a while. But Miss Kate, the children's governess, had succeeded in finding a rich aunt in Paris and had been offered a job as paid companion at a fashionable watering-place.

Sam must have been a very western-looking figure among the smocked painters. The reunion of husband and wife was declining under hidden pressures of silence and discord. In Europe he appeared in Fanny's eyes to be provincial and uncultured; doubtless she seemed to him 'affected and highfalutin'. She wrote to Dora Williams, her great friend in San Francisco, that his company spoiled Lloyd's manners, and she was determined to bring up her son as a gentleman.

Gradually Fanny was regaining her health and her rich unusual beauty. Aged thirty-six and with grey beginning to frost her hair, she was known in the village as *'la belle Américaine'*. Belle was described by the American artist Birge Harrison as 'a bewitching young girl of seventeen, with eyes so large as to be out of drawing'. Several young painters fell in love with her. Will Low wrote of the mother and daughter as 'in appearance more like sisters; the elder, slight, with delicately moulded features and vivid eyes gleaming from under a mass of dark hair; the younger of more robust type, in the first precocious bloom of womanhood.'

Like countless other Americans, Fanny was entranced by Old World culture and manners. 'Art and life were synonymous with us in those days,' wrote Will Low.

The painters scorned the sunshine, but on grey days they went out to work in the meadows under a mushrooming of enormous white umbrellas, and one or another of the men always carried Fanny's easel and paintbox. When she was not feeling well they strolled with her in the flickering forest. They competed for her society. At odd moments they made sketches of her mouth, her expressive eyes, her arms. Always learning, she soon picked up the more sophisticated ways of the cosmopolitan group, and mingled a sort of masculine *camaraderie* with the coyness of her generation. No one knew as yet that her marriage was breaking up. She was a proper matron chaperoning her student daughter. The young men always treated her as a 'lady', which in a way was no mean achievement in Bohemia.

The Osbournes had been hearing tales of the two legendary Stevenson cousins – and also, it was hinted, their menacing prejudice against women in the colony. 'Always in our minds', Lloyd reported many years later, 'was a vision of those dreadful Stevensons returning to drive us forth.'

Then one morning he and his mother were looking down from their upstairs window into the paved courtyard. They saw Belle speaking to someone in a velvet jacket, flowing tie and *mustachios*, whom they recognized from description as Bob Stevenson. He was a 'dark, roughly dressed man as lithe and graceful as a Mexican *vaquero*'. He was smiling pleasantly, big black hat in hand. But the watchers were somewhat disquieted by his 'habitually mocking expression'. 'Then [Belle] ran up to our room, laughing with excitement, to tell us that "Bob" was a most agreeable and entertaining man . . . and my sister's eyes were shining. . . .'

He soon became 'very much a friend', in Belle's understatement, and the family grew less timid if not less diverted by the prospect of the unknown Louis. 'Bob', confirmed Will Low, in his memoirs, 'was at this time the dominant figure. . . . His genius (no other word suffices) for talk was greater than I have known in any man.' Many years later Fanny was to write, 'Whenever my husband wished to depict a romantic, erratic, engaging character, he delved into the rich mine of his cousin's personality. . . .'

But though Bob was the senior partner, the two Stevensons were jointly admired. Everyone at the inn told the Osbournes, 'Wait until Louis gets here!'

Lloyd wrote that he never forgot a soft sweet dusk in early July when the sixteen or eighteen guests were all dining in the lamplight at the long table. His mother and sister were the only women and he the only child. There was a sound at one of the open french windows, and into the room there vaulted a thin young man with a dusty knapsack on his back. The whole company rose with delighted cries and outstretched hands. The newcomer was led to a chair in a hubbub of chatter and laughter. Then he was introduced to the Osbournes.

'"My cousin, Mr Stevenson," said Bob, and there ensued a grave inclination of heads, while I wriggled on my chair, with shy peeps. . . .'

Afterwards the gallant Louis himself, in common with Fanny and his more sentimental biographers, claimed that he had fallen in love with her at first sight when he had paused to peer in through the window at the company at the long table. Perhaps he did, more or less; he certainly preferred to think so. An immediate shock of liking would have been in character for Fanny too, since most of her powerful affinities for special friends – male or female – seem to have begun with an instant recognition. Debunking biographers claimed that the couple fell at once into each other's arms, but in fact this must have been many months later. For one thing, Sam had not yet gone back to America and was still there at his wife's side. In the second place, Louis had to return to Britain after a few days and did not revisit Grez until September. In the third, Fanny's letters home showed her friends that during the first season she was more attracted to Bob than to Louis.

Soon Sam started back to San Francisco. There must have been a strange parting behind the bedroom door. No date was set for his family's return. Only Belle went along in the diligence to see him off at the station. 'On the way, he stopped and bought me a little silver purse. When I came back home and looked into it I found a twenty-dollar gold piece.'

One of the painters in the community was a twenty-year-old Irishman named Frank O'Meara, 'an artist of peculiar delicacy and charm,' according to Low. A handsome youth with curly hair, blue eyes and a fine voice for Irish ballads, he appeared in rough tweeds and blue beret, carried a thorny shillelagh and spoke with a brogue to match. He came from the wealthy landed gentry, but being one of a large Catholic family he had only a small allowance. He and Belle fell promptly in love.

It was customary for the painters to take a dip in the river before the midday meal. The long table was spread in the garden under the grape arbour, and a score or so would sit down to the *plat du jour* in what were then 'the lightest of costumes'. The food was simple but wonderfully well cooked: *pot-au-feu* served in a heavy yellow bowl, yard-long loaves of bread, chickens roasted on a spit before the open fire, lettuce salad flavoured with garlic and tarragon, cheese made in the village, and bottles of good red wine. 'We finished off with tall glasses of black coffee,' wrote Belle, 'and often sat talking for hours.

And such talk – gay, inspiring, electric. . . . We argued, we beat the table, we shouted to be heard. . . .'

Fanny, thriving upon fresh air, art and attentions, gradually grew out of her very real deep grief for Hervey. Her letters indicated that she was conscientiously trying to keep it alive – which might seem hypocritical today but was idealistic and faithful then. She took pleasure in the happy time her surviving children were having. ' . . . I was exquisitely conscious also', remembered Lloyd, 'of my mother's tenderness and of the growing consolation she found in me.'

Writing home, she showed her central role in the picturesque male group with entertaining gossip about the two Stevensons and the rest. Bob's name was mentioned more than any other.

'He is exactly like one of Ouida's heroes,' she told Rearden, 'with the hand of steel in the glove of velvet. . . . He is the best painter here, a charming musician, speaks all languages, does all sorts of feats of strength and has no ambition. . . .' Once, alas, he got drunk.

Pampered by so many men, and dazzled by Bob, her dead-end marital role would have been disheartening to any attractive and vital woman, but it must have been doubly frustrating to one of her passionate possessiveness. More than the average woman she must have wanted a congenial man of her own to love and cherish. For all she could foresee, as long as she lived this could never be.

When Louis Stevenson returned to the Continent in September, he and Sir Walter Simpson made their venturesome trip in two sailing canoes from Antwerp along the Scheldt and the Belgian canals to the upper Oise. The journey was later to be turned into the lilting water-music of Louis's first little book, *An Inland Voyage*. In the first chapter there is an early reflection of Fanny: 'If a man finds a woman admires him, were it only for his acquaintance with geography, he will begin at once to build upon the admiration.' And at the end of the book he was to write: 'You may paddle all day long; but it is when you come back at nightfall, and look in at the familiar room, that you find Love or Death awaiting you beside the stove; and the most beautiful adventures are not those we go to seek.'

By now Fanny's intimates at Chevillon's could not fail to know that her marriage was a shell. But her head was still turned by the dark dynamic Bob when Louis reappeared. In her letters he continued to be 'the other Stevenson'.

Belle wrote home about him too. 'There is a young Scotchman here, a Mr Stevenson, who looks at me as though I were a natural curiosity. . . . He is such a nice-looking ugly man and I would rather listen to him talk than read the most interesting book I ever saw. We sit in the little green arbor after dinner drinking coffee and talking till late at night. Mama is ever so much better and is getting prettier every day.'

One might have thought that Louis would have been more attracted to the enchanting and eligible Belle. He found the American girl such a phenomenon that he wrote a magazine sketch about her. But Belle was eight years younger than he, while Fanny – as he preferred – was more than ten years older. She was, wrote her sister, Nellie Sanchez, 'so foreign to his race' in historic Edinburgh that her experiences 'threw about her an atmosphere of thrilling romance that appealed to Stevenson'. 'Dark as a wayside gipsy, Lithe as a hedgewood hare . . .' he was to describe her in a poem. From the first he was much more strongly drawn to her than was Bob.

The piquant fact is that there was almost a *Midsummer Night's Dream* situation among that little group in the forest: Louis was falling in love with Fanny, who was fascinated by Bob; while Bob was strongly attracted by Belle, who was in love with O'Meara. More than three years later Bob was still writing to his cousin about Belle, '. . . of course if she really took to me I would go for her'. Whether Fanny knew that Bob preferred her daughter is doubtful.

One October day the Chevillons were alarmed when Fanny and Bob were very late in returning from a walk through the forest with its first flitting golden leaves. They had taken a wrong turning and got lost. She made an anecdote of this little adventure in a letter to Rearden. Apparently he taunted her about it, for she replied, weeks later: ' . . . You spoke of my getting lost – for the purposes of flirtation. I would hardly do that with one considered a madman, though his conversation seemed to my limited understanding quite logical and sensible. I think if you had heard it all you would hardly call it flirtation, though. Of course, I know less about such things than a man of your varied experience. This is what he was saying to me: that I was a stunning good little girl, not a "toothless old hag", though that was a politeness, I dare say. And that he wanted to tell me something . . . that I would make no mistake in cultivating the acquaintance of his, Mr Stevenson's, cousin Louis. "You must have nothing to say to *me*," he said, "for I am only a vulgar cad, but Louis is a gentleman, and you can trust him and depend upon him." And he thanked me for not laughing at Louis, whose faintings and hysterics were caused by ill health. And then . . . we found we had taken the wrong path. He was so much more troubled about it than I was and made me walk so fast that I was almost tired to death when we arrived at home, and found them all in a state of consternation because I was lost with "Mad Bob". So that, with a little desultory talk, was our "flirtation".

'I took his advice because it was honestly given and kindly meant, and I think I should like him better than some of the other men, except that he reminds me in some curious ways of you. He was right about his cousin, whom I like very much, and who is the wittiest man I ever met. Only I do wish he wouldn't burst into tears in such an unexpected way; it is so embarrassing. One doesn't know what to do, whether to offer him a pocket hankerchief, [sic] or look out of the window. As my hankerchief [sic] generally has charcoal upon it, I choose the latter alternative. He will be in Paris in January on business connected with some dramas of his that have been translated into French, so I suppose Belle and I will go to the theatre, sometimes, with him. I don't care anything about going but since the doctor said I was to be amused, I am taken to all sorts of places whether I want to go or not. I cannot understand French well enough to feel much interested in a French play, anyway. . . . F.'

After such a chivalrous intimation that she was wasting her time if she hoped for a romance with Bob himself, Fanny took the hint and began to pay more attention to 'the other Stevenson'. Louis's name appeared oftener in her letters home.

Lloyd recalled that soon 'even a child could see' that Louis and Fanny were attracted – though perhaps he was partly exaggerating by hindsight, since she was still bemused by the smiling fascination of Bob. Indeed, as before, Louis partly courted the mother by courting the child, and Lloyd adored his fanciful nonsense and nicknamed him 'Luly'. The boy noticed that sometimes, when the other painters were out of the inn, his mother and Luly sat and talked long and earnestly on either side of the dining-room stove.

There is no record of any qualms of vanity or sense of insecurity which Fanny may have felt about the difference in their ages. Her tiger-lily beauty was at its height. Old photographs show a face so strong that one is surprised to realize that she was petite and still slim.

Her compatriot Birge Harrison remembered her at Grez as 'a grave and remarkable type of womanhood, with eyes of a depth and somber beauty that I have never seen equalled – eyes, nevertheless, that upon occasion could sparkle with humor and brim over with laughter. Yet on the whole Mrs Osbourne impressed me as first of all a woman of profound character and serious judgment, who could, if occasion called, have been the leader in some great movement. But she belonged to the quattrocento rather than to the nineteenth century. Had she been born a Medici, she would have held rank as one of the most remarkable women of all time. . . .

'Mrs Osbourne was in no sense ordinary. Indeed she was gifted with a mysterious sort of over-intelligence, which is almost impossible to describe, but which impressed itself upon everyone who came within the radius of her influence . . . . She was therefore both physically and mentally the very antithesis of the gay, hilarious, open-hearted Stevenson, and for that reason perhaps the woman in all the world best fitted to be his life comrade and helpmate. . . .'

Though Fanny was later to write much about her life as Mrs Robert Louis Stevenson, she was naturally very reticent concerning the first few years of her association with Louis, during which she was Mrs Samuel Osbourne. She and Stevenson both discreetly withheld or destroyed their early letters to each other. Hers must have been much more sensitive than her letters to Rearden, since they pleased Louis.

She drew a realistic head and bust of him, with his Indian embroidered smoking-cap, his longish hair and his thin hand – a skilful likeness, it was said. She could, in fact, draw very well.

One of his poems, written in that year or more likely in the next, tells of floating downriver in a canoe below the many-arched stone bridge, one blue afternoon:

Deep, swift and clear, the lilies floated; fish
Through the shadows ran. There, thou and I
Read kindness in our eyes and closed the match.

Chapter IV
Love, poverty and Victorian conventions

Fanny and her children went back to Paris in October. Lloyd was
overjoyed when she told him, 'Luly is coming too.'

She returned with Belle to Julien's atelier. Her doctors thought
she was not yet strong enough to keep house, so she took a small
apartment up four flights of slippery waxed stairs at 5 Rue Douay in
Montmartre. Several other respectable American and British women
lived there – artists, musicians, writers.

Louis, in a letter to her years later, recalled the happiness of 'the
day when I came to see you in Paris after the first absence'. And the
American artist Will Low reported, '. . . His daily pilgrimage from
our quarter to the heights of Montmartre told the story clearly, and
for male companionship Bob and I were left alone'.

Louis wrote to his mother that he dined almost every day at a
modest *crèmerie* 'with a party of Americans, one Irishman, and
sometimes an English lady: elderly, very prim'. In another letter he
further pulled, or tried to pull, the wool over Mrs Stevenson's
gentle eyes when he told her about a party – without alcoholic
drinks – at the studio of a wealthy art student, and for the first time
discreetly mentioned Fanny. 'One of the matrons was a very beautiful woman indeed; I played old fogy and had a deal of talk with her
which pleased me.'

One winter dusk the Osbournes, O'Meara and one or two others
were gathered around the fire in Fanny's shabby little *salon*, when
Louis came bounding up the slippery stairs waving a magazine. He
opened it and breathlessly read aloud a very favourable review of his
work. Readers were advised to keep an eye on a rising young author,
referred to as 'one Stevenson'. That became his nickname for months.

Once the group were dining in a restaurant when Louis, tasting the burgundy, declared that it was corked, and ordered another bottle. The *sommelier* apologized, carried off the offending bottle, and came back deferentially with another.

The customary sample was poured into the bottom of Stevenson's glass. He sniffed, sipped and rolled it about on his tongue. Suddenly he stiffened with fury. The second bottle was corked also. He felt sure that he had been tricked – that the management had contemptuously sent back the rejected wine, thinking the *Anglais* would not know the difference.

His friends, the waiters, the proprietor, all tried to dissuade and soothe him. But he rose, white and silent, seized the bottle by the neck, whirled it around his head – not caring that the wine was pouring down his sleeve – strode across the room until he came to a wall, and dashed the bottle to pieces. Then he marched calmly back to his table, and after a few uneasy moments the dinner went on as usual.

No one could deny that it would take courage for a woman to ally herself with a man who had such a temper. Moreover, like Bob, he sometimes gave way to hysterical fits of laughter or tears.

By January 1877 he was giving Fanny's apartment at 5 Rue Douay as his forwarding address – though he certainly would not have lived there. In the February issue of *Cornhill* appeared his essay 'On Falling in Love' (later to be published in *Virginibus Puersique*). The evidence indicates that Fanny was beginning to respond to this most appealing of love letters.

'. . . Love should run out to meet love with open arms,' he wrote. 'Indeed, the ideal story is that of two people who go into love step for step, with a fluttered consciousness, like a pair of children venturing together into a dark room. . . . The feeling is so plainly shared, that as soon as the man knows what it is in his own heart, he is sure of what is in the woman's. . . . It seems as if he had never heard or felt or seen until that moment . . . He is practically incommoded by the generosity of his feelings. . . . The essence of love is kindness; and indeed it may be best defined as passionate kindness: kindness, so to speak, run mad and become importunate and violent.'

In April, Fanny wrote to Rearden:
'Bob Stevenson is the most beautiful creature I ever saw in my

life, and yet somehow, reminds me of you. He spent a large fortune at the rate of eight thousand pounds a year, and now he has only a hundred pounds a year left; he graduated from Cambridge with high honors and won all the boat races and everything of that sort, studied music and did wonderful things as a musician, took holy orders to please his mother, quit in disgust, studied painting and did some fine work, and is now dying from the effects of dissipation and is considered a little mad.

'Louis, his cousin, the hysterical fellow, who wrote the article about Belle, is a tall, gaunt Scotchman with a face like Raphael, and between over-education and dissipation has ruined his health, and is dying of consumption. Louis reformed his habits a couple of years ago, and Bob, this winter. Louis is the heir to an immense fortune which he will never live to inherit. His father and mother, cousins, are both threatened with insanity, and I am quite sure the son is. His article about Belle was written as she says, for the five pounds which he wanted to give a pensioner of his in the hospital and was done when he had a headache, and badly enough we knew as well as he . . . .

'You are quite right. I shall miss my bohemian friends when I get home . . . but the two mad Stevensons who with all their suffering are men out of spirits, but so filled with the joyfulness of mere living that their presence is exhilarating, I shall never see again. I never heard one of them say a cynical thing, nor knew them to do an unkind thing. With all the wild stories I have heard of them fresh in my mind, I still consider them the truest gentlemen and nothing can make them anything less. . . .'

Presumably Mrs Samuel Osbourne was understating to Rearden the extent of her friendship with the two Stevensons, and now especially Louis.

Between February and May he was spending much time in the black frosts of Edinburgh, chilled alike by the stern company of his parents and by his chronic chest ailments. Bob was also at home for a while, and ill.

Fanny told Rearden, '. . . I have received 2 very characteristic letters from the Stevensons. Bob says, "I implore you to write a little letter to my poor cousin in that prison house of his in Edinburgh. I am only a poor cad but Louis is a true and good man and your letters may cheer him for he is said to be dying, God help me."

Louis says, "They tell me dear Bob is not long for this world. I know him better than anyone and the good that is in him, and you need not fear to write to him. Pray do, to please me as well as for his sake." That is so sweet of them both – of course, I shall write. I think they will care for my letters more than you do, and that I am wasting my time writing to you, which would be better spent upon them. If you have anything more malicious to say, say it about me, and I won't mind, but not about my friends. You needn't, as I have before remarked, call me "My dear". I don't think I am coming home in the spring. Fanny MO.'

Unhappy and unsettled as Louis was over his love for Fanny, in Scotland in that year or the next he may have sought emotional escape in a couple of amorous adventures. His friends' accounts vary as to the timing, and it may be that the tales belong to an earlier period. One girl was said to be the fair-haired daughter of a carpenter, the other the blonde daughter of a village blacksmith. Whether or no, many months later Louis still felt obliged to write ruefully to Henley that he was recovering from the problem of 'an enchanting young lady whom you have seen, or rather from her inspiration . . . letters threatening exposure, etc. . . .'. She may, however, have still been blackmailing him over an affair which occurred before he met Fanny.

His parents found out belatedly about his sexual indiscretions, and his father, firmly chivalrous – like R.L.S. himself – towards all women whether virtuous or unvirtuous, is said to have told him that if he had seduced a respectable girl he should marry her. This is believed to have been the reason, or one of the reasons, for his first disclosing to his parents the equally unpalatable information that he was deeply and seriously in love with someone else – a married woman.

The mild Mrs Stevenson was no longer so willing a buffer between her husband and her son, now that questions of religion and morals were involved. 'My mother is my father's wife', Louis had once remarked bitterly. 'The children of lovers are orphans.'

To escape from the fierce disapproval at home he left for London and France, and hastened to complete *An Inland Voyage* because he 'wanted coin so badly'. The maturity of his first real love had added a new dimension to his work, but so far he had not yet earned more than fifty pounds for all his writings in any one year.

Naturally, Stevenson's flood of letters to Mrs Sitwell diminished in spate and in depth. ('It is to be noticed', he had written in the essay 'On Marriage', 'that those who have loved once or twice already are so much the better educated to a woman's hand.') Soon, from Paris, he confessed to Fanny the First his growing attachment to Fanny the Second, and unburdened his painful social and financial difficulties. Wise restraint seems to have been shown by both ladies – the usual tact by the subtle Fanny Sitwell and a more than usual forbearance by the vigorous Fanny Osbourne.

'Look here, you and Colvin are God's angels', he wrote to Mrs Sitwell after her sympathetic response. And the brief note was signed by Fanny as well as himself.

Literary historians have argued for decades about the actual time at which Louis and Fanny first became lovers. Though it may possibly have been during those late autumn or early winter months together in Paris, it was probably a good deal later. Most likely her warm blood was well teamed with his. But in the 1870s a physical affair was, of course, a desperate step for a respectable woman, even in the Paris art colony, and she must have hesitated to cut herself off from what scant and shaky security she had. She had seen too much of life as a desirable woman flattered by many men to be sure that any one of them might not be fickle. She was constantly harassed by her lack of money, and it was not easy to be in love with a sickly, impecunious young man. Sam's contributions were small and erratic, and now seemed to be dwindling. But it would be surprising indeed if Stevenson, so generous with others whom he loved less, did not help her and her children from his fast-diminishing thousand pounds.

Few even of her enemies have suggested that she was a 'gold-digger'. Though she was shrewd and far more practical than Louis in domestic improvisations, as a financier she was not much better qualified than he.

The Osbournes spent the summer at Grez, and early in the autumn Fanny returned to Paris. Her modest new apartment was at 5 Rue

Ravignan, and Louis again had his mail addressed there, presumably still as a convenience.

At the atelier her paintings managed to imitate the mannerisms of the Barbizon school and were fair enough to justify her presence. But there was never much doubt that her gifts were more for crafts than for art. As with most amateurs her talent was not compulsive – unlike Stevenson's, whose life and work were one.

In October Louis caught an eye infection so severe that he nearly went blind. Rising above discretion, she insisted that he should stay at her apartment where she could nurse him – surely a brave and generous act in those times.

By the first of November he was no better. Terrified of what might happen, and of her own responsibility, she telegraphed to Bob to come to Paris and take him home. Anxious days passed and there was no answer; she could not know that Bob himself was away from Edinburgh and neurotically ill. In desperation she boldly wired to Sidney Colvin – whom she had never met – to say that she herself was bringing Louis to London for care and treatment. There, with his doctors and his friends, his eyes soon began to improve.

It was her first visit to England but she saw little. A foot injury incurred at Grez had never quite healed and now got worse again, so she was forced to undergo surgery. The admirable Mrs Sitwell took her away from her cheap lodgings and into her home. It would have been fascinating to be present at the meeting of the two Fannys.

Louis had coached her as to how to behave with his great friends, who were more than kind and tactful. He had warned her not to smoke, but she did and was caught. Urbanely, her hostess and Mr Colvin showed no sign of shock, but even sent a servant out for tobacco and papers, and had her demonstrate the rolling of cigarettes.

Decades later, Colvin gallantly named strength and staunchness as her ruling qualities. 'Her personality was almost as vivid as [Stevenson's]. She was small, dark-complexioned, eager, devoted; of squarish build – supple and elastic; her hands and feet were small and beautifully modelled, though busy; her head had a crop of close-waving thick black hair. She had a build and character that somehow suggested Napoleon, with a firm setting of jaw and beautifully precise and delicate modelling of the nose and lips; her eyes were full of sex and mystery as they changed from fire or fun to gloom or tenderness.' He noticed her 'fine pearly set of small teeth, and the clear metallic accents of her intensely human and often quaintly individual speech'.

This account of her voice as 'metallic' is at variance with a later description by her sister Nellie. 'Her speaking voice was low, modulated, and sweet, but with few inflections, and her husband once compared it to the pleasantly monotonous flow of a running brook under ice.'

One afternoon Fanny received a caller who was later to be her bitter enemy: William Ernest Henley. The young big-bearded, loud-voiced cripple heaved into Mrs Sitwell's house with two crutches propelling his powerful torso and withered legs. ('To converse with him is a physical no less than an intellectual recreation', grumbled Oscar Wilde who, years later, was knocked down by Henley with his crutch.)

Henley had become editor of the magazine *London,* to which Louis was the leading contributor, necessarily almost unpaid. Stevenson was perhaps the first of the promising writers then known as 'Henley's young men', who were to include Kipling, Conrad, Barrie, Hardy, Henry James, Wells, Yeats and Shaw. Henley's physical sufferings made him seek sublimation in a burly masculinity and a scorn of the aesthetes. Aubrey Beardsley was reputed to have run off in fright at the first glimpse of him. Nevertheless Fanny knew of his obverse side, the feminine streak of tenderness and delicacy shown in his great friendship for Louis – and in the lyrical verse which was putting him among the best of the late Victorian poets.

She had felt slightly uneasy at confronting this formidable personality, but though details are not known, the meeting was said to have gone well.

When Fanny returned to France, she shepherded Bob, who had finally turned up, still weak and nervous. In Paris she and their mutual friends humoured and coddled him until he was better in mind and body.

Louis, spending Christmas and New Year at home, devoutly thanked Mrs Sitwell for her kindness to Fanny. 'F., in a letter which did me much good, sent you her love. . . . Her letter to me was mostly about you.'

Fanny waited and brooded until he rejoined her in January.

Shortly after his return there is the first definite proof that by this time the lovers' relationship had become physical, as well as 'a romance of destiny', as he called it. He wrote to Henley during a visit to Edinburgh: '. . . I'm a miserable widower, but so long as I work, I keep cheerful. . . . And do I not love? and am I not loved? and have I not friends who are the pride of my heart? O, no, I'll have none of your blues; I'll be lonely, dead lonely, for I can't help it; and I'll hate to go to bed where there is no dear head on the pillow, for I can't help that either, God help me; but I'll make no mountain out of my little molehill and pull no damnable faces at the derisive stars. . . .'

Fanny was putting a frank and courageous front to their liaison before their circle in Paris and his more sophisticated friends from Britain. He was deeply moved by her sacrifice. For a woman in 1878 it meant making him a gift of her lifelong reputation, but having taken the fatal step she did it spontaneously and ungrudgingly.

His allowance had recently been increased to a hundred pounds a year, but this was barely enough to keep himself, much less a mistress with two children. The thousand pounds would soon be gone. Torn in two by his poverty and his devoted obligation towards Fanny, he tried guardedly to explain to his parents a little of what he called 'the new complications in my life.'

He wisely asked Mrs Sitwell and Colvin to say a word on his behalf, knowing that Thomas Stevenson respected and admired them both. He wanted them to assure his family that Fanny was not just another of his light loves. He was acutely ashamed of his past philandering which could cheapen her in their eyes. His two friends did a masterly job of mediation.

In February he asked his father to come to Paris so that he could talk to him personally. 'Don't be astonished,' he told Colvin, 'but admire my courage and Fanny's. We wish to be right with the world as far as we can.' And he added, 'Three days from hence, I shall know where I am, and either be well off or quite a beggar.'

The good old man answered his call. It is unlikely that he met Fanny or was told that she was his son's mistress, but Louis tried to convey something of the full seriousness of his attachment. She meanwhile waited tensely in her apartment for him to come and tell her how the meetings had fared. Proud as she was, it was an intolerable humiliation to be regarded as an undesirable companion, above all for the object of her great love and sacrifice.

Thomas apparently found a little wry consolation in the fact that the infection was confined to 'immoral' France. He might have been less amenable if the talks had taken place in Edinburgh. At any rate, the woman was legally tied. It seemed a likely bet that this improbable affair with an older matron from remote barbaric America would fade out in time. He was prepared to be patient. Meanwhile he was stoically decent to his ailing son.

'My dear friend,' Louis wrote to Mrs Sitwell, '. . . I know no way of thanking you for all you have done. Perhaps, after all, the confident trust with which I came to you was better than any thanks after the event. At least, so I try to think. I am afraid Fanny is not very bright in health, but she says she is taking care. . . . Indeed you need be under no surprise if you have made a very enthusiastic friend of her. She could not be honestly less. . . .'

More toleration of himself at home, however, still did not extend to 'that woman'. Obliged to meet his father's conciliation half way, he left Fanny for the Easter holidays and spent them with his parents. But a few weeks later he was with her again in Paris.

'I have two invalids instead of one to look after,' he wrote to Mrs Sitwell, 'and I feel so tired you wouldn't believe. . . . I have had a deal of writing and telegraphing with my people; they are behaving awfully well. . . . I am ashamed to be stiff, where I find them so full of concessions. . . . Fanny really must be excused; I wish I could say she is well; her nerves are quite gone; one day I find her in heaven and the next in hell. We have many strong reasons for getting her out of Paris in about a month.'

All spring she was in a dark fever of indecision as to whether she ought to go home to the United States. Surely her relationship with Stevenson was leading only to a *cul-de-sac* of disgrace and destitution – a calamity for her children as well as herself.

It must have lain on her mind that one day her impoverished young author might grow tired of a too difficult tie and marry some eligible girl of his own age. And if she, Fanny, had thrown away everything else, where would *she* be? At any rate it was a godsend that she kept her head and did not go off to live with him in open sin, as they must sometimes have been desperately tempted to do. Such defiance would not only have ruined them socially and lost all support from his family, but also it would have blasted his career.

Stevenson's first book, *An Inland Voyage*, was released in London in May 1878. Proceeds: twenty pounds from the publishers, and a few good reviews which he did not expect. Always his own cool critic, he underestimated the work as 'not badly written, thin, mildly cheery and strained'.

In that same summer he held his first and only regular job. Professor Jenkin was a juror at the International Exhibition in Paris, and engaged him as his private secretary. Louis appeared like a stranger in a new clean suit. It was his nearest approach to the bourgeoisie – but not very near. 'I had many letters from Jenkin in Paris,' wrote the principal, Sir Alfred Ewing, 'but none were written in the handwriting of the secretary.'

This was Stevenson's best year so far for literary earnings – partly because he was reaping the payment for work previously done and only now being published, and partly because he was beginning to write short stories which, appearing in *London* and *Cornhill*, were helping to build his reputation. 'Will o' the Mill' was praised by Henry James. He was also turning out pot-boiling sketches for Henley and other editors. Fanny, more than his father, was anxious for him to make a living from the work he loved – hardly a culpable wish, as some have charged. Her influence had already begun to exert itself on his career. Like most people who write a little, she felt that she was qualified to speak the language of someone born to write a great deal. She was eager for him to produce more fiction, which in their generation was far better paid than non-fiction, and at which he had been trying his hand since he was sixteen.

For the third summer running, the Osbournes spent much of the season in the shady peace of Grez, and Louis joined them when he could.

Fanny's character – or at any rate her personality – had altered and solidified since the first summer. Her naïve American charm was putting on the weight of a fanatic dedication to what she believed and wanted herself and her life to be. In some ways she was disarmingly honest and modest; she knew that she was no genius in painting or writing, as she would have loved to be. But she felt that she was noble, gifted and infallibly wise in divining character and values. She played this wishful role with such conviction that, like a compelling actress, she conveyed it to at least half of her audience. Those who did not respond were the more ruthless because they felt it to be false. But it was not false. It was a dream of self-hypnosis.

In July, with dramatic abruptness, she finally made up her mind to leave for California the next month. Undoubtedly one strong reason was that Sam had had enough of supporting his absent family and had stopped sending money, with an ultimatum that they were to come home. There seemed no possible way in which she could maintain herself and her children, especially in a foreign country, though Louis was trying his best to help her by raising a little money through his literary connections.

Mr and Mrs Stevenson were relieved beyond words that the strange American woman was going back to the ends of the earth before she had turned their son into a social outcast. They quietly expected that she would soon be forgotten.

The Osbournes hurried up to Paris to pack. Fanny gave no explanation to her children. Belle was stunned – and so was O'Meara. 'This beautiful adventure was over and I thought my heart would break.' If only he had proposed! But he did not.

O'Meara gave his departing sweetheart two presents. One was a portrait of himself by another young art student named John Singer Sargent. The other was a little pug dog with the Irish name of Barney. He was to live for years and travel across the Atlantic and later the Pacific, making, Belle recorded, 'a great sensation wherever he went'.

In August the Osbournes stopped in London for a few weeks *en route* to their transatlantic steamer. Fanny faced the interlude with stoical despair.

Louis was unable to be in town for their arrival, probably detained by his job in Paris, but Bob met them at Dover and took them up to London to cheap lodgings in Chelsea.

Louis soon arrived, and he seemed more mature and well-dressed, rather fancying himself as a journalist. He was tidy in a new blue suit with double-breasted coat and a stiff felt hat. He was helping

Henley to edit the weekly *London*, and spoke importantly about dashing off copy, reading proofs and going to press.

The magazine had almost no money to pay contributors, and as Fanny later recalled in a Preface to Louis's works, 'It often happened that an entire number of *London* was written by Mr Henley and my husband alone. . . . As verses filled space more readily than prose, poem after poem would be dashed off by Mr Henley and my husband until the blanks were filled. ''Hurry, my lad,'' Mr Henley would shout; ''only six more lines now!'' My husband would scratch off the six lines, hand them to the printer's devil, who stood waiting; and the situation was saved for another week.'

Most of Stevenson's stories to be collected in *New Arabian Nights* first appeared in *London*. They included the 'Suicide Club' series, some of which he read aloud in manuscript to Fanny and the children in their bleak little parlour. The series was based on an idea which Bob had expounded in his mother's Chelsea drawing-room. He had, wrote Fanny, 'described the advantages of a suicide train, where persons weary of life might engage a compartment,' scheduled to hurtle over a precipice in an hour. Bob himself figured as the young man with the cream tarts.

Fanny and Louis must often have been tempted to cancel her reservations before it was too late. 'Meanwhile', recalled Lloyd in his memoirs, '. . . I had not the slightest perception of the quandary my mother and R.L.S. were in, nor what agonies of mind their approaching separation was bringing. . . .'

The boy's last picture of that London visit was of Stevenson seeing them off on the boat train. His mother was trying not to weep as they strained their eyes to follow his long thin miserable figure in a brown ulster striding away down the platform without looking back.

Part 3

California
A lover's pilgrimage 1879 - 80

Chapter I
Fanny's dilemma

In America the Osbournes stopped to visit the family in Indiana, where there was more sadness, for Mr Vandegrift had died. Fanny's widowed sister Josephine, formerly Mrs Marshall, was married again, to a banker in Danville.

When Fanny left with her children for California on the new transcontinental railroad she took along her sister, the young blue-eyed Nellie. Nellie was 'an odd earnest girl', as Belle said, with a fringe of 'bangs' on her brow and a long braid of fair hair down her back. She was prim, bookish, demure, and she adored her eldest sister. Fanny was then, recalled Nellie, 'in the full flower of her striking and unusual beauty, and so youthful in appearance that she, her daughter and I passed everywhere as three sisters'.

The travellers rejoined Sam in the cottage at East Oakland. He had a good job as a court stenographer in the Bureau of Mines. After the wit of R.L.S. and his friends, her husband's bland heartiness got on Fanny's nerves more than ever. But both their children were warmed again by his mellow charm. Belle recollected, 'He was as gay and entertaining as ever, but at home there was a perceptible chill between him and my mother.'

For that whole next year Fanny was at a loss as to what to do. During the first half she seldom wrote to Louis, in her seething uncertainty. Matrimonial stiffness and gloom were varied by 'scenes' behind closed doors.

In that spring Belle and Nellie were surprised when they were sudenly told that the husband and wife were going away together for a 'little trip'; they did not say where, but promised to let them know. The couple had quarrelled and made up, and presumably wished to slip off quietly and talk over their situation. Fanny was still worn out and unwell from strain and worry, and wanted a change in more impersonal surroundings. A week later the girls were excited to get a telegram asking them to bring Lloyd and join the elders in Monterey, the drowsy old coast town about a hundred and fifty miles south of San Francisco.

From the narrow-gauge railroad the three young people gazed at the peculiar and distinctive beauty of the Monterey coast, its forested hills curving down to rocky headlands with live-oaks and strange wind-twisted cypresses in the spray. (This shore was later borrowed in part by Stevenson for *Treasure Island*.) The little train stopped at some distance from the old ex-Spanish capital, and dumped out its passengers in a dusty road without even a platform. Several carriages were waiting – Sam in one – and a group of horsemen calling out in Spanish.

While the hack driver stowed away the luggage, one of the riders jumped off his horse and came over to greet the party. Belle said, 'He looked like a young German with his twisted yellow moustache and close-cropped hair.' It was Joe Strong, back from studying art in Munich and now among San Francisco's most promising young painters. He was one of several artists who had 'discovered' the quaint charm of Monterey – first Spanish, later Mexican, and at this time only slightly Americanized.

The carriage took the newcomers into the main street. High walls hid the graceful houses of sun-baked *adobe*, with red-tiled roofs and gates and balconies with iron grilles, where the few proud old Spanish-speaking families still lived in reduced circumstances.

Before one of these houses, Señora Bonifacio's, the carriage stopped and Fanny was waiting at the door to embrace her family. Sam had rented a whole wing, with a parlour opening into the large garden full of fruit trees, fuchsia and floribunda roses. The whitewashed walls were three feet thick, the ceilings supported by hand-hewn beams.

Osbourne went back to his job in San Francisco – and also, his wife soon learned, to his current 'lady friend'. Belle wrote in her memoirs, 'It shocks me now to remember how little I noticed that my father's visits grew fewer and fewer. At first, he joined us over the weekends, going back to San Francisco on Sunday nights; then several weeks would pass, and often when he did come, Nellie and I would be sent away while he and my mother held agitated conferences. I know now they were discussing a divorce.'

Apparently Fanny confessed to her husband a good part of what he must have suspected. Lloyd remembered, 'Once as I was studying my lessons in an adjoining room and felt that strangely disturbing quality in their subdued voices – reproaches on her side and a most affecting explanation on his side of his financial straits at the time of my little brother's death – I suddenly overheard my mother say, with an intensity that went through me like a knife, "Oh, Sam, forgive me!"'

Osbourne continued to be very reluctant to have a legal dissolution of the marriage. He was always see-sawing back and forth between his generosity and his instability. Though no one could deny that he had been unfaithful – well, so had she, now – he loved his home-life and did not want to cause a scandal for himself or his beloved children or his strict Methodist family, who would be as horrified as the Vandegrifts – or indeed the Stevensons.

Nevertheless Fanny's health improved in the soft sea air. The liberal Sam had bought three little Canadian saddle-horses for her and the girls and a pony for Lloyd. She was often seen galloping in her flowing riding skirt along the roads between the mountains and the Pacific on her small mustang, Clavel – Spanish for carnation.

Meanwhile, Belle and Nellie were having a radiant summer, for both had acquired devoted suitors, the former in Joe Strong, the latter in Adolfo Sanchez, the most popular young man in Monterey. He was the son of one of the old aristocratic Spanish-Mexican families, but they had lost their great wealth with the coming of the gringos, and Adolfo now earned his living by keeping the local saloon.

In midsummer Nellie and Adolfo announced their engagement, and Belle and Joe were pining to do the same. 'But', Belle wrote, 'we both knew a young artist with nothing but a number of orders for portraits hadn't a chance of meeting with my mother's approval. So we decided to wait.'

Probably Belle did not find out until later that Fanny was not averse to making use of the scorned suitor: she arranged for Louis Stevenson to address his letters to her in Joe's care.

Then one autumn day Fanny made a crucial mistake which threw the obliging young man into a panic. He claimed that she told him she was arranging 'a very good marriage' for her daughter. At least, that is what he understood her to say, though she may – or may not – have put it more vaguely as a plea not to stand in Belle's way of a better match.

Joe caught the train and hurried up to San Francisco to talk to Osbourne. Sam was warmly sympathetic; he was always ready, like an actor, to please, to charm at the moment. He did not pause to consider, as Fanny did, that the summer's romance was very new and Belle's heart had recently been broken over another temperamental young artist. Still less did he wait to discuss the matter with his wife.

On the way back to Monterey Joe stopped at Salinas, the county seat, and got a marriage licence. Hurrying to Señora Bonifacio's, he took Belle out for a walk on the beach, and told her that her father had given him his consent. He begged her to marry him at once 'without telling anybody' – notably her mother. They could, he said, go to the cottage in East Oakland to get her clothes and other belongings, and then they would find rooms in San Francisco.

The startled Belle could not bear to say no. Hand in hand the elopers climbed over the rocks until they came to a place called the Pacific Grove Retreat. Joe led her to a cottage where a minister and his wife were waiting – and they were married. The bride wore an old grey dress and shabby scuffed shoes which she kept for walking on the beach. Then they boarded the train for East Oakland.

There, the next day, Fanny followed to confront them and berate them for their treachery. The defiant Belle, knowing little of her mother's own hidden torment, could not realize how acutely it must have hurt her that her daughter had turned to Sam and not to herself.

Meanwhile Sam had found an apartment for the runaways in San Francisco. 'Papa met us there after the painful interview with my mother. My dear father! When I remember him, it is always with his arms open wide to love and comfort me. He helped us arrange the rooms, invited us to dinner at Frank's, and when we parted, filled my handbag with twenty-dollar gold pieces. Bless him!'

Chapter II
'Broke', ill, and a 6,000 mile journey

Across the Atlantic, meanwhile, Thomas Stevenson's son had not got over his Parisian wild oats as the father hoped. The elder Stevenson had, the younger wrote in his essay of reminiscences, 'a hot-headed chivalrous sentiment for women. He was actually in favour of a marriage law under which any woman might have a divorce for the asking, and no man on any ground whatsoever'. But it was something else for his son to be pursuing a woman who was still legally another man's wife. In fact, Louis regarded himself as already married to Fanny, with the honourable sense of permanence which was a part of the Victorian morality. He seems not to have hesitated as much as she; but as a man he had less to lose.

In early September he went back to France for a walking tour through the Cévennes, from which came his delightful little book, *Travels with a Donkey*. 'Lots of it', he wrote Bob, 'is mere protestations to F.'

Surely it was one such 'protestation' when he wrote of his amusing struggles with Modestine, his stubborn little donkey. 'Once, when I looked at her, she had a faint resemblance to a lady of my acquaintance who formerly loaded me with kindness.'

On publication the book had a good press, in spite of one critic who misnamed it *Travels OF a Donkey*. It earned a few pounds more than *An Inland Voyage* and pleased Louis's father, though the incorrigible author used up nearly all the proceeds in buying twenty pounds' worth of copies to give his friends.

He had declined any money from home except his allowance of £25 a quarter – which he had not even cashed for two quarters, trying to live without asking his father for more help. 'I must save,

save, *save*', he wrote to Henley in the winter. £350 must be made and laid by ere I can breathe freely.' Doubtless he hoped to help Fanny with her divorce and to subsidize their reunion. He was ill, but he tried to write as much as he could – in Scotland, England and France. 'I sit and sit, and scribe and scribe, but cannot get my back into it.'

In the winter he told Colvin, '. . . to F. I never write letters. . . . All that people want by letters has been done between us. We are acquainted; why go on with more introductions? I cannot change so much, but she could still have the clue and recognize every thought. . . .'

His friends waited dourly for him to get over his infatuation.

In the spring Stevenson wrote a frank passage in an essay on 'Lay Morals', which went discreetly unpublished until after his death:

'Thus, a man is tormented by a very imperious desire; it spoils his rest; it is not to be denied; the doctors will tell you, not I, how it is a physical need like the want of food or slumber. . . . But let the man learn to love a woman as far as he is capable of love; and for this random affectation of the body there is substituted a steady determination, a consent of all his powers and faculties, which supersedes, adopts, and commands all the others. . . . Life is no longer a tale of betrayals and regrets; for the man now lives as a whole . . . through all the extremes and ups and downs of passion. . . .'

He applied to *The Times* of London for a job which might pay his passage to California, to write a series of articles, but the editor declined. He also tried to collaborate with Henley in a play based on his own earlier drafts for *Deacon Brodie* – the beginning of an unsuccessful playwriting partnership.

'I can do no work . . .' he wrote to Gosse from Edinburgh in the spring – and enclosed a five-pound note from his own flat wallet. 'I want – I want – I want – a holiday; I want to be happy; I want the moon or the sun or something. I want the object of my affections badly anyway. . . .'

And again to Gosse: 'I envy you your wife, your home, your child – I was going to say your cat. There would be cats in my home too if I could but get it. I may seem to you "the impersonation of life", but my life is the impersonation of waiting, and that's a poor creature. . . .'

In June he had Baxter send twenty-five pounds from his account to Fanny's brother Jake, who had moved to southern California for his health; whether the money was meant for Jake or for Fanny is not clear.

Almost a year after her departure, a cable arrived from her. The piece of paper has not survived, nor did Louis apparently tell anyone her exact words. Generations of Stevensonians have wondered whether it was a *cri de cœur*, an appeal for him to come, or a mere stoical statement of bewilderment and despair. At any rate, it was enough for him to make up his mind to go to her.

He hurried to London to raise enough money for his fare. To save every scant penny, he determined to travel emigrant style. Steerage in the *Devonia* would cost six guineas, but he paid two guineas more for a cramped dingy cabin with a table to write on.

His close friends tried their best to dissuade him from going – perhaps only to be disinherited, and certainly to sacrifice his work and contacts in London just as his career was taking shape. They even withheld financial co-operation, but he managed to scrape together thirty pounds in cash – for a journey of six thousand miles – and to wring from Charles Baxter a credit for £150 on work not even written. Only Baxter was given his address: c/o Jos. D. Strong, Monterey, California, USA – 'and tell no one, not even the Queen'.

'No man is of any use until he has dared everything,' he wrote to Colvin. 'I feel just now as if I had, and so might become a man.'

On the day he sailed he wrote to Bob, 'F. seems to be very ill. At least I must try and get her to do one of two things. I hope to be back in a month or two; but . . . it is a wild world.' And from the steamer he wrote to Colvin, 'At least if I fail in my great purpose, I shall see some wild life in the West. . . . But I don't know yet if I have the courage to stick to life without it. Man, I was sick, sick, sick of this last year.'

The only deliberately cruel thing he seems ever to have done – apart from many thoughtless ones – was not to have told his parents before he embarked. With the letter to Colvin he enclosed a note to them. Unfortunately it has not survived. But it brought to Colvin an anguished appeal from Thomas Stevenson:

'For God's sake use your influence. Is it fair that we should be half murdered by his conduct? I am unable to write more about this sinful mad business. . . . I see nothing but destruction to himself as well as to all of us. . . .'

Louis's sacrificial hardships led to the two hard-won little books, *The Amateur Emigrant* and *Across the Plains*. The journey permanently broke his health, but it marked a growing-up of the author from his early personal lyricism.

Mingling in the squalid steerage, himself a shabby emigrant rather than a young gentleman in a battered velvet coat, he was shocked to find that many of his companions were not the hardy pioneers he had expected, but failures – often alcoholics – who had been unable to succeed in Europe, and were shuffling off to the New World to cadge a makeshift living. Yet he was furious at the supercilious slumming of a party of first-class passengers.

Most of his shipmates were revoltingly seasick in public. But at his pitching table he did a superhuman amount of notemaking, and drafted 'The Story of a Lie'. In it was an autobiographical passage: '. . . The woman I love is somewhat of my handiwork; and the great lover, like the great painter, is he who can so embellish his subject as to make her more than human . . . the woman can go on being a true woman, and give her character free play, and show littleness or cherish spite, or be greedy of common pleasures, and he continue to worship without a thought of incongruity.'

Skinny enough before, he lost a stone and acquired an 'itch', as he called it. In New York, down-at-heel and drenched by muggy rain, he was hardly a propitious salesman of his manuscripts in his calls on publishers. Worse still, as he wrote to Henley from his shilling Irish boarding-house, he had found a letter with bad news.

'F. has inflammation of the brain and I am across the continent tonight. . . .'

The immigrant train took twelve grim days from New York to San Francisco. The stench became so foul that he took the hazard of squatting on the platform or even on the roof in baking heat or in rain. He was an admirer of Walt Whitman, and from his high blowy perch he managed to write jauntily to his friends about the landscape of the grass-root plains, then the pine-forested ravines and foaming rivers. 'My body, however, is all to whistles.'

Loss of appetite, insomnia, torpor and semi-delirium followed in suffering stages. He was a mere wisp of himself as he tottered off the ferry at chilly San Francisco on 30th August, and asked how to get to Monterey.

Chapter III
A precarious reunion in Monterey

Fanny had resumed something of her former terms of prickly confidence with her two old beaux in San Francisco, John Lloyd and Timothy Rearden. John Lloyd, now a rising banker, was still willing to be useful, if he must, in a stiff dependable way – attracted, but obviously congratulating himself that he was not entangled with her, and seeking to improve her conscience like his own.

'My dear Mr Rearden', she wrote in September from Monterey. 'You always say that I never come to you except when I want something done. . . . I hear that my literary friend from Scotland has accepted an engagement to come to America and lecture; which I think great nonsense. . . . He has a line that belongs to him alone and would be an idiot to leave it for money and flattery. Later on if he works and lives he will get both fame and money. . . .' She hoped Rearden – who must have made a face at the suggestion – would take an interest in the literary friend. His curiosity must have been intense.

Lloyd recalled a morning in the Osbourne's parlour at Señor Bonifacio's, when 'my mother looked at me rather oddly, and, with a curious brightness in her eyes, said, "I have news for you. Luly's coming."'

Stevenson arrived in Monterey the next day, in his seedy blue serge suit and bowler hat. His first act, even before he went to find the Señora's house, was to step into a bar and stave off collapse with a strong drink.

Lloyd said, 'I remember him walking into the room, and the outcry of delight that greeted him, the incoherence, the laughter, the tears; the heart-welling joy of reunion.'

Fanny had not let her daughter know that Louis was in America until, coming home from the beach, the bride opened the parlour door to the sound of voices and found him sitting there. He purported to be travelling as 'The Amateur Emigrant', but, she said, 'he was there because he loved Fanny Osbourne. All of his talk was to her; Nellie, Lloyd and I hardly existed.'

'Now,' wrote Lloyd, 'he looked ill even to my childish gaze. . . . His clothes, no longer picturesque but merely shabby, hung loosely on his shrunken body; and there was about him an indescribable lessening of his alertness and self-confidence.' But soon the impression passed. 'We never thought of him as an invalid,' Belle said. 'He was so gay, so full of vitality, his brown eyes sparkling with fun and interest.'

Louis wrote guardedly to his friends at home that he found Fanny's health much better, but at first he had little else to report. No one knows what the two said to each other in private. No doubt she was powerfully touched to find that he had risked everything to come so far for her sake. But she cannot have failed to feel some consternation when the broken scarecrow loomed up in her doorway, with his cough, his 'itch', his one valise containing chiefly a six-volume history of the United States, and his flat purse – which his father was unlikely to fill again. She was already a subject of gossip, with her short hair, her cigarettes, her husband's infrequent visits and her daughter's elopement with an artist. The black-clad Señora Bonifacio was cold and stiff, and other ladies, Mexican or American, did not call on 'that Mrs Osbourne'. They watched her strolling with the eccentric newcomer in the street or on the beach. She spread the word that he was a British author on a lecture tour – an unlikely tale, they could see.

Having been unable to make up her mind about a divorce in her talks with her husband, Fanny seemed even more uncertain when confronted by Stevenson at the lowest ebb of his fortunes. She had learned from her disillusion with Sam that she and her children could not live by charm alone.

Even Lloyd remembered wondering 'what was to become of poor Luly, who daily looked thinner and shabbier. But afterwards my mother reassured me, and I was thrilled to hear of what "experience" meant to a writer'.

Fanny's indecision shook Louis so much that on the pretext of his health, and to save rent, he hired a horse and a light wagon to go wandering off through the aromatic mountains above the Carmel Valley. Eighteen miles south of Monterey he collapsed. 'Two nights I lay out under a tree in a sort of stupor, doing nothing but fetch water for myself and horse, light a fire and make coffee.' He was found nearly dead by two backwoodsmen from a goat ranch – an old bear-hunter and an Indian – who took him home and cared for him. He convalesced there for two weeks, trying to repay his hosts in the mornings by teaching the children to read. Unquenchable, he also started to mould his shipboard diary into *The Amateur Emigrant*. When he was able to handle the reins he drove back to Monterey.

He knew that he had almost died, and drafted the first version of his famous poem, *Requiem* ('Under the wide and starry sky –') which he sent to Colvin for his own epitaph.

Discovering that she had nearly lost Louis, Fanny learned how much she loved him. She finally made up her mind to the madness – sickly and penniless herself – of marrying the destitute invalid.

It put the heart back into his shattered body. 'I want to be married . . .' he wrote resolutely to Colvin three weeks after his return from the hills. 'In coming here I did the right thing; I have not only got Fanny patched up again and in health, but the effect of my arrival has straightened up everything. As now arranged there is to be a private divorce in January . . . and yours truly will be a married man as soon thereafter as the law and decency permit. The only question is whether I shall be alive for the ceremony.'

Not long after he sent Henley all nine chapters of *The Pavilion on the Links*, his most ambitious piece of fiction to date. 'Carpentry, of course, but not bad at that. . . . May it bring me money for myself and my sick one, who may need it, I do not know how soon.'

Leslie Stephen bought the manuscript for *Cornhill*, an early stroke of luck which was to be the last for months.

Since Fanny had so strongly opposed her daughter's match she could hardly expect Belle's blessing for her own vulnerable plans. However much the girl had first liked 'the young Scotchman' at Grez, she could hardly welcome his attentions to her mother, even while she knew that Sam was an undependable husband both amorously and financially. She admitted years afterwards, 'Though

I admired Louis and respected him, there had always been a hidden antagonism between us. Perhaps because I had adored my father I was unconsciously critical of him.'

Lloyd never forgot one afternoon when Stevenson asked him, alone, to go for a walk on the beach. The volatile man was strangely quiet.

Finally he said, 'I want to tell you something. You may not like it, but I hope you will. I am going to marry your mother.'

Lloyd was struck dumb. He walked along on the sand for a few moments. But at length a slim young hand stole into Louis's. Giving each other little reassuring squeezes, they trudged back in silence to the Señora's.

It had not been easy for Louis to find a lodging in Monterey because the flagrant 'itch' on his hands alarmed the landladies. At length he had been taken in by a French-Swiss who kept the French Hotel, an old *adobe* house on the hillside – long and low, with shutters and climbing roses. (It is now preserved by the State of California as The Stevenson House.)

'Each day', he wrote Colvin, 'I take one of my meals in a little French restaurant; for the other two, I sponge.'

The restaurateur, Jules Simoneau, was 'a dear and kind old man'. As Louis's lack of cash grew more desperate, Simoneau gave him credit with a casual delicacy which he himself had often used towards his own friends when he was in funds. He even got the other boarders to club together, poor as they were, and make up a salary of two dollars a week which one of them – Bronson, editor of the town's weekly newspaper – ostensibly paid him for writing articles for it. Stevenson never knew that this salvation was a gift from people almost as hard up as himself.

Understandably he was anxious to praise his new *milieu* and to justify his visit in the eyes of his frowning friends. His parents felt so disgraced that they even thought of moving away from Scotland. But via Baxter they promised their son money if he would come home. Thomas brooded himself into bad health and sent word that he was desperately ill. But Louis wrote back that Fanny was very ill too: 'I won't desert my wife.'

Fanny braced herself and broke the news to Rearden that she meant to divorce and remarry. As she must have foreseen, he was shocked and condemnatory, like most of her other intimates. A chaste little flirtation – with himself, for example – was one thing; flouting convention and breaking up a family was another. Again they quarrelled by post.

Then Rearden himself came down to Monterey and – a momentous day – walked on the beach with the 'literary friend'. They apparently got on well enough, and in time found much in common. The lawyer – standing by Fanny at a pinch, like John Lloyd, however grudgingly – even allowed himself to be engaged to file the suit for divorce.

Now Fanny sometimes went up to Oakland to see about the action. It was Osbourne's turn to baulk and haver with doubts, worries and second thoughts. His threatened change of mind set all their nerves on edge with suspense and frustration. The strain caused a setback to Fanny's health.

At last he yielded, and let Rearden start the unpleasant business. Having done so, he was said to have been courteous and affable throughout the whole proceedings. Indeed, Fanny's course might have been easier if he had been a brute. He was very popular in the community. Many persons insisted that she had exaggerated his infidelities. They felt that he had been imposed upon in having had to support his wife and children for those three years while she was enjoying herself in Europe.

In mid-October 1879 Fanny, with Nellie and Lloyd, left Monterey for good and returned to East Oakland. This was done partly to preserve some shreds of decorum and partly so that she could be on hand for the court arrangements. She was to live in the cottage, which Osbourne planned to put legally in her name. California law required a husband to support his wife during the divorce proceedings, and Sam further agreed to do so until her remarriage. She in turn was not to hurry the wedding, to allow a decent interval for the sake of all three families.

The tension of argument and scandal brought on a relapse of Fanny's neurasthenia. She again had severe dizzy spells, and at times she was appalled to find herself almost blind and deaf. She laid the symptoms to exhaustion. The alarming news inevitably caused a deterioration in Louis's health while, an exile, he wrote and coughed and waited in his unheated room in Monterey.

In the cold fogs of early winter he developed pleurisy and stayed in bed all day because he 'had no other means of keeping warm for my work'. Nursed by the Simoneaus, he got better only at 'fitful times'. 'I am going for thirty now,' he wrote to Gosse, 'and unless I can snatch a little rest before long, I have, I may tell you in confidence, no hope of seeing thirty-one.' And to Henley: 'I have to get money *soon* or it may have no further interest for me.' To add to his misery, his teeth were decaying and aching, but he could not afford dentistry.

'With my parents', he told Baxter, 'all looks black.' He quite expected them to disinherit him. And in that whole year of 1879, with so much illness, he earned only a hundred and nine pounds.

About the middle of December he left the tattling little town with relief, and went to San Francisco to wait for Fanny and, he hoped, the divorce.

Chapter IV
San Francisco on forty-five cents a day

Lloyd was sent to boarding-school while Fanny, slowly recuperating, lived with Nellie at the cottage. She cooked, sewed, painted, read and rode. She had an elderly Chinese 'boy', and still kept two of the frisky saddle-horses, possibly for health reasons; like Stevenson she had streaks of extravagance along with the most conscientious economy. Anyhow, she loved animals.

It was arranged that she and Louis were to meet discreetly and to lunch or dine together two or three times a week at small back-street restaurants in San Francisco. Louis succeeded in renting a workman's room for the equivalent of six shillings a week, at an Irish boarding-house in Bush Street. Mrs Carson, the landlady, was first suspicious, then kindly. From her husband Louis took the character of Speedy in *The Wrecker*.

On Boxing Day he wrote to Colvin, 'For four days I have spoken to no one but my landlady or landlord, or to restaurant waiters. This is not a gay way to pass Christmas, is it? . . . If I could work, I could worry through better. But I have no style at command.' His critical friends at home were indignant that Fanny should so neglect him. But obviously she could not leave her family alone on Christmas Day to dine in a restaurant with her lover.

'It's a waiting race; slow, but that is all . . .' he assured Henley. 'F. is so much better, so almost quite well – in spite of another fit; I count these fits like coffin nails – that my heart is very light.' Stevensonians have worried about the mention of 'fits' and some have even interpreted them as epilepsy. In the perspective of recent evidence, it seems most likely that he was referring to relapses of her neurotic illness. In any event her spirits always seesawed between exuberance and morbid depression – as indeed did his.

For the first month he budgeted his meals to a 'self-imposed penury' of seventy cents a day. He allowed himself a ten-cent breakfast consisting of coffee with a roll and butter. His main meal was a full fifty-cent lunch, including a half bottle of cheap red wine and a nip of brandy. Supper again cost ten cents: soup or coffee with a roll or doughnut.

January brought the one lucky break: the divorce. Louis wrote triumphantly to Gosse, 'I am now engaged to be married to the woman I have loved for three years and a half.' And he went on, '. . . as few people before marriage have known each other so long or made more trials of each other's tenderness and constancy . . . . I do not think many wives are better loved than mine will be.'

Then Osbourne lost his government job with the Bureau of Mines. He had never bothered to save money and he could not contribute even temporarily to his wife's maintenance. It now fell to Stevenson's lot – with about forty pounds in hand, on which he had meant to subsist indefinitely – to support the Oakland household as well as himself: Fanny, Nellie, Lloyd at school, the Chinese servant and the horses. Belle and Joe Strong too were very poor; Joe earned even less than Louis.

'I . . . who have hitherto made so poor a business of my life, am now about to embrace the responsibility of another's . . .' he wrote to Colvin.

At the end of January he reduced his expenses by having a twenty-five cent dinner instead of a fifty-cent meal. This gave him a budget of forty-five cents a day. Notes show that he was giving ten dollars and then four dollars to Fanny when he was giddy with hunger himself. He broke up the coal in his fireplace to make it last to the final puff, and wrote or read by candlelight in the chilly evenings.

He tried without success to get a job on *The San Francisco Bulletin*, though he later sold that newspaper a couple of articles on speculation. Famished, cold and unwell, he was writing more desperately hard than ever. Along with shorter pieces, he completed *The Amateur Emigrant* and worked on the first draft of *Prince Otto*. He lost precious time by beginning a play called *The Slate*, which 'both Fanny and I have condemned utterly; it is too morbid, ugly, and unkind; better starvation'. Feeling himself too worn to work well, he even had the will-power to take a week's holiday – an amazing feat of perspective for the worried self-employed. He further took the painful step of asking Baxter to sell his books at home and send him the proceeds.

'Do not defer expostulation because he is ill', Henley wrote toughly to Colvin. '. . . Come back he must and that soon. . . .'

Now, to Fanny's helpless alarm, he was afflicted with feverish shivering bouts of ague on top of everything else. Somewhere in his travels the 'amateur emigrant' had picked up malaria. He and Fanny almost 'got married right away' so that she could take care of him. '. . . I have to ask you frankly, when you write,' he told Colvin, 'to give me any good news you can, and chat a little, but *just in the meantime*, give me no bad.'

Very soon after his arrival in San Francisco Fanny had taken him to call on Dora Williams. The next afternoon he went again, alone, to retrieve something which he had characteristically forgotten. Virgil Williams came home from his art school to find the stranger leaning against the mantelpiece in his shabby velvet jacket. Williams 'glanced at him very curiously', according to Dora. '. . . He afterward told me he thought some tramp had got into the room and I could not get him out.' After a conversation about European art and literature, 'they became fast friends. . . . He often came . . . to talk over the ever new theme of "*The* Marriage", as with a lover's fond egotism he called the approaching event.'

During these calls, though 'he was always gay, eloquent and boyish', Mrs Williams wondered at his physical weakness. It did not occur to her that he had had only the scantiest breakfast and lunch; she would have been glad to serve him a hearty afternoon tea.

The fiancés often dropped in at the young Strongs' apartment. They lived in what was then the *Quartier Latin* of the city, with many artists' studios tucked among office buildings which were dark at night. Their life was hard up, happy-go-lucky, hospitable and bohemian. The walls were hung with Joe's paintings and with curios from their travels. A sequence of young Chinese boys did the housework for a dollar a week, long enough to learn English. Belle was a clever cook like her mother, and Joe's rum punch was all too famous. He never saved a penny. At a table by the window Belle worked at illustrations, sketches, posters, book jackets and greetings cards.

When the Strongs entertained Oscar Wilde he cried, 'This is where I belong! This is my atmosphere! . . . I didn't know such a place existed in the whole United States.'

In March 1880, Louis reported to Colvin, 'my dearest Fanny is as bright, well and happy as ever.' He said that they were both content to wait for the marriage, though not quite relieved of anxiety yet – 'when we meet we laugh at each other for our apprehension'.

'Marriage', he had written in the essay 'On Falling in Love', 'is like life in this – that it is a field of battle, and not a bed of roses . . . . Times are changed with him who marries; . . . the road lies long and straight and dusty to the grave. . . . Once you are married, there is nothing left for you, not even suicide, but to be good. . . . And yet, when all has been said, the man who should hold back from marriage is in the same case with him who runs away from battle. . . .'

Then his landlady's four-year-old son Robbie was stricken with pneumonia. The mother was already overburdened with a house full of lodgers; and so, though Louis was staggering with feebleness, he undertook to help nurse the 'poor innocent'. '. . . O, what he has suffered!' he wrote Colvin. 'It has really affected my health. O, never, never any family for me! I am cured of that. . . .'

Robbie survived, but Stevenson broke down. He was on the verge of galloping consumption, with prostrating coughing spells, 'sinking fits' in which he was unable to speak, ague and high fever.

As soon as he showed signs of recovery, Fanny moved him to

a hotel in Oakland where she could more easily come in to look after him. It was ruinously expensive, and he needed constant care. Now came a black milestone: he had his first haemorrhage.

So she again rose bravely above conventions and took him home to nurse him in her cottage. It was a godsend that the divorce had been granted; and she purported to be chaperoned by Nellie. She fought for his life as she had fought for little Hervey's, and this time she won.

After six weeks' silence, he told Gosse in April, '. . . I have cause to bless God, my wife that is to be, and one Dr Bamford . . . that I have come out of all this . . . with some new desire of living.' To his boyhood friend Walter Ferrier he wrote, 'I fear I am a vain man, for I thought it a pity I should die. . . .'

He went on significantly, '. . . It is so difficult to behave well; and in that matter, I get more dissatisfied with myself, because more exigent, every day.' Evidently he was referring to the belated troubling of his conscience now that he was a guest and a patient in Samuel Osbourne's house. He must have felt his position to be doubly dishonourable since Osbourne was behaving well.

Somehow, living rent free, the household scraped along with the last of his few dollars. Sam got another job and was able to help a little more than Fanny had dared to hope. But Louis's recovery, dragged down by anxiety, was very slow, doubtless not least because even when he was near 'the grey ferry', as he called it, he managed incredibly to keep on writing, against the doctor's orders.

Even before their son's collapse, Mr and Mrs Stevenson had been deeply upset to learn from Baxter and Colvin of his ill health, semi-starvation, and a poverty so desperate that he had asked Baxter to sell his books at home. Thomas wrote to Louis, '. . . We have had all our letters including £20 returned from New York. . . .'

The fact that Fanny was now legally free let the first glimmer into the black night of their disapproval. Mr Stevenson admitted that 'the case was not what he supposed', and hinted that if the marriage was delayed as long as possible, he was 'prepared to do his best'.

It is hard to guess what the lovers would have done in the even greater predicament of Fanny too having British nationality. Divorce was bad enough in America, but it was less difficult, scandalous, expensive and lengthy than in England – and above all, in Scotland.

Even for the Stevenson parents, a court case was a little less painful to accept as a *fait accompli* at six thousand miles than in the conspicuous courts of London or – unthinkable – Edinburgh.

In despair Fanny wrote to Colvin of their grim immediate need, hoping that he would appeal to the Stevensons. And then, in April, Louis was able to send Colvin the news which had suddenly given an impetus to his survival: 'My dear people telegraphed me in these words: "Count on 250 pounds annually."' An advance draft was being wired. Soon a letter followed, in which the parents told him that they would receive his wife. They even sent her kind messages.

'I remember the day this word came from his father', wrote Nellie, 'and the exceeding happiness it gave him.'

Fanny must have felt radiant with relief, not only about the money but at being regarded as respectable at last. This time she did not break down from the strain of her 'sleepless care', though her health was still far from hardy. Some of their friends wondered if either of the pair would live to be married.

Chapter V

A marriage *in extremis*

In Oakland Fanny's flimsy wooden cottage, which, as Louis wrote, 'seemed indissoluble from the green garden in which it stood', amused him, for its sides blew in and out like a balloon on windy nights, as no solid stone house had ever done in Scotland.

She prepared tempting trays for him, with nourishing soups, fresh eggs and cream, custards and home-preserved fruits, often served on the sunny lawn. He strolled in the garden, or sat in a big armchair on the veranda with its canopy of roses, while she read aloud to him. They were joined by her four cats and two dogs, one a sentimental setter-cum-spaniel called Chuchu.

Stevenson tried his hand at verse – though he was never self-deceived as to any greatness in that medium – and produced some of the attractive little poems eventually collected in *Underwoods*. He asked Henley to send back the manuscript of *The Amateur Emigrant* for revision. His main project, however, was the first draft of *Prince Otto*, his Ruritanian novel of manners, which he later dedicated to Nellie in appreciation of her services as amanuensis. The character of Princess Seraphina was partly based on Fanny. It was not flattering. Her eyes 'were her most attractive feature, yet they continually bore eloquently false witness to her thoughts; for while she herself, in the depths of her immature, unsoftened heart, was given altogether to manlike ambition and the desire of power, the eyes were by turns bold, inviting, fiery, melting, and artful, like the eyes of a rapacious siren . . . '.

While he was dictating, he paced up and down the room, walking faster and faster as his thoughts gained momentum. Fanny was afraid that this habit would tire him, so the sisters cunningly re-arranged the chairs and tables to pen him in. Whenever he sprang up, he found himself baulked by obstructions on all sides, and sank back into his seat.

Nellie wrote, 'But above and beyond his wife's care for his physical wellbeing was the strong courage with which she stood by him. . . . Her profound faith in his genius before the rest of the world had come to recognize it had a great deal to do with keeping up his faith in himself.'

Moreover, with far-reaching results, 'he had begun even then', recorded Nellie, 'to submit all his writings to her criticism'. Here indeed was a sore point for her opponents.

At last Stevenson could afford to go to a dentist with his painfully decaying teeth. The resultant work filled out his mouth and improved his profile. However, his convalescence was so slow that Fanny was sometimes alarmed. He was almost transparently thin. 'My affairs and the bad weather still keep me here unmarried; but not, I earnestly hope, for long,' he wrote to Colvin.

If ever a long courtship had become unglamorous it was theirs, with the sordid details of illness and poverty. Yet they both always made a great story of their 'romance of destiny' – as if it were the charming operetta which they and their admirers liked to think. As long as he lived Stevenson claimed gallantly that he had wanted to marry Fanny from the first moment he saw her through the window in the lamplit inn at Grez.

With her usual headlong determination Fanny decided that they had better marry sooner than they had conventionally meant to do, so that she could take care of Louis in a higher, drier climate. He told Gosse, 'I shall be married in May and then go to the mountains, a very withered bridegroom.' In May he wrote, 'My doctor took a desponding fit about me, and scared Fanny into blue fits; but I have talked her over again.'

He wrote afterwards to the Scots art critic P. G. Hamerton, 'It was not my bliss that I was interested in when I was married; it was a sort of marriage *in extremis*; and if I am where I am, it is thanks to the care of that lady, who married me when I was a mere complication of cough and bones, much fitter for an emblem of mortality than a bridegroom.'

Perhaps now in illness the partly maternal bond which had conditioned Louis's capacity for love drew the pair far closer than the decorative poses of courtship. The early hot blood which had first made them lovers had been cooled by hard luck.

'I am trying to take care of my dearest boy,' wrote Fanny to Colvin.

Yet the surprising cast of masculinity in the tiny woman's character gave her the extra dimension of companionship which he so whole-heartedly enjoyed with his men friends, and which a more fully feminine wife would not have offered. Perhaps above all there was her gift of listening, which raised his *élan* as man and as artist. He seemed to recognize this in 'Talks and Talkers': 'Women are better hearers than men, to begin with; they learn, I fear in anguish, to bear with the tedious and infantile vanity of the other sex. . . .'

Fanny was therefore part comrade, part mother, part dependant, part lover – though no longer much of the last – and part the indefinable *x*, the embodiment of blending personalities which makes people like to be together, in spite of passing irritations, even for life.

Finally the rains stopped as usual for the whole summer, the fields of buttercups withered and the grassy coastal hills began to turn brown. The weather was safe. Still very shaky, Stevenson went alone one day by horse-car and ferry to San Francisco. He bought a marriage licence, and made arrangements with a fellow Scotsman, the Rev. Dr William A. Scott, minister of St John's Presbyterian

Church. He also bought two plain silver wedding rings, in the way of French peasants; he could not afford gold.

On 19th May the gaunt weak man and the tiny tense woman crossed the bay alone on the ferry. They could not afford a hansom cab, so they boarded a cable car uphill to the Williams's home. They were always grateful to these friends, Louis told Colvin, as 'the parties who stuck up for us about our marriage'. Virgil was out of town, but Dora joined them. The three then walked to the home of Dr Scott on Post Street. Dora, reported the groom, was 'my guardian angel, and our Best Man and Bridesmaid rolled into one'. Dora and the parson's wife were the only witnesses.

The register shows the entry in the minister's handwriting:

Married by me at my residence 19th May 1880, Robert Louis Stevenson, born Edinboro', Scotland, white, single, 30 years old, resides in Oakland, Cal.

Fannie Osbourne, born Indianapolis, Indiana, 40 years, widowed, white, resides in Oakland.

Certificate to be sent to Mrs Virgil Williams, 719 Geary Street, City.

It is touching that Fanny, though bravely admitting to '40 years', lost courage and described herself as 'widowed'.

The bride and groom spent two days in San Francisco before they returned to the cottage to collect their bags for their mountain honeymoon. *En famille* as in most of their married life, they rented rooms in the same building as Belle and Joe. Nellie moved in with the Strongs until her marriage.

Stevenson could not afford a tangible wedding gift for his bride, but he gave her one that she cherished far more. It was a group of love poems which he had been writing for her in the last shadowy half year. (They were printed – privately at first – some years after his death.)

One poem was a sonnet, containing the lines:

Hope is so strong that it has conquered fear;
Love follows, crowned and glad for fear's defeat.
Down the long future I behold us, sweet,
Pass and grow ever dearer and more dear. . . .

Chapter VI
Squatters' honeymoon

Three days after their wedding the honeymooners, with Lloyd and Chuchu the setter-spaniel, trooped north by ferry and train towards the mountains. Reconnoitring, they stayed first at the big white hotel in Calistoga Hot Springs, the spa village in the fertile Napa Valley, with its vineyards and orchards, its scattered ranches, its steep roads winding up forested canyons on the vast bulk of Mount St Helena. 'This is a land of stage-coaches and highwaymen', wrote Louis with gusto in his notes.

The problem was to find the cheapest possible quarters in mountain air. Fanny, after her experience in western mining camps, knew that many of the holdings had petered out and become ghost towns. She had suggested that they might find some old miner's shack and live in it as squatters. Her husband called her 'the forty-niner'.

The local Jewish storekeeper, a great character, recommended an abandoned silver mine on the shoulder of the mountain and drove them up in his trap for a look. 'Silverado!' The name glinted in R.L.S.'s imagination as the title of his planned book *The Silverado Squatters*. 'Silverado be it', they said. The storekeeper himself appeared in the pages as the genial and canny Kelmar.

One fine morning the bride and groom set out in a double buggy, accompanied by Chuchu and by Lloyd on horseback. The narrow stony road wound up among pines, oaks and madronas. 'A rough smack of resin was in the air,' recorded R.L.S., 'and a crystal purity.'

Half way up the mountain they stopped at the Toll House, a low wooden building at which the stage-coaches made regular halts. At one end lived the Stevensons' nearest neighbours, also squatters: the lean and taciturn hunter called Rufe Hanson, with his wife and children and his oafish brother-in-law whom the newcomers nicknamed Caliban. ('Beautiful as a statue', Louis wrote of him. 'Too lazy to spit', said a local matron.) These characters were also to figure in the book. The Hansons had agreed to provide their fellow squatters with milk, eggs and meat, the last usually being venison shot by Rufe.

Hanson was supposed to follow the Stevensons up from Calistoga with his team and wagon, bringing their bags and boxes – mostly books – and a second-hand stove, but though they waited, he did not appear. It seemed a likely bet that he was playing poker. So they decided to go on, and puffed their way up the deep ravine by a perpendicular path, rocky and overgrown. At about two o'clock they scaled a wooden ladder and took possession of Silverado – 'a world of wreck and rust, splinters and rolling gravel'.

The chaos of the deserted mine was wedged against the mountain, perilous with tunnels and deep shafts. Here on the rubble was the triangular 'platform' on which they were to live. They had to wade through poison oak among the stones, and all summer no one could take a step without the rocks shifting and crunching underfoot, ruinous to shoes. Rattlesnakes, 'whizzing on every side like spinning wheels', kept Chuchu in terror, though not Louis, who did not know what they were. 'A tremendous wind was blowing over the mountain', he noted. The platform was bare and glaring except for a clump of dwarf madronas near the old forge. But in front they looked out on 'a great realm of air' with forested hill tops and the distant valley.

Silverado had once been a camp of many hundreds of people, but all the wooden houses, stores, even hotels, had been carted away. All that was left was a tumbledown shack once used as an assayer's office and miners' dormitory, the rooms perching at different levels. The lower room, the office, contained a barrel, a table, some yellowed papers, a plate-rack, some old boots and a hole in the leaky roof for the smoke from a fire. Above, the dormitory held nothing but the skeletons of nine old three-tier bunks. It had to be entered perilously as if by walking the plank on a board balanced between the red rock-face and the open door, while one clutched at sprays of poison oak for support. There were no windows or doors left, not even casings, but luckily the whole summer is dry in that region.

The rooms were full of rubbish, dead leaves, mine-dust and a formidable sapling of poison oak. The new arrivals had no choice but to start cleaning out the mess; at least, Fanny did, while Louis helpfully got in the way.

The shadows of the mountain ranges spread over the valley, and still no Rufe Hanson appeared with their belongings. There was nowhere to sit but on the splintery table. 'Chuchu whimpered for a softer bed.' They could not lie down until Rufe brought up a load of hay to spread in the bunks. The heat cooled off with mountain swiftness, and they built a camp-fire in the forge.

Famished, they had the idea of getting some bread from the Toll House. 'Fanny has about as much locality as a toothpick; Lloyd rather less, and there was whooping-cough at the Toll House, so he could not go. . . .' That left only the weary Stevenson to toil down the dusky path and back. Lloyd had broken his watch-chain and had put the watch in his stepfather's pocket; it was the great pride of the boy who was already entranced by mechanical devices. (Louis himself never wore watches; in his youth, he 'thought them only to be pawned'.) Carrying the treasure, he fetched the bread, and 'returned up the trail – a breathing wreck, the mere offal of myself'. Fatigue settled on the party like a nightmare. The fire had gone out. 'Hay or no hay, we must go to bed.' He put his hand in his pocket: there was no watch.

'Lloyd's face became a picture . . . I saw myself face to face with another excursion down the cañon, not to speak of coming up again, and a hunt by lantern light for an object about two inches and a half in circumference. Fanny lit the lantern; it was a weird affair . . . it begged to be broken.' (One wonders that she allowed him to go; probably he insisted with the headlong intensity – not unlike her own – which she was to find so hard to bridle.) He set forth down the steep track, bent double, looking right and left among dead leaves and rocks. At last, within sight of the Toll House lights – incredibly – he found the watch in the middle of the path.

He got back at about half past seven, and was quickly followed by Rufe Hanson and his hulking brother-in-law with their gear. The watchers winced at the weight of the books on the ladder. There indeed was the stove, but the men had forgotten the chimney and lost one of the plates along the road. There too, were the boxes, 'piled higgledy-piggledy, and upside down, about the floor'. But what, for once, of the efficient Fanny?

'My wife had left her keys in Calistoga.'

The men went down the dark trail again, but the shivering squatters still could not go to bed until the hay came. Sitting on the boxes, they waited by the fluttering of the one candle, while the sharp night air poured through the empty doors and windows. Finally, about nine o'clock, Rufe and 'Caliban' clambered up once more with the load of hay, with which they filled the two bunks next to the door, 'to keep us out of the draught'. Then in silhouette the trio walked the plank to the family bridal chamber.

In the morning Louis was weary but able to get up. The campers built a good fire in the forge and Fanny cooked porridge and bacon and made coffee. He rested, and when he went across to the house, he 'found the broken door and the frameless window were all mailed up with white calico' . . . to keep out the wind and let in the light . . . 'and there was Fanny on her knees hammering up a door of the same material for the gaping eastern doorway'. Needing hinges, she sent him off to hunt for leather among the rubbish, and he found a pair of old boots. They were *too* old, however, and day or two after her clever work all the hinges parted, and the door blew in upon the stove and upset a frying-pan of onions.

Louis, that 'handless man', could hardly drive a nail. But 'wood and iron, nails and rails' lay scattered about the platform, and 'the forty-niner' used them to repair the worst holes in roof and floor. She banged, sawed and pounded. The wooden packing-cases became stools and cupboards. There was never a chair; Louis had to retire to his bunk to rest his thin bones. Nevertheless, he recorded in *The Silverado Squatters*, the ruined shanty was soon transformed, 'with the beds made, the plates on the rack, the pail of bright water behind the door, the stove crackling in a corner, and perhaps the table roughly laid against a meal'.

After a few weeks Belle, Joe and Nellie came up by stage-coach – white as statues with the dust of the dry season – to stay a while. 'The old bunkhouse', admitted Nellie, 'seemed to me an incredibly uncomfortable place of residence.' Fanny must have slaved like a squaw in the primitive camp.

'We had our meals out of doors,' Belle recollected, 'and as there never was a better cook than Fanny Stevenson, they were good ones. She used the mouth of the old Silverado mine for an ice chest and storeroom; here hung sides of venison, pigeons, wild ducks and other game . . . and cans of fresh milk brought up the mountain each morning.' Wine, dried peaches and other fruits were kept cool in the tunnel, and the storekeeper in Calistoga sent up tinned foods by stage-coach.

Stevenson – always an early-bird writer – was the first to rise in the crystal mountain mornings, with the sun on the heights but the mine in shadow. He drew water from the precious spring in the red rocks, and chopped up some kindling. 'Thenceforth my wife laboured single-handed in the palace, and I lay or wandered over the platform at my own sweet will.'

The rocky platform was baking hot in the daytime. Louis sat with his writing-case or his books on a boulder in the sole patch of shade under the stunted madronas. He pored over his manuscripts for four or five hours a day, though he was too weak to accomplish much. At eleven o'clock and at three Fanny brought him a rum punch, frothy with cream and sprinkled on top with cinnamon. The others shared it, for she did not, Belle said, treat him as an invalid.

So far *The Silverado Squatters* was taking only the form of notes. Stevenson seldom wrote about a place until he had left it, but he had the habit of keeping several projects going, according to mood, and was revising earlier work. It is obvious that in *The Squatters*, as in his other writings about America and Americans, his wife must have coached him from her own experience of the scene and people.

It was always a relief when the glaring sun went down and the party could sit on their platform in the shadow, pungent with the night-scent of bay and nutmeg trees. 'Our day was not very long,' wrote Belle, 'but it was tiring' – especially with no chairs and almost no shade. They amused themselves by tossing stones down the deep chute to hear them fall far below; they dared not venture inside the tunnel. Stevenson wonderfully described the 'hurly-burly of stars', and in time the moon over the vast mountains and the valley. 'We sat around the camp fire talking,' wrote Belle, 'but soon the chill that always came at night, even after the hottest day, drove us to our beds.'

During those two months, at any moment the dump might have slid downhill, carrying the squatters along in the avalanche; or a crack of rotten wood might have been the only warning that the platform had caved in and fallen into the shaft underneath; or a wedge might have slipped, with the splintered camp disappearing under hundreds of tons of mountain.

'Doubtless she is not the daughter-in-law that I have always pictured to myself', wrote Mrs Thomas Stevenson to a woman cousin.

Louis had told his parents, 'If you can love my wife, it will, I believe, make me love both her and you the better.'

They had written kind, reserved letters of welcome to Fanny, and she was exchanging a careful correspondence with his mother.

'I do try to take care of him,' she told her mother-in-law. 'The old doctor insists that my nursing saved him; I cannot quite think it myself, as I shouldn't have known what to do without the doctor's advice, but even having it said is a pleasure to me. . . .

'I do not believe that any of Louis's friends, outside of his own family, have ever realized how very low he has been; letters followed him continuously, imploring, almost demanding his immediate return to England, when the least fatigue, the shortest journey, might, and probably would, have proved fatal; and, which at the moment filled my heart with bitterness against them, they actually asked for work.'

'Taking care of Louis', she observed in another letter, 'is as you must know, very like angling for shy trout; one must understand when to pay out the line, and exercise the greatest caution in drawing it in. I am becoming most expert, though it is an anxious business.'

Later Mrs Stevenson indicated that she did not quite believe her new daughter-in-law's cheerful assertion that they had spent 'a jolly summer' in such a rough spot. Fanny replied: 'You may wonder at my allowing Louis to go to such a place. Why, if you only knew how thankful I was to get there with him! I was told that nothing else would save his life, and I believe it was true. We could not afford to go to a "mountain resort" place, and there was no other chance. . . .'

She described a few of her makeshifts in carpentering and catering, which must have seemed odd indeed among the ancestral mahogany of Heriot Row. And she added, 'Louis says nothing about the flowers, but the beauty of them was beyond description, to say nothing of the perfume. At the back door was a thicket of trees covered with cream-coloured and scarlet lilies. . . .' Flowers, in fact, did not much attract her husband except for their scent. He preferred a 'nobler effect'.

Louis himself wrote gratefully and affectionately to his parents. 'Since I have gone away', he said of his father to Colvin, 'I have found out for the first time how I love that man; he is dearer to me than all, except Fanny.'

Now that their son's marriage was irrevocable the elder Stevensons naturally longed to meet his wife. All summer their letters begged him to bring her home.

Louis wrote of her to her brother Jake: 'I know I am on trial; if I can keep well next winter, I have every reason to hope the best; but on the other hand, I may very well never see next spring. In view of this, I am all the more anxious she should see my father and mother; they are well off, thank God, and even suppose that I die, Fanny will be better off than she had much chance of being otherwise. . . . I am an author but I am not very likely to make my fortune in that business, where better even than I are glad to get their daily bread.'

'. . . I am truly better,' Louis assured his mother at the end of June; 'I am allowed to do nothing, never leave our little platform in the canyon nor do a stroke of work. . . .'

'As to my dear boy's appearance,' Fanny told Mrs Stevenson in July, 'he improves every day in the most wonderful way, so that I fancy by the time you see him you will hardly know that he has ever been ill at all.'

On 16th July she was able to announce, '. . . Now, at last, I think he may venture to make the journey without fear, though every step must be made cautiously. I am sure now that he is on the high road to recovery and health, and I believe his best medicine will be the meeting with you and his father, for whom he pines like a child. I have had a sad time through it all, but it has been worse for you, I know. I am now able to say that all things are for the best. Louis has come out of this illness a better man than he was before; not that I did not think him good always, but the atmosphere of the valley of the shadow is purifying to a true soul; and though he may be no nearer your hearts than before, I believe you will take more comfort in your son than you have ever done. I trust that in about two weeks we shall be able to start. . . .'

Many years later, on the mine dump, the clubwomen of Napa County placed a monument. It was a slab of Scottish granite shaped like an open book, and was inscribed to mark 'the site of the cabin occupied in 1880 by Robert Louis Stevenson and bride'. Ann Roller Issler, the expert on R.L.S. in California, wrote: 'Children and children's children have been brought up on *The Silverado Squatters*.'

In contrast to Louis's painful rattling across the continent on the roofs of railroad cars, this time he and Fanny and Lloyd went first class all the way. But the conventional mode of travel yielded no 'copy'. They embarked from New York on 7th August, a year to the day after he had sailed from home.

Part 4

Scotland and London
On trial with the family
and friends 1880

Chapter I
Meeting the parents

'Please remember', Fanny had written with candid charm to her mother-in-law, 'that my photograph is flattering; unfortunately all photographs of me are; I can get no other. At the same time Louis thinks me, and to him I believe I am, the most beautiful creature in the world. It is because he loves me that he thinks that, so I am very glad. I do so earnestly hope that you will like me, but that can only be for what I am to you after you know me, and I do not want you to be disappointed in the beginning in anything about me, even in so small a thing as my looks.'

She confessed to her intimates that she was terrified of meeting Louis's parents. Not so much the gentle Mrs Stevenson, since they had begun to know each other through letters. But she felt apprehensive of Thomas, whose photograph rather alarmed her with his stern stocky face, firm mouth and long upper lip.

'Your fancy that I may be a business person is a sad mistake,' she cautioned Mrs Stevenson. 'I am no better in that respect than Louis, and he has gifts that compensate for any lack. I fear it is only genius that is allowed to be stupid in ordinary things.'

The parents could scarcely fail to be disarmed. As Fanny wrote of herself later to her mother-in-law, the little girl with the curl in the middle of her forehead 'may well have been a Stevenson': 'When she was good, she was very, very good, But when she was bad she was horrid.'

'Stevenson returned from America', reported a sour critic, 'with some admirable travel sketches, a fading middle-aged woman and tuberculosis.'

The opponents of the marriage were even more amused after they learned that Louis's bride was soon to be a grandmother. Belle was expecting a baby in the spring.

The docking of the *City of Chester* in the grey Mersey at Liverpool meant an emotional half hour alike for the younger Stevenson couple waving from the deck and the older from the quay. Thomas and Margaret had come down from Scotland to meet the prodigals, and were joined by Colvin, who went out in the tug and scrambled up the ship's ladder to the deck.

'I daresay it made things pleasanter my being there,' he wrote to Henley. 'And I'm bound to say the old folks put a most brave and most kind face on it indeed.'

Everyone behaved wonderfully. Fanny – the bohemian artist, the pistol-shooting pioneer – now acted the part of a cosy and sensible little matron. She was about half way between the ages of her mother-in-law and her husband. However, her mature respectability was at least a relief to the parents after their son's adventures with the tarts of Edinburgh and Paris. Their politely smiling eyes must have lingered on her hair, which she had cut short, an incredibly *outré* act at that time; no doubt she put off smoking for as long as she could bear it. But they were on her side in so far as they were pathetically anxious for the match to be the best of a bad bargain.

Colvin stayed with the party only for lunch at the hotel. Lloyd, he told Henley, 'distinguished himself (it should be said in passing that he is not a bad boy) by devouring the most enormous luncheon that ever descended a mortal gullet'. Fanny put first things first and did not bother much with Colvin; it was vital that she should make her impression on the parents, especially the formidable father, before courting the cronies.

But now Colvin told Henley that Louis's mother looked the fresher of the two women. And he confided, 'When I had him alone talking in the smoking-room it was quite exactly like old times; and it is clear enough that he likes his new estate so far all right, and is at peace in it; but whether you and I will ever get reconciled to the little determined brown face and white teeth and grizzling (for that's what it's up to) grizzling hair, which we are to see beside him in future – that is another matter.'

'Fanny is very entertaining,' wrote Mrs Stevenson in her diary, 'and Lloyd a pale-faced, delicate looking boy of twelve; he rather made a commotion in the hotel and at last a chambermaid dashed breathless into my room and cried out, "Oh, if you please, ma'am, is it possible that that young gentleman is your son's son?" He was really so much liker Louis than his mother that bets had been made on the subject on board the vessel.'

In handsome Edinburgh, Fanny was impressed by the elegant eighteenth-century house and heirloom furniture. Chameleon-like, she adopted the ways and wills of the household. Black stockings had just come into fashion, but when her father-in-law frowned on them as indelicate, she demurely wore white ones in his company.

Louis wrote to James Cunningham, a new Scots friend made on shipboard, about 'my whole family having to be rigged out with wedding garments – what my mother significantly calls "getting a few things together in the meantime"'. The trio from California had apparently made heads turn in the staid grey streets of the 'Athens of the North'. Mrs Stevenson opened cupboards and trunks for Fanny's benefit, generously sharing her own conservative but opulent wardrobe. She turned over a long accumulation of Louis's clothing which had been too gentlemanly for his rakish tastes: suits, coats, smoking-jackets, dressing-gowns, even some silk net underwear which his bride made him wear. Fanny's letters home purred with a happy boasting which did not escape her amused bridegroom.

'[We] are taking so much and will never be able to give anything,' she wrote Belle. 'They are so sweet to Lloyd too.' Luckily 'Uncle Tom' and 'Aunt Maggie' liked him, and were not sorry to have a boy in the house again.

The servants were excited and mystified. A maid assured 'Mrs Louis', as she was called in the family circle, that she 'spoke English very well for a foreigner'. One day she heard two of them gossiping about a Scot who had just come home from Africa. 'He's merrit a black woman,' said one. The other, in a mirror, was seen to point to Fanny's back and put her finger to her lips.

Like any solid Scottish family, the party went *en masse* to church. Fanny was glad to remember that she too was a Presbyterian. No doubt there was much peeping over the hymn-books at the new daughter-in-law. Louis confessed to his new friend James Cunningham that he and Lloyd, sitting side by side, had 'gently elapsed' in the middle of the sermon.

He could now submit to the family piety with a good-natured shrug. Since he had had his own way over his career and his marriage, he no longer needed to fight against his parents' religious austerity.

The difference in background kept Fanny ever watchful to please. One day, her hands still hard from manual labour at the mine, she was surprised to hear her mother-in-law ask if she never 'worked'. She learned that this was the British abbreviation for fancy-work. When next the two went shopping they bought all that was needed for a piano cover to be embroidered with roses. She plied her expert needle with her usual vigour, and a few days later displayed the completed masterpiece. Shocked, Mrs Stevenson threw up her hands. 'Oh Fanny!' she cried. 'How could you! That piece should have lasted you all summer!'

None the less, 'Fanny fitted into our household from the first', wrote Mrs Stevenson in her diary. 'It was quite amusing how entirely she agreed with my husband on all subjects, even to looking on the dark side of most things, while Louis and I were more inclined to take the cheery view.'

Louis was soon heard to say that he had never seen his father so completely subjugated. Probably, as with the son, it was her talent as a listener which worked much of the magic.

Sir Walter Simpson, Louis's canoeing companion, gave the bride a young black Skye terrier for a wedding present. The little dog was, said Colvin, 'remarkably pretty, engaging, excitable, ill-behaved', with clever eyes peeping drolly from a fringe of overhanging hair. This redoubtable character was to rule the Louis Stevensons with iron irascibility for his full six years. He was first named Wattie for Walter, but the name degenerated into Woggs, Woggy and Wiggs, and finally became Bogue. Fanny now joined her father-in-law as the two most impassioned dog lovers of the household. Louis claimed to agree with Professor Blackie's dictum that dogs interrupted conversation – though his actions belied the complaint. 'An auto-maton he certainly is,' he theorized in his essay on 'The Character of Dogs', 'a machine working independently of his control, the heart, like the mill-wheel, keeping all in motion. . . .'

Soon Mrs Stevenson senior wrote in her diary, 'That Louis might have more mountain air we went first to Blair Atholl and then to Strathpeffer. The first morning at the latter place when I went into our sitting-room I found Louis and Fanny both hard at work writing with the table covered with papers. When I asked for Lloyd I was told that he was in his bedroom as there was no room for him at the table. When I followed him I found him on his knees before a chair busy writing a magazine article! So said I: "This is what it is to have a literary family."'

Fanny smothered her misgivings and tried to pretend that the raw cold air was good for Louis, for the sake of his parents. But he had already written, 'I must flee from Scotland. It is, for me, the mouth of the pit.'

There was the inevitable resort gossip about the lit'ry fella and the divorced woman. But Fanny's success with the family gained momentum. Louis's maternal uncle, Dr George Balfour – a stalwart character – watched her keenly.

'Yes, Louis, you have done well,' he presently told his nephew. 'I married a besom myself and I have never regretted it.' Thomas too often teased her, 'I doot ye're a besom'. This Scots word for the old-fashioned twig broom, indicating a bossy woman or a 'handful', was used affectionately, though it was turned against her by her enemies. Thomas soon had a variety of pet names for her. He called her 'The Vandegrifter', and sometimes 'Cassandra', for her mystic claims as gloomy prophetess and seer. She pleased him by saucily talking back, and called him Uncle Tom or Mr Tommy or even Master Tommy. But though others found her 'bold' and 'presumptuous', she managed not to overplay her role as tactful daughter-in-law.

'. . . the most masculine and direct of women', her husband had generalized in *Virginibus Puerisque*, 'will some day, to your dire surprise, draw out like a telescope into successive lengths of per-sonation.'

As for Louis, in those early months Fanny's letters to Dora
Williams showed an almost incredulous gratification at finding him
so kind and fond. Cunningham said that she told him, 'There's no
one like Louis, is there?' ('Lou-us', she always pronounced her
husband's name, with a casual midwestern slur.)

Though Stevenson was planning a history of Scotland, a practical
project urged by his father, he was able to produce little. Thomas,
reading *The Amateur Emigrant*, was so ashamed of its revelations of
his son's desperate poverty and hardships that he bought it back
from the publisher.

The family returned to Edinburgh in mid September. Louis was
laid low with acute catarrh and extreme weakness. '. . . soon after his
marriage,' recorded Graham Balfour, Louis's second cousin and
official biographer, 'though his wife was the most devoted and
capable of nurses, on the outbreak of an illness, like a child he
turned to his mother and would be satisfied with nothing short of her
presence.'

His doctor uncle, George Balfour, was alarmed by his emaciation
and the congestion in his lungs. The new Swiss theory of treating
tuberculosis was being adopted, and Dr Balfour recommended
Davos-platz, in the Grisons in south-eastern Switzerland.

'It is settled', wrote Maggie Stevenson in her diary, 'that Louis
is to winter at Davos, so after seeing a good many Edinburgh friends
the trio leave on 7th October for London, Fanny with a dog in one
basket and a cat in another.'

Chapter II
The test with the London circle

The Stevensons travelled south just as the autumn mists were
dimming the gas-lamps in London. They stayed for some days to see
a few publishers – and many friends, whose welcome was the more
heartwarming because they thought the 'gay beloved Stevenson'
was dying.

Now at last was the time when Fanny made her debut in Louis's brilliant inner circle. Eager to like and ambitious to be liked, she began well. Towards each one she projected her magnetic personality like a divining-rod probing for water. In this first enthusiasm she claimed to understand and appreciate her husband's friends as if they had been her own discoveries rather than his. She was described by some as 'brooding', listening with little comment.

'. . . she was one of the strangest people who have lived in our time,' Edmund Gosse summed her up years later to Edward Marsh, 'a sort of savage nature in some ways, but very lovable – extraordinarily passionate and unlike everyone else in her violent feelings and unrestrained way of expressing them – full of gaiety, and with a genius for expressing things picturesquely, but not literary. I think R.L.S. must have caught some of his ways of feeling from her. . . .'

Beginning her chore of regular bulletins to her mother-in-law, Fanny wrote sharply: 'For no one in the world will I stop in London another hour after the time set. It is a most unhealthful place at this season, and Louis knows far too many people to get a moment's rest. . . . Company comes in at all hours from early morning till late at night, so that I almost never have a moment alone, and if we do not soon get away from London I shall become an embittered woman. It is not good for my mind, nor my body either, to sit smiling at Louis's friends until I feel like a hypocritical Cheshire cat, talking stiff nothings with one and another in order to let Louis have a chance with the one he cares the most for, and all the time furtively watching the clock and thirsting for their blood because they stay so late. . . .'

The scintillating Bob, though also short on money and health, spurred his cousin to respond as in the old days of their pranks and poses. But the worst offender, first and last, was the big, lame, noisy, whisky-smelling, devastatingly clever Henley. She forgot his devotion to Stevenson and his help in placing his manuscripts, as he stayed on in booming repartee. At her heavy hints, he obviously thought her a sort of Old Woman of the Sea squatting on the back of the once lightfooted Louis.

'Germs' were a new idea, and Fanny, as amateur physician, had noticed that whenever her husband was exposed to anyone with a cold he caught it. Therefore she 'kept guard over him like a fiery little watch-dog', in Nellie's phrase. If she herself had a cold she stayed away from him, and she expected his relations and friends to do the same. 'Fiends disguised as friends,' she termed them, when they thought her a faddist.

The heedless visitors could not realize what those nightmare years of tuberculosis meant to Fanny, as Lloyd was later to describe them: '[Louis] would put a handkerchief to his lips, perceive a crimson stain, and then sooner or later there might be a haemorrhage of the lungs, with all its horror and suspense, and its subsequent and unutterably dejecting aftermath of having to lie immovable for days and nights on end. . . .'

'Marriage often puts old friends to the door', R.L.S. had declared in *Virginibus Puerisque*. And undoubtedly – to protect him – his wife sometimes gave the door an extra slam. Colvin wrote of her, however, that '. . . the more considerate among [his friends] she made warmly her own and was ever ready to welcome.'

Colvin was complacently aware of being one of the favoured few. Fanny had figured out that he and Baxter – the punctilious scholar and the conscientious legal adviser – were better than the improvident *literati*. She therefore sought to cultivate those two at the expense of the others – especially of Henley, with whom she had a cat-and-dog antipathy. Now she turned the same confidential appeal upon Colvin (and with him, Mrs Sitwell) which she had used on Thomas Stevenson. Few men could have remained detached under her deference.

'She had deep and rich capacities alike for tragedy and humour,' he reminisced in *Memories and Notes*. 'All her moods, thoughts, and instincts were vividly genuine and her own, and in her daily talk, like her letters, there was a play of character and feeling and choice and colour of words.'

Already some of the London literary clique had begun to argue that Fanny's influence on her husband's career weakened his works and lowered his potential place among the great authors. At the same time she felt that she was discovering genius, with her usual precognition, before the rest of the world had had the sense to perceive it. For a man struggling against illness and chilled by the cold water thrown by his prejudiced friends on anything he had written in America, this can hardly have been other than heartening. Talent and the creative will are touchy and egoistic plants. If she had withered his *amour propre* as an artist over a long period, it would have frosted his love more than all their outward troubles. By this most sensitive of tests she lifted him up more than she pulled him down. In any event, after strenuous argument, he usually wrote as he pleased.

On the whole he must have found her company – her presence – 'good' for his work, by the stark proof that, after four years' intimate trial, he married her, and stayed inseparably married for the rest of his life.

With extravagant living and entertaining, the couple's hotel bill for the week came to the exorbitant total of forty-six pounds. They were broke before they had even left London.

The disgruntled Colvin managed to get together ten pounds which would take the trio and their dog and cat as far as Paris, later repaying, with difficulty, the full fifty pounds he owed Louis. Thomas Stevenson, already so generous, had to reopen his cheque book at once.

What of the sage caretaking of the Vandergrifter? She guiltily apologized to the parents with the weak excuse that it was due to her inexperience in English hotels.

In mid October the bridegroom – a wreck from fog, chatter, burgundy, tobacco smoke and excitement – was bundled off none too soon across the Channel.

Part 5

Switzerland

A lunger's resort in the Alps 1880 - 82

Chapter I
Snow, sunburn and gossip

The Stevensons and Lloyd took two weeks to reach Davos by easy stages and with skimpy funds. On 4th November the party boarded one more train, puffing up the darkening Alps, and took a diligence over the frozen road to the lights of the Hotel Belvedere and the chalets hanging on the mountainside at Davos.

While Fanny was looking at rooms upstairs, Louis waited below, and a good-natured landlady told him, 'Your mother will be down soon.' Luckily Fanny did not hear this dreaded phrase. (A fellow guest reported it.) Her husband, moreover, never lost his way of looking boyish and younger than his age. The great Dr Ruedi, while examining him, bluntly told Fanny she was too fat, said it was caused by 'a disease of the stomach', and put her on a diet. When Louis teased her about her plumpness she took it in good part.

He wrote to his mother, 'We got to Davos last evening, and I feel sure we shall like it greatly. I saw Symonds this morning, and already like him; it is such sport to have a literary man around.' This was the consumptive John Addington Symonds – the expert on the Renaissance and classical literature – to whom Stevenson had brought a letter of introduction from Gosse. The Symondses were building themselves a chalet, accepting a permanent exile of invalidity.

Davos, a mile high, was a scattered little town with several pointed church steeples, three large hotels and a charity sanatorium. Even the shops were kept by consumptives in this strange lofty desert of the sick. The peaks of the windy valley rose straight up from the icy river. Louis described the scene, in the *Pall Mall Gazette*, with a newcomer's optimism: '. . . a world of black and white – black pine woods, and white snow . . . and a few score invalids marching to and fro upon the snowy road, or skating on the ice rinks . . . . The place is half English, to be sure, and the local sheet appearing in double columns . . . but it still remains half German . . . The row of sun-burned faces round the table can present the first surprise . . . in the rare air, clear, cold and blinding light of Alpine winters, a man . . . is stingingly alive. . . . [With] this sterile joyousness of spirits . . . you cast your shoe over the hill tops. . . .'

Soon the early stimulus faded. 'You weary before you have well begun,' wrote Stevenson. As for the professional writer, 'all his little fishes talk like whales'. He called the place 'a cage'. 'The mountains are about you like a trap. . . . You live in holes and corners, and can change only one for the other.'

Fanny too pined for more warmth and colour and contact with nature. She wrote to her mother-in-law, 'I have been so tired and worn out with so much to do that I broke down a little.'

She sent to Zürich for a clock to time her husband's regimen, and mounted guard. His writing was restricted to two hours in the morning and perhaps one in the afternoon. He became deadly bored with the same limited walks, the dull straight river, and soon the deep, deep snow. He said that the only touch of colour was the frozen yellow patch of dog's urine met at the same place and time each day. But his mechanical promenades were made more bearable by the pattering company of Woggs. As he wrote in his essay on 'The Character of Dogs', '. . . To follow for ten minutes in the street some swaggering, canine cavalier, is to receive a lesson in dramatic art. . . . To be a high-mannered and high-minded gentleman, careless, affable, and gay, is the inborn pretension of the dog. . . .'

Fanny did not often share even these brief outings, for the high altitude disagreed with her heart and she usually felt too unwell to go out. She spent much of her time lying on a couch. The room was warmed by a huge porcelain stove 'like a monument' which reached from floor to ceiling.

'But the great thing', she told the parents, 'is that the climate is

doing Louis good. To have him recover entirely will be so splendid
that I must not murmur at nothing.'

The majority of the Hotel Belvedere's guests were well-to-do
Britons, and again the Stevensons felt out of step with conventional
people, buzzing about Fanny's divorce. They disapproved of Louis's
long hair and 'un-British courtesy of manner'. 'Life is most monotonous here,' she wrote, 'which is after all the best thing for Louis,
although he tires of it sometimes. We have had a few badly acted
plays and one snowstorm; there was a quarrel between a lady and her
son's tutor, and a lady lost a ring. Otherwise the current of our lives
flows on without change. . . . I have made a couple of pretty caps for
the ladies' bazaar, and if I can get the use of a sitting-room will paint
them some things. . . . '

A great many patients died while the Stevensons were there –
'died discreetly', as Lloyd remembered later. Meanwhile they
counterfeited a gay and animated life. But there were reckless
breakaways from the routine, mad love affairs, jealousies, cliques,
intrigues, feuds and eternal gossip forever falling like the fresh snow.

'It is depressing to live with dying and suffering people all about
you . . .' Fanny wrote to Mrs Stevenson. She spoke also of 'little
kindnesses that warm the heart', one of which she prophesied with
her occultism. One morning she told Louis that she had dreamed
that a fellow guest named Cornish had made him a present of his
toboggan. As soon as Louis went out, Mr Cornish came up and gave
him the toboggan. 'I had never thought of such a thing,' she added,
'and don't see why I dreamed it.'

The Stevensons were frowned upon because they allowed Lloyd to
call his stepfather Louis. Lloyd recollected that a 'fussy officious
person' once ventured to criticize Louis for the way he was bringing
the boy up. 'Of course I let him read anything he wants,' Louis
retorted. 'And if he hears things you say he shouldn't I am glad of it.
A child should early gain some perception of what the world is
really like. . . .'

At first Stevenson tried to tutor Lloyd, but then turned the job
over to some tubercular young men who were glad to earn a little
money. He paid forty pounds for the winter's tutoring, plus more to a
dying Prussian officer who taught the boy German 'with the aid of a
pocket-knife stuck down my throat to give me the right accent'.

Lloyd, in his own word, 'idolized' his stepfather. He did more than anyone else to open a door for the sick man into the world beyond the sanatorium. Louis had a rare gift for slipping back into a child's *milieu*.

A lad who had died at the Belvedere left Lloyd his toy theatre. Fanny painted scenery for it, and Louis, wrote Lloyd, 'helped me to give performances, and slide the actors in and out, as well as imitating galloping horses, or screaming screams for the heroine in distress. My mother, usually the sole audience, would laugh till she had to be patted on the back, while I held back the play with much impatience for her recovery. . . .'

Four months after Sam Osbourne had bade his son goodbye in San Francisco, he wrote to plead with him – as he was often to do, 'I am very glad indeed to hear from you; and if I don't get a letter every week or ten days I commence to feel that my little boy – not so very little though – has forgotten me'.

He wrote kindly of his son's mother, but complained if she neglected to forward a letter sent to the lad in her care during brief separations. Apparently he and Fanny were in direct touch, at least for a time. There were business matters to settle, and they still jointly owned the cottage in East Oakland. Some months later Louis had to write to Rearden asking him to engage a lawyer to see that the property was not sold for taxes. Sam did not contribute towards the maintenance or education of his son, though sometimes he sent him a little pocket money.

Louis's allowance of £250 from his father was hardly half enough for the support of three people plus his own and Fanny's heavy medical bills and Lloyd's schooling. The boy remembered that his mother's face was 'often anxious'; sometimes he would find her crying. Once, with consternation, he heard his stepfather say in a tragic voice, 'Good heavens, Fanny, we are spending ten pounds a week on food alone!' While he sat studying his lessons in the room which they all shared, he 'grew used to hearing a sentence that struck at my heart. "Fanny, I shall have to write to my father."'

Thomas Stevenson responded to each apologetic plea. From year to year the paternal allowance must have been doubled. As Louis once put it, 'I always fall on my feet, but the legs are my father's.'

Slowly Stevenson's health improved, despite occasional haemorrhages. In time he was able to skate a little and became mad about
tobogganing, especially – and rashly – by moonlight. (Ski-ing had
not yet appeared at Davos.) As a fellow-convalescent observed, 'He
stayed in bed when he should have been out of doors and when he
should have been in bed he played the fool with a toboggan.' The
elder Mrs Stevenson wrote to tell her daughter-in-law that it was
'absurd to light the candle every time Louis coughs in the night'. And
Sidney Colvin grumbled to Baxter about her 'love of harrowing her
own and other people's feelings'.

'Louis and Mr Symonds are, so to speak, Siamese twins,' Fanny
informed Colvin early in their stay. But even this compensation
wore thin like the air, though the two dissimilar writers remained
landmarks for each other in the perpendicular waste of snow. The
father of four daughters whom he adored, Symonds was one of the
few homosexuals among Stevenson's friends, and consorted with the
Swiss peasants. In time Louis observed to Colvin that to be with him
was 'to adventure in a thornbush', but 'his mind is interesting'.

Fanny might have been expected to hobnob with Mrs Symonds
while their literary husbands were fraternizing, but the two women
disliked each other. As Stevenson described the lady in a letter to
Colvin, '. . . for Mrs S. I have much pity but little sympathy. A
stupid woman, married above her, moving daily with people whose
talk she doesn't understand. . . .'

With the mellowing of time, however, Symonds recalled the
Stevensons' stay: '. . . it has been so full of innocent jollity and
beautiful bohemianism . . . – the beautiful companionship of the
Shelley-like man, the eager, gifted wife, and the boy for whom they
both thought in all their ways and hours.'

'Louis is worried because he thinks he cannot write as gracefully
as he used to,' Fanny reported to the parents, 'but I believe his
writing is more direct and stronger, and that when he is able to join
his old style with the new he will do better work than he dreams of
now. His later work is fuller of thought, more manly in every way'.

She also told Mrs Stevenson, 'Louis is learning to be very quiet
and sedate, and does not give way to excitability about small things
so much.'

He was permanently afflicted with writer's cramp and, especially when he was weakened by illness, his wife was glad to act as amanuensis. Gradually she took over part of his personal correspondence as well, and had unquestioned access to his desk. This sometimes altered the tone of his letters to and from his old friends, even the many letters which he himself still penned.

She wrote most often to Sidney Colvin, telling him particular details about Louis and his condition, and asking his advice. She was careful to show a high esteem for Mrs Sitwell, with whom she conducted most of the correspondence.

In January Colvin came to Davos to pay his friends a visit, and Fanny rose from her couch to glow upon him and seek his counsel. Woggs bit him when he stroked his fur the wrong way. However, the cross little animal once bit even his doting mistress. 'Woggs is ill-tempered, and obstinate, and rather sly, but he is lovable and intelligent', wrote Fanny – and some might say that this was almost a description of herself. 'I imagine that it is with dogs as with people – it is not for being good alone that we love them.'

After Colvin left, the Stevensons were joined, unexpectedly and poignantly, by Mrs Sitwell and her eighteen-year-old son. The adored Albert – Bertie – had just left school at Marlborough, only to be stricken with galloping consumption.

Fanny was reminded of her own long agony in the loss of the golden-haired Hervey, and had the warmest sympathy for the worried mother, already once bereaved. She and Louis both tried to do what little they could to help and comfort her. There followed the familiar alternations of hope and despair, while the Stevensons marvelled at Mrs Sitwell's courage and fortitude.

'. . . I know the thing to be terribly perilous, I fear it to be now altogether hopeless', Louis wrote to Colvin. '. . . in her true heart, the mother hopes no more. . . . It has helped to make me more conscious of the wolverine on my own shoulders . . .'.

Virginibus Puerisque was being printed for spring publication, with the author's dedication to Henley, later to seem so ironic: '. . . as I look back in memory, there is hardly a stage of that distance but I see you present with advice, reproof, or praise. . . . I hope that our sympathy, founded on the love of our art, and nourished by mutual assistance, shall . . . with God's help, unite us to the end.'

The ebb of the winter, when spring was opening the buds in

lower lands, brought even heavier snow, making the roads almost impassable and the isolation more marked. One by one, familiar faces had been quietly disappearing, with funeral after funeral; and new invalids took the scrubbed rooms.

In a letter to her mother-in-law Fanny confessed, 'I cannot deny that living here is like living in a well of desolation. . . . But may Davos forgive me! It has done so much for Louis that I am ashamed to say anything against it.'

They decided reluctantly that a tuberculosis resort was not a good place for a healthy boy of thirteen, and sent Lloyd to a clergyman's small school in Bournemouth: another expense for Louis, via his father.

Fanny had been ill, and in late March she went down to Paris for a costly ten days to see a doctor. 'Bertie is dying . . .' wrote Louis to his parents. 'I do so wish Fanny were here.' She returned in time for the boy's death, in his mother's arms, on 3rd April. He had lasted unmercifully long. Mrs Sitwell, quiet and brave, went back to England and the faithful Colvin.

The Stevensons were shaken more by this intimate loss than by the many others. Fanny humbly counted her blessings. R.L.S. wrote his touching poem, "In Memoriam: F.A.S.", reprinted in many anthologies. It began:

> Yet, O stricken heart, remember, O remember
> How of human days he lived the better part.
> April came to bloom and never dim December
> Breathed its killing chills upon the head or heart. . . .

Dr Ruedi had estimated eighteen months at Davos for Louis's cure, but the patient felt that he could not endure the long stretch unbroken. At the end of the month he and Fanny decided to go home to Scotland for the summer.

Meanwhile in San Francisco, on Easter Monday, Fanny's grandson, Austin Strong, had been born to the thrilled and happy Belle.

Chapter II
The origin of *Treasure Island*

To escape the altitude, Fanny went ahead to France, and her husband joined her there with Woggs in the time of the lilies of the valley. First they stopped at Siron's inn at Barbizon, to renew memories of the forest of Fontainebleau. Faulty drains and a scare of an epidemic drove them into Paris. There they explored the odd little by-streets and junk shops. Once Louis insisted on spending almost his last sou for an antique watch which Fanny had admired. 'Now we'll starve', she said. But when they got back to their modest hotel, he chanced to put his hand in the pocket of an old coat and drew out an uncashed cheque which he had forgotten.

From Paris they went to St Germain, in fresh air above the Seine, with the terrace of its magnificent sixteenth century château – where for the first time they heard a nightingale sing. But alas, Louis had a relapse and another haemorrhage which alarmed and discouraged them both.

Again they were out of funds. The landlord became insolent, even insulting, at their inability to pay their hotel bill, plus the 'general suspicious appearance of Louis's wardrobe' – particularly, Fanny thought, his coloured flannel shirt. Then suddenly the unfailing manna descended from the skies of Scotland. They left their baffled host 'in the belief', according to Fanny, 'that he had turned from his doors the eccentric son of a wealthy English nobleman'.

They started for Edinburgh very slowly, for Louis's welfare. Arriving at the end of May, they left for Perthshire a few days later with Lloyd and Mrs Stevenson.

Louis had written his parents to ask that their summer quarters be 'a house, not an inn, at least not an hotel; a burn within reach; heather and a fir or two'. They found these for two months at a small farmhouse called Kinnaird Cottage, outside the hamlet of Moulin near Pitlochry. Behind, beyond a glen, a great purplebrown moor, scented like honey, reached to Ben Vrackie.

The party arrived on 7th June to find 'nothing but cold rains and penetrating winds', wrote Fanny, in a Preface, and the bad weather continued all summer. 'Between showers [my mother-in-law] and I wandered over the moor and along the banks of the burn, but always with umbrellas in our hands, and generally returning drenched.'

The invalid was a prisoner by the fire in the sitting-room with its one small window. 'The only books we had with us', continued Fanny, 'were two large volumes of the life of Voltaire. . . . Even these, removed from us by my husband's parents one dreary Sunday as not being proper "Sabba'-day reading", were annexed by the elder couple, each taking a volume.'

So all they could do was to write stories and read them to each other. They meant to devise a joint book of eight tales. Fanny wrote 'well', but her writing trots: it does not gallop, like her husband's. His friends scolded him for debasing his own work by collaboration with such lesser talents. But he was indulgent towards them and enjoyed the creative companionship. Since her bent was for horror tales – probably developed in childhood by her grandmother – he fell in with what she could do. 'Crawlers', he called them. '. . . at last', he told Gosse, 'I am at work with that appetite and confidence that alone make work supportable'. He produced 'The Merry Men', 'The Body Snatchers', and that brooding, compelling story in Scots dialect, 'Thrawn Janet', which Henry James was to pronounce a masterpiece.

Fanny further recalled the evening it was begun: '. . . the dim light of our one candle, with the acrid smell of the wick that we had forgotten to snuff, the shadows in the corners . . . the driving rain on the roof close above our heads, and the gusts of wind that shook our windows. . . . By the time the tale was finished my husband had fairly frightened himself, and we crept down the stairs clinging hand in hand like two scared children.'

She herself wrote a horror tale called 'The Shadow on the Bed', which has not survived.

Acutely anxious to be independent and support his family, Louis applied for the chair of History and Constitutional Law at Edinburgh University, with a stipend of £250 for only three months of lectures in the summer. His father and friends mustered all possible 'pull' but he was not accepted. Fanny confided to Dora Williams that she hoped he would not get the professorship: she wisely saw that he was not cut out for a don.

In fact, the closing of this door meant the opening of another. Always liking to hold forth to an audience, he had conscripted his young stepson to sit and listen while he practised lecturing on constitutional law, 'every now and then stopping to make sure that his class was following his meaning'. 'No wonder', recollected Lloyd, 'that my mother smiled.' At last the bored captive asked him glumly if he couldn't try and write 'something interesting'. This plea stuck in the author's mind. Having obliged Fanny with weird stories, he was soon in the mood to amuse Lloyd. But not yet.

Then he caught a cold and began to spit blood: 'Bluidy Jack' was on his back again. 'Weather wet. . . . Bad weather. . . . Still wet. . . . Afraid to go out. . . . Pouring rain. . . .' ran the entries in his mother's diary. So the party decided to move to beautiful Braemar, which they hoped would be milder.

After they arrived, Louis urged Gosse to come for a visit, but added, 'If you had an uncle who was a sea captain and went to the North Pole, you had better bring his outfit. . . .' He himself ventured out eccentrically in a white hat and a plaid.

Mrs Stevenson reported in her diary, 'I had Kate Greenaway's children's birthday book. Lou took it up one day and said, "These are rather nice rhymes, and I don't think they would be difficult to do," and he proceeded to try.'

He then gradually wrote about fourteen of the little poems which were to comprise *A Child's Garden of Verses*. His stepson was too 'old' for them, and some of his friends disapproved, but they were to become part of the early consciousness of generations of English-speaking children.

> When I am grown to man's estate
> I shall be very proud and great.
> And tell the other girls and boys
> Not to meddle with my toys.

One day he found Lloyd painting a map he had drawn of an imaginary island. Louis loved charts and joined in, adding a number of swashbuckling place-names such as Spyglass Hill and Skeleton Island. In the top right-hand corner he wrote 'Treasure Island'. Something lit up his mind like a smuggler's lantern. In five minutes he had jotted down a list of chapter headings. 'Then,' remembered Lloyd, '. . . he put the map in his pocket, and I can recall the little feeling of disappointment I had at losing it.'

'On a chill September morning,' wrote Stevenson, 'by the cheek of a brisk fire, and the rain drumming on the window, I began *The Sea Cook*, for that was the original title.'

He wrote to Henley: '. . . I am on another lay for the moment, purely owing to Lloyd, this one, but I believe there's more coin in it: *The Sea Cook, or Treasure Island : A Story for Boys*. If this don't fetch the kids, why, they have gone rotten since my day. . . .'

'Next day . . . three chapters. All now heard by Lloyd, Fanny, my father and mother, with high approval. It's quite silly and horrid fun . . . with the chorus "Yo-ho-ho and a bottle of rum!" . . . No women in the story, Lloyd's orders; and who so blythe to obey?'

Henley was disgruntled; he wanted his friend to write plays. But Louis exulted at the possibility of earning some quick money at last. 'If it nets me £50 promptly, I have gained the battle for just now.'

Lloyd wanted only one exciting episode after another, and kept his stepfather to the mark. Thomas Stevenson took a surprising interest in the plan. 'I had counted on one boy', said Louis. 'I found I had two in my audience.'

Louis, Thomas and Lloyd puzzled for hours over the details of the island and the gear. Fanny was indulgently pleased to watch her husband working so happily with his father and her son, like three lads playing pirates. However, she did not care for *Treasure Island*; she thought it a pity for Louis to waste his great talent on a boy's adventure story.

He had meanwhile begged a number of his intimates to come and stay: Colvin, Gosse, Baxter – and Henley. The last declined, though in liking the horror stories he had even included Fanny's.

Louis had promised Gosse, 'You will like my wife because she likes cats. . . .' But very soon Fanny was telling Dora Williams that 'Mr Gosse and I are at daggers drawn.' He had tried to belittle her and she had put him in his place. He was the first of Stevenson's circle of close friends with whom she quarrelled.

In his book *Critical Kit-Kats* Gosse described his visit, with the sleet howling outside, all the household ill, and Stevenson's cold deteriorating with chest pains and loss of voice. 'After breakfast I went to Louis's bedroom, where he sat up in bed with dark, flashing eyes and ruffled hair.' They played chess. 'Not a word passed, for he was strictly forbidden to speak in the early part of the day. As soon as he felt tired – often in the middle of a game – he would rap with peremptory knuckles on the board as a signal to stop; then Mrs Stevenson or I would arrange his writing materials on the bed. . . . I would see no more of him till dinner time, when he came down, smiling and voluble. Then after dinner, he would read us what he had written during the day. I wrote to my wife, "Louis has been writing . . . a novel of pirates and hidden treasure, in the highest degree exciting."'

By a lucky chance Dr Alexander Japp, the journalist and scholar, was next invited to the cottage, to talk of Thoreau, about whom Stevenson meant to write a book. He was taken upstairs to the picture gallery in which Louis and Lloyd worked. 'Stevenson said to me with a sly wink and a gentle dig in the ribs, "It's laugh and be thankful here."'

'His wife,' wrote Dr Japp, 'an American lady, is highly cultured, and is herself an author. In her speech there is just the slightest suggestion of an American accent, which only made it the more pleasing to my ear. She is heart and soul devoted to her husband, proud of his achievements, and her delight is the consciousness of substantially aiding him in his enterprises. . . .'

Japp too was impressed by the nightly readings of the pirate tale. He thought that his friend James Henderson, editor of *Young Folks* magazine, might buy it as a serial; and he carried off the first sixteen chapters in his portmanteau.

When Henderson received these early chapters, he changed the name to *Treasure Island* and accepted the work at space rates. The payment added up to only £34 7s 6d instead of the £50 for which Louis had hoped, but though 'not noble', any cash was welcome. Certainly Fanny and her father-in-law more than agreed, surprised though they were at the unexpected turn which Louis's gift had taken. The triumphant author estimated to Henley that the serial was earning '£2 10s a page of 4,500 words. . . . Each three chapters is worth £2 10s. So we have £12 10s already . . . Yo-heave ho!'

The story was to be published under the *nom de plume* of 'Captain George North', but even so, Stevenson's literary friends reproached him for hacking with a boys' adventure yarn. Louis sputtered back to Henley, '. . . let them write their damn masterpieces for themselves and let me alone . . .'.

After a chapter a day for sixteen days, the writing got stuck in the middle and the author had to stop. He anxiously tried to force a few more chapters but they went badly. Henderson did not know that he often put unfinished work aside for a long time, and confidently began to publish the serial in the issue of 1st October.

Meanwhile the weather became so cold and stormy that on 23rd September the party had to flee to Edinburgh – the younger members *en route* back to the snow-peak prison of Davos. After a few days in Heriot Row, Louis and Fanny travelled down to London. They were accompanied not only by Woggs but by Lloyd, whom they could not afford to keep in boarding-school.

Louis went to call on Mr Henderson, the editor who had accepted *Treasure Island*. 'It was', he wrote to Colvin, 'a very amusing visit indeed; ordered away by the clerks, who refused loudly to believe I had any business; and at last received most kindly by Mr Henderson.'

On the way to Davos, wrote Fanny later, 'We carried the unfinished novel with us on the journey, as we rather expected to stop and rest en route. But we also carried a toy theatre for the lad, who had preceded us with his tutor; also sheets of unpainted sets, *penny plain*, and a fine large box of water colours, for Lloyd.'

'The first night we stopped we opened the package of manuscript, which also contained the theatre sets and the paints. I began idly trying the colours on one of the *plains*. My enthusiasm rose with action, and I was soon absorbed in the sport. My husband watched me for a moment, and then he too fell a victim. We painted on and on, until the night was almost spent, only ceasing with the end of our material, and *Treasure Island* went back into the parcel as it came out.'

Chapter III
The icy cage of Davos again

For the winter of 1881–2 the Stevensons returned to Davos and took the Châlet am Stein, a small bleak wooden house scaling the mountainside. It proved costlier than hotel life, but it was more homelike and blessedly free from the gossip. They engaged a disagreeable German maid. Fanny was too unwell to devise her usual domestic comforts, and Mrs Symonds deplored her house-keeping.

Louis was seriously worried about his barren spell with *Treasure Island*. Money was short; the early instalments had been printed in *Young Folks* – and what if he could not complete the serial? Then one October morning he sat down, '. . . and behold! it flowed like small talk'. He finished it at the renewed rate of a chapter a day.

It did not sell any more copies of the magazine, and some readers turned up their noses. After its publication Louis wrote to Colvin, 'F. has re-read *Treasure Island*, against which she protested; and now she thinks the end about as good as the beginning; . . .' However, she still maintained in a letter to Ellen Gosse that she disliked the story. He revised it before it was published in book form a couple of years later.

On 2nd November Symonds wrote of Louis to the historian Horatio Brown: 'He was lying, ghastly, in bed – purple cheek-bones, yellow cheeks, bloodless lips – fever all over him – without appetite – and all about him so utterly forlorn. "Woggs" was squealing . . . Mrs Stevenson doing her best to make things comfortable.'

The next week Louis was better, but Fanny was taken very ill. '. . . she has, it is thought, drain poisoning,' her husband wrote to Mrs Sitwell; 'she had diarrhoea very bad, pain, great weakness, spotted throat, and I know not all what.' In early December she was ordered away for four weeks' treatment, first in Zürich and then in Berne. It was found that she had passed a gallstone. The doctor was 'very glum' and feared ulceration of the bowels. She in turn was worried about being away from her post with Louis.

'We have been in miserable case here,' Louis wrote to Baxter, 'my wife worse and worse, and now sent away with Lloyd for a sick nurse, I not being allowed to go down. . . . I don't care as much for solitude as I used to: results, I suppose, of marriage.'

He went down to Berne to fetch Fanny and Lloyd on Christmas Day. For seven hours they drove up the steep ridges in the snow in an open sleigh, which was all they could get. Incredibly, neither of the convalescents was the worse for the long exposure. But back at Davos Louis slipped and fell and badly hurt a knee. Fanny too had a sharp relapse, and they both were ill in bed on New Year's Eve, though they could not sleep, Louis told Colvin, for 'shouts of stifled laughter all through the watches'.

It was in the essay on 'Talk and Talkers' that Louis wrote, after eighteen months of matrimony, his well-known definition of the state: 'Marriage is one long conversation, chequered by disputes. . . . But in the intervals, almost unconsciously and with no desire to shine, the whole material of life is turned over, ideas are struck out and shared, the two persons more and more adapt their notions one to suit the other, and in process of time, without sound of trumpet, they conduct each other into new worlds of thought.'

Luckily that winter was fairly mild, except for an occasional *Föhn*, the violent south wind which shook the snow-piled roof. Fanny was able to stick out the season with two more brief respites in the lower altitude of Berne. 'I shall be damn glad to get you back again and meanwhile send you a kiss,' her husband told her. To Dr Japp he wrote, 'I was ill – I did really fear my wife was worse than ill.' 'Art and marriage are two very good stand-by's . . .' he informed Baxter on 22nd February. 'My wife is better again. . . . But we take it by turns; it is the dog that is ill now.'

In those six months of improving health at Davos, Stevenson wrote thirty-five thousand words. He produced several essays, worked on *Prince Otto* and completed *The Silverado Squatters*, which was strangely hard labour after the facile dash of *Treasure Island*.

'I am still far from satisfied about Fanny,' he told his mother in April. '. . . I had her persuaded to leave without me this very day (Sat. 8th), but the disclosure of my mismanagement broke up that plan; she would not leave me lest I should mismanage more. . . .'

One morning they heard a bird sing. The snows on the sunlit heights began to melt, floods of water rushed down the streets, and abruptly, Fanny noticed, the slanting meadows around the châlet turned 'as white with crocus blooms as they had been in their winter covering of snow'. One day Louis sat singing beside his wife while she was writing to his mother, and she added, 'I do not care for the music, but it makes me feel so happy to see him so well. When I wake in the morning I wonder what it is that brings such a glow to my heart, and then I remember!'

Louis was able to write to Henley, 'My lungs are said to be in a splendid state . . . Taïaut! Hillo! Hey! Stand by! Avast! Hurrah!'

To their great relief Dr Ruedi allowed them to leave the bleak crystal cage for ever. He recommended the palatable alternative of the South of France, 'fifteen miles as the crow flies from the sea, and if possible near a fir-wood'.

Meanwhile in San Francisco Belle had by no means forgiven her mother for divorcing darling Papa. Towards the end of 1881 Fanny wrote to Dora Williams: '. . . Except a cold note asking me to sign a deed, I have not had a letter from Belle since the middle of last summer. I wrote to Belle till I got tired, and then to Joe, but got no answer. They know how ill I have been, too. . . . Ingratitude is not warming to the heart. You wonder at my patience with them; after all they belong to me whether or not, and I probably spoiled Belle by over-indulgence and have to blame myself somewhat for her selfishness. . . . I feel greatly distressed about Joe's health. . . . I am afraid he does not live in as wholesome a way as so delicate a person should. . . . The worst of helping Belle and Joe is that it is so hard on Louis. Every penny must be coined in Louis's mind. . . .'

Belle was perhaps not the more pleased because Fanny's original opposition to the Strongs' marriage had been justifying itself. Joe had plenty of commissions for portraits at several hundred dollars each, but he was unreliable about his work and squandered his earnings and his wife's. Belle stood up for him loyally, and she too seemed to enjoy the feckless life of late nights and studio parties. Soon Fanny was deploring to Dora Williams the 'coarse flavour' of her daughter's letters. Colvin, Baxter, Henley et al. were shocked and disgusted that Louis should have to send money to such a shiftless couple.

Luckily the baby was thriving. Sam reported to Lloyd, 'Baby is ugly but he is nice – like you are.' And later, 'Belle worships little

Austin, who is a delightful little cuss, just commencing to walk.'

Some prominent San Francisco business men thought it a pity that young Strong was wasting his talents with too much convivial company. Since Joe came from a pioneer missionary family in Hawaii, Mr Spreckels, the tycoon of a big shipping company in Honolulu, suggested that he go there and paint island scenes for the firm's offices. The Strongs were eager to accept, but it was more than a year before – with the Stevensons' help – they could finally afford to make the move, in September 1882. Fanny wrote to Dora Williams that her daughter was annoyed with her for not sending more money. Belle seemed to feel that since Louis had broken up the Osbourne family it was the least he could do to subsidize them all. As for Joe, he had no sense of financial pride or obligation; he merely grabbed the money – any money – like a small child.

None the less, in giving a letter of introduction to a friend who was going to Europe, Belle assured him that her mother and stepfather were 'the most entertaining folks alive'.

Part 6

The French Riviera
The first success   1882 - 84

Chapter I
'A garden of paradise' – and plague

The Stevensons joined first the parents in London and then Katharine de Mattos in Surrey. She was separated from her husband, who had not only left her very poor but had been greedy as well.

As for Bob, in the previous summer he had been married at last – to an attractive girl named Louisa Purland. She fitted well into his restless dreaming, being a 'new woman', with a job (the pair always needed more money), and an interest in the artistic life.

In late June the family went to Stobo Manse in Peebleshire. Again the weather was bad, and the Manse was shut in by trees. Louis had a haemorrhage, so in only a fortnight he had to go down to London to see Dr Andrew Clark. On his advice the party tried Speyside – a cottage at Kingussie near 'a golden burn that pours and sulks'. It was the last full month they were ever to spend in his beautiful native land.

Stevenson's creative energy slackened again, though he wrote most of 'The Treasure of Franchard'. More blood-spitting sent him back to London and Dr Clark. Fanny had feared that the specialist might order him to Davos, but luckily they were allowed to go as planned to the South of France.

Fanny too had remained rather an invalid all summer, and she was now too ill to travel. Lloyd was sent back to the clergyman's school in Bournemouth. Louis was not well enough to go to France alone;

so in mid September Bob accompanied him to the Midi to look for a
house.

In Montpellier Louis had a haemorrhage. The convalescent
Fanny was intent on joining him, though she had never been to the
Riviera and was still almost mute in French. He wrote her in early
October:

'. . . If my mother is not to come with you to Paris, I don't know
that I want you to come at all. I cannot bear to have you travelling
alone. . . . Tell her she has to come to Paris with you, no excuse will
serve. . . .

'And you can then come and produce a tonic effect on your
papa. . . . If you think I don't want to see you, you are a great baby;
kiss my Wogg; I like him to be bad.

'I am going to wear beautiful rich clothing always new *on condition
that you do*. When you come you shall have a kiss.

From your loving husband,

Louis.

[PS.] 'I am no good at all. Marriage does soften a person. I have
neither pluck nor patience, and I must own I have wearied awful for
you. But you will never understand that bit of my character. I don't
want you when I am ill. At least it's only half of me that wants you,
and I don't like to think of you coming back and not finding me
better than when we parted. That is why I would rather be miserable
than send for you.'

Bob had to return to England, and Louis managed to go on to
Marseilles, which he liked, with its nautical vitality and pretty
women. His wife got out of bed to follow him. 'Fanny joins him,
travelling alone from Edinburgh,' reported her mother-in-law's diary.
'We are anxious about her but "through idiocy and being an American she made it out",' as she said. She reached Marseilles on 11th
October in an 'alarmed and fatigued condition'. Louis wrote to Bob,
'F.'s arrival here, after our separation, was better fun to me than
being married was by far'.

In a few days they found, outside the suburb of St Marcel, a
lovely spacious house called Campagne Defli, which they both
thought ideal. The rent was only £48 per year. Set in a large estate,
the house looked south over a valley of beautiful white cliffs and
woods. They sent for their household goods and planned to stay for

several years at least. Fanny wrote jubilantly to her mother-in-law: '. . . It is a garden of paradise, and I cannot tell you how I long to have you here to enjoy things with us. . . .'

She marshalled the servants in repairing walls, scrubbing, hanging curtains over draughty doors, re-covering old furniture, and planting flowers and vegetables in the neglected garden. Once when she was standing on a ladder, hammering a nail to hang a picture, she heard one maid whisper to another outside, 'Elle est folle.' As the two came in she shook the hammer at them and cried indignantly, 'Pas folle! Beaucoup d'intelligence!' Then she lost her balance and fell over, ladder and all, while the women fled shrieking.

The new tenants – especially Louis – looked forward to welcoming their friends. But then an episode occurred which showed how sensitive they still were. Stevenson had been in friendly correspondence with William Dean Howells, the American editor who had bought some of his verses for *The Atlantic Monthly*. R.L.S. urged him to come and stay at St Marcel. But before Howells could make any plans, Louis happened to read his new book, *A Modern Instance*, and got the idea that its author was strict about marriage. He took up his pen:

'Dear Sir,

I have just finished reading your last book; it has enlightened (or darkened?) me as to your opinions. . . . I find myself under the unpleasant necessity of intruding on your knowledge a piece of my private life.

'My wife did me the honour to divorce her husband in order to marry me.

'This, neither more nor less, it is at once my duty and my pleasure to communicate . . . after the kindness which you showed me in your country and the sympathy with which many of your books have inspired me, it will be my sincere disappointment to find that you cannot be my guest. I shall bear up, however; for I assure you I desire to know no one who considers himself holier than my wife.

'With best wishes, however it goes, believe me
Yours truly
Robert Louis Stevenson.'

Mr Howells did not reply.

Alas, the climate of St Marcel proved deadly to Louis. He sagged with fever and exhaustion and worked very little. Soon Fanny had to write home, 'I am sorry to say that Louis has had another haemorrhage. . . .'

But the patient improved a little and they looked forward to Christmas together in their château. On 23rd December Louis wrote his mother, 'Fanny is away into town to meet Lloyd, who arrives at five o'clock tomorrow. I am dreadfully lonely, I must own. . . .'

After the holidays an epidemic of enteric broke out in the village. Fanny thought it was typhus, and panicked. Funeral bells rang all day in the village, corpses were carried on coffin-lids past the house and one (she claimed) was left to bloat in the sun outside their gate. She insisted that Louis should go off at once to Nice. 'Just at that time', she wrote Symonds, 'there was not money enough for the two of us, so he had to start alone, though I expected soon to be able to follow him.' She stayed a few days to guard and pack their belongings, 'armed with a revolver . . . the situation being lonely, and reports of robberies and even murder having reached us.

'I was to have a despatch from Toulon, where Louis was to pass the night, and another from Nice, some few hours further, the next day. I waited one, two, three, four days, and no word came. Neither telegram nor letter. The evening of the fourth day I went to Marseilles and telegraphed to the Toulon and Nice stations and to the bureau of police. I had been pouring out letters to every place I could think of. The people at Marseilles were very kind and advised me to take no further steps to find my husband. He was certainly dead, they said. It was plain that he stopped at some little station on the road, speechless and dying, and it was now too late to do anything; I had much better return at once to my friends. "Eet ofen 'appens so", said the Secretary, and "Oh, yes, all right, very well", added a Swiss in a sympathetic voice.'

All night she waited in Marseilles without an answer, then returned to St Marcel and found none there. At eight in the morning she and Lloyd started off to travel by Louis's route, meaning to get out of the train at every station and inquire for him until they reached Nice. Luckily Lloyd could act as interpreter. She telegraphed again at Toulon and finally got an answer the next day. Her husband was at the Grand Hotel in Nice. 'I never received any of the letters

Louis had written to me, and he was reading the first he had received from me when I knocked at his door.'

The change of air and doctor had helped him. He was meanwhile working on *Penny Whistles*, later called *A Child's Garden of Verses*, and informed his old nurse Cummy that he was going to dedicate the volume to her.

Fanny left him still in bed and went back to pack up and dispose of the house. 'My nerves are so shattered by the terrible suspense I endured that memorable week that I have not been fit to do much,' she told Symonds.

To her husband she sent an arch scolding: 'Don't you dare to come back to this home of "pizon" until you are really better . . . deserting your family as you have done and being hunted down and caught by your wife. . . . You are a dear creature and I love you, but I am not going to say that I am lonesome lest you come flying back to this den of death.'

Louis was lonesome too and wrote couplets to her, illustrated with drawings.

> When my wife is far from me
> The undersigned feels all at sea.
> R.L.S.

> I am as good as deaf
> When separate from *F*.

> I am far from gay
> When separate from *A*.

> I loathe the ways of man
> When separate from *N*.

> Life is a murky den
> When separate from *N*.

> My sorrow rages high
> When separate from *Y*.

> And all things seem uncanny
> When separate from Fanny.

> Where is my wife? Where is my Wogg?
> I am alone, and life's a bog.

He had disquieting visions of her trying to cope with the move with her few words of French. To her annoyance he disobeyed her orders and turned up, though she made him sleep in Marseilles. 'He became filled with the idea that it was shirking to leave me here to do all the work,' she wrote his mother. 'He was a good deal hurt, poor boy, because I wasn't pleased. . . . It is so surprising, for I had never thought of Louis as a real domestic man, but now I find that all he wanted was a house of his own . . . and it was like pulling up roots to get him away. . . .'

At this time the couple received from New York the *Century* magazine – which had declined *The Amateur Emigrant* but was accepting *The Silverado Squatters* for a hundred pounds. The current issue contained an enthusiastic review of Stevenson's collection of stories, *New Arabian Nights*, recently published in London. 'The person was evidently writing in such an ecstasy of joy at having found out Louis,' Fanny told her mother-in-law. 'I am so pleased that it was in the *Century*, for every friend and relation I have in the world will read it. I suppose you are even prouder of Louis than I am, for he is only mine accidentally, and he is yours by birth and blood. Two or three times last night I woke up just from pure pleasure to think of all the people I know reading about Louis. . . .'

Chapter II
The enchanted cottage

The intimates in Britain, not for the first or last time, were annoyed at Fanny's false alarm about her husband. 'I will never let myself be frightened by that maniac partner of his again, and she may cry "Wolf" till she is hoarse,' Colvin had written to Baxter. A similar implication from the parents made Fanny downcast. 'No,' Louis told them, 'Cassandra was not Cassandra, as you imagine. . . .' He asked them to write her a word of comfort: 'What she is to me, no language can describe, and she can never learn.' Though in one letter he told his mother that his wife was 'as cross as Two

Sticks', in another to Colvin he signed himself 'Uxorious Billy'.

Since the climate of Nice had benefited him, the couple decided to look for a place in that part of the Riviera. By the first of March they were signing a lease in Hyères, which was then well known as a tuberculosis resort.

The Châlet la Solitude was unique. It climbed the Rue de la Pierre Glissante half way between the high old town with the Saracen fortress and the new town at the base. 'The loveliest house you ever saw,' Louis described it to Mrs Sitwell, 'with a garden like a fairy story, and a view like a classical landscape'. 'A most coquettish little place', Lloyd remembered. It had been a model Swiss châlet at the Paris Exposition of 1878, and was meant to be reproduced on a larger scale. A prosperous resident of Hyères had bought it and rebuilt it on his own property. With three tiny rooms below and four above, 'it is the smallest doll's house I ever saw,' Fanny wrote to Mrs Stevenson, 'but has everything in it to make it comfortable. . . .

'Our life in the châlet was of the utmost simplicity,' she wrote, 'and with the help of one untrained maid I did the cooking myself. The kitchen was so narrow that I was in continual danger of being scorched by the range on one side, and at the same time impaled by the saucepan hooks on the other, and when we had a guest at dinner our maid had to pass the dishes over our heads, as our chairs touched the walls of the dining-room. . . .'

The maid was a blessing. Fanny had advertised in the local newspaper, and a strong blonde girl named Valentine Roch applied for the job. She had been born in Switzerland of a large French family who now lived in Hyères, where her father was a railway employee. Though untrained, she learned very quickly. Lloyd remembered her as 'a charming girl, far above her class, with a sparkling sense of humour, who reviewed the whole neighbourhood and nightly brought its annals up to date'. In time she even joined the family circle of literary criticism, and her loyalty and devotion became legendary among the invalid's friends. Stevenson nicknamed her Joe when she was on her usual good behaviour and Thomasina if she was moody.

Louis's health seemed better for a while. A sure sign was the fact that he ventured to have his hair cut short. He even wore what Lloyd called 'presentable clothes', with a straw hat and a short black *pèlerine*, or cape, which he always preferred to an overcoat and which raised no eyebrows in France. He had become 'very French', with the little tuft of an *impérial* on his chin. He must, however, have looked eccentric enough, for when he and Fanny visited Monte Carlo he was refused admittance to the Casino.

While her husband wrote in the mornings Fanny worked in the house and grounds. After lunch, with the good *vin du pays* and a salad which he relished, they discussed and criticized his morning's output. Then they walked in the garden and enjoyed their song-birds, trees and flowers; or, with Woggs scampering ahead, they strolled up the hill to the ruined castle. At home again they opened and answered the day's correspondence. After 'an excellent dinner', they talked or read. At night, he told the painter Will Low, in 'the most aromatic airs', there was 'the most wonderful view into the moonlit garden . . . with the flutes of silence . . .'.

They found that they could just manage to live on their income so long as there were no costly illnesses. They planned to send Lloyd to school at Toulon. 'Last year', Louis told Henley, 'I pocketed £268; but it needn't be so always, and besides – well, it might do for an exceptionally chaste bachelor. But for a married man, who is sick, and has a sick wife, and a boy at school, it is scrimp.'

On 5th May he wrote to his parents that Fanny was still 'quite out of sorts', but he had 'not the heart to be dispirited about anything. I have a great piece of news. There has been offered for *Treasure Island* – how much do you suppose? I believe it would be an excellent jest to keep the answer till my next letter. For two cents I would do so. . . . No – well – a hundred pounds, all alive, O! A hundred jingling, tingling, golden minted quid. Is not this wonderful? . . . It does look as if I should support myself without trouble in the future. If I have only health, I can, thank God. It is dreadful to be a great, big man, and not be able to buy bread. O that this may last! . . .' And he ended, 'Your loving and ecstatic son, Louis.'

To Henley he wrote, 'I will now make a confession. It was the sight of your maimed strength and masterfulness that begot John Silver in *Treasure Island*. Of course, he is not in any other quality or feature the least like you; but the idea of the maimed man, ruling and dreaded by the sound, was entirely taken from you.'

He considered the hundred pounds for the book 'a sight more than it is worth', having hoped for only half as much. But then – though he had once written that 'if a man be not frugal he has no business in the arts', he knocked a good chunk out of the proceeds in buying Fanny a set of Hokusai prints.

She was less than delighted when her former husband beguiled their machine-loving son with the gift of a bicycle for which the boy had yearned. Osbourne did not, of course, share the cost of the boy's tutor – named, by coincidence, Louis Robert. Nevertheless Sam did not hesitate to urge, at no expense to himself, that his son should study chemistry and metallurgy to become a mining expert in California.

Some sketches by Joe Strong had appeared in *Harper's* magazine. But Belle wrote from their new home in Honolulu that Joe was seriously ill, and she again begged for financial help. The Stevensons were dubious. 'Do, please,' Louis wrote to Dora Williams, 'try and find out if Joe Strong is really very ill.'

Soon Louis was reporting to Henley 'a shower of small troubles'. A new stove was necessary. And he incurred 'a huge vague debt' when it was discovered that the ground under the exquisite châlet was 'riddled with cesspools' which needed cleaning. 'A word in your ear: I don't like trying to support myself. I hate the strain and anxiety and when unexpected expenses are foisted on me, I feel the world is playing with false dice.'

Chapter III
Red wine and 'Bluidy Jack'

In mid May Stevenson caught what he defined to Colvin as 'a whoreson influenza cold'. Again for several weeks he hovered between life and death. Valentine was trained by Fanny in the nursing which the girl was to share so ably and unselfishly for six years. Day or night she took turns in the watches, and in his strangling coughing spells she lifted him, pillows and all, in her muscular arms.

Gradually she was beginning to find her mistress 'difficult', though her devotion to Louis was never in doubt. But when she herself fell ill, Fanny nursed her in turn with all her skill and care, and Valentine stayed on and on.

Henderson of *Young Folks* asked Stevenson to write another serial for boys, and he launched upon *The Black Arrow, or The Outlaws of Tunstall Forest*, a story of medieval warfare by 'Captain George North'. He spoke of these swashbuckling tales as 'tushery', but again his pen flowed along easily and profitably. Fanny, not in sympathy with such potboiling by a genius, refused even to read the manuscript.

Resuming *Prince Otto*, he told Henley: '. . . To feel as I felt today, when I turned the corner of my story, was the reward of a lifetime. It came next, and but some thousand miles behind, love.' An intricate and romantic comedy of a small court in the Black Forest, the novel was revised and polished several times, and one chapter seven times – the next to the last draft being done by Fanny. She wrote to her mother-in-law about their 'combats' over the work. This was Stevenson's last big youthful experiment. The hero showed traits of himself and of Bob. Fanny's part-portrait as Seraphina was not – for whatever reason – as attractive, and certainly not as convincing, as the vivacious Countess von Rosen. She was drawn from the elder of the two Russian sisters at Menton, and was one of his few successful female characters. He wrote to Henley: '. . . triumph of triumphs, my wife – my wife who hates and loathes and slates my women – admits a great part of my Countess to be on the spot.'

Two other books for adults have not survived. One was *The Travelling Companion*, which a publisher turned down as 'a work of genius but indecent'. Stevenson later decided that it had 'no urbanity and glee, and no true tragedy', and burned it. About the other, of which little is known, a legend has grown up. It was said that it was a more or less autobiographical novel about a street-walker; and that Fanny had disapproved and thrown the manuscript on the fire. Colvin is understood to have confirmed the incident. Mr J. C. Furnas, the most nearly omniscient biographer of R.L.S., has deduced that this attribution may have been confused with Louis's later burning, after an argument with his wife, of a much more important manuscript to come.

A second legend, also centred on Fanny, assumed for over half a century that the rumour of the destroyed novel gave Henry James the idea for his story, 'The Author of Beltraffio'. It is about a writer whose wife allows their adored sick child to die rather than let him grow up and read his father's 'immoral' books. But Mr James did not yet know the Stevensons, though he had doubtless heard them described.

Professor F. O. Matthiesen, who a generation later had access to Henry James's unpublished notebooks, finally disclosed that it was Mrs Symonds's attitude to her husband's writing which was the inspiration. At any rate, Louis and Fanny acknowledged no reflection of themselves. He praised the story, while she particularly admired James's skill in creating child characters, saying that the boy in 'The Author of Beltraffio' reminded her of her own little Hervey.

'I. . . am merely beginning to commence to prepare to make a first start at trying to understand my profession. . . .' Stevenson wrote to Henley. 'I sleep upon my art for a pillow; I waken in my art; I am unready for death, because I hate to leave it. I love my wife, I do not know how much, nor can, nor shall, unless I lost her; but while I can conceive my being widowed, I refuse the offering of life without my art. I *am* not but in my art; it is me; I am the body of it merely.'

In June, 'The boy has just come, to our great delight', reported Fanny to her mother-in-law. On 1st July the trio left the Midi to summer in the higher air of the Auvergne. They set out by easy stages, with the incomplete manuscript of *The Black Arrow* in their luggage. The first instalment had already appeared in *Young Folks*. '. . . Writing for serial publication in haste', recalled Fanny, in a Preface, 'is a somewhat precarious occupation. I remember, when we once stopped for a day or two at Lyons, my husband's dismay when he sat down to write a chapter . . . to find that he had forgotten how to extricate his hero from an apparently impossible position. He could only make a new, somewhat lame invention to take the place of what was meant to be a most thrilling and ingenious escape.'

They settled at Royat, a small spa near Clermont Ferrand. It had comfortable hotels, and lay in peaceful landscape among the dome-shaped grassy mountains – the extinct volcanoes of the Massif Central. They admired the ancient fortified cathedral, and the wooded cliffs and waterfalls rising on the Puy de Dôme behind the town.

Caesar himself had bathed in the healing waters of Royat spa, and the Empress Eugénie had sponsored the vogue of the arsenical springs. 'One *source* had a flavour . . . of weak chicken broth', said Fanny, 'and another effervesced, when you plunged into it, like champagne.'

There were long drives on the Puy de Dôme road, and in the evenings the trio strolled in the gardens of the Casino, where a string band played in a small kiosk. They were so enthusiastic about the place that the elder Stevensons came out to join them.

By now Mr Stevenson could not fail to acknowledge his son's gifts and his growing recognition as a writer, and had become resigned to his making the work a full-time profession. Ironically, after his early opposition, he considered Fanny's head the more practical. 'On literary subjects,' wrote Mrs Stevenson in her diary, 'they thought so much alike that before my dear husband's death he made Louis promise that he would never publish anything without his wife's approval.'

Though Thomas still seemed outwardly a vigorous middle-aged man, the younger couple were disturbed to find him failing in body and mind. His business affairs were deteriorating, perhaps to the detriment of the Louis Stevensons' fortunes.

Thomas and Lloyd enjoyed *The Black Arrow*, though Fanny boycotted it. It continued smoothly and easily, and each new chapter was posted to Henderson almost as soon as the ink was dry. The manuscript was completed by the end of the summer.

'No one', Fanny wrote later, 'could accuse my husband of showing a mercenary spirit in the sale of *The Black Arrow*, for which he accepted Mr Henderson's offer of about three dollars a thousand words, just after receiving two hundred and fifty pounds from Mr C. J. Longman for the magazine rights of *Prince Otto*.' However, since *Treasure Island* had not been very successful as a serial, Louis was anxious to 'capture this audience' with *The Black Arrow*. He succeeded: the readers of *Young Folks* preferred it to the pirate tale.

In September the younger Stevensons went back to Hyères, the elder to Edinburgh, and Lloyd to the clergyman's school at Bournemouth. Sam Osbourne and his new wife Paulie had meanwhile been in Europe, and he had arranged for Lloyd to join him on a walking tour in the South of France, on an itinerary suggested, at

Sam's request, by Louis. Fanny deplored his hearty hand on the boy.

Osbourne had remarried not long after the divorce. His ex-wife had known the girl in the old days. Later, when grumbling about Fanny and her fame, Sam's sister Cynthia wrote to her son: 'He and Aunt Paulie visited at our house soon after their marriage. I have heard Mama say that it seemed that he chose a wife as much like Fanny as he could find. There was a strong resemblance between them. But while Aunt Paulie was sweeter, she lacked the keen-mindedness of Aunt Fan, and then her deafness must have been a trial to both of them. Mother always thought that grief for her son really hastened her death. I have not expatiated upon the alienation of the children – but it must have been bitter indeed to Sam. So much was made of Louis's affection and kindness to them. . . .'

Belle, however, emphasized that she and Lloyd were always devoted to their father – especially herself, who had known him better. She liked Paulie too: Miss Rebecca Paul, 'a slim, black-eyed, curly-haired woman who adored him'. Sam still worked and lived in San Francisco, but he was buying on mortgage a vineyard in Sonoma County, near Silverado, and was putting it in his new wife's name. Belle had written of once meeting them in the street and noticing that Sam was carrying Louis's latest book under his arm. 'He and his wife discussed it and expressed great admiration for R.L.S.'

Treasure Island was released in book form in London at the end of November 1883, and the author's years of heartbreaking struggle began to be rewarded by his first glimmer of success. Andrew Lang was not the only one to whom the book gave 'several hours of unmingled bliss'. Even the Prime Minister, Mr Gladstone, sat up most of the night reading it, though Louis, no partisan of his, sniffed that he might have been better employed in affairs of state. Lloyd, the 'American gentleman' to whom the tale was dedicated, sported a copy at school. Though naturally Fanny was pleased, she was astonished that 'tushery' for boys should be better received than worthier works. 'It seems to be making a sensation', she marvelled to her mother-in-law. Stevenson himself wrote cautiously to his parents, 'This gives one strange thoughts of how very bad the common run of books must be. . . .' Even so, it was not a fast seller, and no more than 5,600 copies were sold in Britain in the first year.

American readers soon took up the tale, but unfortunately in those days before international copyright the publication was largely pirated and the proceeds were small.

'Until the unexpected popular success of *Treasure Island*,' said Fanny in a Preface, 'my husband had hoped or looked for nothing more to follow from his work than a modest livelihood, and perhaps a *succès d'estime*.'

R.L.S. was writing steadily and well through those last months of 1883. Several articles were published in British magazines, and *The Silverado Squatters* appeared as a book in London.

'*Prince Otto*', continued Fanny, 'had been sent on offer to publishers. My husband was asked by Mr Longman to put a price on his work [as a serial for *Longman's* magazine]. With much perturbation he answered, naming a sum absurdly small. I insisted that this should be changed to a larger amount; but how earnestly I wished I had not interfered when days passed without a word in reply. My husband's mortification was acute. He said he felt like a cheat. . . . He actually had the pen in his hand to write a telegram retracting the terms in his letter when a hurried note came from Messrs Longman, saying that they considered £250 a very moderate price for the story, which should go to press immediately.'

The Christmas holidays drew near, and Lloyd travelled north to spend them with Uncle Tom and Aunt Maggie in Edinburgh. Fanny wrote that she would miss him, but she was gratified that they were fond of the boy. Tall, blond, polite, and 'of the embryo intellectual type', he would soon be sixteen.

'What a Christmas of thanksgiving this should be for us all,' she told them, 'with Louis so well, his father so well, everything pointing to comfort and happiness. Louis is making such a success with his work, and doing better work every day. Dear mother and father of my beloved husband, I send you Christmas greetings from my heart of hearts. . . .'

On 1st January Louis further exulted: 'A Good New Year to you. The year closes, leaving me with £50 in the bank, owing no man nothing, £100 more due me in a week or so, and £150 more in the course of a month; and I can look back on a total receipt of £465 os 6d for the last twelve months.'

The holiday respite was short. At the beginning of 1884 Baxter and Henley came out for a visit. Lacking room in the châlet, they slept at the Hôtel des Îles d'Or in the next street down the hill. By day the doll's house fairly burst its walls with hearty male talking, smoking and drinking. Fanny was no more enamoured than before of burly, booming Henley, with his scorching frankness. Louis had offered to help to pay his expenses. She intensely begrudged this and other small gifts or loans which her husband made to him, though Henley continued to act as Louis's unpaid literary agent; it was he who had arranged the hundred-pound advance on *Treasure Island*, and other payments.

The next week Stevenson suggested that he and his companions should go together to Nice for a change. After several days of the bland moist air and the cafés of the Promenade des Anglais, Louis caught a cold. It seemed slight and his friends started back to Britain. But before he could go home, he developed an acute congestion first of the lungs and then of the kidneys. Two doctors and a nurse helped his wife to fight for his life.

He was almost insane with suffering, as if he were at war with another self. Once in delirium he seized Fanny furiously. She wrote to his parents the next day: 'If I write like a mad creature do not be surprised, for I have had a period of awful wretchedness. Louis fell ill, and when the doctor came he beckoned to me to follow him, and then told me Louis was dying and could not be kept alive until you could get here. That was yesterday. I watched every breath he drew all night in what sickening apprehension you may guess. . . .'

The British doctor told her that she had better send for some male friend or relative to stand by her in case her husband died. She wired to Bob, who hurried to pack his bag and come as soon as he could.

Even before he started, however, Louis had passed his crisis. Already on the second day she was writing to the Stevensons, 'Today another doctor, Dr Drummond, was called in, and says that Louis may well live to be seventy, only he must not travel about. He is steadily better and is reading a newspaper in bed at this moment. I, who have not slept a wink for two nights, am pretending to be the gayest of the gay, but in reality I am a total wreck, although I am almost off my head with relief and joy.'

Bob arrived to join them at Hyères, and Fanny wrote, 'I can never be grateful enough for what he did for me then. He helped me to nurse Louis, and he kept me from despair as I believe no one else could have done; he inspired me with hope when there seemed no hope.'

The invalid's convalescence seemed only to crawl along. 'I survived, where a stronger man would not. . . . Pain draws a lingering fiddle-bow', he wrote Bob. '[The doctor] told me to leave off wine, to regard myself as "an old man", and "to sit by my fire". None of which I wish to do. . . .'

Fanny looked after him like a tough little watchdog. '. . . While he sat for photographs I stood near, guarding him from fatigue or draughts as much as possible. Sometimes the unexpected opening of a door would send a chill into the room, when I would snatch at anything at hand to throw about his shoulders.' This habit was noted by their friends to the end of his life.

For Fanny, forty-four in March, there was a brief personal crisis that spring. 'I must tell you a joke,' her husband wrote to Simpson. 'A month or two ago, there was an alarm; it looked like family. Prostration: I saw myself financially ruined. I saw the child born sickly, etc. Then, said I, I must look at this thing on the good side; proceeded to do so studiously; and with such result that when the alarm passed off – I was inconsolable.'

These words seem to endorse the complex fact that the frail couple did not intend to have children, though it meant that Louis's great paternal longing must go unsatisfied. While Fanny was very much a mother and indeed a grandmother, her fanatic dedication to her husband's talent and a wish to give it immortality might have made her even more devoted to a little Stevenson than to the young Osbournes. Certainly Louis's parents would have rejoiced to have an heir, but it is probable that they never knew of the brief likelihood.

Chapter IV
'I was only happy once – '

In late April news came from London that a scurrilous gossip columnist named Edmund Yates, whose work Stevenson loathed, had been sued, convicted of criminal libel and imprisoned. (Years before, he had made an assault on Thackeray, with the support of Dickens.) Fanny described ruefully how her husband celebrated the sentence. In the evening they placed a candle in each window and lighted a bonfire in the garden. Louis, Fanny and Valentine clasped hands and danced around it, shouting and laughing. 'We did not notice', she wrote, 'that a mistral was blowing until we were all chilled to the bone.'

A relapse followed. 'This has been a fine well-conducted illness', Louis wrote to Gosse. 'A month in bed; a month of silence; a fortnight of not stirring my right hand; a month of not moving without being lifted . . . devilish like being dead.'

Fanny always kept a small bottle of ergotin and a minim glass at his bedside in case a haemorrhage struck. Late one night in early May there had come the most violent blood-spitting ever. She was at his side in a moment and for once she was trembling with fear. He was choked by the flow of blood and unable to speak. So he made signs to her for a pencil and paper.

'Don't be frightened', he wrote in a firm neat hand. 'If this is death it is an easy one.' He took the bottle and glass away from her, measured the dose carefully and steadily, and gave them back to her with a reassuring smile.

The doctors said later that if she had not always had the emergency dose ready and known just what to do, her husband could not have lived. She also had to administer the dangerous morphine or aconite, which he detested.

'. . . I cannot read'; he spelled out to Colvin, 'so much of the time (as today) I must not speak above my breath, that to play patience, or to see my wife play it, is become the be-all and the end-all of my dim career. . . .'

'I am very dim, dumb, dowie and damnable. I hate to be silenced; and if to talk by signs is my forte (as I contend), to understand them cannot be my wife's. . . .' Their vague code of hand signals kept Fanny under constant frustration and strain.

The old town of Hyères was very dirty, and a few weeks previously Louis had written a letter to the mayor, pointing out the disgusting state of the streets. The mayor had had them cleared out, and the workmen dumped the rubbish in front of Rosemount, the cottage of an Englishman who was away from home. The Stevensons had to pass the heap on their way up and down the hill. Louis again protested to the mayor, and unluckily mentioned also that the road outside his own house was in need of care. So this time the pile of refuse from Rosemount was spread in front of La Solitude. There had been a contagion of Egyptian ophthalmia in the town; and probably from the filthy dust blowing off the street, Louis's eyes were infected.

When the disease was diagnosed by the doctor, Fanny felt that it was more than she could bear. She slipped into another room and, as she put it, 'sat and gloomed'. Then Louis rang his bell and she went in to him. 'Well,' she said bitterly, 'I suppose that this is the very best thing that could have happened!'

He took a pencil and pad of paper from the bedside table. 'How odd!' he scribbled. 'I was just going to say those very words.'

Some days later she wrote to his mother: 'I am not very good at letter writing since I have been doing blind man's eyes, but here is a note to say that the blind man is doing very well, and I consider the blindness a real providence. Since he has been unable to read or do anything at all a wonderful change has come over his health, spirits, and temper, all for the better. . . . I wish you could see him with his eyes tied up and singing away like mad; truly like mad, as there is neither time nor method in it, only a large voice. . . . Our Wogg is an invalid, having got himself badly mangled in several fights, the maid is ill with symptoms of pleurisy, and altogether we are a forlorn household, but with all this Louis and I are in high spirits.'

While R.L.S. lived he must write – even silent and flat in a darkened room, with his right arm bound to his side to prevent haemorrhage. 'Across his bed', explained Fanny, 'a board was laid on which large sheets of paper were pinned; on these, or on a slate fastened to the board, he laboriously wrote out in the darkness, with his left hand, many more of the songs of his childhood.'

This was the series finally published as *A Child's Garden of Verses*, the timeless musing singsong of the very young. '. . . I am quite blind and giddy', he wrote Colvin. '. . . What am I to do with my beastly little girls?'

To inveigle his wife into having some fresh air, he got her to take an hour's walk every day and meanwhile to make up a tale to tell him when she came back. At that time the London newspapers were recounting a series of attempted bomb outrages on behalf of Home Rule in Ireland. One of Fanny's weird inventions later became 'The Dynamiter'. Along with one or more other ideas born in those walks, which the couple eventually worked out together, the story was included in the collection to be published as *More New Arabian Nights*.

Lloyd now came out from school to rejoin his mother and step-father after nearly a year away.

'I was aware of a curious change in my family,' he recalled, 'while in reality the change was in myself. I had expected to take up things where I had left off, and felt a little baffled and lonely. . . . It is not that R.L.S. was not extremely kind, or that anything was lacking in the warmth of his welcome. But somehow he had receded from me; and though my mother stuffed me with delicacies, and overflowed with confidences about the new life and new interests, she had receded, too. Woggs . . . alone met me on the old basis . . . ; he jumped all over me and smelled the same boy . . . ; it was at least the only time in my life when Stevenson and I were not delightfully intimate . . . ; too old for any childish appeal, and too immature for any other. . . .'

'. . . I was only happy once; that was at Hyères', Louis wrote nearly a decade later in the South Pacific. Though perhaps it was an overstatement in a low mood, the words are now inscribed on a plaque on the veranda of La Solitude.

'I often think it was a mistake he ever left Hyères. . . .' continued Lloyd. 'The reason was absurd.' Fanny, always a home physician and now avid to be up to date about medicine for her husband's sake, subscribed to *The Lancet* from London, and superstitiously took up every new health fad. When a doctor published a theory that vinegar was detrimental, she banned it from Louis's salads, which she also suspected of being full of tapeworms' eggs. (In fact, he later had a tapeworm.) 'It was the worst reading in the world for her. . . .' said her son.

Because they lived so quietly she was among the last to know that the current epidemic of cholera had reached that stretch of the Riviera. In a letter home she described how they watched a cloud gathering over the horizon above nearby Toulon, where it hung heavy and lowering for days. They felt that it was somehow ominous and depressing. Later they were told that great fires had been burning in the streets, on the mayor's orders to clear out the sources of infection.

'. . . When the climax came', continued Lloyd, 'in an outbreak of cholera in the old part of the town, with a terrible death-roll, she fell into a panic and began to work on R.L.S. to abandon Hyères as a place too dangerous to live in.'

She resolved to get him away. So in June she moved him by short journeys to Royat spa again. At the end of the month they decided to see the specialists in London and find out where he stood. Gingerly the trio crossed the Channel, accompanied by Valentine and Bogue (ex-Woggs).

Part 7

Bournemouth
'Revolt into respectability' 1884-87

Chapter I
A home of their own

The Stevensons joined the parents beside the Thames at Richmond just in time for Fanny to go into central London for the first night of *Deacon Brodie*. R.L.S. had collaborated on the play with Henley, whose brother Edward enacted the Deacon. ('It is about Henley, not *Brodie*, that I care', Louis had written to Colvin.) The opening was fairly well received.

Cholera lingered in Hyères, so the couple could not return. In London two specialists said that the southern English climate would be bad for Louis, while two others thought it would be all right. Uncertain, they went down to the south coast to visit Lloyd in school at Bournemouth. They first took lodgings above the beach and then rented a house in wooded Branksome Park.

'It was lovely autumn weather when R.L.S. and my mother arrived', Lloyd recalled. 'They were in the highest spirits; everything pleased them; and although they . . . had neither home nor plans . . . they seemed not to have a care in the world. . . .'

Mr and Mrs Henley came to stay with the Stevensons, he with his big red beard and his crutch. 'And he had come to make us all rich! . . .' Lloyd recollected. Henley and Louis were to collaborate on more plays, and began *Beau Austin* and *Admiral Guinea*.

'. . . Mr Henley', said Fanny in a Preface, 'had an extraordinary faculty of infecting others with his own enthusiasm. I even found myself unwittingly drawn into the whirlpool. I remember being promised a ruby bracelet, to be bought from the proceeds of the first performance, for a suggestion for *Admiral Guinea*. . . . The plays were invented and written in the fervid, boisterous fashion of Mr Henley, whose influence predominated, except in the actual literary form. . . . "That'll make 'em jump, my boy!" Mr Henley would shout. . . . "No, Henley", my husband would protest wearily, "you're too violent."'

Fanny was so keen on *Admiral Guinea* that she wrote Henley about lying awake at night and repeating every line – after which she proposed revisions. The play was drafted in only four days, an alarming session of argument and laughter. But Lloyd, who adored Henley, was moved to tears when the big cripple read the script aloud – 'so movingly, so tenderly. . . . He was the first man I had ever called by his surname, the first friend I had ever sought and won. . . .'

Fanny showed a habit of salvaging discarded literary ideas. 'Louis and Henley had decided against using *The Hanging Judge*, so, emboldened by my husband's offer to give me any help needed, I concluded to try and write it myself.'

For many months Fanny and Henley both tried hard to get on well together. She called him Buffalo William, and kept nobly inviting him down to stay – with his gentle Anna, whom she liked and always treated kindly. 'You know we love you in spite of your many faults', she wrote him, 'so try and bear with our few.'

In January the two authors wrote a fourth play, *Macaire*. Herbert Beerbohm Tree was inveigled down to read their scripts but was politely uninterested. For one thing, the dramatists knew little of stagecraft. Louis now had to catch up with other neglected work, and he realized how weak the plays were. 'Mr Henley,' wrote Colvin, 'who had built hopes of fame and fortune on their collaboration, was very unwilling to face the fact.' Louis told Henley in March, '. . . I have come unhesitatingly to the opinion that the stage is only a lottery. . . . It is bad enough to have to live by an art – but to think to live by an art combined with commercial speculation – that way madness lies.'

Eventually all the plays were performed but none succeeded. The irony was that though Fanny had agreed with Henley in this waste of time, he later blamed her influence for the abandonment of the playwriting.

He wrote to Baxter, 'Louis has grown faster than I have; and then there's the Bedlamite [Fanny]. I love her; but I won't collaborate with her and her husband, as I begin to feel that the one means both.' At length he entreated her, 'Have a little charity, do! . . .' He did say, 'I admire your courage. . . .' And he tried to sell a short story of hers, without success. But at length he snorted, 'I think, Mrs Louis, that we'd better give up corresponding on any save the commonest subjects. . . .' When Stevenson later developed further haemorrhages, she wrote grimly to Mrs Sitwell, 'Henley must not come to him now with either work or business unless he wishes to kill him.'

Next the Stevensons began to put together the second series of *New Arabian Nights* from the stories which Fanny had made up to amuse the invalid at Hyères. Literary historians have claimed that the title story of 'The Dynamiter' alone was her very own. This seems to be shown by the piece itself. Though in letter-writing her style was often attractive and even graceful, when she laid her hand on fiction it had a coarse texture and synthetic manner which one does not find in those of her husband's works in which she was not a collaborator.

Meanwhile in November young John Singer Sargent had come to stay at the house and paint Louis's portrait, as a commission from the rich and admiring Mr and Mrs Charles Fairchild of Boston. '. . . a charming, simple, clever, honest young man; he has delighted us', Stevenson described him to his mother. When the seated likeness was finished, however, Louis told Will Low, '. . . it is a poetical but very chicken-boned figurehead. . . .' Fanny and others – including the artist himself – disapproved of it, and he arranged to try again later.

Louis had read Henry James's essay on 'The Art of Fiction' in *Longman's* magazine, and now the December issue printed his own reply, 'A Humble Remonstrance', pleading for 'story' above form. Heretofore neither James nor Stevenson had taken the other very seriously. At Davos, Louis had enclosed a bit of doggerel in a letter to Henley. Entitled 'H. JAMES', the first stanza ran:

Not clad in transatlantic furs
But clinking English pence
The young republic claims me hers
In no parochial sense. . . .

And the last verse:

Yet I'm a sentimental lot
And freely weep to see
Poor Hawthorne and the rest who've not
To Europe been like me.

Fanny indulgently defended her countryman. At the time she admired his writings more than her husband did, perhaps because she understood them more deeply under the skin. After all, to this day Henry James speaks better than anyone else for the American expatriate in Europe.

Now James wrote a courteous letter in reply to Stevenson's article, and their argument was carried on in a personal correspondence – friendly but forceful, since they were probably the two men then writing in English who were most intensively devoted to the practice of fiction. R.L.S. was aged thirty-four and James forty-two.

Stevenson's horror story, 'The Body Snatchers', was published in the Christmas number – inappropriately – of the *Pall Mall Gazette*. Macabre as even Fanny could wish, it was one of the tales they had written at Pitlochry in 1881. Sandwichmen paraded through the streets of London to advertise it with posters so gruesome that they were suppressed by the police. Louis now told Colvin, '. . . I long ago condemned [it] as an offence against good manners.'

Both Louis and Fanny fell ill again, but the parents came for the holidays.

'. . . If you *could* come to stay with me a few days,' sighed Fanny to Mrs Sitwell, 'I cannot tell you what a comfort it would be to me. Louis is ill again, *not* this time with haemorrhages, but a cold, a present from his mother . . . in spite of all my entreaties . . . and [she] went off saying, "Now that Louis has entirely recovered his health, we shall expect him to spend his summers in Scotland with us. . . .'' Colvin told Henley, 'Fanny, on her account, is evidently nearly off her head also.'

Both Fanny and Louis always considered every move they made with the most devoted solicitude for Lloyd's welfare. Early in 1885 the lad went north with the elder Stevensons to live at Heriot Row as a science student at the University of Edinburgh. Fanny wrote in agitation to Dora Williams that Sam had been trying to persuade his son to come and run the ranch in Sonoma County. 'I should like his father to know that if he takes Lloyd he also takes his maintenance and his future prospects upon his own shoulders and that I shall be no more responsible.' Lloyd, however, thought he would like to be apprenticed to the Stevenson family firm.

In February 1885, to persuade Louis and Fanny to stay in Bournemouth, the ailing Thomas Stevenson presented his daughter-in-law with a house and five hundred pounds with which to furnish it.

The secluded place stood above the chalk cliffs on the outskirts of Westbourne. It was a tall trim villa of yellow bricks with a blue slate roof, set in more than an acre of land. The ivy-grown house faced south onto a lawn which touched the edge of a narrow ravine called Alum Chine. On the slopes, laurel and rhododendron grew lush among the heather and gorse and pine which reminded Stevenson of Scotland, with a tiny stream below.

Enchanted, Fanny wrote to Mrs Sitwell: 'It is very comfortable to know that we have a home really and truly, and will no more be like Noah's dove, flying about with an olive branch. . . .' She thought the garden 'delicious', with 'even a little studio for me to dabble paints in. . . . When we are rich enough (if I am not too fat by that time) there is a stable all ready for my horse. A fine dog-house awaits my Bogue.' There was also a dovecote, and 'through all my memories . . .' wrote Lloyd, 'runs that melodious cooing and flutter of wings on the lawn'. (In Westbourne's quiet residential region the house was almost the only building to be destroyed by a bomb in World War II.)

The couple moved at Easter time. Louis changed the name of the house to Skerryvore, after the famous lighthouse built by the family firm. He erected a model of Skerryvore at the street entrance, with a light showing every evening, and put a ship's bell in the garden. Soon the energetic Fanny planted fruit trees, hydrangeas, roses and tiger lilies, and introduced Indian corn and tomatoes, then rare in England. On the slopes of the chine she worked out what she called 'a seductive little labyrinth' of paths, stairs and arbours, and placed seats where Louis could write with a board on his knee.

'I am now a beastly householder', grumbled R.L.S. to Colvin. Lloyd, in a memoir, wrote '. . . they paid rates and taxes, and were called on by the vicar; Stevenson, in the word he hated most of all, had become the "burgher" of his former jeers. . . .' Yet contrarily he was enthralled by the place. The free spirit who had once scorned even to carry a comb was nicknamed 'the Squire'.

As for Fanny, she wrote to her mother-in-law, '. . . I could only ask one thing more to have the most perfect life that any woman could have, and that is, of course, good health for Louis. . . . I should be perfectly appalled if I were asked to exchange his faults for other people's virtues.'

Chapter II
A suburban middle-class couple

In the resort town with its sedate population of retired officials, widows and invalids, a bashful, sugar-sweet girl named Adelaide Boodle heard that there was an extraordinary-looking man coming to the neighbourhood. He was a writer – 'just an animated bundle of shawls and wraps, with long, thin hair and burning eyes'. She had literary yearnings, and in the first few days she persuaded her mother to take her to call. Mrs Boodle was very shy, and when they found the bell-wire out of order and had to wait a long time for an answer to their knock, she began to cry. The Stevensons thereafter christened their front porch 'The Pool of Tears'.

Valentine appeared at last, and admitted the callers by mistake. The master and mistress were unpacking their possessions, Louis in a velvet coat and dark red tie, Fanny in a painting-apron. They urged the Boodles into the only two chairs while they squatted on packing-cases, and ordered tea. Adelaide became a worshipful errand girl to them both, and later wrote a naïve but observant book about their Bournemouth stay, gushingly entitled *R.L.S. and His Sine Qua Non.* (The phrase was taken from the inscription of a copy of *Rab and His Friends* which its author, the Scots essayist Dr John Brown, had given the couple.) Louis's cousin Graham Balfour said in the preface to Miss Boodle's book, 'The great thing . . . is that whenever she quotes any saying, any direct words of either of them, I can always hear it in his or Fanny's voice. . . .'

On meeting Fanny the girl was struck by 'the depth and tenderness that glowed in her unfathomable eyes. But . . . [at] the mere mention of cruelty . . . I have seen her quivering with passion, alight with fury. . . .'

The acolyte admitted that her two idols had occasional awful rows – 'when the casual looker-on might have felt it his duty to shout for the police . . . with cries of "Murder!"' . . . But soon they calmed down.

Miss Boodle also confessed that, being so very young, she was 'disposed to imagine the disparity in their years much greater than it actually was'. She therefore thought that 'their mutual love and understanding was a source of wondering delight'. One day after Stevenson had had a haemorrhage, she found his wife sitting with a remote look in the shadows of the Blue Room. She told Adelaide, 'I said it would be impossible for me to live without Lou-us, but he said I must live to see his biography through the press. . . .'

In Westbourne the Stevensons' chief friends were two elderly couples: the poet's son, Sir Percy Shelley and his wife, and Sir Henry and Lady Taylor with their daughters. Lady Taylor, a stately character, presented Louis with the South American poncho, dark red and quickly ink-stained, which he wore in bed and at table and in the garden, until the mysterious garment became part of the Stevenson mythology.

Callers, Fanny told Colvin, 'pour in upon us in droves, but they are all alike. . . . After speaking of the weather and kindred topics, they generally observe, "Your husband is quite literary, I understand! . . .'

'Mrs Stevenson, a most brilliant talker', wrote Miss Boodle,

'shone even more as a listener. . . .' The girl described her as listening
to the long conversations 'with her matchless patience' – the recurrent
if contradictory theme in the continuing success of the marriage.

But she had to watch her husband becoming hoarse and hysterical
while the visitors stayed on and on in the drawing-room, and the
whisky in the decanter went down and down – especially when
Henley was there. He was supersensitive and she infuriated him when
she finally put the decanter away as a hint that it was time to let
his host go to bed. (Louis was still supposed not to drink or smoke.)
Henley also took it as a personal affront when she exiled him from
her husband's presence if he had a cold – though she did the same
with everyone, even herself.

Those whom she affronted could not know that she often felt
intense remorse. One day Miss Boodle ran up to her bedroom and
found her in an abstracted mood. She put down her sewing and
caught the girl's hand in 'a specially tender, protective fashion
peculiar to herself. "I have made everybody miserable", she said in a
tone of deep despondency . . . and went on passionately, "I could
not help it; I should do it again. I *had* to do it! They were all seething."' She then told Adelaide that she had been sitting with her
husband and three literary friends in the sheltered stable courtyard,
when they had been gossiping and making fun of some absent person.
She had listened in silence, and finally burst out, 'Are you men? Are
you Christians? Have you no shame?' But afterwards she herself had
been overwhelmed with compunction. 'Am I a woman? Am I a
Christian? Had I no pity, no compassion, for these shame-stricken
menfolk?'

In June Louis had a shock from the death of his earliest sponsor,
Professor Jenkin. Unwell as he was, he wrote to the widow, offering
any possible help from himself or Fanny, and adding, '. . . I was so
pleased that he and my wife made friends; that is a great pleasure.'

The end of the year brought another death still more disturbing to
Fanny, that of Virgil Williams. She had had a premonition of it two
days before Dora's letter came.

Sidney Colvin was appointed Keeper of Prints and Drawings at the
British Museum and had a house there. When Colvin entertained,
Mrs Sitwell acted as his hostess with perfect propriety in the Shavian
tradition. And Fanny referred to her as 'my dearest friend'.

The invalid rarely ventured to London, even under Colvin's wing, and when he did he was laden with cautions and precautions from Fanny.

She was proud when the new collection of stories appeared in May 1885 as *More New Arabian Nights: The Dynamiter*, by Robert Louis Stevenson and Fanny Van de Grift Stevenson. She exulted at the 'great advertisement' which the book received when the Fenians, the Irish agitators for Home Rule, chanced to perpetrate some fresh dynamite blasts at the time of publication, and soon there were two reprints. However, as she told her mother-in-law, she felt 'some mortification' at the way the reviewers hardly noticed the collaboration. 'I thought in the beginning that I shouldn't mind being Louis's scapegoat, but it is rather hard to be treated like a comma, and a superfluous one at that. And then in one paper, the only one in which I am mentioned, the critic refers to me as "undoubtedly Mr Stevenson's sister". Why, pray? Surely there can be nothing in the book that points to a sister in particular.'

Miss Boodle's heartwhole intention was to be a literary disciple of R.L.S. With timid nerve she dared to ask if Mr Stevenson might criticize her writing.

Fanny naturally wanted to protect her overworked invalid from this soft little parasite. She said kindly, sadly – as reported by Adelaide: 'My dear child, he would try with all his might to help you, but probably, in the attempt, he would break your heart. . . . Probably I could, to begin with, [help you] as well as my husband. If you will come round to Skerryvore and read the tale, I shall soon see where you are; and I might, if it seems worth while, talk it over with him. I write too, a little, and he reads all his work to me. It is always a help, you know, to have an experienced listener at hand. . . .'

The next day there began a series of cosy literary sessions at Skerryvore. Sometimes the lessons were cut off by the furtive entrance of Stevenson who, when he was not well enough to work at full stint, 'would glide into the room like a stage conspirator, with finger on lips, and beckon me away'. The first time Miss Boodle glanced inquiringly at Fanny, who said with a smile, 'Oh, yes! Of course you must go. Louis is tired of being alone. He wants another child to play with him. Run along, both of you!'

One day she greeted her pupil by asking to be excused from the lesson. 'I am writing for my life,' Adelaide remembered her saying, 'or rather, it may be, for the life of another woman. I have this minute finished a story to go [to New York] by the next mail; I must get a legible copy ready for the post tonight. Money is needed for a dear friend of ours who is expecting another child soon. All sorts of things will be wanted, things she can ill afford to provide. . . .'

Adelaide offered to do the copying. She took the manuscript home, worked for hours, and posted the copy just in time. The story was accepted by *Scribner's* magazine, and in due course a cheque for the equivalent of thirty pounds was added to the fund. The title was 'Miss Pringle's Neighbours', appearing in June 1887. The fairy tale was all she had previously published until she leaned on her husband for her share of *The Dynamiters*.

Stevenson had written in *Virginibus Puerisque*, 'Certainly, if I could help it, I would never marry a wife who wrote. The practice of letters is miserably harassing to the mind, and after an hour or two's work, all the more human portion of the author is extinct'.

Valentine remained the mainstay of the ménage. She had soon learned English, and she rather shocked the seemly British visitors by exclaiming 'My God!' as casually as she would have said 'Mon Dieu!'

Years later an interviewer asked her about Stevenson, and she said, discreetly, 'I remember once when it had been a little harder than usual I came to him, summoned by his bell. He looked at me – so sad – and when I tried to justify myself, he said, "Hush, Joe! You know when one tries to justify oneself, one puts someone else in the wrong – and life is not possible under these conditions."'

A scandalous rumour arose in California because Fanny had written to friends that when she was away, Valentine slept by the fire in Louis's room to be on guard against haemorrhages. This was misinterpreted. The best witnesses have vouched for the propriety of the arrangement.

Chapter III
'Poor barbarous lady'

In the spring of 1885 a portly bearded gentleman called at Skerryvore. Valentine mistook him for a tradesman who was expected to call to apologize for a lapse, and he was kept waiting.

'We have had a very pleasant visitor. . . .' Fanny wrote to her mother-in-law. 'One evening a card was handed in with "Henry James" upon it. He spent that evening, asked to come again the next night, arriving almost before we had got done with dinner, and staying as late as he thought he might, and asking to come the next evening, which is tonight. I call that very flattering. I had always been told that he was the type of an Englishman, but, except that he looks like the Prince of Wales, I call him the type of an American. . . .' To Colvin she wrote, '. . . I think there is no question but that he likes Louis; naturally, I have hardly been allowed to speak to him, though I fain would. He seems very gentle and comfortable, and I worship in silence – enforced silence. . . .'

James had come to Bournemouth to spend some weeks with his invalid sister Alice. Soon he was calling at Skerryvore almost every evening, and his favourite big blue armchair from Heriot Row was reserved for him as 'Henry James's Chair'. 'We are devoted to him', Fanny told Colvin.

Intuitively courteous and understanding, but deeply inquisitive about people and their lives, he admitted to mutual friends that he was fascinated by the Stevenson marriage. He would have won Fanny's praise if only by the sensitivity with which he never tired Louis or stayed too long, and sympathized with her problems over those who did.

'Character, character is what he has!' he wrote of Stevenson. He also said, 'His feelings are always his reasons.' The same was surely true of Fanny.

The two writers each admired the other for qualities opposite to his own. James – heavy and deliberate, probing the air for the perfect word – was a contrast to the sprightly figure of R.L.S. Even in their affinity of shop-talk, James almost never neglected to be tactful and attentive to Fanny. Probably, too, he and she respected each other because they were both listeners. Also, as a fellow American her matriarchal vitality did not seem as alien to him as to the British, and he knew better how to respond to it. He was the only member of the Stevenson circle with whom she never quarrelled.

Less flattering, his sister Alice wrote after meeting Mrs R.L.S. that either 'Nature or Providence' had made her 'an appendage to a hand-organ!' Miss James conceded that Fanny was said to have 'great wifely virtues' and had written some excellent letters to Henry. But the invalid spinster deplored 'such egotism and nakedness!'

While Fanny confided in her compatriot, so did her husband. Once he wrote to him, 'My wife is peepy and dowie. . . . She is a woman (as you know) not without art: the art of extracting the gloom of the eclipse from the sunshine; and she has recently laboured in this field not without success or (as we used to say) not without a blessing. It is strange; "we fell out my wife and I" the other night; she tackled me savagely for being a canary-bird; I replied (bleatingly) protesting that there was no use in turning life into *King Lear*; presently it was discovered that there were two dead combatants upon the field, each slain by the arrow of truth, and we tenderly carried off each other's corpses. Here is a little comedy for Henry James to write! The beauty was that each thought the other quite unscathed at first, but we had dealt shrewd stabs. . . .'

There seem to be flavours of Fanny here and there in the cannibal stew-pot of the skilled American fiction writer. Surely the Stevensons partly inspired his story, 'The Lesson of the Master', which first appeared in 1888, three years after he met them. There recurs the incident of an author's wife, Mrs St George, who had burned her husband's autobiographical novel because she 'didn't like it'. And yet, widowed, St George laments, 'She took everything off my hands, off my mind, and I was free, as few men can have been, to drive my pen. . . .'

Years later James wrote of Fanny that he felt 'a sneaking kindness for her'. He certainly showed that he liked her. But she would have been devastated if she had known that the master was one day to describe her as a 'poor barbarous and merely *instinctive* lady'.

Meanwhile in the summer of 1885 John Singer Sargent had come back to do a better portrait of Stevenson. Stressing elusive movement more than form, the result was considered the most living likeness ever made of him by brush or camera. The sitter himself described the painting to Will Low: 'Sargent was down again and painted a portrait of me walking about in my own dining-room, in my own velveteen jacket, and twisting as I go my own moustache; at one corner is a glimpse of my wife, in an Indian dress, and seated in a chair that was once my grandfather's, but since some months goes by the name of Henry James's. . . . It is, I think, excellent, but it is too eccentric to be exhibited. I am at one extreme corner; my wife in this wild dress, and looking like a ghost, is at the extreme other end . . . touched in lovely, with that witty touch of Sargent's; but of course, it looks damn queer as a whole.'

Fanny disliked this fantastic rendition of her husband and of herself dim in the corner. She wrote Colvin that she had said to Sargent, 'I am but a cipher under the shadow', and she saw the wry joke when he 'too eagerly assented'.

Under her Indian sari – added for colour – he had painted a glimpse of one tiny bare foot. From this circumstance apparently came the legend that Mrs Robert Louis Stevenson used to go to dinner parties in London without shoes and stockings.

But, by chance in a single summer, the two masters of character, James and Sargent, may have learned and interpreted more of the Stevensons and their marriage than anyone before or since.

Chapter IV
The English literary life

'In the small hours of one morning,' wrote Fanny, 'I was awakened by cries of horror from Louis. Thinking he had a nightmare, I awakened him. He said angrily, "Why did you wake me? I was dreaming a fine bogey tale."'

In vivid scenes with many details he had dreamed *The Strange Case of Dr Jekyll and Mr Hyde*.

For several days Fanny and Lloyd, who was at home for the vacation, found him preoccupied and mysterious. He was kept in bed after a haemorrhage, and was not allowed to talk except for 'cautious minutes'. But he scribbled away with phenomenal zeal, and then summoned them to the usual hearing. In a rich voice he read aloud the rough draft.

Lloyd was enthusiastic, Fanny more reserved. 'I was thunderstruck by her backwardness', her son continued. She felt that Louis had missed the allegory; the story should be more than just a 'crawler'. He had made Dr Jekyll a bad man who posed as being good, whereas he was really 'Everyman' who had both a good self and a bad self.

'Stevenson', Lloyd went on, 'was beside himself with anger. . . . His voice, bitter and challenging, overrode my mother's in a fury of resentment. . . . I went away. . . . When I came back my mother was alone. She was sitting, pale and desolate before the fire, and staring into it. . . .'

Presently Louis's bell rang, and Fanny went to him. She found him sitting up in bed with a thermometer in his mouth, pointing with a long thin finger at a pile of ashes in the hearth.

She cried out in dismay and alarm. But he had not burned the manuscript to spite her. He saw that she was right, and had destroyed it so that he would not be tempted to refer to the original draft, but would rewrite it wholly.

Again he worked superhumanly for three days. ('I drive on with Jekyll; bankruptcy at my heels', he told Colvin.) Fanny was afraid to protest much for fear the story would be lost altogether. But strangely, Lloyd said, 'far from exhausted, he seemed refreshed and vitalized; he looked better than in months'.

This time Fanny applauded the new draft. Louis worked hard at revising and polishing for another six weeks or so (not, as per legend, a few miraculous days), and sent the manuscript to Longman's. They issued it as a shilling paperback, but the bookstalls were full of Christmas reading and the trade was not interested. The book was withdrawn until January, and again largely ignored, until *The Times* of London gave it a major review and it was the theme of a sermon in St Paul's Cathedral. In the next six months nearly forty thousand copies were sold. In America, besides the authorized edition, it was widely pirated, and probably sold a quarter of a million copies in the writer's lifetime – if not to his own profit.

At last R.L.S. was well on the way to success – not least, perhaps, because he had acted on his wife's criticism. The phrase 'Jekyll and Hyde' quickly became an idiom in the English language. The author himself was sardonic about it. In a letter to his mother he signed himself, 'I hope, Jekyll, I fear, Hyde.'

Also writing to Mrs Stevenson after this hard-won battle of wits, Fanny said, 'If I die before Louis, my last earnest request is that he shall publish nothing without his father's approval. I know that means little short of destruction to both of them, but there will be no one else. The field is always covered with my dead and wounded, and often I am forced to compromise, but still I make a very good fight.'

It was later to turn out a poignant irony that Stevenson dedicated *Dr Jekyll and Mr Hyde* to his cousin Katharine de Mattos. Without a husband and often hard up, she and her children were always welcomed at Skerryvore. Like Bob she had a vivid gift of expression; and – like Fanny and others in the orbit of R.L.S. – she was inspired to write a little. Louis, always pleased to encourage his intimates, often criticized her manuscripts.

Miss Boodle noticed that 'when Bob was near, Mr Stevenson seemed younger, gayer and more extravagantly amusing'. Lloyd later called this mood of Louis's 'Bobism'. It must have been somewhat the same with Katharine, for she was said to share the magnetism of her brother. Her mind has been described as 'incisive' and 'astringent', but she appears to have been something of an April character, with wayward changes. In the collection of verse called *Underwoods* Louis included a poem entitled 'Katharine' and a second 'To K. de M.'. The latter remembered her in their Scottish childhood: 'A lover of the moorland bare/And honest country winds you were. . . .' The former was a lyrical characterization – 'Elfin and human, airy and true. . . .'

He sent her a copy of *Jekyll and Hyde* with its rhymed inscription, together with a letter written on New Year's Day, 1886:

'Dearest Katharine,

Here, on a very little book and accompanied with lame verses, I have put your name. Our kindness is now getting well on in years; it must be nearly of age; and it gets more valuable to me with every time I see you. It is not possible to express any sentiment, and it is not necessary to try, at least between us. You know very well that I love you dearly, and always will. I only wish the verses were better, but at least you like the story; and it is sent to you by the one that loves you –

Jekyll, and not Hyde.'

Henry James, urged by Louis and Fanny, was at Skerryvore for three days in the autumn. He backed up his burdened hostess by writing to Colvin, 'My visit had the gilt taken off by the somewhat ponderous presence of the parents – who sit on him much too long at once. (They are to remain another week, and I can't see why *they* don't see how they take it out of him.) . . . If he could be quite alone on alternate, or occasional, weeks, it would be a blessing.'

Thomas had been honoured by being elected president of the Royal Society of Edinburgh, though he was ageing fast. His wife made a show of being bright and cheerful, but her placidity was inevitably tried by her husband's swift decline. After a long visit Fanny reported to Colvin that Louis's mother fussed hysterically, and 'having crushed and exhausted him . . . left him the legacy of an influenza cold'. She added, 'If Louis dies it will be murder.'

Gradually Fanny was winning obedience to if not belief in her newfangled germ theory, among her husband's friends. She was gratified when she sometimes got a message which said, in effect, 'I can't keep my engagement to see Louis today, for I have a cold, but as soon as I am over it I shall let you know.'

Stevenson had few diversions except to dine occasionally at his neighbours', the Taylors or the Shelleys. When the weather was dry he walked in his flapping plaid and wide hat on the seaside cliffs. Lloyd recalled one evening after his stepfather had been cooped up in the house by several days' rain. At sunset, when the sky finally cleared, he entered the Blue Room in his cloak and meekly asked Fanny for permission to stroll in the garden.

'Oh, Louis, you mustn't get your feet wet', she implored him.

In silent despair, he yielded.

Sometimes, almost out of his head with fever or haemorrhage or both, he swore at Fanny when she tried to nurse him. With her odd contrariety she was wise enough to take these delirious outbursts in her stride. Perhaps that was a big reason why the marriage was not seriously racked by the violent quarrels which so intimidated onlookers; to two high-tempered people their mutual rages were more or less cathartic.

'... We had a dreadful overhauling of my conduct as a son the other night,' Louis wrote his father, 'and my wife stripped me of my illusions and made me admit I had been a detestable bad one. Of one thing in particular she convicted me in my own eyes: I mean, a most unkind reticence, which hung on me then, and I confess still hangs on me now, when I try to assure you that I do love you.

Ever your bad son, R.L.S.'

Though he was ostentatiously loyal towards Fanny with the grunting Henley, more than once when he was cross with her his guard slipped and he could not resist grumbling to the man who would most heartily agree. He wrote, 'I got my little finger into a steam press called the Vandergrifter (patent) and my whole body and soul had to go through after it. I came out as limp as a lady's novel, but the Vandergrifter suffered in the process, and is fairly knocked about.' And he added, 'I am what *she has made me*, the embers of the once gay R.L.S.'

For years Louis had been increasingly in love with music, with almost no chance for education or performance. It was a pity that, though Mrs Jenkin, Mrs Sitwell and Mme Garschine, the Russian lady at Menton, were all musical, his wife was the only one of his four mature loves who was not. Lloyd was interested in musical instruments as in other devices, and played the tin whistle to his stepfather's two-finger accompaniment. As Nellie wrote, 'Music was "as a closed book" to Fanny; she could not sing a note nor hardly tell one tune from another.' But Louis was so fascinated that his music even made him neglect his writing – beyond his sacred early-morning stint. He wore himself out. Fanny told Colvin: 'I am afraid the piano is *not* good for him. . . .'

If she had no ear for music, her husband had no eye for gardening. He hardly knew one plant from another. Miss Boodle wrote that he was otherwise such a keen observer that 'for a long time I thought his ludicrous mistakes were only made in fun'.

Once when Fanny had to go up to London on business, she lamented the need of leaving just when she was ready to prune her raspberries for the first time. While she was away, Miss Boodle saw 'the Squire' in the garden, hot and tired but triumphant, with bleeding fingers and a long knife in his hand. He had 'hacked the plants to pieces'. The next day she joined Fanny in the raspberry patch and found her in distress. Every promising shoot was cut off; there would not be a berry. 'She did so love everything her hands had planted.' Suddenly they heard a step. 'Hush!' she warned the girl. 'Louis must never know what he has done. He did it to surprise me and thinks it has been a splendid day's work.' The next moment, 'she was radiant, and I do not think he had one doubt of his success. . . . He often talked eagerly about the raspberries they hoped to harvest'.

Stevenson could not often venture away from Bournemouth, and when he did, even in the warmer months, he usually fell ill. In late August 1885 they went to the West Country for a little change, and particularly to meet Thomas Hardy at Dorchester. As for Mrs Hardy, Fanny wrote, 'What very strange marriages literary men seem to make'.

On the way back, at Exeter, Louis became desperately ill with haemorrhages. Stranded in a hotel room, Fanny could not take him home until 12th September. She wrote Mrs Sitwell that 'my back is broken altogether', for she had had to lift him in and out of bed ten times in one night with his furious delirium.

'The *Prince* [*Otto*] has done fairly well,' Louis wrote to Gosse at the New Year, 'in spite of the reviews, which have been bad. . . . That is the hard part of literature. You aim high, and you take longer over your work, and it will not be so successful as if you had aimed low and rushed it. . . . I know that good work sometimes hits; but, with my hand on my heart, I think it is by accident. . . .'

He had been commissioned to write another boys' adventure story for *Young Folks*, and launched upon what he first called *David Balfour* – later *Kidnapped*. 'I have no earthly news', he wrote his father on 25th January 1886, 'living entirely in my story, and only coming out of it to play patience.'

Fanny agreed with Colvin, Henley and the author himself that *Kidnapped* was 'far the most human of my labours hitherto. . . . As to whether the long-eared British public may take to it', he told his father in April, 'all think it more than doubtful . . .'. Even with his growing reputation he received only thirty shillings per thousand words for the serialization. When it was published in book form Matthew Arnold was among its delighted readers. '*David* seems really to be going to succeed,' Louis wrote to his mother. 'I am, I believe, floated financially; a book that sells will be a pleasant novelty.'

Bogue's ailments, often from battle, made the local veterinary surgeon an *habitué* of Skerryvore. At length the warrior was so badly mauled that he had to be sent to the pet hospital. He broke loose and, injured and bandaged as he was, attacked another dog much bigger and stronger than himself. 'Poor wee man,' Louis wrote to Cummy, 'he died . . . in a fight, which was what he would have chosen; for military glory was more in his line than domestic virtues.'

He was buried in Fanny's garden, with a Latin inscription on the tombstone.

Back in Edinburgh the step-grandparents liked having a lad living in Heriot Row again, now as a science student. Lloyd, however, like his stepfather before him, secretly chafed at the primness and the Sabbath piety of the old house after the casual stimulus of a home with his mother and Louis.

'I find in the contemplation of the growth of Lloyd much benefit,' Louis told Henley. 'He is a dam [sic] fine youth. Happy am I, to be even thus much of a father. . . . Perhaps . . . the age of paternity coming, a demand sets in. Thus perhaps my present (and crescent) infatuation for the youth Lloyd; but no, I think, it is because the youth himself improves so much, and is such a dam, dam, dam fine youth.'

To the alarm of all the family, when Lloyd was taking his exams in Edinburgh his eyes seemed to be failing. For a time the doctors feared that he might go blind. Fanny reproached herself for having deplored his childhood lack of interest in scenery. With a tubercular husband, it was appalling to picture herself also improvising a life for a blind son. Lloyd, brave as his mother – or his stepfather – resolved to teach himself to use that newfangled contraption, the typewriter, so that he could at least write a little.

'. . . I fear the doctors were right about his eyes', Fanny told Dora Williams. '. . . He is taking it very well, and talks quite composedly about making arrangements for the time when he shall not see at all. He is trying to learn the piano, and we are to get him a typewriter. There are times, especially at night, when I think I cannot bear it. Already his life is shorn so very close. Mr Henley, who has just left us, said: "At least it is God's mercy that he is in Louis' hands." I said, "It is God's mercy that we both are."'

In time Lloyd was given very strong spectacles, and his sight was saved.

Sam Osbourne could hardly be blamed for having come twice to England to see his son, except that his former wife suspected – with reason – that he wanted to get him away from her. He took his son off for a visit, once on a walking tour from which Fanny complained that Lloyd had returned quite vulgarized for a while. The lad was growing up to resemble his father in being tall, blond, blue-eyed and big-boned, but he had his mother's curly hair, and his tastes were more highbrow than Sam's.

Osbourne was now trying to persuade his son to come back to California and learn to run the new vineyard near Silverado. Fanny worried and fumed. Understandably, living under the constant fear of losing Louis, her fierce love clung all the tighter to her son. '. . . when I see other people's boys, I am very thankful for my own,' she had told her mother-in-law.

Meanwhile Belle and her husband and child were settled in Honolulu, for Joe's commissions as a painter. When their ship had sailed towards the pretty little capital set low among its coconut palms and flowering trees, with white villas under the purple hills, Joe had exclaimed with dismay, 'I can't paint that . . . It's all done in primary colours.' But he managed.

There were no resident artists in the Kingdom of Hawaii and the attractive young couple created a diversion. Well-dressed ladies, gloved and veiled, arrived in smart carriages to leave visiting cards. The Strongs had the alternative of joining either the Missionary Set, with its tea parties, or the Royal Set, with gay balls at the Palace and parties on the visiting warships of many nations. Obviously they plumped for the Royal Set, and were soon a popular success, carefree and extravagant.

One afternoon Belle was sitting on the veranda of her flowery cottage in Nuuanu Avenue when her old friend from California, the painter Jules Tavernier, came up the walk and – a sign of agitation – addressed her in French. He showed her a San Francisco newspaper which had just arrived by the morning's steamer. Across the front page she was shocked to read her father's name. Samuel Osbourne had vanished – no one knew where. A prominent and respected man, his disappearance caused a sensation. His business affairs appeared to be in order. Was he dead? Had he run away?

On a visit to California soon afterwards Belle went to the vineyard to see his wife, Paulie, who was pale and thin, her black hair powdered with white. 'Paulie told me that my father went to court for a night session, asked her to have supper for him at midnight, kissed her, and went off down the street, whistling. . . . From that day to this he has never been heard of. He left the court-house a little before twelve o'clock, in his usual good health and spirits, and disappeared for ever.'

Many persons, including his children, maintained that he had been shanghaied in a dark street, or robbed and murdered. Years later there was a report that he had been seen in South Africa. But most people felt fairly sure that it was suicide; he had always been known to be unstable under his charm. Moreover, eventually a small pile of clothing was found on the beach, too much worn by time and weather to be positively identified, but believed to be his.

Fanny wrote in confidence to Colvin: '. . . The papers say that there are "evil rumours" concerning him, one being that he has deserted his miserable wife and fled with a young girl employed in his office. . . . That he probably brought the girl to grief, I do not doubt, but it was not in him to do more. . . . It is either murder, in which case some ugly story is at the back . . . or it is suicide . . . or he has absconded. It is more hard on the boy than words can express, for he has my own pride that Louis has always called devilish pride. The wife, who is left in absolute destitution, in debt beside . . . seems to have been more or less prepared for something. . . . The first shock of it was dreadful to my poor boy. All that Louis could think of was to offer him some money to send the wife. He thanked Louis and kissed him, and lay down in his bed, having before that been wandering about alone in the darkness. The next morning he wrote one of the most beautiful letters I ever read to a lawyer in San

Francisco, sending the money Louis gave him, saying that he owed the ability to do this to Mr Stevenson, to whom he also owed everything else in his life. . . . Why could the man have not died a decent death at least . . . ?

'My poor boy is very brave, and has braced himself for the worst, hoping for the best which is suicide. . . . All sorts of nightmare thoughts fly through my head, as I know they do through Lloyd's. . . . Lloyd, who is the only real sufferer, takes it best. Except for his trembling hands, and a more demonstrative affection for Louis no one could detect anything. . . . He, Lloyd, seems to be really learning to write. Louis has been delighted with his last attempts. He always had plenty of invention and imagination, but it was a question whether he could use them. The typewriter is a great thing for him. He already uses it with much dexterity. . . . I believe, in spite of everything, that Louis feels a sort of joy in knowing that the boy now belongs to him entirely. . . . Please tell nobody, and try and say Lloyd.'

The last sentence refers to the fact that at this time the youth, who heretofore had been called Sam, adopted his middle name, which to avoid confusion has been used throughout this book.

Chapter V
A mad scheme of martyrdom

'No insanity', wrote G. K. Chesterton of R.L.S. at Bournemouth, '. . . is so interesting to the psychologist as the shock of Stevenson going sane . . . his revolt into respectability.'

Fanny was a co-revolutionary. She played her new role of passionate respectability in her headlong way – house-proud with her suburban villa and the local intelligentsia in her salon. Always a chameleon, she became quite 'English', or so it must have seemed to her. Old timers who knew her then have said that most of her American accent had disappeared. Yet the future wife of Graham Balfour was to write of her, 'She was wholly un-English, but she made allowances for every English tradition.'

Despite continuing illness Stevenson managed to keep up his prolific output of essays, short stories, books and poems – perhaps partly because of the complete quiet of his life with Fanny to shelter him from the world. Nevertheless for those three years at Bournemouth his literary income still averaged less than four hundred pounds.

His first popular successes brought the familiar reaction: his friends, among other critics, gave him more adverse reviews. 'There must be something wrong in me,' he replied to a sting from Gosse, 'or I would be popular'. Even his literary adherents, like Fanny and his father, could not keep up with his aim (though Henry James did) in always reaching out to extend his range rather than to repeat the proved patterns. At the same time his vindication of himself as a writer gave him great comfort in his frail world with 'Bluidy Jack' upon his back.

He agreed to write a memoir of the late Professor Fleeming Jenkin, and the widow – the first charmer of his youth – came down to Skerryvore to help. 'She is not generally liked, but I like her,' Fanny wrote to Dora. The work went well and he was gratified to find that Mrs Jenkin approved.

He also accepted an invitation to give a course of lectures to young writers at the British Museum. (A heavy haemorrhage eventually prevented its delivery.) One morning Fanny turned up at the Boodles' house at a surprisingly early hour. 'Louis is asking for you', she told Adelaide. 'Can you come?' The night before, he had sat up with a high temperature and demanded that the girl be sent for. 'He is so full of ideas for those lectures that he must vent it upon somebody,' Fanny explained. '. . . He thinks you will just suit his purpose. Of course I had to ask the doctor. He said it was useless to thwart him. . . . Do try to keep him as calm as possible'.

As they walked to Skerryvore she added, 'I am still half afraid on your account. But if ever you feel frightened, you must come to me. Remember that I shall always be somewhere close by, generally in the next room.'

Miss Boodle was only too happy to have instruction from the Master.

At Skerryvore they found him, to Fanny's 'surprise and (well-disguised) dismay', downstairs in the Blue Room. He sat before a blazing fire, wrapped in his maroon poncho, with books on his lap and others on the floor. He set his eager pupil an exercise by telling her a short anecdote and ordering her to write it in the styles of several different authors – the 'Sedulous Ape' method of temporary imitation by which he had taught himself to write.

She 'toiled most of the night', and the next day returned to the Blue Room. 'For once' she found the Sine Qua Non lying on the divan, apparently asleep. 'With a red silk pillow as her background, she looked so superbly beautiful that, for a moment, my attention wandered. Suddenly there was a low rumble of thunder. "Oh, but this work is disgracefully bad! It could hardly be worse! . . ."

'I choked back my tears and tried to make an airy apology. Mrs Stevenson, like a crouching lioness bereaved of her whelps, sprang to the rescue. She reared her glorious head, and from the divan at the far end of the room rang out, "Louis! You are a brute! I told you it would kill the child – and it *will*!" "No, it won't," I gasped. "I don't mind a bit. I *will* learn to write!" In a moment he was on his knees beside me on the hearth-rug, my trembling hand firmly clasped in his own. "*Of course* you are! Fanny is right. I really am a brute. But I'm going to teach you!"'

He did – but the inoculation did not 'take' very well. (The 'little brown deer', as Fanny pet-named her, eventually became a primary school mistress and then a missionary in the Far East.)

The elder Stevensons had taken a furnished house in Bournemouth for the winter of 1886–87. Fanny had been obliged to endure a further strain for her invalid with Thomas's alternation of dark 'Hyde moods' and periods of clinging gentleness. As the old man's mind wavered he often spoke to his Lou as if he were a small boy. At bedtime he kissed him good night, adding reassuringly, 'You'll see me in the morning, dearie.' And when they parted he added, 'Take care of yourself, my dearie.' 'It was', wrote Fanny, 'just like a mother with a young child.'

R.L.S. gave so much companionship to his father that for the first time his writing was neglected. 'Louis fancies that he feels some stirring of the intellect', Fanny told Colvin as the winter wore on. 'I hope he does, for it was growing alarming. I began to fear he would never work again.'

Margaret Stevenson was sometimes hysterical from bearing the brunt of her husband's disintegration. He kept her awake to share his restless gloom. Finally one night they both fell asleep. But he soon roused her and announced, 'My dear, the end is now come; I have lost the power of speech.'

It was understood that the old man was dying, and would rather be at home, so his wife took him back to Edinburgh.

In April too Fanny was extremely alarmed by her husband's 'Irish folly'. In Ireland the crusade for Home Rule was then in a full tide of resistance, often with mob violence. In the previous November a farmer named John Curtin had been murdered by a party of 'moonlighters' at his farm on Castle Island, County Kerry. His grown sons and daughters had rallied bravely and one of the murderers had been shot. For this the Curtins had been boycotted; they were refused any contact with the community – even the most necessary trading for supplies. Louis was sympathetic with the Home Rule aim but, influenced by the morality of Tolstoy, he wanted to jolt both the English and the Irish peoples to do their duty with law and justice. Having always longed to be a man of action – a knight errant – he now seriously planned to go, with Fanny and the half-blind Lloyd, to live with the Curtins on their farm and share their ostracism, to write of their cause, and even, if fate willed, to be assassinated for its sake.

His incredulous friends expostulated only less than his wife and stepson, who could hardly believe their ears and had not the least wish to be mobbed and martyred. After violent arguments Fanny gave in, brave and loyal even in the hardest test of all. As for Lloyd, he allowed himself to be included, even while he felt a grudging indignation at being offered for assassination at the age of nineteen. 'Indeed,' he recalled, '[Louis] was in the deadliest earnest, and my mother scarcely less so, unbelievable as it then seemed to me. . . .'

Stevenson argued out his plans pro and con in a midnight letter to Mrs Jenkin. '. . . Now, my work can be done anywhere, and a writer being murdered would . . . throw a bull's-eye light upon this cowardly business. . . .'

'I am married. "I have married a wife!" I seem to have heard it before. . . . My wife has had a mean life (1), loves me (2), could not bear to lose me (3). I admit; I am sorry. But what does she love me for? and she must lose me soon or late. And after all, because we run this risk, it does not follow we should fail. . . .'

'I see what a dreary, friendless, God-forgotten business it will be. . . . Yet I see quite clearly how all points to nothing coming, to a quite inglorious death by disease. . . . I do not love this health-tending, housekeeping life of mine . . . do not falsely counsel me to put my head under the bed-clothes. And I will say this to you: My wife, who hates the idea, does not refuse. "It is nonsense," says she, "but if you go, I will go." Poor girl, and her home and her garden that she was so proud of! I feel her garden most of all, because it is a pleasure (I suppose) that I do not feel myself to share. . . .'

This wild scheme might actually have been carried out but for a sudden worsening of Thomas Stevenson's condition. Louis abandoned the idea with reluctance, to Fanny's infinite relief.

Early in May, wrote Fanny, 'we were summoned by telegram to Edinburgh, where my father-in-law was fighting death inch by inch. His memory gone, his reason shattered, nothing remained but his determined will. It was a terrible figure we found sitting grimly in the drawing-room of the house at Heriot Row. . . .' Mr Stevenson had always vowed that he wanted to die on his feet, so he was sedately clad in a broadcloth suit and cravat, smoking his pipe in an armchair. However, he did not recognize them, not even Lou – which was a great shock to his son. '. . . it was not until an hour or two before his death . . . that he could be persuaded to lie upon his bed, and then only after a narcotic had been administered.' On 8th May, at midday, in the words of his wife's diary, 'he fell gently asleep'.

Louis had caught a cold, and his doctor-uncle forbade him to go to the funeral with his mother, Fanny and Lloyd – the two women heavily veiled in black. Later, however, he received the mourners when they came back from the cemetery to Heriot Row.

'The funeral would have pleased him', Stevenson wrote of his father to Colvin; 'it was the largest private funeral in man's memory here.' He added, 'Now I . . . can say that I am glad. If we could have had my father, that would have been a different thing. But to keep that changeling – suffering changeling – any longer, could better none and nothing. Now he rests. . . . He will begin to return to us in the course of time, as he was and as we loved him.'

The couple stayed with the widow until the end of May. It was a difficult time. Louis was too unwell to leave the house, and there were problems about the will and the business. It seemed at first as if Thomas had taken seriously his son's burning embarrassment at being financially dependent. His earlier will had bequeathed most of his assets to the Church of Scotland, leaving Louis only three thousand pounds promised in his mother's marriage settlement, which in fact was all he was to receive at present. However, a codicil provided that Mrs Stevenson should have two thousand pounds outright plus the income from the estate of about £26,000 for life, and afterwards the inheritance was to pass to his son, his son's wife if she survived him, and then to his son's stepson. To Fanny this ultimate recognition of her flesh and blood was as deep a gratification as any in her life.

Louis, now being head of the family, had been enjoined by his father to help his late brother Alan's children, Bob and Katharine, if they were ever in need.

The newspapers annoyed Louis and Fanny by proclaiming them rich, the heirs to a large fortune, but even the actual three thousand pounds seemed to them a big sum to put into Baxter's care. In the perverse way of money it chanced to come when at last it was no longer so urgently needed, as Louis's own earnings increased.

'I abandoned college at the end of my second year', recorded Lloyd, 'and returned to Skerryvore, with the intention of becoming an author myself under R.L.S.'s tuition.'

He went back to Bournemouth soon after Thomas Stevenson's funeral, while his mother and stepfather remained in Edinburgh. 'In the course of time two letters arrived, the first from my mother – such a heartbroken letter – saying that the doctors had ordered R.L.S. to leave England at once for Colorado . . . England was ended for him. . . . She wrote of her "little nest" and the unendurable wrench it would be to leave it. "Life had been too happy at Skerryvore – the envying gods had struck it down."'

Lloyd expected to find his stepfather's letter echoing a similar note of tragedy, but when it came a day or two later it was 'cheerful, almost jubilant. . . . He was plainly glad to be off, and the sooner the better'.

There was no more talk of the Irish escapade. Fate had put other adventures in his path. He had another bout of his 'leaking haemorrhage' even in midsummer, so it was indeed urgent to go to high dry air.

As for Lloyd, unlike his mother he was still an American citizen. Fanny assured Dora Williams that the thought of his father was a 'nightmare horror' to him. But after seven years abroad it seemed time to return to his own country, and he was happy to travel and write. Valentine also decided to accompany the family.

Margaret Stevenson reported in her diary, 'Louis wished me to go with them; at first I said it was impossible, I was not in spirits . . .; then Fanny wrote to say, "The doctor says that Louis *must* go and he won't go without you." So of course I gave in and I never regretted it.' She proposed to help with finances, and further funds were to come from the letting of Skerryvore.

Louis's cronies were disappointed at his again going so far away as America, though everyone, including the Stevensons themselves, assumed that it was only for the winter. He was upset, however, because there was an eleventh-hour quarrel between Fanny and Colvin, its cause unrecorded. On his last day in Bournemouth (Fanny had gone ahead to London) he wrote his old friend, '. . . There was no essential unkindness in any of our minds; some muddle, some trouble. . . . I have told Fanny, who was cut to the heart with fear and alarm, that I would disculpate her. It was certainly not her doing, beyond meddling; wherein I cannot excuse her; and if we have grown to count on your indulgence very largely, yours is the fault. I wish I had a word of peace to take to her tomorrow. . . .'

The faithful Colvin forgave her, and turned up the next day when a few friends went to say goodbye at the hotel near the London docks. Louis called for a lawyer (on Sunday) and made his will, though Gosse found him 'radiantly humourous and romantic'. But Colvin was the only one to see the Stevensons off in a small boat to the ship's side, as he had been the only one to welcome them seven years before. On board was a case of champagne, sent as a seasick remedy by Henry James.

'They are a romantic lot, and I delight in them,' he wrote to a friend when they had sailed away.

Part 8

Saranac

Snowbound in the 'Adirondack Wilderness' 1887-88

Chapter I
Frontier life in the 'Hunter's Home'

Fanny, shopping for a thrifty passage to New York, had booked the party aboard a tramp freighter with roomy cabins. The *Ludgate Hill* proved to be 'shabby and dirty', but 'Louis and Lloyd have longed for adventure', wrote Margaret Stevenson – whose prim serene diaries and letters to her sister 'Auntie' Balfour were to register the family chronicles for the next six years.

When the ship called at Havre, the cargo turned out to consist of stallions, cows, apes (for zoos) and matches. Fanny was indignant because the shipping firm had not let her know. At night pandemonium echoed with the neighing of horses, lowing of cattle, squealing of monkeys, and shouting of French and English sailors. There was a smell of the stable, not the sea.

Fanny was very seasick, and Lloyd and the servant Valentine only less, but the Stevenson mother and son were born sailors. Louis romped about in mid storm, dispensing Henry James's champagne to green-faced passengers. 'O, it was lovely on our stable-ship, chock full of stallions', he exulted to Colvin. 'She rolled heartily, rolled some of the fittings out of our stateroom. . . . But we enjoyed it to the masthead, all but Fanny, and even she perhaps a little. . . . I (at least) made a friend of a baboon . . . whose embraces have pretty near cost me a coat. . . .'

The ship ran into thick fog off the Newfoundland Banks, and

Louis caught a heavy cold. Even so – alas for his landlubber wife – he told Bob, 'The sea voyage proves the sea agrees heartily with me, and my mother likes it, so she will likely hire a yacht for a month or so in the summer. Good Lord! What fun! Wealth is only useful for two things: a yacht and a string quartet. . . .'

To his wife's gratification, Stevenson reached America to find himself famous. *Treasure Island*, *Kidnapped* and especially *Dr Jekyll and Mr Hyde* had all made a sensation, though most of the heavy sales were in pirate editions. Even before land was sighted the family learned that the boarding pilot was nicknamed 'Hyde' while his better-tempered colleague was 'Jekyll'.

They were welcomed by the Lows and editor E. L. Burlingame of *Scribner's* magazine. Louis found a telegram from Mr Fairchild, his rich admirer in Boston, telling him that a suite was prepared for the party as the Fairchilds' guests, and a carriage from the Victoria Hotel was waiting at the pier – in contrast to his previous threadbare arrival. Fanny hustled her husband to bed at once, but even so he was interviewed by eight reporters, the last somehow getting in after he was asleep. 'My reception here was idiotic to the last degree', the lion wrote to Bob. '. . . America is a fine place to eat in, and a great place for kindness, but Lord! What a silly thing is popularity! If it ever paid. . . .'

The cheerful Maggie Stevenson – then fifty-eight, and considered 'old' – was a success with her new American acquaintances. She was always a neat upright figure in her black dress and white starched widow's cap with the two long streamers, as in the later pictures of Queen Victoria. She and Fanny attended the first night of *Dr Jekyll and Mr Hyde*, with Richard Mansfield as star, but Louis was too unwell to go. The dramatist T. R. Sullivan called on the Mesdames Stevenson and, wrote Maggie, 'gives up the author's box to Fanny saying that he has no right to it'. Lloyd, arriving late, had to see the play from the back of the box, but Fanny and her white-capped mother-in-law sat on either side of their escort, Will Low.

Louis and Fanny were incredulous to find themselves prospering under the patronage of the rich. 'Publishers made him offers for work, so large that he was afraid to accept them. . . .' she recalled. Fan-mail poured in. The sculptor Augustus St Gaudens began work on a medallion of Louis, shown sitting up in bed and writing in his old red poncho. The original pose with a cigarette was later changed to a pen for the reproduction in St Giles Cathedral in Edinburgh.

A dynamic American publisher named S. S. McClure – still a slim fair young man in his twenties – had written to Stevenson at Bournemouth, but Louis had lost the letter and did not know how to reach him. In New York Lloyd went to the office of his Syndicate and explained the lapse. Mr and Mrs McClure hurried over and called on the Stevensons, to find the author writing in bed – as in the St Gaudens sculpture. For the time being, however, Charles Scribner had got in ahead. He had promised Louis $3,500 for twelve monthly articles for his magazine. 'I am now a salaried party; I am a bourgeois now . . . but the sum was irresistible', R.L.S. told Henley. Mr Scribner also offered a good price for *The Black Arrow*, and voluntarily paid royalties for the earlier books he had published, although there was no international copyright. Louis then signed a contract which gave Scribner the rights in all his work in the United States.

Now that he was 'second to no novelist in England or America', wrote Lloyd in a Preface, 'he exulted; it did much to keep him alive; gave him a new assurance and authority.' But whereas before Fanny had had to encourage him in failure, now she found it her mission to protect him from his success – from the time-wasting interruptions of public acclaim. She was still the guardian at the door.

Louis was tired in New York and the autumn had come. Someone recommended the Adirondack mountains in upper New York State. Reconnoitring, Fanny and Lloyd went north by river boat and train, marvelling at the brilliant foliage of early October, to Loon Lake at the end of the railroad line. They took a buggy and team for twenty miles to Saranac Lake, about 1,600 feet up in the so-called Adirondack Wilderness near the Canadian border. At an isolated logging and trapping village a sanatorium for consumptives had been founded in 1882 by Dr E. D. Trudeau, who had himself arrived there on a mattress and recovered to win fame as a pioneer expert in his own disease. Fanny rented half of 'Baker's house', a guide-trapper's white wooden cottage, crudely carpentered, with green shutters and a veranda around it. Set high on a forested ridge above the river, it was only ten minutes' walk from the backwoods village of log cabins and frame houses. It had a small corner study for Louis and a garret 'for hardy visitors', the less rugged being put up at the inn.

The newcomers telegraphed for the other three and sent a buggy to meet them. 'When we reached Saranac', wrote Mrs Stevenson, 'Fanny met us in a petticoat and jacket, busy cooking our dinner!'

Fanny toiled and improvised to make everything snug in the Hunter's Home, as they nicknamed it. The house-keeping was 'very like camp life'. 'We are living', she wrote Miss Boodle, '. . . in the most primitive fashion. The maid does the cooking (we have little beyond venison and bread to cook) and the boy comes every morning to carry water from a distant spring for drinking purposes. . . .' All the water for washing had to be carried up from the river by their landlord, Mr Baker. 'It is already very cold, but we have calked the doors and windows as one calks a boat. . . .'

Stevenson quickly settled down to work, often bundling up to pace the veranda in the piercing air and think out his stories. He began to produce, among other works, the twelve monthly articles for *Scribner's* magazine, though he mistrusted anything done to order for a deadline. Fanny or Lloyd carefully checked the American pieces for accuracy in background and speech.

'. . . From the next room,' he told Henry James, 'the bell of Lloyd's typewriter makes an agreeable music as it patters off (at a rate which astonishes this experienced novelist) the early chapters of a humorous romance; from still further off – the walls of Baker's are neither ancient nor massive – rumours of Valentine about the kitchen stove come to my ears; of my mother and Fanny I hear nothing, for the excellent reason that they are sparking off, one to Niagara, one to Indianapolis. . . .' Fanny was visiting her spry little mother in Indiana.

On her return to Saranac she travelled by way of Montreal, the nearest city, and bought for her whole household a supply of 'extra-ordinary garments' made by the Canadian Indians to keep out the cold; coats and robes and rugs of buffalo hide, fur caps and snow-shoes. It became so cold that it was impossible to touch metal without being burnt; and Lloyd or Fanny drove with three pairs of gloves, while each of the many-layered passengers had a hot soap-stone for the feet and a smaller one in the pocket to warm the hands. After a drive or a walk (in Canadian moccasins) or a little skating on

the pond, Louis usually lay down until six, when the family dined.
They talked, read aloud or played cards by the fire – Aunt Maggie
was always the champion at card games – or Louis and Lloyd played
duets on penny tin whistles. Everyone went to bed early with a hot
soapstone to keep warm.

Louis and Fanny were both impressed when William Archer sent
them a novel called *Cashel Byron's Profession*, by a new young writer
named George Bernard Shaw. 'I have read your friend's book with
singular relish', wrote Louis. '. . . It is full of promise; but I should
like to know his age. . . . It is *horrid fun*. All I ask is more of it. . . .
(I say, Archer, my God, what women!). . . .'

Fanny was elated when Henry James wrote to praise the 'elegance'
of her letters. Mr James sent to Owen Wister, the American author of
The Virginian, a note of introduction to 'dear Louis Stevenson'.
He told Wister, '. . . You will find him a young, unique, dishevelled,
undressed, lovable fellow. There is a fresh, youthful complacent
Scotch mother, a poor sightless (or almost so) American stepson,
& a strange California wife, 15 years older than Louis himself, but
almost as interesting. If you like the gulch & the canyon you will like
her. . . .'

One very dark night while Stevenson was pacing the narrow
veranda, buffalo-coated, astrakhan-capped and Indian-booted, with
the icy air stinging his nostrils, he drew out of past impressions the
novel which was to become *The Master of Ballantrae*. Another
good-and-evil study, about two conflicting brothers in love with the
same woman, it was the major work of the winter.

He told the story through the stern Scot, Mackellar, partly to
lighten it and partly to spare the need of going too deeply into the
character of the heroine, 'because I am always afraid of my women,
who are not admired in my home circle . . .'.

S. S. McClure came up several times to see the new literary hero,
hoping for the Stevenson name in his *New York World*. He liked
both Louis and his wife. Once in Fanny's absence he told him that
he wanted to publish *The Black Arrow* in syndicated form. R.L.S.
'said he didn't know; his wife didn't like the story, but he would
send to her for a copy and consult her. . . . So it was done.'

McClure also probed out the information that Stevenson had two novels in mind, one a sequel to *Kidnapped*. He asked how much he wanted for the serial rights, and Louis said $800. 'Well,' announced McClure, '. . . I am going to pay you $8,000. . . . He was somewhat reluctant, and blushingly said that he didn't feel he ought to take so much money, and was he worth it. . . . He must consult his wife and Will Low, and if they approved, he would make the contract. . . . He was unlike any other author I ever met. . . .'

And so Louis wrote jubilantly to Baxter, '. . . I'm awfu' grand noo, and long may it last!'

Having signed the agreement, it was several weeks before he suddenly remembered that he had made a contract with Charles Scribner for all his American works. Fanny too was appalled. He wrote to Scribner with a pained apology, explaining that he was so absent-minded about business that earlier he had even forgotten to sell the American rights in *Jekyll and Hyde*, which had left the whole lucrative field to pirates. Naturally Scribner was annoyed and suspicious; neither he nor McClure could be expected to know that Louis was the kind of man who had repeatedly forgotten to cash cheques even when he thought himself penniless.

Henley had heretofore saved his friend the trouble of marketing most of his writings. Louis confessed to him sheepishly, 'I find myself in the worse scrape of being a kind of unintentional swindler.' After this shock, he put all his financial arrangements in the hands of the patient Baxter.

The Black Arrow was duly made ready for American publication. Since Fanny had always disapproved of this fine medieval adventure story, her husband, with tongue in cheek, dedicated it to her: 'No one knows but myself what I have suffered, nor what my books have gained, by your unsleeping watchfulness and admirable pertinacity. And now here is a volume that goes into the world and lacks your *imprimatur*; a strange thing in our joint lives; and the reason of it stranger still! I have watched with interest, with pain, and at length with amusement, your unavailing attempts to peruse *The Black Arrow*; I think I should lack humour indeed if I let the occasion slip and did not place your name in the fly-leaf of the only book of mine that you have never read – and never will read.'

Though he never used a typewriter, saying the noise distracted him, he did not mind the clicking of Lloyd's. That aspiring young man was writing a novel to be called *The Wrong Box*, an amusing tale about a mistaken identity of a corpse in a barrel. 'I quite chortle over some of it,' Louis wrote to Fanny while she was away. 'Some of it, of course, is incredibly bad.' When it was finished, the proud mother reported, 'He read it aloud to the family, a few chapters each evening. It seemed to us all a rather creditable effort for a boy of that age, and my husband remarked that it would be very easy to pull it together and "make it go".' They hoped that the joint work might earn some quick money for a yacht cruise. With his urge to collaborate with those he loved, Louis was generous in giving his stepson the prestige of his reputation in launching the book. Burlingame, who paid them a visit, declined it for *Scribner's* magazine, but McClure said he would publish it if Stevenson thought it was worth while, though he advised him in vain against putting his name to it. Lloyd's American citizenship, however, had the advantage of getting a copyright for United States publication. Fanny too continued to lean on Stevenson's time and talent for collaboration. She resumed work on the play called *The Hanging Judge* which she had taken over from Louis and Henley in Bournemouth, and got her husband again to help her with the script, 'amid much acrimony and general dissension', she told Colvin. They completed it in Saranac but it was never produced, though more of Louis's time had been wasted.

'Louis has not, since he left England, brought up one drop of blood from his lungs', Fanny wrote joyfully to Colvin. She deported Lloyd to stay at the village inn until he got over a cold. As for herself, she was suffering from 'breathlessness'. The doctor ordered her to have another change of climate.

Again she was in one of her uncommunicative moods of neurosis, and did not write even to her worried mother, so Louis had to do it on 31st January. '. . . she has been away upon her own devices for nearly two months . . . she has been pretty ill in her absence. . . . You must not blame her if she does not write: the doctors, I know, would rather she did not write at all. . . . She has been to New York and to Philadelphia where she saw her cousin and Walt Whitman – the latter, I believe, a great disenchantment after his works; she has a story coming out in next month's *Scribner* . . .' This was the ill-fated tale, *The Nixie*.

While the polar wind skirled and the icicles crashed, the shivering family longed for sun and warmth. When McClure paid another visit to Saranac, Stevenson told him that he always felt better at sea and wanted to fit up a yacht for a half year's cruise.

'Well,' the publisher later quoted himself as saying, 'that's easy. If you get a yacht and take long sea voyages and write about them, stories of adventure and so forth, I'll pay all the expenses of the yacht.' (He added, 'I was young and bold.') When he returned to New York he tried to find a suitable yacht, but none turned up.

Meanwhile Louis and Lloyd bought sailing directories, maps and charts, and in the snowy fireside evenings, like two schoolboys, they dreamed of far-off places – Bermuda, the Aegean, the Azores, the Indian Ocean, even the Pacific. Fanny, veering between altitude-sickness in the mountains and seasickness on the ocean, had little choice.

'The more I saw of the Stevensons,' McClure recalled long afterwards, 'the more I became convinced that Mrs Stevenson was the unique woman in the world to be Stevenson's wife. . . . When he met her her exotic beauty was at its height, and with this beauty she had a wealth of experience, a reach of imagination, a sense of humour, which he had never found in any other woman. Mrs Stevenson had many of the fine qualities that we usually attribute to men rather than to women; a fair-mindedness, a large judgment, a robust, inconsequential philosophy of life, without which she could not have borne, much less shared with a relish equal to his own, his wandering, unsettled life, his vagaries, his gipsy passion for freedom. She had a really creative imagination, which she expressed in living. She always lived with great intensity, had come more into contact with the real world than Stevenson had done at the time when they met, had tried more kinds of life, known more kinds of people. When he married her, he married a woman rich in knowledge of life and the world.

'She had the kind of pluck that Stevenson particularly admired. He was best when he was at sea, and although Mrs Stevenson was a poor sailor . . . she accompanied him on all his wanderings . . . with the greatest spirit. A woman who was rigid in small matters of domestic economy, who insisted on a planned and ordered life, would have worried Stevenson terribly. . . .'

Later, on a visit to London, McClure met a number of Steven-

son's literary intimates. He said that he found them jealous and
critical of Louis's great success – all except Henry James, who was
generous.

At last there was a thaw. The eaves dripped, the icicles melted.
The weather became bewilderingly changeable. On 26th March
1888, Fanny started out for a visit to California, leaving the others to
pack up for good and return to New York. She expected to rejoin
them there, though Louis had told her to look for a yacht if she
could find one.

Again, on 12th April, it was Louis who had to inform Mrs Vandegrift of her daughter's arrival in San Francisco. '. . . It was rather an
anxious business letting her go alone: but the Doctor would not hear
of my trying the journey. . . .' She had stayed in her berth with
rheumatism, until Belle, who had come from Honolulu to see her,
met her on the ferry, 'looking well and fat', and took her to poor
rooms in a lodging-house where Fanny shared the housekeeping.

Austin, Belle's son, Fanny described to Louis as 'a little, little
child, very ugly, very delicate, and most affectionate and touching.
He is very quiet and shy but I do not think at all stupid. Last
evening, he was out playing on the veranda with some children. I
heard them say, "Come on, Austin, what are you doing? why don't
you play?" I heard his little fingers picking at the venetians, as he
said, "I must look in to see if she is there yet." He gave an audible
sigh of relief when he saw me still sitting by the fire, and went on
with his play'.

The Saranac party went to New York on 13th April. (Fanny had
warned Valentine 'not to kill herself in the moving'.) Louis liked
to sit on a bench under the budding trees in the Early American
atmosphere of Washington Square, talking to the children. His
most memorable pleasure was an afternoon which he spent there
with Mark Twain, whose *Huckleberry Finn* he greatly admired.

But he soon grew tired. 'Low, get me out of this', he begged his
friend. So Low sent the party across the Hudson to a little white
colonial inn on the Manasquan River in New Jersey, where Louis
rested, tried to write, and sailed a catboat with Lloyd.

News came that Fanny had hardly settled down among her old
friends when she was again ill in bed. She had developed an alarming

growth in her throat, which might or might not be malignant. She would have to have an operation.

Even before he left Saranac Louis had been in trouble too. His mother wrote in her diary, 'On 21 April Louis gets some worrying letters which upset and depress him very much and he stays much in bed'.

Fanny had unwittingly started what has been called 'one of the great literary quarrels of the generation'.

Chapter II
Fanny's famous quarrel

A year or so before, in 1887, Fanny and Louis had been present at a conversation at the Henley's house, a centre of what she called 'the Shepherd's Bush gang', in London. Among the guests was Louis's cousin Katharine de Mattos who, with her acutely cultivated mind, was much more accepted as 'one of us' than was Fanny. Henley, like Louis, had been helping Katharine in her efforts to write. She had been working on a story about a meeting in a train between a poetic young man and a girl who turned out to have escaped from a lunatic asylum. Fanny, used to volunteering suggestions and criticisms, urged her to make the young woman a nixie, or water sprite. Fanny also offered to collaborate, but Katharine wanted to write her own story in her own way.

Henley tried to sell the manuscript to a number of magazines, but it was rejected. Later, at a gathering at Skerryvore, Fanny again intruded. Since Katharine's version had failed, Fanny asked if she might take over the story and rewrite it with her nixie idea.

Mrs de Mattos consented, but so reluctantly that everyone understood it as only a polite way of saying No – everyone except the eager Fanny. Katharine glumly kept her word and gave Fanny the rejected manuscript, though Louis himself asked his wife to go no further. But Fanny was attracted as usual to a tale in which she could bring in the supernatural, and acted on the weak permission. She rewrote the manuscript, using much of Katharine's material, and it became her third published story, appearing in *Scribner's* magazine for March 1888: 'The Nixie', by Fanny Van de Grift Stevenson. Louis, in fact, had one of his monthly articles, called 'Beggars', in the same issue. His friends were probably right in inferring that her feeble little tale had been accepted only because she was Mrs R.L.S.

What followed might have been avoided if she had done the simple and decent thing: shared the 'by-line' with Katharine de Mattos and sent her half the payment. Apart from the fairness of co-authorship, Katharine was poor, and Thomas Stevenson in his will had asked his son to give financial help to his niece and nephew in case of need. Fanny's impulse was most probably sheer greed for recognition – not money. She could never give up her hankering to be a literary lady in her own right.

The magazine was read by Henley who, even if he had been a less truculent character, would hardly have beamed at seeing a story which he had failed to sell for a friend in England, opulently sold by an enemy in the United States. Like Stevenson, Henley was unwell and highly strung in his work. On 9th March he wrote his friend a long, depressed, ruminating letter, ominously headed *Private and Confidential.*

He began: 'Dear Boy, If you will wash dishes and haunt back-kitchens in the lovely climate of the Eastern States, you must put up with the consequences. . . .' He went on with some gossip and chaffing about Louis's recent election to the Athenaeum Club, and added, 'I am out of key today. . . .' Then came the short paragraph – only six lines – which sped from his poisoned pen into Stevenson's bloodstream:

'I read *The Nixie* with considerable amazement. It's Katharine's; surely it is Katharine's? There are even reminiscences of phrasery & imagery, parallel incidents – que sais-je? It is also better focused, no doubt; but I think it has lost as much (at least) as it has gained; and why there wasn't a double signature is what I've not been able to understand. . . .'

He then discussed the failure of their joint play, *Deacon Brodie.* 'Lewis, dear lad, I am dam [*sic*] tired. . . .' He added: . . . 'What I want is the wings of a dove – a soiled dove even! – that I might flee away and be at rest.

'Don't show this to *anybody*, and when you write, don't do more than note it in a general way . . . deal vaguely with my malady. Why the devil do you go out and bury yourself in the bloody country of dollars and spew? . . . However, I suppose you must be forgiven, for you have loved me much. Let us go on so to the end. . . . Forgive this babble, and take care of yourself and burn this letter. Your friend, W.E.H.'

Fanny had left for the West just before the letter reached Saranac, so Louis was spared her flaming fury. He groaned and paced the floor for several days and tried out draft after draft of his answer. Not the least of Henley's malice was his forbidding his friend to show the letter to 'anyone' – meaning the woman whom he was accusing of plagiarism. He could cunningly imply that he did not want anyone to know he had called himself a soiled dove. Louis was the more ready to give his wife the benefit of the doubt since he himself had just been unintentionally dishonoured by forgetting a contract with one publisher and signing with another.

He finally answered the letter: 'My dear Henley, I write with indescribable difficulty . . .; you are to remember how very rarely a husband is expected to receive such accusations against his wife. I can only direct you to apply to Katharine and ask her to remind you of that part of the business which took place in your presence and which you seem to have forgotten; she will doubtless add the particulars which you may not have heard. . . .

'I am sorry I must ask you to take these steps; I might take them for myself had you not tied my hands by the strange step of marking your letter "private and confidential". . . . I must go farther and remind you, if you have spoken of this to others, a proper explanation and retraction of what you shall have said or implied to any person so addressed, will be necessary.

'. . . it is hard to think that anyone – and least of all my friend – should have been so careless of dealing agony . . . You will pardon me if I can find no form of signature; I pray God such a blank will not be of long endurance. Robert Louis Stevenson.'

Apparently Louis obeyed the 'Confidential' injunction and did not send Fanny the actual letter from Henley, but for her protection he wrote her about the contents. The spiteful little drama was well advanced before she heard of it – ill in bed with possible cancer of

the throat. She wrote back in a frenzy of rage and alarm. Nevertheless after a while she pulled herself together and, less headlong than
usual, managed to send a friendly message to Mrs de Mattos, to
emphasize that as a matter of course all was well and Katharine would
indeed support her against Henley in saying that she had handed
over the story to Fanny.

Henley in turn was many days in bracing himself to reply. Then,
in Manasquan, New Jersey, Louis received a letter from the elusive
and erratic Katharine, to whom Henley had spoken of her cousin's
charge. She said: 'As Mr Henley's very natural but unfortunate
letter was written without my wish or knowledge, I have refused to
let him go further in the matter. He had a perfect right to be
astonished but his having said so has nothing to do with me. If
Fanny thinks she has a right to the idea of the story I am far from
wishing to reclaim it or to criticise her in any way . . . It is of course
very unfortunate that my story was written first and read by people
and if they express their astonishment it is a natural consequence and
no fault of mine or any one else . . . I trust this matter is not making
you feel as ill as all of us.'

Louis was devastated. If Katharine would not confirm – though she
did not quite deny – that she had given Fanny permission to use her
story, then he had no backing in demanding an apology from Henley.
The good Baxter tried hard to mediate between the two men. Louis
told him, 'God bless you for your letter . . . Suppose that I am
insane and have dreamed all that I seem to remember, and that my
wife has shamefully stolen a story from my cousin, was this the class
of matter that a friend would write me? . . . And such an accusation –
a theft of money and of reputation? . . . It is of course quite true
that Katharine's attitude absolves him of three parts of what I had
against him, but the fourth part that remains – that willingness
to seethe up against me and mine in my absence and that
heartless willingness to wound me . . . O, a little kindness will go
far. . . .'

He overlooked the fact that if Henley now voiced a chivalrous
retraction on Fanny's behalf it would make Mrs de Mattos appear to
have lied in not endorsing it.

In the meantime Henley's reply had arrived at last. 'My dear
Lad: – Your letter is heart-breaking; & I do not know how to reply

to it, for it convicts me (I now see) of a piece of real unkindness, unworthy of myself and of our old true friendship. . . .

'You must not believe, though, that I struck to hurt. . . . I thought the matter of little consequence. It seemed right that you should know how it looked to myself, & that there might well be the end of it. I was elbows deep in the business from the first & I had (I thought) a right to make remarks. It was surely as well (I assumed) that you should hear of certain coincidences from me as well as from another quarter. . . .

'. . . I make haste to own that I spoke without a full sense of the regard that was due you, & that I beg your forgivenness. . . . Ever your friend, W.E.H.'

Thus Henley had apologized for having hurt Louis's feelings, but not for having insulted his wife – nor even mentioned her name.

The two men had already quarrelled several times. They were drawing farther apart on the literary seesaw – of which Stevenson's end was rising higher. Henley, passionately possessive as Fanny herself, could not wish his beloved friend well in a success which he had not lately had a hand in creating. Over the years he had become more and more angry at the interference of this 'semi-educated woman', as he called her, with her 'presumption and arrogance'.

On her side, she undervalued his services as unpaid literary agent and begrudged him the 'loans' her husband had made, while they each blamed the other for the playwriting fiasco. In turn she confided her Jovian wrath to poor Baxter. To her it seemed simple and absolute that she was the innocent victim of persecution – a complex which was growing with the years. Her husband's desperate efforts to save his friendship with Henley and with Katharine maddened her the more.

In these weeks of writing she had her throat operation. Blessedly the growth was not cancerous. If only she could be sure that it would not reappear! After some days of soreness she recovered.

There was a trough between the waves of the quarrel when for a time she thought it was ebbing. 'I hope you are not worrying about those people in England', she wrote Louis. 'If you are, I shall – I don't know what – write and apologize – or something equally dreadful. I have cast it out of my mind only in so far as it affects you. That sounds ambiguous, but you know what I mean. My dearest

Louis, whom I love with all my heart, I send you every good wish. . . .'

But she was not to recuperate in peace. When she learned that Katharine had backed down, and Henley did not withdraw his charge, and she herself stood exposed in her intellectual avarice, and her invalid husband was upset for weeks, then she became livid with anger and frustration. The fury of her letters drove him on to insist on saving her face. Apparently he did not even chide her with 'I told you so'. He seemed to care the more for her now that his chivalry had been called upon to protect her from her own mistake.

He lectured Katharine on her equivocation, concluding, 'I counsel you if you wish peace of mind, to do the right thing and do it now. . . .' She must have resented his eagerness to sacrifice her for Fanny. Her reply was again ambiguous: 'If I have failed to understand anything said to me at Bournemouth, or put a wrong construction on things, I am more grieved than ever, but I *cannot* say it has been intentional.'

To Louis's protest that she was evading the facts, she returned only a three-line note from a cocoon of camouflage: 'That was best. I am afraid to speak or breathe. There is devilry in the air.'

Of the four parties to the quarrel – Henley vindictive, Fanny greedy, Katharine weak and Louis unreasonable – his behaviour was the least ungenerous, and it was he who suffered most and longest. 'I wish I had died at Hyères', he told Baxter.

At length he wrote again from Manasquan to San Francisco: 'My dearest Girlie, I have not written to you for some days; all my energies have gone in writing and destroying letters to Henley; but I have now decided after two sleepless nights to do nothing. And if (as I believe they will) things take the worst course, simply to let "silence be the rest" . . . .

'I see no other way out of it, either with health or dignity; . . . I envy you flimsy people who rage up so easily with hate; the days go, and this is the more dreadful to me. Excuse my little bitterness with "flimsy", it is a tap in return from my thousands, and I don't believe it, dearest. . . .

'Well, this is the next morning. I have slept and I wash my hands of these hobgoblin figures, once my friends, for just now. But indeed I find it hard to think or write of anything else; my work is at a

stand. . . . Say nothing of it to anyone, please. . . . I am, my dear,
Your Louis.'

Young Lloyd was not much comfort to his stepfather. It was a
great shock to his proud sensitive nature to endure a quarrel over the
literary integrity of his mother, and he had hero-worshipped Henley
second only to Louis himself.

By this time the incident was abroad in the London clubs and far
beyond. All of Louis's intimates – except one – had had their turn
at sampling Fanny's temper. The one was Henry James, who
dissociated himself from the row with a dignified rebuttal. The wives
of the Victorian great were preferred to be seen rather than heard,
and now the quarrel about the divorced, foreign Mrs Robert Louis
Stevenson spread through the gossip columns. Both men lost caste
in their literary reputations – until private correspondence was made
public, decades later.

Baxter wrote confidentially to Colvin of his estimate of Henley:
'. . . a dangerous friend . . .; he seems born to leave himself un-
friended in the long run.'

Louis sent Baxter a codicil to his will. Hinting at Fanny's enmity,
he said that 'there may be war among my heirs'. In deference to his
father's admonition about Katharine as his ward, he arranged on
Baxter's advice for an annuity to be provided for her little girl. As to
Henley – 'I could only leave him a legacy, which he would throw
into the sea at once'. But he had already asked Baxter to find a way
of making Henley a very small allowance which might appear to
come from 'anybody but me'.

Fanny, as potential executrix, was informed of this legal turning
of the other cheek. She was blind with anger at the prospect of
sharing Thomas Stevenson's heritage with Katharine's child. She
snorted to Baxter that any such charity should be handed out as *she*
might see fit. As to Henley – such a gift was beyond belief. 'Already
the hands that dealt me the cruellest blows are held out to be
filled. . . . I am not likely to change my feelings of resentment. The
wrong can never be condoned, nor do I ever wish to see England
again. It is most probable that I never shall. Every penny that goes
to them, any of them, goes with my bitterest ill will'.

Naturally she was appalled to learn that the affair had been called
'an international incident'. '. . . As it is', she wrote Baxter, 'they

have nearly, perhaps quite, murdered [Louis]. It is very hard for me to keep on living! I may not be able to, but I must try, for my dear Louis's sake. If I cannot, I leave my curse upon the murderers and the slanderers. . . . I think it is almost better that we both were out of such a world. I never go to bed now but I am tempted sorely by the morphia and the arsenic that stands beside my bed.

'. . . If it so happens that I must go back to perfidious Albion, I shall learn to be false. While they eat their bread from my hand – and oh, they will do that – I shall smile, and wish it were poison that might wither their bodies as they have my heart.'

Though Fanny's final letter of malediction was the last recorded item in the Stevenson-Henley quarrel, the affair was to echo for years, and even beyond the grave.

Later in the same summer, 1888, Henley's collected verse was published, and the Stevensons read the volume. Louis still held – and continued to hold – to the belief and hope that the break with his old friend was not permanent. He wrote to Baxter: 'I wish you would tell Henley how heartily I have enjoyed his verses. My wife and I were both rejoiced to see him at last do something worthy of himself. . . .'

Inconsistent though the reference to Fanny may seem, it may well have been a fact; for in fairness it is important to remember, as most of those whom she offended could not know, that she often suffered heavy bouts of remorse for the discord she had caused. Nellie wrote of her sister: 'But as she loved, so she hated, and as she endowed her friends with all the virtues, so she could see no good at all in an enemy. Yet, just when you thought you were beginning to understand her nature – with its love and hate of the primal woman – her anger would suddenly soften, not into tenderness, but into a sort of dispassionate wisdom, and she would quote her favourite saying, "To know all is to forgive all" '. Thus, Fanny wrote to Baxter to apologize for the witch-like imprecations which she had cast on her enemies in her letters to him. She excused herself partly on the grounds that she had been worried about the possible malignancy of her throat condition.

Included in Henley's newly published *Poems* was one which he had first drafted in 1876 after Louis's early devotion to him in the

1. Fanny Osbourne at about the time when she first met Stevenson in France. He was to describe her piercing gaze as 'like the sighting of a pistol'.
  – *From the Stevenson Collection, Beinecke Library, Yale University.*

2. R.L.S. at the age of twenty-six in 1876, from a drawing by Fanny Osbourne, soon after they met in Grez-sur-Loing, France. He is wearing his old Indian embroidered smoking-cap.
– *From the* Life of R. L. Stevenson *by Graham Balfour, Methuen, 1901.*

3. 'The Bridge at Grez-sur-Loing', painted by Fanny Osbourne in 1876–7.
– *From the Stevenson Collection, Lady Stair's House, Edinburgh.*

4. Stevenson in 1879, after he followed Fanny Osbourne to California. – *From the Albert E. Norman Collection, California Historical Society, San Francisco.*

5. Fanny Osbourne before her marriage to R.L.S. in 1880.
– *From the Stevenson Collection, Lady Stair's House, Edinburgh.*

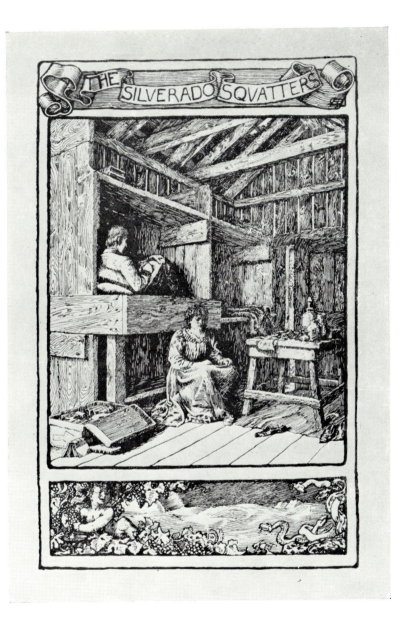

6. R. L. and Fanny Stevenson as squatters on their honeymoon at the Silverado mine, California, 1880. From an engraving by Fanny's son-in-law, Joseph D. Strong, Jr.
  – *From the Edinburgh Edition of the* Works *of R. L. Stevenson, 1895, British Museum Reading Room, London.*

7. Fanny Stevenson in the mid 1880's at Bournemouth. The photograph shows her nimble little 'boy's hands', as R.L.S. called them.
– *From the Stevenson Collection, Beinecke Library, Yale University.*

8. Fanny's favourite likeness of her husband: R.L.S. in the medallion by Augustus St Gaudens, New York, 1888. The invalid is wearing his old red poncho. The original cigarette in his hand was changed to a pen for the copy in St Giles's Cathedral, Edinburgh.
– *From the Stevenson Collection, Lady Stair's House, Edinburgh.*

9. At Saranac Lake, New York State, 1887–8: Valentine, the French-Swiss maid; a local 'help'; Lloyd Osbourne, Fanny's son; Fanny and R. L. Stevenson.
– *From the Stevenson Collection, Lady Stair's House, Edinburgh.*

10. Lloyd Osbourne, Fanny Stevenson's son, aged twenty, in 1888 in San Francisco.
 – *From the Stevenson Collection, Lady Stair's House, Edinburgh.*

11. In Honolulu in 1889. *Seated:* Ah Fu, the Chinese cook; R. L. and Fanny Stevenson; Lloyd Osbourne, her son. *Standing:* Mrs Margaret Stevenson, mother of R.L.S., and Belle Strong (*née* Osbourne), daughter of Fanny.
 – *From the Stevenson Collection, Lady Stair's House, Edinburgh.*

12. A native feast given by the Stevensons for the King of Hawaii and his sister in Honolulu, 1889. *At head of table:* R. L. Stevenson, Princess Liliuokalani, King Kalakaua, Mrs Margaret Stevenson. Lloyd Osbourne is leaning forward at left, Belle Strong at right.
 – *From the Stevenson Collection, Lady Stair's House, Edinburgh.*

13. Daughter Belle Strong's sketch of Fanny Stevenson's untidy bedroom while getting settled at Vailima, the new house in Samoa, 1891.
– *From the Stevenson Collection, Lady Stair's House, Edinburgh.*

14. Vailima, Samoa, after the second wing (left) was added to the house in 1893. The family group on lawn at right includes R.L.S., Lloyd Osbourne, Fanny Stevenson, cousin Graham Balfour and Belle Strong.
– *From the Stevenson Collection, Lady Stair's House, Edinburgh.*

15. The family group and their servants on the verandah at Vailima, Samoa, 31st July 1892. The white people are: Joe Strong (Fanny Stevenson's son-in-law); Mary, the Australian maid; Mrs Margaret Stevenson; Lloyd Osbourne; R. L. and Fanny Stevenson; small Austin Strong; Belle Strong.
– *From the Stevenson Collection, Lady Stair's House, Edinburgh.*

16. Fanny Stevenson in 1893, at the age of fifty-three.
– *From the Stevenson Collection, Lady Stair's House, Edinburgh.*

17. In Sydney, 1893: Fanny and R. L. Stevenson; Belle Strong; Mrs Margaret Stevenson. The old lady is wearing her streamered white widow's cap, and Fanny a Mother Hubbard in South Sea style.
– *From the Mitchell Library, Sydney.*

18. R.L.S. dictating to his stepdaughter, Belle Strong, who acted as amanuensis, in the library at Vailima, Samoa. Engraving after a photograph.
– *From the Stevenson Collection, Lady Stair's House, Edinburgh.*

19. Fanny Stevenson and a native maid in the 'great hall' at Vailima, before the only fireplace in Samoa.
– *From the Stevenson Collection, Lady Stair's House, Edinburgh.*

20. Fanny Stevenson in old age. From the portrait by Mary Fairchild Low, 1912.

Another glimpse of Mrs Stevenson's intense eyes and extraordinary little hand.

– *From the Stevenson Collection, Lady Stair's House, Edinburgh.*

21. Fanny Stevenson's burial procession on Mt Vaea, Samoa, 1915.
Front row : her daughter Belle; Edward Salisbury Field, carrying the
small casket of ashes; Colonel Logan, the Administrator; Mrs Laulii
Willis.

– *From the Stevenson Collection, Lady Stair's House, Edinburgh.*

Edinburgh Infirmary. The sonnet was later revised and sharpened, but was still a brilliant portrait:

R.L.S.

Thin-legged! thin-chested! slight unspeakably,
   Neat-footed and weak-fingered; in his face –
   Lean, large-boned, curved of beak, and touched
     with race,
Bold-lipped, rich-tinted, mutable as the sea,
The brown eyes radiant with vivacity –
   There shines a brilliant and romantic grace,
   A spirit intense and rare, with trace on trace
Of passion, impudence and energy.
Valiant in velvet, light in ragged luck,
   Most vain, most generous, sternly critical,
   Buffoon and poet, lover and sensualist;
   A deal of Ariel, just a streak of Puck,
   Much Antony, of Hamlet most of all,
   And something of the Shorter-Catechist.

Part 9

Cruising in the South Seas 1888-90

Chapter I
Fanny charters a yacht

Meanwhile in California Fanny had been seeing her former circle:
the widowed Dora Williams; John Lloyd and Timothy Rearden, both
married and rising in their careers; her sisters Cora and Nellie and
their families; old Jules Simoneau in Monterey; and the others.

One morning in San Francisco, Paulie Osbourne, Sam's broken
little wife – or widow – came to see Fanny, and stayed to lunch. Once
pretty in Fanny's own way, she was deaf, lonely, very poor and, in
her own word, 'notorious'. According to Nellie, who heard the
story from her sister (though Belle discounted it), Paulie had fallen
on her knees before her predecessor and burst into bitter weeping,
saying, 'You were right about that man and I was wrong!' Fanny wrote
Louis, 'I can't tell you how sorry I felt for the poor, simple, innocent
creature. . . . Imagine how humble I felt in my good fortune when
I sat side by side with that poor woman whose case might have been
mine – but for you. . . . God bless you, my dear Louis, and my love
to all not forgetting a poor little foreign girl [Valentine], who I hope
is not feeling too foreign. Tell her that all that is dearest to me I have
left in her hands; that I place my trust in her. Ever yours, Fanny.'

'If Fanny can find us a yacht in San Francisco,' Maggie Stevenson
had written from New York to her sister, 'we *may* go and sail about
the Pacific next winter.'

Will Low recalled in his memoirs that he had been lunching with the party one May day at the shady white inn at Manasquan, when a telegram was brought to Louis. He uttered an exclamation and then tossed the yellow paper across the table to his mother. 'Read that aloud', he told her.

The message said: 'Can secure splendid seagoing schooner-yacht *Casco* for seven hundred and fifty a month with most comfortable accommodation for six aft and six forward. Can be ready for sea in ten days. Reply immediately. Fanny.'

While the telegraph boy waited, Louis dashed off his answer: 'Blessed girl, take the yacht and expect us in ten days.'

Since Louis and Fanny had left California as squatters, it seemed – and was – a wild extravagance to be chartering a luxury yacht. He had already written Baxter for two of the three thousand pounds which his father had bequeathed to him, on a desperate gamble for life. 'If I cannot get my health back (more or less),' he wrote, ''tis madness. . . .' If all went well, however, he would prosper from the ten thousand dollars offered by McClure for a series of letters. (In fact his tragic end seemed so likely that the captain privately stowed away all the proper equipment for a burial at sea.)

The yachting dream-come-true was a godsend for Stevenson's depression. In his invalidism he had had too much time to brood about the quarrel. 'Low,' he told his friend, 'I want to live!' He was calm again when he wrote to his wife in mid May:

'My Dearest Fellow, This will not reach you till some time after our wedding day, which as usual has taken me aback; but I mean to send a despatch on the day itself, and this is for dessert. Not that I think so much of that day; if I had some other dates, I could think more of them; but of the day when I looked through the window [at Grez], or the day when I came to see you in Paris after the first absence, for example. But the marriage day we know, and it was a mighty good day for me; for you, I wish I was sure. It would have been better, if my health had been so, that I do believe. The longer I go on, the more I think the worst of me is my health. "The longer you live the more you come to see the truth of the old adage – ". My dear,

if I had the date of the day when you said that, I would think more of
it, God bless you! . . .'

Fanny and Lloyd 'dashed madly about outfitting the *Casco*',
wrote Belle in her memoirs. The yacht was a graceful fore and aft
schooner of seventy tons, ninety-five feet long, with 'lofty masts,
white sails and decks and gleaming brasswork'. The foragers laid in
seven months' supplies for the cruise, with rations for eleven persons
and hundreds of small gifts for the islanders along the way. Lloyd
had a fine new camera.

'My brother Lloyd was twenty then,' observed Belle, 'and very
English in speech and manner. I tried to see in this six-foot stranger
with the lean intellectual face and eye-glasses, the little tow-headed
brother I had parted with eight years before. . . . His witty talk, his
fine manners and his unusually musical voice made a deep impression
on me.'

On Belle's advice Fanny, Aunt Maggie and Valentine each ordered,
from one Yee Lee of Chinatown, a wardrobe of the tropical garments of cool lawn or muslin popularized by the missionaries in
Hawaii and elsewhere. These consisted of a *holoku* or Mother
Hubbard – a long loose gown flowing waistless from a yoke; and
underneath, a *muumuu*, a straight full chemise or nightdress with a
flounce around the hem. Aunt Maggie pronounced herself 'a queer-
looking customer'. Fanny doubly welcomed these odd gowns
because they made it unnecessary to wear corsets; she adopted them
more or less for the rest of her life.

Belle was apparently rather unsettled by the advent of the Stevensons, who now seemed respectable and prosperous. Her own life was
bedevilled by the instability and heavy drinking of Joe Strong;
Fanny was disturbed about her.

Again there were dismayed letters from the literary friends in
Britain as R.L.S. vanished even farther over the rim of the world.
Most disapproved. But Henry James wrote, '. . . This is a selfish
personal cry. I wish you back. . . . The beautiful portrait of your
wife shimmers at me from my chimney-piece. . . . I wish I could
make you homesick – I wish I could spoil your fun.'

The party embarked on 26th June, and the *Casco*, drawn by tugs,
was anchored at the sea wall under Telegraph Hill. Ferry boats
hooted, steamers blew their sirens. The cabin was crowded with

fruit and flowers, friends and reporters. Louis and Fanny gave a farewell party in the evening, expecting to sail the next afternoon. But there were several delays. At 5 a.m., waved away from the wharf by Belle and Dora, a tug finally towed the yacht outside the Golden Gate into the big ground swell, bound sharp south-south-west across three thousand miles of open sea for the Marquesas.

The delay of the departure had been a strain for the mother on board and the daughter on shore. Belle had managed to send out a farewell note with the tug, which brought back an answering letter from the surprised and touched Fanny. The daughter's note must have been a *cri de cœur*, for her mother replied, 'My poor little soul. . . . I feel sick at heart when I think of you. Get away as soon as you can, my dear. There is nothing else you can do, and the sooner you go the better. . . .'

Belle answered with a message, '. . . the letter she sent back to me with the tug tell her I will keep for the rest of my life.'

Chapter II
Sailing among the ex-cannibal isles

The *Casco* was undermanned and oddly crewed. There were four deck-hands – two Swedes, a Russian and a Finn – and a Chinese steward-cook who chose to pass himself off as Japanese. Valentine acted as cabin boy. None of the crew was efficient. The American captain was the only man skilful enough to steer in storms, and his fierce temper vented itself on the men until Stevenson wrote that once if he had not been on deck at 3 a.m. there might have been a murder. The skipper's snorts were also directed at his unwelcome passengers. (He later became the model for Nares in *The Wrecker*.)

Even R.L.S. was unable to come to meals for the first two rough days, while Fanny, Lloyd and Valentine kept to their bunks for three. Maggie Stevenson, like her son, triumphed with perfect sea-legs. Louis grew better and better as the weather became warmer and the sky bluer. Soon he and Lloyd were in singlet and trousers, Fanny and

Valentine in *muumuu* and *holoku* – a relief which Mrs Stevenson was 'putting off as long as I can'. She went so far as to wear boots without stockings while the others were barefoot. 'We are all painfully burned by the sun', her diary reported.

Fanny annoyed Captain Otis by chatting with the steersman. Whenever it was at all stormy he rebuked her by saying cynically, 'Please don't talk to him today, Mrs Stevenson. *Today* I want him to steer'.

Then, and for the next two years of cruising, she was seldom less than half seasick. But she gradually gained even Captain Otis's esteem by improving the chef's cooking, doctoring the crew and mending their clothes.

Stevenson rose early to write. There was breakfast at eight, lunch at twelve, dinner at five. Then they were all on deck for the sunset, 'the great spectacle of the day', and the coming of the night with its 'brilliant phosphorescent water, the air mild'. After dark they played cards, and then put out the lamps to cool the cabin before bedtime.

Though the Pacific was magnificent, Louis wrote that halfway across they were close to hurricane weather, and 'every day for a week or so . . . we have had from three to four squalls. . . . Sailing a ship, even in these so-called fine weather latitudes, may be compared to walking the tight-rope. . . .' The women gained the skipper's dudgeon because they had not taken him seriously about remembering to keep the deadlights closed. A sudden squall, from an innocent-looking cloud, 'fell like an armed man upon the *Casco*. Next moment, the inhabitants of the cabin were piled one upon another, the sea pouring into the cockpit, and spouting in fountains through the forgotten deadlights. . .'. The whole ship might well have been flooded. It took a long time to dry out the cabins.

After a month with only ocean and sky, the seasick Fanny was thrilled by Louis's call of 'Land!' at 5 a.m. on 28th July. Here was Nukahiva, the island of Melville's *Typee*, one of the French-owned Marquesas, where they were to spend six weeks. The natives had until very recently been 'the most inveterate cannibals of Polynesia'.

Anaho Bay was a collection of grass shacks, a few trading stores and one white man, a German merchant. He hurried out in a canoe with the chief, a fine tall man in white linen trousers and coat who loved to shake hands. Soon followed a larger boat with six or seven islanders, bringing coconuts, oranges, bananas and baskets for sale. 'They were', wrote Aunt Maggie, 'in every state of undress. The display of legs was something we were not accustomed to; but as they were all tattooed in most wonderful patterns, it really looked quite as if they were wearing open-work silk tights.'

Meanwhile, the chief, Captain Otis, Louis and Lloyd went ashore, and fourteen natives swarmed over the deck. 'We women were a little frightened.' They had heard the South Sea tales of avid islanders who like locusts had stripped vessels bare. However, the white women bore themselves with polite dignity, and soon the visitors were impressed with the idea that this was the vessel of a rich gentleman with his family, not a verminous trading schooner. There, as later in other archipelagos, Louis was called Ona, a transliteration of Owner.

Lloyd was known as 'the young man with glass in his eyes'. His gold *pince-nez* spectacles with the thick lenses were to furnish him with nicknames in a series of dialects. Later there came aboard an older chief, who was entranced by his typewriter. He insisted on pecking out his own and his family's names with one plump finger, and taking each piece of paper to the bearer as a souvenir. 'He looked such a mild and benevolent old gentleman', wrote Mrs Stevenson, 'that it is difficult to believe he was till quite recently a cannibal. Now he has a large European house.'

Louis, already at an advantage with his fluent French, began at once to use his flair for learning the words and signs of the native languages. The villagers put on a show of dancing, in which many steps reminded the Stevensons of a Highland reel. In turn a boatload of women was invited aboard, headed by the chief's dignified wife. Ecstatic over the luxuries of the yacht, they postured before the mirrors and fingered the velvets and brass. One belle hoisted up her *holoku* and rubbed her bare tattooed backside against the crimson cushions.

The *Casco* ladies were dressed exactly the same as the island women, in Mother Hubbards and (except Aunt Maggie) bare feet on deck. Fanny, with her dark cropped curly hair and chain-smoked cigarettes, was less conspicuous in the exotic South Seas than in Europe or America.

Wrote Will Low: 'In the photographs sent back from the cruise of the *Casco* . . . it is indescribably touching to see, where all the others of their party are seated on the ground and in a sense indistinguishable from their savage hosts, the demure Scots lady, seated erect in a chair, wherever procurable, spick and span, as though newly issued from her Edinburgh home for an afternoon visit to a friend of her own social rank, and coiffed by the widow's cap which became her so well. This cap she carried, I have been told, even on journeys in an open boat around the islands, in a box, ready to don on the first occasion of ceremony. . . .' In fact she had a big boxful of the white caps, so there was always a fresh one with its long organdie streamers immaculately washed and ironed.

For the dangerous inter-island voyaging ahead the captain took on a mate who knew the waters intimately. He was a garrulous Pole who 'talks all the time', and who also spoke Kanaka. The pseudo-Japanese cook had turned out to be a rascal. In his place they were lucky to employ a 'treasure' who was to stay with the Stevensons for two years. Ah Fu had been brought to the Marquesas as a little Chinese bond-boy among a shipload of coolie labourers for the plantations. He grew up tall and strong, abandoned the queue – usually for a flower over the ear – and no longer looked like a Chinese, though his speech combined oriental and South-Sea pidgin English, often profane. He soon became an ardent disciple of Fanny, and with his Chinese flair for cooking – like that of the French – his skill grew under her tuition, though he was rather uncouth as a steward.

After six weeks in the Marquesas they daringly set out for the Paumotus, on the way to Tahiti. The *Casco* was frail for such perilous sailing, but the party wanted to risk it. Once they were lost for a night and half a day. One sunrise they woke to see the yacht heading straight for a big atoll which lay thirty miles off course, and the master and crew had to leap to the ropes and sails barely in time. In a flooding squall even Louis helped, 'judging the possibility of haemorrhage better than the certainty of drowning'.

Finally, after five days at sea, they lay off the official village in the lagoon of Fakarava, the main atoll, a horse-shoe island some eighty miles long and only a couple of hundred feet wide. They anchored opposite the French Residency, but Louis found the sheltered heat oppressive. So they rented a crude little frame cottage on the beach for several weeks. The island, wrote Fanny in her notes, 'lay so little above the sea level that one had a sense of insecurity . . .; the waves had recently swept over the narrow strip of coral during a storm . . .'.

Rising at dawn each day, they walked straight into the warm shallow lagoon for a bath, and cooked their breakfast on a battered American stove which Fanny had picked up on the beach. In the morning they gathered shells on the leeward side and, after lunch and a siesta, more shells on the windward. Louis exulted to Colvin, '. . . I am in for hours wading over the knees for shells. . . .'

After the sultry heat of the day, the sunset brought a gentle breeze. 'It was the time of the moon,' wrote Fanny, 'and the shadows that fell from the coconut leaves were so sharply defined that one involuntarily stepped over them.' They had a simple dinner and a dip in the lagoon and then sat on mattresses on the moonlit veranda, with the only chair reserved for 'our invariable visitor'. Though the pearl-fishing season brought a few French schooners, at the time there was only one European on the island, M. Donat, the half-caste Vice-Resident. '. . . Night after night we sat entranced at his feet, thrilled by stories of Tahiti and the Paumotus, always of a supernatural character. . . .' The occult, of course, was to Fanny's taste. 'I remember one of the stories was of the return of the soul of a dead child, the soul being wrapped in a leaf and dropped in at the door of the sorrowing parents. . . .'

But now, ominously, Louis caught a cold and was forced to take to his bed. There was no doctor nearer than Tahiti, several days' sail away. Fanny bundled him back to the *Casco* and ordered Captain Otis to sail at once. With thundery weather in the offing, he refused. She raged at him, but he would not risk grounding his beautiful yacht on some coral reef. Fortunately the next morning dawned in perfect weather, and the sails were hoisted without delay.

Chapter III
Barefoot in Tahiti

After heading south-west for several days, the *Casco* made Tahiti and
anchored off Papeete, the main town of the Society Islands. Stevenson was very ill, and Fanny waited for the familiar haemorrhage
which the French doctor forecast.

Quietly Louis sent for Captain Otis and, smoking a cigarette,
gave him simple precise orders about what to do with the ship and
the charter if he died. The cynical skipper had gradually come round
to respecting his unwelcome passengers. Now he really liked R.L.S.
at last. Mrs Louis too, as he told friends, he found brave, capable and
devoted. Stevenson also handed Lloyd a sealed letter to be opened in
the event of his death.

On Tahiti the party revelled again in the beauty of the 'high
islands', with the rich tropical mountains sweeping up to bare peaks
striped with waterfalls above the glades of coco palms along the
lagoon. The French town was shoddy, however – 'a sort of halfway
house between savage life and civilization', said Margaret Stevenson.
The party took rooms at the Hôtel de France, but found it cramped
and noisy. So Louis and Fanny moved into 'a little bare one-
twentieth-furnished house, surrounded by mangoes, etc.' near the
old prison where Melville had languished.

Stevenson's feverish cough improved very little, and he and Fanny
were depressed by the heavy air and beachcombing atmosphere of
Papeete – which he later used in *The Ebb Tide*. He was too ill to go out
or to write, though they received the half-caste leaders of society and
toiled at their correspondence for their first mail since San Francisco.

After much heart-searching, since it meant leaving the rather poor
doctors, Fanny made up her mind to take her husband to the other
side of the island. Their principal doctor, fearing that Louis might
be in danger of dying at any time, gave Fanny an emergency phial of
medicine. For three years she carried it about continually, sewn into
her dress.

Most of the *Casco*'s crew had been replaced, because of drunken-
ness or illness, with others almost as inept, but they sailed with a
pilot to Taravao on the south shore.

Taravao was humidly hot and full of mosquitoes, and Louis was now so ill that Fanny was desperate to get him into a more airy spot. She sought what she described to Colvin as 'the largest native village and the most wild'. This proved to be Tautira, on the far opposite end of the island from Papeete. The problem was overland transport for the invalid. Louis and the captain were directed to a surly Chinese who had a wagon and horses, but he refused to hire them out to these suspicious foreigners. No other vehicle was available. So the Vandegrifter set her firm chin. Accompanied by Valentine, she ventured off on foot along a bush trail towards the overgrown shanty of the Chinese. The two women were gone for hours. Speaking neither Chinese, Tahitian nor French (probably Valentine interpreted in pidgin French), she somehow persuaded the owner to yield the full use of his wagon and team.

Meanwhile Captain Otis found that the *Casco*'s jib-boom was sprung, so he remained at Taravao to have it spliced, arranging to sail the yacht around to Tautira later.

The next day the family jogged over the sixteen-mile road, which was crossed by twenty-one streams. Stevenson rode in the wagon, tenderly nursed by Fanny and Valentine and 'sustained by small doses of coca'. The jolting exhausted him, but he managed to hold on until they reached their destination before he collapsed.

Tautira was the picturesque ideal of a South Sea village. Set among elegant fern forests beside the lagoon, it was a cluster of 'bird-cage' houses placed on neat lawns under the coconut palms. Fanny delighted in its 'wildness'. The only two white people were the French gendarme and Père Bruno, a Dutch priest who had forgotten his own language.

Fanny's first act was to rent one of the 'bird-cages', though at an exorbitant cost. For some days, she told Colvin, Louis lay 'in a deep stupor . . . suffering from congestion of the lungs and in a burning fever'. He had eaten nothing. She was gravely worried at her responsibility in having brought him here, cut off from civilization. 'Crushed, I was gazing over the village green, when I saw a tall graceful native woman entering the house of [Areia] the chief of Tautira, amid the acclamations of a great crowd. I remembered that they were expecting Moë, the "great Princess".'

Half an hour later there was a tap on the door and there stood Moë with a plate in her hand. It contained fresh white mullet cut in small strips, soaked in sea water, with a *miti* sauce of coconut milk, lime juice and specks of wild red pepper. The acid of the lime juice 'cooked' the raw fish and made it curl up.

'Speaking perfect English, she told me she had heard that there was a sick foreigner in the village . . . so she had made this dish herself. At first Louis turned his head wearily, but at her advice I slipped a piece between his lips. He opened his eyes and asked, "What's that?"'

'Several times a day the princess came with her plate, [the fish] soon eagerly watched for and devoured by my invalid, and in a week Louis was so far recovered as to walk over to the chief's house, where we took up our abode with him and Moë.'

Fanny wrote home that she felt that Moë had saved Louis's life. To Colvin she added, '. . . I shall never cease to be thankful for my courage, for he has gained health and strength every day. He takes sea baths and swims and lives almost entirely in the open air as nearly without clothes as possible, a simple pyjama suit of striped light flannel his only dress. As to shoes and stockings we all have scorned them for months except Mrs Stevenson.'

The house, locally a 'palace', belonged to the sub-chief, Ori. '. . . Ori is . . . the very finest specimen of the native we have yet seen . . . more like a Roman Emperor in bronze. . . .' A Christian, he spoke good French and fair English, and was 'feared, respected and loved'.

Meanwhile the *Casco* had sailed beautifully into the lagoon, greatly enhancing the 'face' of the party. Louis was again given the title of Ona – Owner. Fanny became known by transliteration as Tapena Tutu because of her boasted descent from Captain Cook.

Her mother-in-law gave a pious party on board for thirty *holoku*-clad women and three children, bearing gifts. They filled the cockpit and sat on rows of chairs outside, sang hymns and made speeches. One woman rose and intoned a prayer for the safety of the ship at sea, 'praying especially that if anything were wrong it might be discovered in time'. Captain Otis sniffed; Mrs Stevenson had been trying in vain to get him to go to church at all the ports where the yacht had called.

Later, when he was inspecting his cherished vessel, he noticed that the main-topmast was sprung. To his – and the whole party's – horror, the spars turned out to be hollow with dry rot. It was a miracle of luck that, in any of their many storms and squalls, the topmast had not cracked off, probably resulting in a loss of all on board. Afterwards Mrs Stevenson triumphantly embarrassed the captain by telling the moral tale even at dinner parties.

There was no choice but to delay. Instead of cruising to Honolulu, Captain Otis had to risk sailing his precarious ship gingerly around the island to Papeete for repairs, while his passengers waited at Tautira – for two weeks, as they thought.

Louis worked well on *The Master of Ballantrae*. In odd hours he blew tunes on his flageolet. He studied Tahitian and collected songs and legends. Moë arranged for exhibitions of singing and dancing to be performed for the visitors in the 'speak-house', or village hall. Lloyd wrote and took photographs.

Everyone went sea-bathing daily. The villagers swam in the river, *en masse*, wearing *pareus*. The children climbed into high trees and 'threw themselves down into the water like ripe fruit dropping'.

'. . . Ori, assuming the duties of a brother,' recorded Fanny, 'took charge of the sack containing our money . . . mostly half and quarter dollars. To Ori the sum seemed a vast fortune, and we, spendthrifts. . . . I remember once asking him for a quarter to pay for a chicken I had bought on credit while he was gone to a distant valley. He spoke to me with much severity, showing me the great bunch of cooking bananas he had carried on his shoulder all that distance for our sustenance.' After that, she 'asked permission before venturing on any foolish extravagance'.

Valentine tried to cook fish in the Polynesian style in an outdoor oven of hot stones underground, but gave up and returned to the small oil-stove which Fanny always carried with them. After several weeks, however, when the *Casco* did not return, the party became deeply worried: there was almost no food left to cook. Their money too was nearly gone; Ori doled it out to them in driblets. Day by day they strained their eyes from the beach for the sail of the *Casco*.

'For over a month we had lived in Ori's house . . .' wrote Fanny. '. . . Areia went to Papeete and came back with a letter saying more work had to be done on the *Casco*. . . . We were playing cards on the floor, as usual, when this message came, and you can imagine the effect. . . . I burst into tears, upon which the princess wept bitterly. . . . Then Ori said . . . with serious dignity, "You are my brother: all that I have is yours. I know that your food is done, but I can give you plenty of fish and taro. We like you and wish to have you here. Stay where you are till the *Casco* comes. Be happy – *et ne pleurez pas*." ' And then Louis too was in tears.

For several weeks the family lived almost entirely on native food. Their favourite dish was *poi-poi* (a sort of porridge of pounded taro-root) with coconut cream. With his affinity for South Sea life Louis did not tire of fish and *poi* and pig, but Fanny and the others began to pine for European fare.

High winds at sea and flooded rivers prevented any contact with Papeete. There was no word of the *Casco*. Finally, against the anxious protests of the Stevensons, Ori insisted on sailing around to the capital with a crew of three to find out the cause of the delay, though there was still 'a raging sea and a storming wind'. He was a week overdue in returning, 'which made us heart-sick', Fanny wrote home. Then he brought back the money and provisions, with a letter from Captain Otis saying when to expect him.

'Amongst the food was a basket of champagne. The next day we gave a commemoration dinner to Ori, when we produced the champagne.' Ori announced that he would have this 'drink for kings' every day, until he asked the cost – when he poured back his refilled glass into the bottle.

Meanwhile in Papeete the captain had found a beachcomber who had been a ship's carpenter, and bought the spars from a wrecked barque. He agreed to an exorbitant charge in return for a speedy job, but he did not allow for the lotus-eating of the South Seas. It was five weeks before he could sail back to his stranded passengers.

Ori gave them a farewell banquet. He 'had such respect for Fanny's cooking powers', wrote Maggie Stevenson, 'that he insisted she should prepare the feast; so she stuffed and cooked a pair of fowls, two roast pigs, and made a pudding.'

After two months' stay, the party sailed on Christmas Day, with hosts and guests alike in heartfelt tears. Captain Otis fired thirteen shots from his rifle and dipped the ensign. Then the *Casco* was off at last to the Hawaiian Islands – still sometimes called the Sandwiches.

Chapter IV
Welcome to Honolulu

The *Casco* took thirty long days to reach Honolulu. 'Our voyage
up here was most disastrous,' Louis wrote to Bob; 'calms, squalls,
head sea, waterspouts of rain, hurricane weather all about . . . we
ran out of food. . . .' Mother Stevenson and her Lou seemed
maddeningly lively to the nauseated Fanny.

When a hurricane breathed hard astern, Captain Otis faced the
dilemma of lying-to and hoping to ride it out with his rickety mast,
or saving time by risking a run before the wind, which might mean
being swamped by a following sea. He stated the equal dangers to
Louis, who again impressed him by saying, 'Run for it'. The hands
were lashed on deck, the best helmsman at the wheel, the passengers
forbidden to leave the cabin, though Louis and Lloyd could not
resist peeping out. Up and down swooped the little white yacht
between the precipices of foam. Once even the pumps ceased
working.

The winds were fiercest of all on the very day when Hawaii was
sighted beyond the fifteen-foot waves. Then, however, the vessel
was becalmed. Even Fanny's culinary skill had no provision with
which to improvise. 'Thirty days of decayed beef and stale biscuits
reduced us to a state of semi-starvation', while the three chain-
smokers ran out of their cherished black tobacco. 'We were nearly a
week hanging about the Hawaiian group', reported Lloyd in a
memoir, 'drifting here and there with different faint slants of
wind. . . . It was a strange experience to see the distant lights of
Honolulu, and then go to bed hungry; to rise again in the morning
and find ourselves, not nearer, but farther off. . . .'

'I have the introspective horrors on me when I think of the
liabilities I incurred . . .' added Louis to Bob. 'My extremely fool-
hardy venture is practically over . . . indeed the cruise might have
cost me double. . . .'

'As for myself,' Fanny wrote to Mrs Sitwell, 'I have had more
cares than I was really fit for. To keep house on a yacht is no easy
thing. When Louis and I broke loose from the ship and lived alone
among the natives I got on very well. It was when I was deathly

seasick, and the question was put to me by the cook, "What shall we have for the cabin dinner, what for tomorrow's breakfast, what for lunch? and what about the sailors' food? Please come and look at the biscuits, for the weevils have got into them, and show me how to make yeast that will rise of itself, and smell the pork which seems pretty high, and give me directions about making a pudding with molasses – and what is to be done about the bugs?" – etc., etc. In the midst of heavy dangerous weather, when I was lying on the floor clutching a basin, down comes the mate with a cracked head, and I must needs cut off the hair matted with blood, wash and dress the wound, and administer restoratives. I do not like being "the lady of the yacht", but ashore – O, then I feel I am repaid for all! . . .'

Long overdue in Honolulu, the *Casco* had been given up for lost. Belle's friends had ceased to speak to her about the yacht 'as a deadly subject'. Then when news came that it was sighted she and Austin dashed out to meet the travellers. 'The *Casco*, all sails set, came flying around Diamond Head at full speed', she wrote in her memoirs. 'Austin and I were in a little open boat directly in her path. Why we were not run down is a mystery. . . . In the midst of shouts and screams we were scooped out of our boat and found ourselves sprawling on the deck, Louis and Lloyd laughing as they helped us to our feet, Aunt Maggie looking on with amusement while mother scolded us roundly for being such idiots.'

She found her mother touchingly relieved, not only because Louis was so much better, but also because the dreaded growth in her throat had not returned.

Belle's popularity had prepared a colourful niche for the Stevensons among the 'royal set' in Honolulu, where her fortunes had been full of sun and shadow. Her admiring patron, King Kalakaua, was tall, broad, stately, moustached, well-educated, hard-drinking, and deeply interested in native lore and arts. He wore immaculate white suits and straw hats with a band woven of the white stems of peacock feathers; or operetta-like uniforms on state occasions. He was known as 'The First Gentleman of the Pacific'. When he returned from his round-the-world trip to visit foreign royalties, including Queen Victoria at her Jubilee, he had modelled his little subtropic capital on

European courts. It had an opera house with red velvet, gilt, electric light, Italianate scenery and a royal box. Honolulu actually had a telephone system – long ahead of more sophisticated cities. His Majesty was the centre of elegant riding picnics, court banquets and balls, and parties on visiting men-of-war. The Strongs had been invited to the handsome coronation and its evening ball in the palace gardens. There they had met all the island aristocracy – brown, white, oriental or half-caste – in magnificent costumes, the ladies with trains, bustles, jewels and feathers.

Joe seemed to prosper for a time, and his vivacious wife took part in theatricals and taught drawing in the government schools. The king commissioned her to design the Hawaiian flag, the royal seals, and the star of the Royal Order of Oceania – of which he made her a Lady Companion.

At home, Austin sat in his little rocking-chair under a big *hau* tree, while Hawaiian passers-by often leaned over the paling fence to drop a *lei* around the child's neck or thrust a spray of fragrant ginger flowers between the slats.

In time a baby brother arrived and was given the ill-fated name of Hervey. When he was eleven months old the family went to the island of Maui to visit the McKees, who owned a splendid sugar plantation between the extinct volcano Haleakala and the sea. The laughing baby, with his curly hair and rosy cheeks, lay with his Portuguese nurse on a tarpaulin under a big tamarind tree in the lush terraced gardens and held court among the Hawaiian retainers.

One morning Belle was alarmed to notice his 'drooping head and languid eyes'. A servant was sent around the island on a forty-mile ride for the doctor, who was delayed by the epidemic of dysentery (he himself died a few days later). He advised the anxious mother to let the child sleep.

'My baby slept, but he never woke again.'

Now Cassandra's early pessimism about her daughter's marriage was being fulfilled. The trouble with Joe was more than drink and parties.

One bright day he neglected his painting as usual and went out for a day's fishing on the coral reef off Waikiki Beach. His bare right arm became so swollen with sunburn that for weeks he was threatened with blood poisoning. He grew thin, pale and despairing; in constant pain, he could not work. He had a nervous breakdown. Belle nursed him and taught her art classes, until he was sent off to a sanatorium in the country.

'Some days later', she wrote in her book, 'it occurred to me that Joe's pistol shouldn't be left in its box. Opening it, I saw a mass of papers that had been carelessly thrown in. To my dismay I found they were unpaid bills. . . . What I earned myself I always gave to Joe, even the hundred a month I got for my teaching. If we had money, we spent it. . . . Now . . . I was appalled. . . .' They were behind with the rent and the grocer; there were bills – months old – for artist's materials, for carriage hire, for dinners at the hotel.

Belle urgently wrote to the Stevensons for help – which she received – and set herself to pay off the debts. She opened dancing classes for children. Kindly Honolulans gave her commissions to draw place-cards and caricatures. She also wrote the 'Society News' and occasional articles for *The Honolulu Advertiser*. Once a week she drove out in a borrowed carriage to visit her husband. Then came an alarming period when the doctors refused to let her see him. She was terrified for his sanity. But at last they sent for her. 'Mr Strong is waiting for you in the garden.'

In agitation she followed the doctor along the path. 'And there stood Joe, completely recovered in body and his mind at peace.'

Shortly before Joe's mother-in-law swept impressively into port with a smart yacht and a famous husband, King Kalakaua had sent young Strong to Samoa as official artist with a Hawaiian delegation. Its mission was a futile effort to establish a federation of the various Pacific archipelagos. The *opéra bouffe* embassy was a bibulous farce; but Joe's part, and the King's, were important in rousing the Stevensons' interest in Samoa.

Chapter V
The Stevensons and the King of Hawaii

Louis and Fanny had been waiting almost fearfully for an accumulation of mail in Honolulu – the first for many months – to find out
whether they were solvent or not. But – 'No money, and not one
word as to money!' Louis wrote to Baxter. '. . . which leaves me in a
fine uncertainty and quite penniless on these isles. . . .' However,
after many days of suspense and frustration a bundle of mail turned
up, bringing news that his works were selling well.

Polynesia tempted them with its promise of health and experience.
They therefore planned tentatively to remain for a few months in the
Pacific where Stevenson could work hard until it was warm enough
to return to Britain. So they paid off the *Casco* – an expensive deal –
and looked for a house.

The faithful Ah Fu had followed the family ashore to remain as
cook. He was still devoted to Fanny. Not so Valentine who, after
helping to settle her employers, abruptly took a steamer back to
California. Louis told Colvin that it was 'the usual tale of the maid
on board the yacht'. She took a job as housekeeper in a San Francisco
hotel, and married. Her only son was named Louis.

The Stevensons took a cottage, four miles out of Honolulu at
Waikiki, which was then a lazy scattering of twenty or thirty summer
houses among the coconut palms along the beach. A giant *hau* tree
marked for many decades this further Stevenson House. It was an
hour's drive from town to the end of the mule-car line. There, one
crossed a causeway and walked through a garden with pink oleander,
scarlet hibiscus and tall algaroba trees whose fallen thorns drew
yells of pain from the barefooted tenants. The Strongs came out every
weekend. Joe set up his easel and did more and better work in such
creative company, though he and his family were still largely supported by Stevenson.

The Master of Ballantrae had been published in England in
September, and Andrew Lang wrote in a review: '. . . Mr Stevenson
makes a gallant effort to enter what I have ventured to call the
capital of his kingdom; he does introduce a woman, and confronts
the problems of love as well as of fraternal hatred.' In the 1880s

Louis could not have gone far in detailing a woman's physical passion for her brother-in-law. Fanny was later blamed by hindsight for his enforced reticence – and probably she would have agreed at least in part with her contemporaries about what was then 'good taste'. Stevenson himself commented, 'I have never pleased myself with any woman of mine – except for two minor characters, Countess von Rosen in *Prince Otto* and Mme. Desprez in "The Treasure of Franchard".'

All Honolulu society flocked to call on the newcomers. The family admired the gentlemen, white or brown, dressed in white duck or flannel with bands of shells or peacock feathers on their straw hats. The ladies were elegant in morning attire of Mother Hubbards trimmed with lace or ruffles, under wide-brimmed hats with ostrich plumes and gay little parasols. In the afternoon they appeared in waspy European dresses, bowling along behind liveried coachmen. Smart riding parties in white linen reined up in front of the gate and sent in their cards. Fanny and Louis were driven to the expedient of having a regular 'day' when they 'received', to avoid continual callers.

Belle observed that 'Louis's guests always stayed on till my mother broke up the party. . . . At the first sign of fatigue on his face the guests departed, in spite of Louis's entreaties to stay. . . .'

'My wife is no great shakes', Louis wrote – as usual – to Baxter. 'She is the one who has suffered most. . . . I do not know myself – sea-bathing, if you please, and what is far more dangerous, entertaining and being entertained by His Majesty here, who is a very fine intelligent fellow, but O, Charles! what a crop for the drink! He carries it, too, like a mountain with a sparrow on its shoulder. We calculated five bottles of champagne in three hours and a half (afternoon), and the sovereign quite presentable, though perceptibly more dignified at the end.'

King Kalakaua had read *Treasure Island* and *Dr Jekyll and Mr Hyde* long before Belle's prompt presentation of her family at court. The Stevensons entertained the King and his sister, Princess Liliuokalani, at a party with much champagne on board the *Casco* before it was sent back to San Francisco. His Majesty reciprocated by asking the family to a breakfast at Iolani Palace, stone-built in European style. They were regaled by the music of the Royal

Hawaiian Band, under its German bandmaster. When the King asked Aunt Maggie how she liked it, she replied that it was very nice and didn't disturb her in the least.

Thereafter the monarch often dropped in at Manuia Lanai, followed by his chamberlain carrying a load of books. He loved to talk to R.L.S. about the South Seas, and tell him of Hawaiian history and archaeology. Through his influence Louis took lessons in the native language, and the King tried hard to persuade the Stevensons to settle in the kingdom. ('He son-of-gun fine fella', Ah Fu approved.)

The Missionary Set and some of the rich plantation clique were trying to oust the monarchy and make Hawaii an annexation of the United States. The Stevensons felt this an injustice, and Louis began to meddle on behalf of the kingdom – going off half-cocked in letters and articles for the British press, with an inexperienced haste which was to prejudice his later and more seasoned writings on Polynesian affairs.

Furthermore, Fanny wrote to Colvin about an argument over her husband's book on the South Seas. 'I am very much exercised by one thing. Louis has the most enchanting material that any one ever had in the whole world for his book, and I am afraid he is going to spoil it all. He has taken into his Scotch-Stevenson head that a stern duty lies before him, and that his book must be a sort of scientific and historical, impersonal thing, comparing the different languages (of which he knows nothing really) and the different peoples. . . . Think of a small treatise on the Polynesian races being offered to people who are dying to hear about Ori à Ori, the "making of brothers" with cannibals, the strange stories they told, and the extraordinary adventures that befell us!' And the good wife added, 'Louis says it is a stern sense of duty that is at the bottom of it, which is more alarming than anything else. . . . I am going to ask you to throw the weight of your influence as heavily as possible in the scales with me. . . . What a thing it is to have a man of genius to deal with! It is like managing an overbred horse! Why, with my own feeble hand I could write a book that the whole world would jump at. . . .'

At home Colvin expressed to Baxter his disapproval of R.L.S.'s life in the South Seas, his 'drinking with dusky majesties' and his 'isolation from anything like equals'. He went so far as to tut-tut at 'the presence of Bell [sic], a really degrading connection. . .'.

After Mother Stevenson sailed for Scotland in the spring her son wrote to her, 'Joe's debts are getting thinner'. But though young Strong was talented, winsome and affectionate, Louis and Fanny were repeatedly driven to the breaking-point by his unreliability and self-indulgence, with drink and with opium which he got from the Chinese. Belle's nerves were worn. She had not fully lost her inner resentment of her mother's remarriage and was much more ready to accept her stepfather's money than his guidance, even about Joe.

With so much social life the Stevensons complained that they were seeing 'too many *haoles*', or white people. Louis needed more material for the McClure 'Letters'. So twice he went off for a week alone, once to the unspoilt windward shore, and again by overnight steamer to the Big Island named Hawaii. He stayed near the sleepy bay where his wife's ancestor Captain Cook had been massacred more than a century earlier, and got the backgrounds for two stories, 'The Bottle Imp' and 'The Isle of Voices'.

In May he went by special permission to the island of Molokai to visit the famous leper colony tended for many years by the Belgian priest Father Damien, who had just died of the disease. He wrote poignant letters to Fanny about his stay in 'this marred and moribund community, with its idleness, its furnished table, its horse-riding, music, and gallantries under the shadow of death'. He talked to the nuns and mingled with the patients, especially the children with their games and play.

At home on the *lanai* he told his enthralled family of his compassionate adventure. Belle recalled, 'When he spoke of shaking hands with the lepers and using their mallets when he played croquet with them, my mother said anxiously, "Oh, Louis, I hope you wore gloves!"

' "Of course not", he said. "The Sisters advised me to, but as they didn't, how could I?" '

Months afterwards they saw in a Sydney paper a letter from a Protestant clergyman in Hawaii attacking the late Father Damien's character and motives in the leper colony. Louis wrote a sizzling letter of defence and denunciation which he, as a lawyer, well knew to be libellous. It was reprinted in many parts of the world and published as a booklet. (The royalties were sent to Molokai.) He first read the letter to the assembled family, and asked if they would accept the probability of being poor again through ruinous libel suits. 'Throwing the manuscript on the table,' recorded Belle, 'he turned to his wife. She, who never failed him, rose to her feet and, holding out both hands to him in a gesture of enthusiasm, cried: "Print it! Publish it!" '

Luckily the clergyman, though offended – as were many other people in the strongly Protestant Kingdom of Hawaii – did not sue, and Louis later regretted his own ferocity.

Fanny, with her childhood bent for horror tales, wrote a short story with a leper background, 'The Half-White', which was published the next March in *Scribner's* magazine.

In the spring Louis had told his waiting friends that the party were not coming home for another year. 'I think it good for Fanny and Lloyd. . . . And even here in Honolulu I have withered in the cold', he wrote to Henry James, 'and this precious deep is filled with islands . . . and to draw near a new island, I cannot say how much I like. . . .'

James wrote back, 'This is really dreadful news, my dear Louis. . . . I miss you shockingly. . . . A wonderful, beautiful letter from your wife to Colvin seemed, a few months ago, to make it clear that *she* has no quarrel with your wild and wayward life'.

Fanny explained to Mrs Sitwell, . . . 'It seems a pity to return to England until [Louis's] health is firmly re-established, and also a pity not to see all that we can see quite easily. . . . Of course there is the usual risk from hostile natives, and the horrible sea, but a positive risk is so much more wholesome than a negative one, and it is all such joy to Louis and Lloyd. As for me, I hate the sea, and am afraid of it (though no one will believe that because in time of danger I do not make an outcry – nevertheless I *am* afraid of it, and it is not kind to me), but I love the tropic weather, and the wild people, and to see my two boys so happy. Mrs Stevenson is going back to Scotland in May, as she does not like to be longer away from her old sister who has been very ill. And besides, we do not feel justified in taking her to the sort of places we intend to visit. As for me, I can get comfort out of very rough surroundings for my people. I can work hard and enjoy it; I can even shoot pretty well, and though "I don't want to fight, by jingo if I must", why I can. . . .'

Louis even talked of buying an island of their own. And so in the spring they were again looking for some sort of transport among the Line Islands – near the Equator.

'One noonday', recalled Lloyd, 'R.L.S. came driving in from Honolulu, his horses in a lather . . . wildly excited. "I've chartered a schooner!" he shouted even before he jumped down, and we all crowded about him. . . . "I arranged the details and signed the charter-party as she was casting off. . . ." '

'She' was the *Equator*, sixty-four tons, and due back from San Francisco in a month to pick up the Stevensons for the Gilbert Islands. A new trading schooner, she would ply about in Micronesia, and while the captain loaded copra and bargained with the local chiefs for the merchandise in her trade room, the party could explore ashore. Louis paid a lump sum down for a four months' cruise with privilege of renewal, and with extra stops to be arranged at an added charge per day.

Ah Fu and Joe Strong were also included in the *Equator* party, the latter in the hope of getting him away from his weaknesses. But shortly before sailing Fanny confided to 'My dear ones' – Mrs Sitwell and Colvin – that she and her husband had had an 'unpleasantness' with Joe, 'who was driving about in carriages while Louis walked . . . just the usual thing that that sort of person (one that you always love, worse luck) invariably does. It ended by my forcing Louis's hand . . .; he explained to poor Joe with the brutal frankness that I advised that he was to spend no money without permission, that abject obedience . . . was to be expected from him. . . . Of course that ended Joe's connection with the cruise for the time.

'Late that evening he came back to us, I am pretty certain only to say goodbye to us before destroying himself. I never saw anyone appear to better advantage, dignified and sorrowful, and affectionate still. He thanked us for the kindness we had shown to one so unworthy, begged us to forgive him. He said he had had an opportunity to retrieve his life offered him . . . and he had wantonly thrown it away. And that, even, was not what he cared the most for, but the happiness of living with us as he had done for the last three months. With that he kissed us both and walked away. . . . Had he been maudlin and wept . . . or tried to defend himself, I should have still held out against him. Louis – I agreeing – went after him and offered him another chance. . . .

'Those who know him best, say that there will be no further trouble now. . . . No one can help loving the creature, yet I would push him on to his death sooner than he should harm Louis. . . . Then there are many things to the poor soul's credit. I fully expected that he would fly to what had been his solace in the past, either drink or opium, but he has kept away from both. He has signed a paper drawn up by a lawyer in terms so frank that Louis was shocked by them, placing himself and his affairs absolutely in Louis's hands, and binding himself to obedience. He is as sweet and affectionate as ever. . . . It was an ugly gulf he looked into that evening. . . . I cannot understand why such almost criminal weakness should go hand in hand with unfaltering courage. . . . I believed there was still a chance, and that only was why I bade Louis to call him back. . . .'

Belle wrote of her husband, 'After his illness he was never the same again. A man cannot go through that experience without bearing scars. He and I began to get on each other's nerves more and more, till it was a positive relief to see him sail away on the *Equator*. He was in good hands, enjoying a new adventure, and I felt that I didn't have to worry about him any more.'

She had expected to stay with her son Austin in Honolulu. He was too young for the schooner trip, and she could not bear to leave him in a boarding-school. 'One afternoon,' she wrote, 'only a week or two before they left, I was called to Louis' cottage where he and my mother were waiting for me. Then, as head of the family, Louis told me the plans that he had made for me, my mother agreeing to everything he said. I was to leave Honolulu by the next steamer. Tickets had been bought and a cabin engaged for Austin and me on the *Mariposa* to Sydney, Australia. When there, we were to put up at a boarding-house already chosen, and draw on Towne and Company, bankers, for a certain sum every month. "And what do I do then?" I asked. "Wait till called for", said Louis.

'. . . It was a stormy interview. . . . I loved Honolulu. I had many friends there, and I could earn my own living. . . . But nothing I said made any impression on either my mother or Louis. I know now that they had been told that my friends were altogether too lively and I'd be much better away from their influence.'

While the Stevensons were waiting in Honolulu, they were thrilled by the landing of a number of castaways who had been picked up on Midway Island from the wreck of the brigantine *Wandering Minstrel*, 'a mysterious vessel with a dubious errand', as Fanny wrote. The castaways had been desperate, but before helping them the captain of the rescuing ship first ascertained what money they had. He took the several thousand dollars from the crew's wages and all the captain's savings, and dumped them penniless in the nearest port, Honolulu. People there thought that something seemed 'fishy' – with the very high rate of the crew's pay, et cetera. Louis and Lloyd were fascinated by the speculation.

'. . . the *Equator*', Fanny wrote to Colvin, 'will come along in . . . June, lie outside the harbour here and signal to us. Within forty-eight hours we shall pack up our possessions, our barrel of sauerkraut, our barrel of salt onions, our bag of coconuts, our native garments, our tobacco, fish-hooks, red combs, and Turkey-red calicoes (all the latter for trading purposes), our hand organ, photograph and painting materials, and finally our magic lantern – all these upon a large whaleboat, and go out to the *Equator*.' Lloyd was also taking his taro-patch fiddle – a Hawaiian instrument not unlike a banjo – Louis his cherished flageolet, Joe his accordion, and Fanny her guitar – oddly, since she had no ear for music.

On 24th June 1889 *The Honolulu Advertiser* announced: 'Robert Louis Stevenson and party leave today by the schooner *Equator* for the Gilbert Islands. . . . It is to be hoped that Mr Stevenson will not fall victim to native spears; but in his present state of bodily health, perhaps the temptation to kill him may not be very strong.'

Chapter VI
Islanders amok

Fanny was the only woman among fifteen men on board the little
Equator. The trading schooner was new and clean, though over-
crowded and very uncomfortable. The captain had given the
Stevensons his cabin, where a second bunk was built for Fanny,
while two more new bunks were installed in the trade room for Lloyd
and Joe. The crew included a big Norwegian mate, a Finnish second
mate, a Russian former sea captain, a New Zealand parson's runaway
son as cook, and Ah Fu.

Captain Denis Reid, aged twenty-three, was described by Fanny as
'a small fiery Scotch-Irishman, full of amusing eccentricities, and
always a most gay and charming companion'. He was an expert
skipper and player of draughts. More Scottish than Louis himself,
he wore his national bonnet even on the torrid isles, and his sole but
unrelenting musical repertoire consisted of 'Annie Laurie' and 'In
the Gloaming'. He got on well with the Stevenson party from the
start.

They had a long run of brilliant days and moonlit nights, close to
the sea on the little low schooner, so that, Fanny said, 'we began to
feel that the sea belonged to us and we to the sea'. The fine weather
was a mercy for her seasickness, while Louis was more than ever in
love with the ocean life, he told Colvin, 'except for the expense'.
He now decided to make his home in the South Seas and buy a
schooner, 'half-yacht, half-trader, and wholly self-supporting'. Lloyd,
if not Fanny, was enchanted. They would pick the schooner up at
intervals for cruises, captained by Denis Reid. They eagerly planned
to ply among the Pacific islands, paying their way by selling the
usual cargo of sewing-machines, revolvers, calico and cheap trinkets
to the natives. The vessel was to be named the *Northern Light* and
the firm – probably – Jekyll, Hyde & Co. Reid said the schooner
would cost about fifteen thousand dollars.

Now and then the talk returned to the strange loss of the *Wandering
Minstrel*, whose survivors had intrigued the family in Honolulu.
Suddenly Louis and Lloyd had the idea of collaborating on a novel
to pay for the trading schooner – the tale of a sea captain who forced

some castaways to give him everything they owned for their rescue. 'One fine moonlight night,' wrote Fanny in an introduction, 'the fresh trade wind blowing in their faces, the two men sat late on deck, inventing the plot of *The Wrecker*. Louis decided to cut short his cruise, and charter the *Equator* to Samoa, where there was a good service of mail steamers, making serial publication of *The Wrecker* possible. We were to stop in Samoa until the $15,000 were earned and the schooner bought.'

They made landfall near the equator in the Gilberts, some sixteen low flat islands, all monotonous with coconut palms and pandanus on the sand. The flatness, however, enhanced the radiance of sky and clouds and sea. The dense population was of Micronesians – shorter, darker and more intense than the Polynesians, with black blood and a very different group of languages.

Captain Reid disembarked his passengers at Butaritari on the island of Great Makin, while the *Equator* went off here and there to collect copra in exchange for goods. Normally the crude little town, with its streets of thatched huts, was safe enough, but for the Stevensons this was probably the only time when they were in real danger ashore. (Louis described it in a chapter of *In the South Seas*).

Most of the missions and trading posts were American, and the natives took a bizarre way of celebrating the national Independence Day, 4th July. Some nine days before the Stevensons arrived the surly brutish King Tebureimoa had lifted the taboo on alcohol. The *Equator* visitors landed to find that he, his wives, his court and most of his subjects were wildly drunk. The two American traders were each afraid of refusing to sell him *din* (gin) and *paranti* (brandy) for fear that the other would profit; or, if they should both agree to close, that a fiendish mob of drunks would break into their bars.

The Hawaiian missionary Maka and his wife Mary were away at the time, and the Stevensons ventured to rent their comfortable little wooden bungalow. Thus obligated to the missionaries, they felt a constraint on their usual hobnobbing with the heathen – even any who were sober. They thought the bungalow would be a 'nice quiet place to write', but Louis did little work, for it was next to the Sans Souci bar. The trader finally closed the doors – which was worse than ever, for a crowd gathered round, fighting and yelling for drink.

The King was a sterner sabbatarian even than the absent Aunt Maggie for, though staggering drunk, he piously refused to let the travellers photograph him on a Sunday.

Twice a large stone was thrown at Louis as he sat on the veranda at dusk, just as the lamp was brought out and set beside his chair. There were often shots in the night. Many of the natives had fire-arms, and the King's bodyguard, almost unclad, were equipped with repeating rifles.

The Stevenson party brought revolvers ashore, along with the usual boxes of presents, and ostentatiously practised their marksman-ship on the beach. With so many empty bottles lying about, it was easy to set up a row of targets. Fanny took her turn in shooting at bottle after bottle. Ah Fu hovered about like a faithful watchdog to protect her.

The family agreed that she should not leave the bungalow grounds. But one quiet afternoon she ventured over to the 'weather side' to look for shells. There on the beach, to her unease, she was joined by a strange unkempt man and woman, each dressed in nothing but a dirty piece of old gunny-sack, their faces 'haggard and anxious'. They seized her by the arms and boldly marched her between them onto a narrow path which zigzagged through the heavy coconut woods. As she grimly submitted to being dragged along, the woman, with an appeasing air, paused and drew a clay pipe from 'an enorm-ous hole in her ear'. She stuffed it with strong coarse tobacco, lighted it, puffed a moment, and then tucked it into Fanny's grimacing mouth.

They emerged from the palms to see the town renewing its uproar, with the street in front of the bungalow filled with a 'howling, fight-ing, drunken mob'. She was incredulously relieved to find herself at her own door. Her captors held onto her until they were all safely on the small veranda. Then, to her amazement, the man fell on his knees and began to pray.

The rescuers, it turned out, were Gilbertese converts whom Louis nicknamed 'the baron and baroness'. They became hearty friends of the Stevensons.

Louis now entered upon a little diplomacy with the manager of the rival German trading firm, and persuaded him to stop selling drink to the islanders. Luckily the taboo was accepted, and the soreheaded villagers calmed down. Their sobriety came none too soon, for a day or two later a rival king arrived with a large following from Little Makin for a state visit. There might have been bloodshed; but instead the Stevensons saw a superb ceremonial exhibition of Micronesian singing and dancing.

After more than a month's absence the *Equator* reappeared and the party joined in the trading sorties from island to island.

Chapter VII
'The Napoleon of the Gilberts'

The Stevensons hoped to make their next long stay on Apemama, which interested them as the seat of King Tembinoka, a despot almost legendary in the Pacific. A conqueror in the island wars, he was known as 'the Napoleon of the Gilberts'. It was very doubtful if they could stay. The sovereign allowed no white man to live there except a raffish and cowering poor-white 'prime minister'. The one missionary had been permitted to remain until after he had taught the King an approximation of English, when, dabbling in the royal copra monopoly, he was kicked out. '*I* got *power!*' was His Majesty's well-known boast. He enforced it with crack marksmanship with a rifle, plus an armed bodyguard over his many wives. He was, wrote Fanny, 'an absolute monarch, who holds the lives of his subjects (our own also) in his hand'.

However, he loved Western merchandise. His thatched palace was known to overflow with old clocks, weapons, clothing and gadgets, gradually rusting and mildewing. He was always rowed out into the lagoon to meet any trading vessel – including the *Equator*.

Fanny reported the schooner in a commotion of scrubbing and scouring before he came aboard. The family waited in the cabin with seemly trepidation.

R.L.S. described the tall heavy monarch in *In the South Seas*: 'A beaked profile like Dante's in the mask, a mane of long black hair, the eye brilliant, imperious, and inquiring. . . . His voice matched it well, being shrill, powerful, and uncanny, with a note like a sea-bird's. Where there are no fashions, he dresses . . . "to his own heart". Now he wears a woman's frock, now a naval uniform, now . . . trousers and a singular jacket with shirt tails, the cut and fit wonderful for island workmanship, the material always handsome, sometimes green velvet, sometimes cardinal red silk. This masquerade becomes him admirably. . . .' He also appeared in frock coats, red flannel drawers, top hats and sunbonnets. Nevertheless, he was not ridiculous. He was interested in politics, history and the Western World. He wrote poetry which, as he told the delighted Louis, was 'about sweethearts, and trees, and the sea – and no true, all-the-same lie'.

When he boarded the *Equator* and loftily went shopping, his eye chanced to fall on Fanny's dressing-case and he stubbornly insisted on buying it. The Stevensons refused, until finally they said, 'Very well, take it as a gift'. When they held out in declining payment, he admitted, 'I shamed'.

This loss of royal face in the gift-giving etiquette of the South Seas greatly raised the status of the white chief and his wife. Louis was nicknamed 'Kaupoi' in the Gilberts, meaning the same as 'Ona' among the Polynesian groups. Tembinoka was impressed too – as all the islanders were – by the photograph of R.L.S. with King Kalakaua of Hawaii. But His Gilbertese Majesty was no easy conquest. He hesitated two days, to emphasize the favour of letting the travellers stay.

Ashore, he let them choose a pleasant place to live, near a turgid coral pool, and ordered his men to carry houses and set them up. 'An Apemama house', wrote Lloyd, 'is a sort of giant clothes basket . . . with a peaked roof, and standing on stilts about a yard high. With a dozen pairs of human legs under it, you can steer it to any spot you like. . . . We started with four such houses, forty-eight pairs of legs, and the King, Winchester in hand, firing in the direction – but over the head – of anyone who seemed backward. . . . We settled near a grove of palms, but not too near the falling coconuts. . . . Then a large shed came staggering in that was to serve as our dining-room; and a smaller shed by way of kitchen. . . .' The King finally walked a circle of taboo around the settlement, to ward off theft and inquisitiveness.

Millions of flies swarmed by day and mosquitoes at night. 'There was no escape', said Lloyd, 'outside your mosquito-net. . . . In desperation my mother made a net of prodigious size, a veritable house of mesh, which we hung in the dining-shed, and we not only took all our meals under it, but did all our writing as well. . . .'

The King offered Fanny a sewing-machine, telling her that he had a houseful of them. Since he lacked anchors for his fleet of boats, he used the machines for that purpose. He also lent them servants, including three playful slave girls.

King Tembinoka was passionately fond of European food, and sent the royal cook to learn from Ah Fu. The man was an idle rogue who lounged about, smoking, and passed off Ah Fu's creations as his own. The last straw came when, too lazy to fetch water from the well for himself, he sneaked up behind Fanny while she was watering her plants and snatched a dipperful from her pail.

The Stevensons then reported their grievances to Tembinoka. Shortly afterwards they heard rifle shots from the thatched palace, and met the cook running off and crouching as bullet shots pursued him. The King later explained that he had had no intention of killing the culprit; he merely meant to frighten him.

The couple were a little uneasy about the cook's possible revenge. In the nights that followed, both Louis and Fanny – though they did not tell each other until later – heard someone creeping about the house and a hand feeling cautiously inside their door-flap.

Then one evening the King was very drunk – unusual for him – after the arrival of the copra-bearing schooner *Tiernan*. He arranged a village dance in the speak-house. The clapping, stamping and singing made such a savage din that the Stevensons 'thought some form of riot was going on'. They discreetly remained in their quarters. But Louis got restless and took his flageolet off into the palm woods, playing as he walked. About midnight Fanny was hovering outside the house, anxious for his return. She finally saw him coming along the path – shadowed by a dark figure which flitted along behind him. She called out to warn him. The man ran towards the palace. But Louis, 'a fine sprinter', caught up with him, and the moonlight showed the suavely smiling face of the cook. Louis cursed him with sailor's oaths, and then Fanny saw the cook 'leaping strangely, like a grasshopper'. Louis had kicked him, and he fled.

Now the Stevensons were more worried than ever. They dared not report the man to the King, who would surely kill him. Ah Fu thought he had gone away in fear of his life. 'I have it in my heart to be sorry for the fellow', concluded Fanny, '. . . and we who have brought this upon him belong to the feared and hated white race.' (Some months after the Stevenson's departure the impudent cook gave further trouble, and the King shot him.)

Now 'with many searchings of conscience', Louis bought at a high price the devil-box of Apemama, a shell in a curious wooden box, as a present for Andrew Lang – who had just published his *Blue Fairy Book*. Later the sale of the fetish was blamed for misfortune in the village and an epidemic of measles.

The King robbed his own wives by cheating them at cards, but his strong regard for R.L.S. was extended to Fanny. 'She good; look pretty; plenty chench [sense].' She obliged him by designing a flag for his tiny kingdom: three stripes, green, red and yellow, with a black shark to compliment his ancestor the shark god, who had cohabited with a chieftainess. Fanny eventually had the flags made in Sydney.

Meanwhile as the days passed, inside the big mosquito-tent Louis and Lloyd were collaborating on *The Wrecker*. The *Equator* was to have been gone for only two or three weeks, but the time was more than doubled. As Fanny said in her diary, 'In these dangerous and uncertain waters one is easily made uneasy.' It began to appear sickeningly that the *Equator* was lost. If the party stayed on Apemama they seemed likely to subsist indefinitely on tinned food and little else. They were unwell from malnutrition. All had minor ulcers; Lloyd was limping. Louis decided to book passage in the *Tiernan* for Samoa. This did not work out; Lloyd recalled the reason as being that the price was too high. Fanny attributed it to one of her famous hunches. She had finished packing most of their large camphorwood chests when she had a vision of Captain Reid's face if he arrived to find them gone. 'Louis,' she suddenly whispered, 'I don't want to go.'

Without a question her husband cancelled their passage. The *Tiernan* sailed without them. Some days later the schooner capsized in a squall and sank. The only three survivors nearly died of hunger and thirst before they reached land in an open whaleboat.

Early in November, after two months' absence, the *Equator* turned up, delayed by bad weather and accidents until the hurricane season. The proud tough King was melancholy and emotional in the last few days of farewell. He explained to Fanny that losing the Stevensons was like losing his father. '. . . You no see king cry before. King all the same man: feel bad, he cry. I very sorry.'

'The King took us on board in his own gig, dressed in his naval uniform . . .', wrote Louis. 'That night the palm-tops of Apemama dipped behind the sea, and the schooner sailed solitary under the stars.'

Chapter VIII
'Captain darling, where has your topmast gone?'

While the Stevensons were fascinated by the *Equator*'s business in copra and merchandise, even Louis was cured of his hankering to own a trading schooner – to Fanny's relief, though he and Lloyd were still determined to write *The Wrecker* and go to Samoa. They found that both sides expected to cheat and be cheated with shoddy goods, watered copra, false weights, broken promises and bad bargains. The independent Gilbert Islands were then the final dumping-ground of the white riff-raff of the Pacific – thieves, murderers, turncoats and escaped criminals. Some of this shadowy background Stevenson later used in *The Beach at Falesà*.

Fanny described to Colvin the disgusting reek of fermented copra – an 'acrid steam'. 'The floor of our cabin was so hot that I could hardly stand upon it with bare feet, and to sleep in it was impossible. . . .' Moreover the tropical sun had warped the decks until in the rains her berth was pounded by a leak. Ah Fu had to move her bedding into the small galley-way where she tried to sleep, dressed, under an open umbrella. Lice abounded, and cockroaches 'the size of toads'.

Louis drafted a poem called 'To My Wife, A Fragment'. The first eighteen lines recalled the gentle forest landscape of Grez. The last stanza, incomplete, sketched the life on the schooner. The ending broke off unfinished:

> . . . Assault of squalls, that mock the watchful guard,
> And pluck the bursting canvas from the yard,
> And senseless clamour of the calm, at night
> Must mar your slumbers. By the plunging light,
> In beetle-haunted, most unwomanly bower
> Of the wild-swerving cabin, hour by hour. . . .

'We had a fine alert once . . .' he wrote to his mother, 'a p.d. reef ahead . . . three positions indicated, our own disputed – a very heavy sea running – the boats cleared and supplied with bread and water, our little packets made (medicines, papers, and woollen clothes). . . . It was rather fine going to bed that night; though had we struck the reef the boat voyage of four or five hundred miles would have been no joke.' Fanny held the ship's cat in her arms all night so it would not be forgotten. Another time, after a trading stop, the *Equator* got stuck on a reef, 'and not until she had parted with her false keel would she push on and gain the open'.

The sails were continually being patched – 'we had but the one suit'. Once out of a dead calm a violent squall sprang up so suddenly that it caught the ship with all sails set. It leapt about until the fore-topmast snapped across and the foresail downhaul fouled in the wreckage. The captain was busy elsewhere and the other hands lost their heads. But Ah Fu climbed to the top of the galley with his knife and cut the rope which freed the rigging.

Next morning, however, the signal halyard was missing. Its whereabouts was not learned until several weeks later, when the Chinese presented Fanny with 'a neat coil of the best quality of rope'. He had heard her admiring it, and had taken the opportunity to get it for her as a gift.

Even Louis admitted to Colvin, 'The sea is a terrible place, stupefying to the mind and poisonous to the temper – the motion, the lack of space, the cruel publicity, the villainous tinned foods, the sailors, the passengers.' He dreamed of 'beefsteak and mangoes'. And for once even he had been too uncomfortable to write.

He told his mother just before they reached Samoa in December: 'Fanny has stood the hardships of this rough cruise wonderfully;

but I do not think I could enforce her to another of the same. I've been first rate, though I am now done for lack of green food. Joe is, I fear, really ill; and Lloyd has bad sores on his leg.' Fanny herself wrote home to say what a blessing it was that her mother-in-law had not accompanied them, but added, 'and yet I would do it all over again'.

At any rate she was appreciated, for R.L.S. had written in *Songs of Travel* his famous poem:

TO MY WIFE

Trusty, dusky, vivid, true,
With eyes of gold and bramble-dew,
Steel-true and blade-straight
The great artificer
Made my mate.

Honour, anger, valour, fire;
A love that life could never tire,
Death quench or evil stir,
The mighty master
Gave to her.

Teacher, tender, comrade, wife,
A fellow-farer true through life,
Heart-whole and soul-free
The August Father
Gave to me.

Chapter IX
The first sight of Samoa

On the morning of 7th December 1889, the twenty-sixth day at sea, Fanny called from the deck, 'Come up and see Samoa!'

Her family scrambled out and gazed at the north coast of the long narrow island of Upolu, with its abrupt mountains and the thick jungle looking from afar like soft green moss. They inhaled the land breeze – copra, wood smoke, tropical flowers and fruits, with the 'clean wholesome smell' of breadfruit baking in hot stones. Then they saw the masts and low rooftops of Apia, at the foot of Mount Vaea. They hung over the rail as they entered the bottle-necked coral harbour, the only port on the island. The wrecks of several foreign warships marked a hurricane of eight months before. A few outrigger canoes were soon paddling round the *Equator*, filled with brown men and girls garlanded in wreaths and flowers.

A white man had come out in a small boat to meet the ship. He was Harry J. Moors, a blue-eyed energetic American from Michigan, with whom Joe Strong had made friends on his previous visit and who was expecting the party. Moors had a chain of trading posts in the region and was a leading influence in Samoan business, finance and politics. There was no wharf, and he offered to take the family ashore in his whaleboat. They had to climb over the side and down a steep rope ladder into the boat, which was manned by islanders who sang as they pulled for the little jetty.

The shoddy town wandered for a mile or more along the beach, half hidden by coconut palms. Facing the sea were low white wooden houses with verandas, where the traders lived and sold their goods; several large churches of white-plastered coral blocks; the thatched roofs of the basket-shaped Samoan houses; several bars; and the long pier and warehouse of the so-called 'German Firm', the big trading and planting company of the islands.

The sunburnt, cotton-clad residents – white, yellow and brown – curiously watched the Stevenson party as they stepped ashore. The Rev. W. E. Clarke of the London Missionary Society assumed that they were a troupe of down-at-heel entertainers trying to pick up a few dollars in the town. Fanny, in her Mother Hubbard, wore a wide native straw hat and carried her guitar, while Lloyd had dark glasses and big round earrings and was holding his taro-patch fiddle; in fact they did not dare to trust their instruments with the tune-loving crew. The long-haired Louis was barefoot, with calico shirt, cotton trousers and a yachting cap, while the mustachioed Joe was equally rakish. Ah Fu tagged along familiarly.

The amiable Samoans were strolling around, tall and fine-looking, dressed only in what Stevenson called 'the kilt' – the *lavalava*, which the men wore fastened at the waist and the women just over the bust, their brown skin polished with perfumed coconut oil. The men were tattooed from waist to knee, 'as if they wore lacy drawers'. The white and half-caste population of the town numbered some three hundred people, of whom two-thirds were British and most of the others German.

'Stevenson', recalled Moors in his memoir of R.L.S., '. . . bubbled over with delight. . . . "It's grand!" he exclaimed. . . . When I first brought him ashore he was looking somewhat weak, but hardly had he got into the street (for Apia is practically a town with one street) when he began to walk up and down it in a most lively, not to say eccentric, manner. He could not stand still. When I took him into my house he walked about the room, plying me with questions one after another . . . His wife was just as fidgety as himself, Lloyd Osbourne was not much better. The long lonesome trip on the schooner had quite unnerved them, and they were delighted to be on shore again. . . .'

Before going on to Sydney – and then, they thought, returning via America to England – they planned to stay in Samoa for some weeks. Louis wanted to work on the McClure letters, neglected during the strenuous voyage, and on *The Wrecker* with Lloyd. The one hotel was very poor, and the family were first put up at the home of Moors and his Samoan wife in a hamlet at the edge of the town. They sat and wrote, Louis recorded, 'on his veranda within a few steps of the sea'.

Fanny told Colvin that the voyage had been shadowed by 'the growing anxiety about Joe, who was rapidly developing grave symptoms'. His heart disease was aggravated by the dangers and irritations of the cruises. He urgently needed doctors, so they sent him on from Apia by the next steamer to join Belle in Sydney. '. . . our poor bad child', Fanny added, 'is dying, the best thing he can [do] for himself and the world at large. . . . After he was gone, the doctor told us it was only a question of a very short time. . . .'

Soon Fanny, Lloyd and Ah Fu moved to a small tropic-style cottage in the nearby bush, where Louis rode up to dine with them almost every day. He remained under the trader's roof 'for history's sake', fascinated by his wealth of Samoan experience.

Though Moors noted that Fanny was obviously older than the youthful-looking Stevenson, 'the hand of time had dealt leniently

upon her. She still pleased her talented husband, and never once did
I hear a harsh word pass between them. If there was any divergence
of opinion, I have no doubt the lady had her way. . . . She was
certainly very much attached to him, and I used to like watching the
attention she bestowed on her erratic partner. . . .'

Stevenson still meant to live in England, but he wanted a South
Sea retreat in some healthful place not too bare of the necessities,
and – most important to an author – with regular steamer services to
the outside world. This narrowed the choice to the environs of
Honolulu, Papeete, Suva or Apia.

Fanny wrote to Colvin, 'You told me when we left England if we
found a place where Louis was really well to stay there. It really
seems that anywhere in the South Seas will do. Ever since we have
been here we have been on the lookout for a spot that combines the
most advantages. . . . All things considered, Samoa took our fancy
the most; there are three opportunities each month to communicate
with England. . . . You could hardly believe your eyes if you could
see Louis in his present state of almost rude health. . . . I tremble
when I think of a return to England.'

The Stevensons also appreciated the fact that Samoa was still
independent, though unsettled. Germany, Britain and America were
all intriguing for position, and there had recently been a small native
war among the rival chiefs.

Louis asked Moors to find a suitable property. Apia itself was too
hot and muggy, but on the mountainside the air was fresh and the
nights were cool. Within a few weeks a place was discovered, about
two and a quarter miles from the town – 'not too near, nor yet too
far', said Fanny to Colvin. The Stevensons bought it for ten Chile
dollars an acre, and named it Vailima, pronounced 'Vye-LEE-ma',
and meaning 'five waters'. (In fact there were four.) It was decided
that while Louis, Fanny and Lloyd went on to Sydney, Moors was
to clear the land and build a temporary cottage – 'a very cheap
affair, but three or four rooms'. They would live in this while the
main house was under construction.

Stevenson wrote to Baxter: 'I have bought $314\frac{1}{2}$ acres of beautiful
land in the bush behind Apia; when we get the house built, the
garden laid, and cattle in the place, it will be something to fall back
on for shelter and food; and if the island could stumble into political

quiet, it is conceivable it might even bring a little income. . . . We range from 600 to 1,500 feet, have five streams, waterfalls, precipices, profound ravines, rich tablelands . . . a great view of forest, sea, mountains, the warships in the haven: really a noble haven.' And he added, '. . . If I die, it will be an endowment for the survivors, at least my wife and Lloyd. . . . There is my livelihood, all but books and wine. . . .'

Fanny encouraged her husband in what he so exuberantly wanted to do. But she later poured out her resignation to Mrs Sitwell: 'Because I make my sacrifice with flowers on my head and point out the fine views on the way, do not think that it is no sacrifice and only for my own pleasure. The Samoan people are picturesque, but I do not like them. . . . My time must be so arranged as not to clash with them. I shall be able to get no servants but cannibal black boys. . . . A great part of the housework I shall have to do myself, and most of the cooking. The land *must* produce food enough for us all, or we shall have nothing to eat. I must also manage that. Oh, it makes me tired to speak of it; and I never feel well, then. I don't want to complain. I am not complaining, really, only telling you. . . . I do want Louis, and I do want everybody to think I like going to Samoa – and in some ways I do like it; I don't want people to think I am making a sacrifice for Louis. In fact I *can't* make a sacrifice for him; the very fact that I can do the thing in a way makes a pleasure to do it, and it is no longer a sacrifice, though if I did it for another person it would be.'

Chapter X
Sailing from Sydney

In Sydney Belle was anxious when she had not heard of her seagoing family for more than six months. Meanwhile she too had been having adventures.

When she and her son Austin arrived in Sydney she had walked confidently into the bank and asked to draw the weekly allowance for which her stepfather had arranged. But the staff had never heard of it or him. The manager was brusque and indifferent. So was the American consul. She knew no one in Australia. 'I was tired, discouraged, and more frightened than I had ever been in my life', she said in her memoirs. She hastily left the stuffy red-plush lodgings where the Stevensons had told her to go, and found a large clean room on the top floor of a cheap theatrical boarding-house run by Miss Leaney, a kindly Irishwoman, on the edge of the notorious Wooloomooloo district. Then she had an idea.

King Kalakaua had seen her off with the royal band – delaying the steamer – on the moonlit evening when she had sailed from Honolulu. He had told her that if she should need help, as a Lady Companion of the Royal Order of Oceania she was entitled to apply to his Chargé d'Affaires in Sydney, a Mr Hoffnung. She timidly called at the office and told Mr Hoffnung her story. He believed her and lent her money. She rejoiced to repay him when, with casual tropical delay, her funds arrived from Honolulu by the next steamer.

Loving the stage, she relished the theatrical life at Miss Leaney's. She made other friends and presently wrote articles for *The Sydney Bulletin*. But as the months lengthened alarmingly she took to studying the shipping news: hurricanes, waterspouts, southerly-busters, marooned sailors taken off desert islands, men eaten by sharks.

Then she wrote to Aunt Maggie, 'One morning as I was in bed . . . I heard a wild flying upstairs. . . . It was Joe. . . .' And in February Lloyd burst in with the thrilling news that their mother and Louis were at the Victoria Hotel.

In great excitement she took a horse-cab to the Victoria. As she entered the lobby she saw her stepfather dart out of the lift and stride towards the desk in a fury. She heard him tell the reception clerk that he had asked for a suite on the first floor and had been taken up to the fourth. He wanted two or three large rooms and was shown into one small one. 'And,' he added indignantly, 'you didn't send up my luggage!'

He made one of his sweeping gestures at the conglomeration on the polished floor: two or three cedarwood chests tied with rope, several Tokelau buckets made from sections of a tree trunk scooped out and fitted with covers; bulging palm-leaf baskets, rolls of *tapa* cloth, fine mats, various polished coconut shells and calabashes tied up in fish netting, and sinister Micronesian weapons. To him, Belle explained, this was in all seriousness 'a gentleman's luggage'.

She saw her mother hovering near 'a little anxiously', and realized that 'the two were as odd-looking as their belongings'. Among the wasp-waisted ladies at the hotel, tiny Fanny, brown as a native, was dressed in a flowing grey silk *holoku*, while her husband's suit had been for six months in a cedar-wood chest in the hold of a schooner. Both wore wide floppy straw hats from the Line Islands.

As soon as Belle had embraced them, she suggested that they go to the pleasant but less grand Oxford Hotel. There they were courteously received and given a whole floor of large and comfortable rooms. The next morning the newspapers blazed with headlines, interviews and articles about R.L.S., and the clerk and manager of the Victoria Hotel came to apologize and beg him to return at half-rate. But Louis and Fanny declined. They 'took a mildly malicious pleasure in the fact that the big hotel . . . must send his letters over to the less fashionable Oxford in market baskets'.

In Sydney the Stevensons looked forward to a civilized interlude: bookshops, restaurants with good food and wine, and educated conversation. They mixed with newspapermen and Belle's artist friends, though Louis dodged most of the countless invitations to make speeches and attend social gatherings. '. . . Fanny has an "evening",' he wrote to his mother, 'but she is about at the end of the virtuous effort, and shrinks from the approach of any fellow creature.' She went shopping with Belle, and her husband had himself measured for evening clothes – but he scarcely had a chance to wear them. For though it was February – late summer in Sydney – it was windy as well as balmy: 'chilly' after the South Seas, and there were city 'germs'. Again he caught cold.

Belle's friend Dr Fairfax Ross recommended that Louis should stay at the gentlemanly Union Club for rest and comfort, away from callers. There he sat up in bed, writing, holding court with the housemaids and, at his own request, receiving frequent visits from Austin, his step-grandson. The doorman and footman bowed to the boy and called him Sir, and the housekeeper always brought in a slice of cake or a glass of lemonade.

It was hard on both Fanny and Louis that she was allowed only daily calls at this male preserve and could not nurse her husband night and day. With Lloyd, she joined the Strongs and made another theatrical-looking figure at Miss Leaney's.

'If there are to be hurricanes,' Colvin wrote to Baxter, 'I wish Belle and Joe Strong and all that lot may be at sea in a leaky ship.'

Joe was not dying after all. Financed by Louis, he had resumed painting a little. But the Stevensons' effort to manœuvre him from too much drink and bonhomie in Honolulu to a new life in Australia had got him 'out of the frying-pan into the fire'. He himself, Belle said sadly, wanted to paint well and to be a good husband and father, and was miserable about his own weak will and his thirst; remorse alternated with backsliding. After her respite she was dragged down again to share this humiliating life. 'Belle has her faults and plenty of them', Louis once told Colvin. With all her warm charm and gaiety he had found her extravagant, pleasure-loving and mercenary. But in the disillusionment and exhaustion of her marriage her ways were improving towards her stepfather at last. Perhaps in his childless longing he had spoiled her as well as her brother.

Meanwhile in Sydney the Stevensons and Lloyd went on with the preparations for their visit to England. After two years in their service Ah Fu was also about to travel. He had enthusiastically approved of the new estate in Samoa, but first he wanted leave of absence to go back to see his widowed mother in China. 'Just one trip,' he promised, 'then I come back quick.' His thriftily saved wages, plus a farewell gift of fifty pounds from Louis, were changed into gold pieces. However, he never came back and they never heard of him again.

Stevenson was anxious to push on with *The Wrecker* to earn money for the new estate. But as the autumn cooled he relapsed with fever and coughing, and the old haemorrhages struck hard – after eighteen months' freedom. Fanny almost despaired of saving him. She and Dr Ross agreed that the only hope lay in getting him into the South Seas again. On 10th April he cabled Baxter: 'Return Islands four months. Home September.'

For once the big port of Sydney was not easy to leave. The maritime unions were on strike and the quays were choked with motionless vessels. Fanny went to unladylike lengths in haunting the waterfront from one shipping office to the next.

Then she chanced to hear of the *Janet Nicholl*, an iron-screw steamer of about six hundred tons, fore-and-aft rigged, which belonged to a Scots firm trading in the South Pacific. It was bound under sealed orders 'for the South Seas' – nothing more definite – and was able to sail promptly because the crew were Melanesian 'black boys' and belonged to no unions. She urgently demanded passage. When she was turned down she insisted that it was a matter of life and death for her husband – obviously scaring the shipowners all the more with the prospect of a dying man.

'I was present', recalled Belle, 'when one of the owners, Mr Henderson, called on my mother at Miss Leaney's. She was busily packing, for she had learned the *Janet* was leaving the next day. Her caller, very serious and firm, sat in a big chair, telling her, while my mother continued packing, that he couldn't possibly take any passengers. . . . I left the room on an errand for my mother. . . . When I got back I was astonished to hear Mr Henderson giving instructions how to reach the *Janet* (owing to the strike she was anchored out in the harbour) and warning my mother to be sure her party was on time.'

The next morning, 11th April 1890, the Strongs accompanied the family aboard via an open rowing-boat in a cold drizzle. 'Louis was laid out on a board, rolled like a mummy in a blanket; his wife sat beside him, silent and watchful of his comfort.' The *Janet Nicholl* was painted black – 'long, low and rakish'. She was further blackened by coal-dust. Even at anchor she rolled noticeably – a bad omen for Fanny, who later found that the vessel was known throughout the islands as 'the Jumping Jenny'.

The *Janet* had high bulwarks and it was not easy to get the supine Louis over the side. Anxiously the family watched 'some half-naked black men' carrying him up the narrow gangway and into his cabin. 'As I followed,' said Belle, 'I saw a red-faced, red-bearded man somewhat the worse for drink, lurching about on the slippery deck, making a nuisance of himself in his efforts to help. . . .

'We were heavy-hearted as we left the *Janet Nicholl*. Louis looked so ill we thought we might never see him again. It seemed terrible for him to be going away in that sloppy ship with drunken men and inky-black savages, and I didn't like the thought of my mother being the only woman on board with not even Ah Fu to look after her.'

Chapter XI
Fire and surf in the *Janet Nicholl*

Compared to the *Equator* even the *Janet Nicholl*[1] seemed comfortable, though a man whom the Stevensons met on shore said that the very sight of her made him seasick. 'Think of two bathrooms,' Fanny marvelled to Belle, 'and only one other passenger besides ourselves, a nice long wide deck to walk on, steam to run away from squalls with, and no flopping about in calms.' The food was good. There was a large airy saloon and cabins amidships with the trade room aft. At night the saloon party might sleep in hammocks or on mats or blankets under a huge awning placed over the after hatch, though rain squalls often drove them in. For Fanny four mats were modestly hung in a square; being loose-woven, they did not shut off the air – nor the groans of a mate with nightmares.

The crew consisted of nine white men and forty-odd black boys from the Solomons and the New Hebrides. Cheerful, chattering, hard-working, the boys crawled like spiders among the sails or swam like crabs underwater to scrape the keel. Their people had been cannibals, but they were not pleased when the white crew teased them about it. They sang hymns with rousing piety.

The mess included Mr Henderson, the senior partner whom Fanny had won over, and who proved to be not only courteous and helpful but also a skilful entertainer at sleight-of-hand; Captain Henry, the expert sailing master; Mr Stoddard, the engineer; and Mr Hird, the supercargo. Ben Hird was the red-beard who had alarmed Belle in Sydney harbour, but he was one of the most knowledgeable and respected men in the South Pacific.

There was also their fellow passenger, a handsome young man named Mr Buckland, known as 'Tin Jack', a trader of the company returning to his station. ('Tin' was a South Sea word for 'Mr'.) A flamboyant Australian, he was part Sydney gent and part Gilbert Island beachcomber – 'in alternate layers', as Louis said. He had a certain fixed income which he spent annually on a brief binge in Sydney. Then, broke, he returned reluctantly to his dull trading post for most of the year. 'He was a beautiful creature', Fanny wrote in

[1] Misspelt by Fanny Stevenson, even in her subsequent book, as 'Nichol'.

her notes, 'terribly annoying at times, but with something childlike and appealing . . . that made one forgive pranks in him that would be unforgivable in others.'

The *Janet*'s first port of call, on 19th April, was Auckland, New Zealand. Fanny went shopping for presents to hand out to the people on the islands. Among a seemingly endless supply of piece-goods, beads, etc., she included a bag full of plain gold rings, a number of which she wore on her own fingers each time she went ashore, to give to the women. She had also brought from Sydney four boxes of artificial flowers and fruits which she and Belle had wired into wreaths for her hats, so that later she was continually whisking off the trimming to present it to some local dame – whose eyes, she said, became as round as the mock currants or cherries in the garland.

Tin Jack's shopping included greasepaints, a false nose, a wig and whiskers. These were to provide his favourite joke whenever he went ashore and popped on the disguise in a crowd – either convulsing or terrifying the islanders. 'If I had known,' said Fanny once after he had caused a panic, 'I would have stopped him.'

In Lloyd's company he also bought some cartridges, and a lot of fireworks for the diversion of his native retainers on his own island. The fireworks included ten pounds of 'calcium fire', guaranteed complete with fumes. 'Safe as a packet of sugar', the chemist had reassured the dubious Lloyd.

In the cabin which he shared with Tin Jack, Lloyd put the un-marked parcels on their owner's bunk until he should come below. The *Janet* sailed in the early evening, with the lights of Auckland streaming behind. Between ten and eleven o'clock, the ship was not yet beyond the lighthouse, Louis was resting in his cabin, Tin Jack and Mr Henderson were chatting over coffee, Fanny eating brown bread and butter at the saloon table. Suddenly, from the cabin occupied by Tin Jack and Lloyd, there came, she wrote, 'a spitting puff, followed by gorgeous flames and the most horrible chemical stench'. Red, blue and green rockets burst into the saloon and shot high above the deck.

She ran to her cabin and snatched a heavy red blanket. Henderson followed with a woollen rug, then passed out on the stairs. In the suffocating vapour, laced with vivid flames, she groped blindly for a hand to put the blanket into; one emerged, and luckily it was the captain's. He had known nothing of the fireworks – nor had Louis, who was so flabbergasted by the colourful spectacle that he hardly noticed the fumes.

While the ship drifted dangerously – the helmsman having fled from his post – the captain ordered pump and hose. Crawling into the very centre of the fire with blanket, rug and hose, he succeeded in smothering the flames barely in time to save the ship.

'Had the wind been in a different quarter, or the cartridges exploded', he said later, 'nothing could have saved us.'

Simultaneously Fanny was the heroine of a rescue which has been a highlight of the R.L.S. legend. She saw a couple of black boys about to throw a blazing trunk overboard, and ran forward with a hoarse shout. By a miracle of luck she stopped them just in time. The trunk contained four large boxes full of Stevenson's manuscripts.

Most of the trio's clothing and personal comforts were lost, even their toothbrushes. Lloyd had no clothes left except those he was wearing, and Fanny no other shoes and stockings – so she began to go barefoot as much as possible to save her footwear for 'civilized appearances' ashore. Most of their precious photographs were destroyed.

With her own throat and lungs seared as if by pepper, she feared a haemorrhage for Louis, but none came.

'The annoying thing', she concluded, 'is that Tin Jack has lost nothing whatsoever.'

The Stevensons were delighted when the *Janet*'s sealed orders revealed Apia as an early port of call, so that they could see how the work on their new estate was progressing. Late on 30th April they sighted the familiar green mountain and low roofs. While they dined in the *Janet*, Moors and other people began to arrive in boats to welcome them. In the evening they walked on Apia beach, shaking hands and exchanging greetings of '*Talofa!*' on every side – a word like the Haiwaiian *aloha*, meaning 'Hallo', 'Goodbye', and other amiable sentiments.

Horses were ordered, and the next morning the party went up to Vailima. They could now ride two abreast on the track which Moors had cleared. At the new estate they found a crowd of black boys –

runaways from the German plantations – cutting down and burning trees and brush. 'A good many noble trees' were left standing, Louis noted. A small wooden house had already been run up, and from its balcony they could see the masts of the *Janet Nicholl* at anchor. Later, when they had sailed, 'our little house in the bush was visible to the naked eye from the deck'.

The *Janet* then steamed on to the north east and north-north-west, calling in three and a half months at thirty-three so-called low islands. But the stops were seldom for more than a few hours, and as R.L.S. complained, 'hackney cabs have more variety than atolls'. They missed the beauty and variety of the high islands. More than once the surf was too rough for Fanny even to accompany the men ashore in the boat.

To serve as a record for Louis, she kept a diary of the journey – published years later. It was written 'sometimes on the damp up-turned bottom of a canoe or whaleboat, sometimes when lying face down on the burning sands of a tropic beach, often in copra sheds in the midst of noise and confusion, but oftener on the badly rolling *Janet* . . . to the accompaniment of Tin Jack's incessant and inconsequent conversation'.

'The desire to own an island is still burning in my breast', she wrote – even though she had so recently acquired the beautiful burden of Vailima. In fact, her imagination had fixed by hearsay on the very isle. Named Nassau, it was not far from Samoa, almost uninhabited, but 'unfortunately' owned by a man in Tahiti.

While the *Janet* lay offshore she eagerly surveyed it through a glass: a small high-low triangle enclosing a lagoon. There was no anchorage and to her great disappointment the landing was thought too dangerous for her to attempt, so the men went without her. Louis returned enthusiastic about the loveliness. This was 'a garden-like place', with breadfruit trees, limes, figs, bananas and all the other high-island fruits, and even soft turf, as well as pigs, fowls, green turtles and shell tortoises. The inhabitants – three men, two women and some children – danced 'like jumping-jacks for joy' at the rare visit, rifled Louis's pockets, and sent gifts to Fanny. The Stevensons filed away the dream of the island for later consideration.

On, on steamed the *Janet* from port to port. In mid-June they called eagerly at Apemama and were puzzled when no boat came out from their old friend King Tembinoka. They learned that he was visiting a neighbour island and followed him there, bearing gifts. As the party were rowed along the beach there were cries of 'Pani! Pani!' ('Fanny! Fanny!') from the King's harem, and Fanny was soon seated among the welcoming wives.

Oddly, the King did not seem astonished to see them. He was weak from measles, like many of his subjects – who blamed the disease on the sale of their 'devil-box' to the Stevensons. Nevertheless Tembinoka himself steered the royal boat when he accompanied them back to a meal on the *Janet*. As he approached, Fanny's gift to him was revealed: the bright new shark-god flag which she had designed and made was broken in salute.

He was deeply touched, but not until 'champagne was opened', and he was alone in the cabin with the Stevensons, did he embrace them with tears of joy. He warmed the clairvoyant Fanny's heart by telling them that he had often had visions of their return – which explained why he was not surprised at their appearance. The same morning he had not known whether it was fact or fancy when he had recognized Fanny in a dress which he had given her.

'Then I felt like this', he said, making a gasping sound: 'O-o-oh!'

On 1st July Louis fell ill again, and Fanny suffered and nursed him. He wrote to Colvin that the voyage 'would have been delightful to the end had my health held out. That it did not, I attribute to savage hard work in a wild cabin heated like the Babylonian furnace, four piles of blotting-paper under my wet hand and the drops trailing from my brow. For God's sake don't start in to blame Fanny; often enough she besought me not to go on: but I did my work while I was a bedridden worm in England, and please God I shall do my work until I burst. . . .'.

Fanny herself wrote to Colvin, 'Always, please, fall upon me when his work goes wrong. He will stubbornly hold his own position, but is apt to give way if he thinks I am getting the blame. . . .'

Ten days after Louis's collapse he was lying in his bunk when the ship called at Aranuka, one of King Tembinoka's islands, where they were greeted by the solicitous monarch himself. Henderson agreed to take the royal boat back to Apemama and to give His Majesty a lift with his harem, court and bodyguard – which meant that overnight about two hundred passengers crowded every foot of the *Janet*'s decks.

The loading was a bedlam of noise and a *mêlée* of strange baggage – which included innumerable pandanus bags and baskets, camphor-wood chests, coconuts full of toddy syrup, sewing-machines, rose-wood musical boxes, spades and cutlasses, taro puddings and seaweed ear-piercers. Several old ladies of high rank camped on the bridge, including the King's mother, very drunk on her habitual tipple of gin. The King's favourite wife had a snub-nosed puppy which, when it became peevish, she put to her breast and suckled.

The *Janet*'s black boys were wildly excited, and showed off so much in the rigging before the court ladies that Fanny said it was 'a wonder and mercy none were killed'. Presently the harem were gathered aft and put under a taboo. The females of lower degree – if not Fanny – had more fun, for all night the black boys sang, shouted and danced to entertain them.

On 26th July the *Janet* approached New Caledonia. Noumea was the cruise's first real South Sea town and the last before the steamer was to return to Australia. As the surf ran out to meet them some forty miles from shore, the Stevensons were charmed by a series of lovely bays and miniature islands with hills and coco palms. Louis, though recovered from his illness, was too enervated to write much. He asked Fanny and Lloyd to go on without him to Sydney; he wanted to avoid the cold winter there as long as possible. He also wished to sample the grim atmosphere of the French penal colony (used in *The Ebb Tide*), where the convict band played before the cafés in the square, and to enjoy French conversation and wines with the governor and other officials. It was, too, his only glimpse of Melanesia.

Louis wrote to Burlingame that his health had not improved as much as he hoped, but the others 'seem less run down than on the *Equator*. Mrs Stevenson very much less so'.

Years later, in her ambivalent way, Fanny referred to those stifling rolling days on the little black steamer as 'perhaps the happiest period of my life', which she remembered 'with thrilling interest'.

On the *Janet*'s last lap from Noumea to Sydney she and Lloyd experienced '. . . . a very terrible storm', as she wrote to Colvin, 'lost and drifting, the coal given out, the water swamping the decks . . . our captain very ill with gastric fever. . .'. They were 'very nearly lost on the Australian coast'.

She later told Mrs Will Low that at one time during their South Sea cruises she had been pregnant. But, especially since she was aged fifty when their wanderings ended, those who knew her well were sceptical.

Part 10

Settling in Samoa 1890-94

Chapter I
Jungle pioneers

It was August of 1889 when Fanny and Lloyd returned to Sydney and again took rooms with the Strongs at Miss Leaney's. After Louis followed from Noumea – bringing many casks of French wines to tranship to Apia – he went straight to the Union Club. The family had arrived so quietly that this time the reporters did not know.

In the Sydney winter Louis immediately caught a severe cold. Now he and Fanny both realized heavily that there would be no trip to England – still less a permanent return. It was an incredible blow to them both. Yet he wrote to Henry James: 'I must tell you plainly – I can't tell Colvin – I do not think I shall come to England more than once, and then it'll be to die. Health I enjoy in the tropics; even here, which they call sub- or semi-tropics, I come only to catch cold. . . . How should I do in England? . . . Am I very sorry? I am sorry about seven or eight people in England, and one or two in the States. And outside of that, I simply prefer Samoa. . . . The sea, islands, the islanders, the island life and climate, make and keep me truly happier. These last two years I have been much at sea, and I have *never wearied*. . . .

'*N.B.* Even my wife has weakened about the sea. She wearied, the last time we were ashore, to get afloat again.'

Poor Fanny had thus succeeded all too well in manœuvring her husband into the voyage which saved his life. But now she, like

Louis, half longed for the fertile tropics and yet half yearned for her roots in America and England.

Henry James was again the only one of Stevenson's intimates who 'understood'. As with their domestic life in Bournemouth, he followed the couple's South Sea adventures with painstaking interest. The other cronies, however, were distressed and angry at the Stevenson's barbaric plan. Fanny as usual was blamed, even by the patient Colvin.

She and Louis were both deeply upset by his accusation. She even went to the despairing length of suggesting that they give up staying in the South Seas and go home. Her husband replied to Colvin in her defence: '. . . if I tell you that she cried all night after reading your letter, it is simply to give you a measure of what she thinks of your opinion. And yet she knew all the time that you scarce meant all; . . . and when it became more and more clear to me that I ought to stay in the tropics, my one trouble was about you. . . . I said to Fanny: "I cannot stay here, I must go home to Colvin." She said: "He made me promise to keep you in any place that suited your health . . . I bind it upon you as a sacred duty, and upon another beside you: should you be dangerously ill, I must be summoned. . . ." '

Fanny wrote reproachfully to Mrs Sitwell, saying how touching it was to have Louis wake in the night and tell her that it was wonderful to be able to live like other people, to swim and ride.

The dejected Louis asked Mrs Sitwell to intercede with Colvin. '. . . remember that, though I take my sicknesses with a decent face, they do represent suffering, and weakness, and painful disability. . . . Try and get Colvin, without giving him an idea that he has hurt us, to write a kindlier letter to Fanny.'

The worst of the Stevensons' current problems – second only to Louis's health – was Joe Strong. From Sydney on 1st September Louis told his lawyer crony Charles Baxter of his discovery that Joe had sold some paintings, but 'never a word did he tell me. . . '. Meanwhile, with the three Strongs to support, Louis had given up buying any new clothes in Sydney – 'and my partner Joe should be worrying about his silk handkerchiefs. . .'.

He assured Baxter that 'Belle has behaved really well this time;

if I took notice of anything it would only make him think that Belle has peached; he would only take it out of her worse than he is doing; and the person who would suffer would be the one who has dealt (I must say – and never thought to be able to say it of her –) honestly and kindly to me. So there's nothing to do but grin and bear, and keep the money to a fixed sum. . .'.

Earlier in the year Baxter had disapproved when R.L.S. had generously sent for some money to enable 'a friend of ours to give his wife a holiday. . .'. The friend had been Joe, but now Louis had found out that 'this money which was stolen from me – for he owes me his body, his soul and his boots, and the soup that he wipes from his moustache –' had been spent on pleasures and purchases of which Belle and Austin were given no share. 'It is this which has filled me with an angry bitterness intolerable to endure. And the money for having his child's tooth stopped – O Christ Jesus! it is sometimes too much to have to support this creature. And yet withal he's kind of innocent. . . . He is the place where an innocent child has made a mess on the hearth-rug, and I wish somebody would mop it up. . . .

'Hard is the lot of him who has dependants. But I should not say that. For near six months Belle has been a hitherto unheard-of model of gratitude; by which I mean that she has never said a word of thanks; but gone ahead, and managed the money the way I wished her to, and met my views in every way in her power, against all obstacles. This sort of thing more than repays a man for a little money, which I do not feel, and a great deal of worry, which I own I feel like hell. . . . It ain't charity; I never was guilty of that. Only a person hates to see a pensioner cocking snooks at him, and putting himself up on the top of a monument of mean, greedy-child selfishness. . . . And you can't strike the insane, let alone the dying . . . who (and whose wife and child) is – are – your dependants. . . . But we'll keep our hearts up. . . .'

Having bought the land in Samoa, the Stevensons had to find the money to build their house. After some pangs of hesitation Fanny suggested that they should sell her beloved Skerryvore and use the proceeds. Since Thomas Stevenson had put the place in her name, Louis protested, 'But this money is yours.' In the end he said that he would recompense her in his will by bequeathing Vailima to her, 'with all that it contained'.

Lloyd was sent back to England to sell Skerryvore and to bring out the furniture to Samoa. He had long dreamed of going to Cambridge or Oxford, but he gave up the idea – probably half willingly and half unwillingly. He said that it would add too much to Louis's heavy burden of expense, and also that he wanted to stay and help his mother and stepfather; but in fact the life of travel and writing appealed to him. It was also arranged that he was to escort the senior Mrs Stevenson back to the South Seas. 'Come when you like', Fanny wrote to her. 'Even if we make a temporary shelter you need not be so very uncomfortable. The only question is the food problem, and if in six months I cannot have a garden producing and fowls and pigs and cows it will be strange to me.'

In September she and Louis left Sydney for Apia in the *Lübeck*, the regular German steamer, with their curios and their wine casks. The young pantryman, a plump bald little man called Paul Einfürer, followed them ashore to ask them for a job as a servant, and was engaged, though he spoke very little English. Louis described him as 'a glutton for work, a splendid fellow, but no cook, has twenty thumbs, and we daren't let him go to town (for drink) and he, poor fellow, is afraid to be let go'. Once he fell off his horse when he returned.

They found that Moors had cleared about a dozen acres and completed their temporary cottage. There was almost no furniture except the beds they had brought. But Fanny unearthed from her boxes some rich tawny *tapa* cloth and hung a large flat piece of pink coral over the inner door. Cooking was done, by tropic custom, in a kitchen six or eight yards from the house – with the rainy season starting.

Moors pridefully recorded in his memoirs that he had 'on my own responsibility had a passion fruit arbour erected. . . . with a summer-house on top of it.' Fanny, however, noted drily that there was no shelter for pigs or chicken-house for her Cochins from Sydney. It was up to her to contrive these rustic amenities, though she knew no Samoan – or German – and often had to demonstrate the work with her own small brown hands. But the pigs were soon believed to embody the devils which inhabited the Vailima woods, for they plagued their owners by continually escaping.

Part of the property had once been cleared for cultivation, but the jungle had long since taken over, and the tumultuous undergrowth had to be cut out before the newcomers could see the lie of their own land. In the clearing, great trees were left standing, some of them a hundred and fifty feet high and eight or ten yards in girth, their trunks wound with creepers, orchids growing in the forks of the branches, and their foliage, Louis noted, 'alive with birds, which chatter . . . with rich, throaty voices'. Flying foxes – the great fruit-eating bats – roosted until dusk in giant banyan trees. No other house or roof was visible, though now and then they could hear the cathedral bell from town. On one side the primeval forest rose straight up Mount Vaea, 1,300 feet high, and on the other they could see the distant blue mountains of Atua. The clearing faced the sea over the tree tops, with the dim sound of surf. There was a stream on each side, one of which, fed by a waterfall, became a beautiful clear pool deep enough for swimming and edged by wild orange trees.

In one place the boys uncovered a forgotten banana-planting and a taro-patch, and later a grove of frangipani. Many mummy apples (pawpaws, called papayas in the Pacific) had sprung up through the clearing, 'of which', said Fanny, 'I am glad for the sake of the prospective cow'. (The papayas, bananas and a scented reed later made the butter delicious.) She also found numerous lemon trees in full fruit in the farther hedge, among citron and lime.

Louis called her 'my little blue bogie planter'. She had brought countless seeds from Sydney. For a start she wandered about, scattering handfuls in the bush – melons, tomatoes and bush lima beans – 'as my garden must wait till the weeding is done'. Other seeds she planted in boxes, including cantaloup – 'which one of our boys has been stealing to sell in town'. She set cuttings of the virgin buffalo grass from the American prairies, to carpet the paddock. Their nearest neighbour, the British lawyer Carruthers, sent them two mango trees, and another time some pineapples: 'As soon as we eat them we plant the tops.'

Louis weeded by the hour with a long bush knife to uproot the voracious sensitive plant and other pests. Though he sweated heavily he was triumphantly unharmed except for the blisters on his hands. '*Nothing* is so interesting as weeding', he exulted to Colvin.

In such a state of déshabille and bare cupboards, the Stevensons received their most supercilious visitor: Henry Adams, the eminent historian, a Bostonian friend of Henry James. With his travelling companion, the painter John La Farge, he was brought uphill by the American Consul, H. M. Sewall, to call. Neither Louis nor Fanny though it necessary or becoming to apologize for their temporary state as toiling pioneers. Adams wrote home to Elizabeth Cameron with a most unflattering account, later published in his *Letter*:

'. . . a clearing dotted with burned stumps . . . a two-storey Irish shanty . . . squalor like a railroad navvy's board hut . . . a man so thin and emaciated that he looked like a bundle of sticks in a bag, with . . . dirty striped pajamas, the baggy legs tucked into coarse woollen stockings, one of which was bright brown in color, the other a purplish dark tone. . . a woman . . . [in] the usual missionary nightgown which was no cleaner than her husband's shirt and drawers, but she omitted the stockings . . . her complexion and eyes were dark and strong, like a half-breed Mexican. . . . Though I could not forget the dirt and squalor, I found Stevenson extremely entertaining. . . .'

On 8th November Mr Adams reported: 'Stevenson returned our call the other day. . . . He was cleaner, and his wife was not with him.'

Louis gave Adams a letter of introduction to the royal family of Tahiti, and wrote courteously to Henry James of the 'enlightened society' of his friends: '. . . a great privilege – would it might endure. I would go oftener to see them, but I had to swim my horse the last time I went to dinner, and have not yet returned the clothes I had to borrow. . . . They I believe would come oftener to see me; but . . . we have often almost nothing to eat; a guest would simply break the bank. . . . What would you do with a guest at such narrow seasons? – eat him? or serve up a labour boy fricasséed?'

On 27th November Adams continued: '. . . Last evening [Stevenson] came at five o'clock, and brought his wife to dine with us. Their arrival was characteristic. He appeared first, looking like an insane stork, very warm and restless. I was not present, and the reception fell on little Mrs Parker. . . . Presently Mrs Stevenson, in a reddish cotton nightgown, staggered up the steps, and sank into a chair, gasping and unable to speak. Stevenson hurried to explain that she was overcome by the heat and the walk. Might she lie down? Mrs Parker sacrificed her own bed, and gave her some cognac. Stevenson says his wife has some disease, I know not what, of a paralytic nature, and suffers greatly from its attacks. I know only that when I arrived soon afterwards, I found her on the piazza chatting with Mrs Parker, and apparently as well and stalwart as any other Apache squaw. . . .'

In mid December Adams and La Farge went to breakfast with the Stevensons, sending (by request) their food ahead in a basket. 'We found Stevenson and his wife just as they had appeared at our first call, except that Mrs Stevenson did not think herself obliged to put on slippers, and her night-gown costume had apparently not been washed since our visit . . . both Stevenson and his wife were very friendly, and gave us a good breakfast – or got it themselves, and kept up a rapid talk for four hours. . . . Both La Farge and I came round to a sort of liking for Mrs Stevenson, who is more human than her husband. Stevenson is an *a-itu* – uncanny. . . . Their travels have broken his wife up; she is a victim to rheumatism which is becoming paralysis, and, I suspect, to dyspepsia; she says that their voyages have caused it, but Stevenson gloats over discomforts. . . . Compared with their shanty a native house is a palace; but this squalor must be somehow due to his education. . . . His early associates were all second-rate. . . . He does not know the difference between people. . . .' Mr Adams suggested that instead of buying so much land his hosts might have purchased soap.

After a few weeks there appeared Henry Simile, an educated Samoan chiefling, who had acted as Louis's interpreter-copyist on their earlier visit. He agreed to work for them as an overseer for ten dollars a month and board. He was to help plant trees and ride down to do errands in Apia. He and Louis were to exchange lessons in Samoan and English. He soon proved useful and reliable, and always spoke of 'our house', 'our trees', etc.

Though there were bewildering changes and additions of servants, one was to stay with the Stevensons for a long time: a 'huge mutton-headed Hercules' called Lafaele (Raphael). He became their gardener. Louis characterized him as 'a strong, dull, deprecatory man, splendid with an axe if watched; the better for rowing, when he calls me "Papa" in the most wheedling tones; desperately afraid of ghosts. . . .'

To outwit the devils he painted his face white with lime and added muttonchop whiskers and a moustache in black. He was clever in using herbs to heal cuts or wounds. He came from one of the 'out islands' and knew no English except the few words he was picking up at Vailima. He and Fanny invented a sort of pidgin dialect in which they jabbered to each other, though no one else could understand them. His wife had run away, and he married again and wanted to live at Vailima. 'He says if his new wife does not suit me I am just to kill her . . . and he will continue to work like hell.'

Later Fanny remarked frankly to one of the servants that the Samoans seemed not to feel deeply in such matters. He replied with indignation that indeed they did: when a man's wife ran away he 'felt bad for two or three days'.

Chapter II
Fanny's 'peasant soul'

Several passages in Fanny's diary touched so sore a point that they were over-inked – presumably either by Lloyd, Belle or Nellie, who all handled her papers after her death. But most of the cuts were eventually deciphered by Anne Roller Issler, then curator of Stevenson House at Monterey, by editor Charles Neider and other Stevensonians, with the aid of magnifying glasses and ray techniques. Fanny wrote on 23rd October 1890:

'Louis says that I have the soul of a peasant, not so much that I love working in the earth and with the earth, but because I like to know that it is my own earth that I am delving in. Had I the soul of an artist, the stupidity of possessions would have no power over me. He may be right. I would as soon think of renting a child to love as a piece of land. When I plant a seed or a root, I plant a bit of my heart with it and do not feel that I have finished when I have had my exercise and amusement. But I do feel not so far removed from God when the tender leaves put forth and I know that in a manner I am a creator. My heart melts over a bed of young peas, and a blossom on

my rose tree is like a poem written by my son. . . . After all, I believe
we present our home the best of it [*sic*]: we possess something deep
and strong and never the evanescent sports of the artist. . . . My
things, my house have favoured me, and I cannot loosen the strings
that bind us without something breaking.'

'The soul of a peasant': Louis might have known that nothing he
ever said was likely to have hurt his wife so much. Her longing to
be 'creative' was the driving force of her life and the very power
which made her sublimate her love in tending him and his greater
art.

The tactless remark continued to rankle, and she dwelt on it
repeatedly in her diary. Her entry for 5th November was also over-
inked by a family censor: 'I am feeling very depressed, for my vanity,
like a newly felled tree, lies prone and bleeding. . . . I have been
brooding on my feelings and holding my head before the glass and
now I am ashamed. Louis assures me that the peasant class is a most
interesting one, and he admires it hugely.

'. . . Louis says that no one can mind having it said of him that he
is not an artist unless he is supporting his family by his work as an
artist, in which case it is an insult. Well, I could not support a fly
by my sort of work, artistic or otherwise.

'. . . I so hate being a peasant that I feel a positive pleasure when I
fail in peasant occupations.

'My fowls won't lay eggs, and if they do, the cocks . . . eat them.
The pigs, whom I loathe and fear, are continually climbing out of
their sty and doing all sorts of mischief. . . . I love the growing things
but the domestic beasts are not to my taste. I have, too, such a guilty
feeling towards them, for I know if their murder is not contemplated
that at least they will be robbed of their young at my instigation. . . .'

She made *kava*, the refreshing and slightly intoxicating drink
prepared from the pulverized root – chewed, by the natives – of the
pepper tree, soaked in water. When Fanny's brew was not praised
by a visitor who was a connoisseur, she again referred to herself as a
peasant. And though Paul's clumsy carpentering was a trial, she
wrote, 'I cannot bear to be harsh with him because my own wounded
vanity makes me sensible of disappointments'.

To Mrs Sitwell she wrote that she supposed Lloyd, in England,
had told her of 'my desperate engagements with the man of genius

over the South Sea book. . . . He says I do not take the broad view of the artist, but hold the cheap opinions of the general public that a book must be interesting. How I do long for a little wholesome monumental correction to be applied to the Scotch side of Louis's artistic temperament.'

Her great contribution to her husband's work was one which has been almost unnoticed, even by the Stevensons, though it was eventually suggested by Gosse: the influence of her way of looking at things with such vivid originality and vitality. R.L.S.'s early travel books had a lyric charm. But – apart from contents and maturity – his writing gained a vigour and dash after he joined Fanny, especially in places like pioneer California, Saranac and the various South Sea islands, where she was innately more at home than he. Stevenson the Scot, the European, became Stevenson the Cosmopolitan, not merely by the event of travel, but partly through sharing the interpretations of his colourful companion.

'Work?' wrote Stevenson to Henry James. 'Work is now arrested. . . . Gracious, what a strain is a long book! . . .

'Kipling', he added, 'is by far the most promising young man who has appeared since – ahem – I appeared. He amazes me by his precocity and various endowment. But he alarms me by his copiousness and haste. . . .'

'All morning', Louis told Colvin, 'I worked at the *South Seas*. . . . Fanny, awfully hove-to with rheumatics and injuries received upon the field of sport and glory, chasing pigs, was unable to go up and down stairs, so she sat upon the back verandah, and my work was chequered by her cries.

' "Paul, you take a spade to do that – dig a hole first. If you do that, you'll cut off your foot!"

' "Here, you boy, what do you do there? You no got work? You go find Simile; he give you work. Peni, you tell this boy he go find Simile, suppose Simile no give him work, you tell him go 'way. I no want him here. That boy no good."

'*Peni* (from the distance in reassuring tones): "All right, sir!"

'*Fanny* (after a long pause): "Peni, you tell that boy go find Simile! I no want him stand here all day. I no pay that boy. I see him all day. He no do nothing."

'Luncheon: beef, soda-scones, fried bananas, pineapple in claret, coffee. Try to write a poem; no go. Play the flageolet. Then sneakingly off to farmering and pioneering. Four gangs at work on our place.

'Dinner: stewed beef and potatoes, baked bananas, new loaf-bread hot from the oven, pineapple in claret. These are great days; we have been low in the past, but now we are as belly-gods, enjoying all things.'

Again Louis reported that Fanny had been 'occupied largely with contending publicly with wild swine'. He estimated that the pregnant black sow had cost him from thirty to fifty dollars in days' labour – with the boys chasing her.

'Two Sundays ago, when she had escaped again, Moors and I and Fanny were strolling up to the garden, and there by the waterside we saw the black sow, looking guilty. It seemed to me beyond words; but Fanny's *cri de cœur* was delicious:

' "G-r-r-r!" she cried; "nobody loves you!" '

Meanwhile the Samoans were seeing omens and portents of war. A red eel had been caught, and a dog had interrupted a *kava* drinking. A chief turned up for a visit at Vailima with a fancy pistol strapped to his waist. For the arrival of the new Chief Justice the King had ordered all the reluctant chiefs to do him honour. To protect her pigs and chickens from being pilfered for such feasts, Fanny painted the top of a round meat cask with a hideous face in luminous paint.

In January 1891 the new house was begun. Through lack of money, it was not yet to be as large as the owners had meant, but they would add to it later. An architect in Sydney had designed a house which would cost $20,000 and they could afford only $7,500. So they themselves worked for months at drawing and re-drawing a plan, and called in the local carpenter. They insisted on a chimney – mainly for drying Louis's sheets. It was the only one in Samoa, and with the bricks and haulage it cost $1,000. The cottage had cost the same. Every piece of wood, costly pane of glass, keg of nails, pipe, tool and can of paint had to be imported from America or 'the Colonies', as Australia and New Zealand were called.

Leaving his wife to contend with the builders, Stevenson sailed for Sydney, for 'a change of air' and to meet his mother and Lloyd. 'He was averse to leaving me', Fanny wrote to Mrs Sitwell. '. . . I was not well enough to stand the knocking about of the ship . . . I have been very ill since Louis went, though of course he doesn't know that, and it has been a little alarming to find my head going wrong in the middle of the night, and no one on the premises but an imbecile drunken German man.'

The *Lübeck* had been in port again, and Paul had returned from Apia in his cups, bringing tipsy friends. They swore foully at Fanny when she ordered them away, and one tried to ride Henry Simile down with his horse. After that Henry would never leave his mistress if he knew that the vulnerable Paul was likely to be on a jag.

'Everybody, white, brown or black,' recorded Fanny, 'comes to me with apparently full knowledge that I am able to cure any wound or disease. . . . One day I heard a loud weeping as of someone in great pain; a man had just had two fingers dreadfully crushed. I really didn't know what to do except to go to a doctor, but as the wound was bleeding a good deal I mixed up some crystals of iron in water and washed his hand in that. To my surprise his cries instantly ceased, and he declares he has had no pain since. It was only for the effect on his mind that I gave the iron. . . . It is even more difficult when they bring me their domestic troubles to settle. . . .'

The brother of a chief's wife had been eaten by black boys employed at the German plantation. 'They say', reported Fanny, 'that they only ate one of themselves, as the fact of cannibalism going on at our door is of no moment unless some of ourselves are eaten. A number of black boys have been caught already . . . armed with knives. There are supposed to be a great many [runaways] in our bush. It may be that a cave is hereabouts, in which blacks are living.' The servants reported the walking of the ghosts of persons who had been killed and eaten. Nocturnal noises haunted the stable and kitchen. Fanny herself heard subterranean sounds in the garden – either from a cave or of volcanic origin, for there were occasional earthquakes.

Letters from Sydney dismayed her with the news that as soon as Louis had arrived he had been taken ill as usual with 'a smoking hot little malady'. So he lingered there with his mother as nurse.

In early February Lloyd appeared unexpectedly at Vailima, in company with a new white overseer, a titian-haired, bearded young man named King, whom the Stevensons had met in the Line Islands, and 'tons of stuff, mostly mistakes'. Lloyd was further accompanied by two of the Strongs' cats. The Strongs themselves were expected when the new house was completed.

King had a weakness for spirits and Fanny complained that he and the carpenter wasted time and were presumptuous with their employers' belongings. He also tried to persuade her to send the money for an 'outfit' and steamer passage for his fiancée, who would be a 'companion' for the elder Mrs Stevenson on her arrival – 'but of course no menial work'. Fanny said, 'I told him that *I* will be the companion, and I blacked my shoes today when Paul was busy, and don't mind doing it for all. . . . The bush is no place for fine lady companions. . . '.

Two new servants appeared: a heavy, sulky Samoan woman called Emma, who was to be their laundress, and a small grey-haired Malay whom Fanny named Mat. He had appeared at the kitchen door with insinuating smiles and applied for work.

'What wages do you want?' she asked.

'What you like', he replied. 'I no got Papa, I no got Mamma, you allee same my Mamma.' She wrote, 'I seem to be "allee same Mamma" to a great many people.'

For several days there raged the worst hurricane which Fanny had so far experienced. She had moved bedding, candles, mosquito nets and other necessities to the newly completed stable, which was sturdier than the cottage. Earlier she had trodden on a nail, so Lloyd had to carry her there in the night, dropping her in a puddle while he paused to rest, and she 'standing like a crane on one leg'. They found the stable door locked; King had gone with the key to join Paul in the pavilion. For several days she and Lloyd lived in the stalls, constantly sweeping out the water and lying in wet beds, devoured by mosquitoes. When at last the storm was over she hobbled back to the cottage, which leaned sharply to one side. Indoors everything was wet and mildewed.

Presently the *Lübeck* arrived with Louis, still very ill, and his mother. Mrs Stevenson was surprised and disturbed to find the way of life at the cottage much more primitive than she had been able to visualize. She was shocked by the appearance of good stupid Paul as he waited at table: 'a plump little German', Louis described him to Colvin, 'with a bald head, clothed in a flannel shirt open at the neck, a pair of ragged trousers, particularly dilapidated in the seat and held up by a leather strap around the waist, a sheath-knife stuck in the belt, barefoot, and most likely offering the information in a polite voice that "the meat is tough, by God".'

Fanny reported that Mrs Stevenson 'brought with her a sofa for her own use, which shows that she meant to stay'. But the close quarters, continuous rain, and general discomfort were too much for her. She stayed only until the *Lübeck* left. Then she went on to New Zealand to visit relatives until the new house would be ready.

However much Louis had hurt his wife about her 'peasant soul', he showed now that he appreciated her efforts. Writing in April to a newly engaged girl in Bournemouth, he said, 'I do not think my wife very well; but I am in hopes she will now have a little rest. It has been a hard business, above all for her; we lived four months in the hurricane season in a miserable house, overborne with work, ill-fed, continually worried, drowned in perpetual rain, beaten upon by wind, so that we must sit in the dark in the evenings; and then I ran away, and she had a month of it alone. Things go better now; the back of the work is broken. . . .'

Since R.L.S. by no means denied the strong part which sexuality had played in his younger life, it seems reasonable that this may still have been an important element, subconsciously at least, in the 'whole man' in his mature years when his health was better again. Even Fanny's enemies have conceded her sex appeal. The long periods of his illnesses – and hers – and the many months of cruising without privacy, indicate that bodily union was certainly not the first tie of the partnership. In the words of the American biographer J. C. Furnas, theirs was more a symbiosis than a marriage. But meanwhile their magnetism as man and woman was a state of equilibrium, vital to both.

It seems beyond doubt that Stevenson was never once physically unfaithful to Fanny from marriage to death, with the full Victorian idealism. Too many witnesses – Moors, for instance – would have known and proclaimed any slip. Louis had not lost his eye for sensual male appraisal; Colvin repressed from the *Letters* certain passages such as his description of the maid Faauma's beautiful figure. But he was content with what he had at home: the passionate companionship.

Unpublished then were some poems showing the physical attraction which his wife held for him even in the latter years. His 'love songs' were included in a posthumous booklet called *R.L.S. Teuila* which Belle had privately printed in 1899. In the one called 'Dark Women' she discreetly omitted the last three stanzas. The poem ran:

DARK WOMEN

I must not cease from singing
And leave their praise unsung,
The praise of the swarthy women
I have loved since I was young. . . .
The hue of heather honey,
The hue of honey bees,
Shall tinge her golden shoulder,
Shall tinge her tawny knees.

Dark as a wayside gypsy,
Lithe as a hedgewood hare,
She moves a glowing shadow
Through the sunshine of the fair;
And golden hue and orange,
Bosom and hand and head
She blooms, a tiger lily,
In the snowdrift of the bed.

Tiger and tiger lily,
She plays a double part,
All woman in the body,
And all the man at heart.
She shall be brave and tender,
She shall be soft and high,
She to lie in my bosom
And *he* to fight and die.

Take, O tiger lily,
O beautiful one – my soul.
Love lies in your body
As fire slumbers in coal.
I have been young and am old,
I have shared in love and strife
And the touch of a dusky woman
Is the dear reward of life.

Chapter III
The lady of the manor

'Since Byron was in Greece,' Edmund Gosse wrote to Stevenson, 'nothing has appealed to the ordinary literary man so much as that you should be living in the South Seas.' Elsewhere, however, Gosse observed, 'the fact seems to be that it is very nice to *live* in Samoa, but not healthy to *write* there.'

Fanny was so perturbed by her husband's preference for writing a heavy factual book rather than an entertaining one that she warned him, 'I'll gather together all my letters, and publish them.' Henry James had been further impressed by the liveliness and pungency of her letters and had said that they should be printed. She lacked the discipline for a long book without her husband's collaboration. Yet whether or not she was right, *In the South Seas* proved too much of a compromise to succeed greatly in either field, though there were some evocative chapters.

While the house was being built, Stevenson was much in Moors' debt; once he owed him over $12,000. 'Sometimes it used to worry him,' recalled the trader, 'but I never pressed him, simply asking to be reimbursed for the interest I was myself paying. I never had any security from him . . . he was absolutely upright.'

While Moors served Stevenson well, the trader profited from commissions and sales – too much, Fanny and Lloyd thought. Louis would come into his store and say, 'Bills are a nuisance! Never mind the items, what's the total? Let's have that, and get done with it.'

Harassed by the need of money, Stevenson drove himself to complete his collaboration with Lloyd on *The Wrecker*, which began as a serial in *Scribner's* magazine. He described it to Colvin as 'a violent, dark yarn with interesting, plain turns of human nature'. Andrew Lang pronounced it 'a magnificent yarn . . . because one was always panting after the secret. . . .'

On writing-paper headed 'Vailima Plantation', Louis reported in April 1891 to Gosse, 'We are in our house after a fashion; without furniture, 'tis true, camping here, like the family after a sale. . . .' And to Colvin on 29th April, 'Fanny seems a little revived again after her spasm of work. Our books and furniture keep slowly draining up the road in a sad state of scatterment and disrepair. . . .'

'My mother has arrived, young, well and in good spirits', he announced in mid May. 'By desperate exertions, which have wholly floored Fanny, her room was ready for her, and the dining-room fit to eat in. It was a famous victory.'

Moors, who had also submitted a plan for Vailima, found the new house 'very ill-arranged and inconvenient – but the Stevensons liked it'. The British Consul called it 'a big barn'. It was ugly but plain. Luckily Margaret Stevenson was pleased with it – having helped with five hundred pounds. The wooden house was large and airy in the ample way of the old British tropical architecture. It was painted a peacock blue-green, with a red iron roof. Strongly built, it had shutters against the gales and gauze-screened windows to keep out the insects. There were no doors, only hanging mats or curtains. The verandas extended along the whole north side both downstairs and upstairs. In the bathroom and kitchen the water was piped from storage tanks filled when the rain thundered down the corrugated roof. A new cook-house was being erected – still separate in the South Sea manner, but joined to the house by a covered way.

The dining-room was temporarily the main room, though a large drawing-room was to be added when the owners could afford it. Belle later described the dining-room, done in Fanny's taste, in a letter to Low: '. . . papered with yellowish *tapa*, the woodwork of dull blue, the window and door hung with curious Indian fabrics of yellow silk and silver, a real fireplace in the wide corner . . . a source of never-ending wonder to our people. . . . There are the old leather-covered chairs, the Chippendale sideboard and corner cup-board, the latter containing the most precious of the old china. Some chairs of our own woods . . . and the pictures . . . [including] one of Bob's. The painting of Louis with a conceited smile and a dislocated leg is by Sargent.'

Meanwhile in Sydney for many months Belle had been deeply disturbed. '. . . Everybody seemed to be taking it for granted', she wrote cautiously in her memoirs, 'that we would join the family in Samoa when the new house was finished, and for many reasons I did not wish to do this.' She did not mention the terrible problem of Joe.

Then when Stevenson came alone to Sydney, in February, Belle continued, 'we had the talk that was to influence my whole future life. He always referred to it as "the time we got acquainted" '.

One afternoon he asked her to go shopping with him for supplies for Vailima. Afterwards they strolled through the leafy Domain and, sitting on a bench, watched the famous cow that grazed there taking herself home through the busy streets and carriage traffic for milking time.

'Quite suddenly I burst out with all I had wanted to say. . . . I begged him to let us stay in Sydney . . . we could take care of ourselves. The *Bulletin* had offered me a steady job to write a theatrical column. Friends assured me I could get pupils in drawing and painting, and . . . form a dancing class.' She began to cry.

'Then he gave his side. It is the only time I ever knew him to be despondent in any way. He described the despair he felt when told he could never go . . . home. . . .

' "You and Lloyd are all the family I have", he said. "I want a home and a family, *my* family, round me." '

They talked a long time. She was aware of the 'hidden antagonism' on her father's account which had been mixed with her admiration for Stevenson. 'Even if he was the head of our family, I saw no reason why he should plan my life.

'But now all was changed. He talked with such kindness, such understanding, that every bit of resentment I had held toward him melted away, and I felt myself to be truly his loving daughter.'

In late May the three Strongs arrived in the *Lübeck* at Apia. They were accompanied by Mary Carter, a young Australian maid whom Aunt Maggie had engaged in Sydney. The Strongs also brought their third cat, and Belle's white cockatoo. He often sat on his mistress's shoulder and whispered his one word, 'Mamma, Mamma'.

Lloyd met the small whaleboat at the jetty and led the newcomers to the family, who were waiting in the shade of a big *hau* tree. There were horses for Joe and the inexpert Belle. Cocky rode on her shoulder – a sight which was soon to astonish all the island. Lloyd took the thrilled Austin up behind him. Belle remembered that she 'drew long breaths of pure delight' as they followed first the road between coco palms and bananas and then the steep trail with dense jungle and great trees meeting overhead. A sharp turn revealed Vailima. Peacock-blue and red-roofed under enormous ironwood trees, it rose on a wide sweep of lawn beyond the gate in the low stone wall, which was hidden under greenery and the starry blossoms of jasmine vines. Nearby was a hedge of brilliant hibiscus, many feet high after only a few months.

The Strong trio were housed in the original cottage, which had been taken down and rebuilt with improvements a couple of hundred yards uphill. They took their meals and spent the evenings in the main house, and shared in the work of the estate.

'It fairly buzzed with activity', wrote Belle in her memoirs. Louis was up at dawn writing, and the family had breakfast at six. At seven Lloyd and Joe, overseeing a gang of Samoan workmen, disappeared into the forest where they were cutting out underbrush to plant cacao. Belle assumed charge of the kitchen and the house, freeing her mother for the outdoor work which she preferred.

Strong was to be given another chance to stop drinking, if that was possible – though no one had much hope. 'Joe', wrote Fanny in her diary, 'has charge of the fowls, showing great interest in his department.' However, many of the young chicks soon died, which she attributed to his having fed them lime too soon. He had promptly taken to wearing a bright flowered *lavalava* instead of trousers, with a bandanna knotted over his shirt, and a visored cap. He looked like a pirate with Cocky riding on his shoulder.

Inevitably it was not long before Joe was scrounging drinks and finding excuses to sneak down to Apia. His goings-on put a perpetual strain on the family. They tried to cover it up, but the gossip was rife. His mother-in-law burned with resentful nerves, but Belle reformed at last. She helped Louis stand firm between the dissolute Joe and the seething Fanny, and became her stepfather's 'unspeakable comfort'.

Austin, who quickly learned Samoan, recalled from his childhood how Fanny-Gran would stand and supervise while the workmen completed the house. They were handsome young giants, half naked and wreathed in flowers, singing in their own tongue to the beat of their hammers: 'Let us build this palace for our High Chief Lady, for is she not as beautiful as the little flying cloud which skims the sea's horizon at dawn? Take warning, you who are lazy, she hath eyes round her lovely head; she is to be obeyed.' Their eyes glinted with amusement because she could not understand them.

The Stevensons felt love and pride in returning to their home even after an occasional day in Apia. Then Louis liked to have the lamps all lighted in the house, so that when they rode up the dark road and through the eerie wood, they would find Vailima blazing a welcome.

The furniture from Skerryvore had now all arrived. The piano, the last piece, had been carried up the rocky track, swung on poles from the shoulders of a group of Samoans. The Stevensons gave their first luncheon party, and Louis declared that he was swollen with pride.

Local society was impressed by the imposing display of mahogany, silver, crystal, china, family portraits, hundred of books, and the delicious food and wines. Fanny's vegetable garden, the only one in Samoa, produced artichokes, aubergines, sweet corn, tomatoes, melons and yard-long beans. The islanders were awed by the possessions, the pomp and style of the new white chief's household. Even the most important whites lived in sketchy discomfort; whenever a family left, the others attended an auction sale to pick up leftover pieces. They had difficulty in keeping the untrained native help – and thus prejudiced Fanny into employing white servants indoors. The Samoans neither wanted nor needed to work, in a climate where food, shelter and clothing could be had by reaching out to the trees.

It seemed rather undignified to have the Samoan servants innocently addressing their employers as 'Louis' and 'Fanny'. Partly to circumvent this, and party from whimsy, the family took to being called by their staff, and even by each other, by the names which had been given them locally. Louis, on a tour of the island villages, was introduced by a missionary with the name which became famous: Tusitala, teller of tales. Fanny had two names. One was Tamaitai, meaning 'Madam', customary for the lady of the house, and used by her intimates until the end of her life. The other nickname was Aolele, meaning Flying Cloud: some said politely that it was because of her swift darting, others because of the wagging of her bustle. Tamaitai Aolele was her full title. She was also known as the Witch Woman of the Mountain. Lloyd's own name readily liquefied into Samoan as Loia. Belle was called Teuila, 'adorner of the ugly', because she was always dressing up the Samoan girls with flowers or beads or bows, and devising attractive decorations in the house.

All the family, including Aunt Maggie, went barefoot at Vailima in the daytime. ('Even our highest European dignitaries', recalled Lloyd, 'were apt to scurry for their shoes and socks when callers were unexpectedly announced'.) Except for the old lady, they all chain-smoked, rolling their own Virginia cigarettes. Every afternoon a bowl of refreshing *kava* was passed around at two o'clock and then left on the sideboard. A daily delight was the swimming-pool in its ferny glade under the waterfall, where the family and guests gathered for a late afternoon dip. The unripe fruits from the overhanging orange trees were used as cricket balls for matches on the lawn. In the evening the household dressed for dinner in the usual tropical white – shoes and all – the men with cummerbunds. There was often a cocktail, American style, on the veranda before a meal. They all drank a great deal of excellent coffee, and guests were diverted when this was served after dinner with sugar which had been soaked in burnt brandy.

Though Stevenson often spoke to his wife as 'my dear fellow', he saluted her gallantly one evening when the family party were playing a game called 'Truth'. Each person listed the qualities of the others with a maximum score of ten points for each virtue. Louis gave Fanny ten points for beauty. She protested that he must be honest. But he looked at her in amazement and said, 'I am honest. I think you are the most beautiful woman in the world.'

Chapter IV
Fears and fancies

'The war has very nearly begun several times, but now it seems fairly on its feet', wrote Fanny in her diary in July 1891.

Apia, a neutral municipality, was jointly if discordantly administered by Germany, Britain and the United States. After the recent native war, fought with arms provided by all three powers, these had appointed Commissioners and a Chief Justice named Cedercrantz to deal with the land and laws of the island of Upolu.

The three nations, especially Germany, backed the former king, Malietoa Laupepa, but most of the islanders preferred the high chief, Mata'afa, the rival claimant. Missionaries and traders took sides. The Stevensons championed the romantic Mata'afa, whose seat was at Malie, seven miles west of Apia.

'. . . Mata'afa has declared himself king and has made a stand with an immense number of followers', continued Fanny. 'The guards spend the night in singing and dancing. When news came that the war had really begun, Lafaele immediately blacked his face in the manner of a warrior.

'. . . it was, he assured me, to emphasize the fact that he was prepared to protect "the place" and us. . . .'

'. . . We have landed the weapons this morning', Louis wrote to Colvin, 'and inspected the premises with a view to defence. Of course it will come to nothing; but as in all stories of massacres, the one you don't prepare for is the one that comes off. . . .' He drew a plan of the house and marked its defences. He also listed the Vailima armoury: 'eight revolvers, a shotgun and swords galore. It has been rather a lark arranging.' He put the crack shot Fanny in the first line of defence. He and Lloyd were boyishly thrilled to see their old war games come alive.

Soon R.L.S. was writing impassioned letters to *The Times* of London – wasting his talents in meddling, his friends thought – and making himself unpopular with various white officials, including the British consul. 'We sit and pipe upon a volcano, which is being stoked by bland, incompetent amateurs', he told Baxter.

'Louis is coming round now to my view of his book of travels', Fanny had written hopefully to Colvin. But to the dismay of his old friends, he gave up still more time from his other works to write *A Footnote to History*, a painstaking book on the last Samoan war. His wife, contrarily, approved of this literary detour. 'As it may save Mata'afa, I begged him to do it first, though he will get much less money for it than for the other.'

In early August Fanny took the steamer to Fiji for a little change. She arrived back to find her husband embroiled in Samoan strife. 'I am swallowed up in politics,' he told Colvin; 'a wretched business, with fine elements of farce . . . involving many dark and many moonlight rides, secret counsels which are at once divulged, sealed letters which are read aloud in confidence to the neighbours. . . .' He was feverishly writing to *The Times* to expose what he considered the dangerous stupidity of the white authorities. He had hoped that after Fanny's holiday in Fiji she would be more rested and therefore more serene. But though by the early autumn of 1891 the exhaustion of pioneering had eased off, and she was envied as châtelaine of the best house in Samoa with her whole family around her, she slid into a long phase of brooding and nagging. Joe kept her continually upset, and if he had been her whipping-boy one might not have wondered. But oddly she vented her cantankerous moods on her husband, whose life she had fought like a tigress to save. Sometimes everything he did was wrong. She had lectured Belle on the merits of a low voice, but now her own echoed shrill and strident. Every conversation turned into an argument, then a quarrel.

Naturally the Old Man Virulent was hotly resentful and argued back until he felt sick. Then the black clouds would lift and she would be an agreeable companion as usual – until the next spell of ill humour.

Of Stevenson himself Moors wrote, 'When in a rage he was a study. . . '. And Lloyd recalled his 'fits of irritability that were indeed hard to bear. . .'. He had an 'appalling unconcern' for risk or danger. 'Of all things he hated most were anxious efforts to guard his health or make him comfortable', and Fanny was repeatedly chastised in trying to care for him.

But now in the bad times he took to escaping her by shutting himself up more and more in his study, to write or read or correct proofs, though he was too spent to accomplish as much as usual.

More than ever Fanny was a prey to fears and fancies. Her bizarre imagination was frequently used to win co-operation from her helpers. An old white carpenter came up to ask for a job. 'I like him and he is very poor, so I was glad to have some work for him to do', she wrote in her diary. One task was to cut a small low door into the kitchen from her mother-in-law's room. 'I want you to cut through the boards just as they are, as I cannot match the paint.' He declared that this was impossible. 'But I want a secret door,' whispered Fanny. 'His eyes kindled, and mystery instantly enveloped him. . . . "I can do it – yes, I can do it . . ." said he.'

This architectural peculiarity was a symptom of the strange schemes to which she was becoming increasingly prone. 'The beach' – the term for white and half-caste society in Africa – thought her very queer indeed.

Chapter V
The witch woman of the mountain

FANNY

About my fields, in the broad sun
And blaze of noon, there goeth one,
Barefoot and robed in blue, to scan
With the hard eye of the husbandman
My harvests and my cattle. Her,
When even puts the birds astir
And day has set in the great woods,
We seek, among her garden roods,
With bells and cries in vain: the while
Lamps, plate, and the decanter smile
On the forgotten board. But she,
Deaf, blind, and prone on face and knee,
Forgets time, family and feast
And digs like a demented beast.

R.L.S.

'My mother, in a blue *holoku*,' recalled Belle, 'planted innumerable seeds in little baskets filled with earth.' (Sometimes Fanny even wore modest full-cut trousers – an innovation to set tongues wagging.)

She was in correspondence with the botanical garden staffs at Colombo and at Kew and with a grass expert in Washington – by all of whom her experiments were soon taken seriously. The Colombo botanists sent her many tropical plants and trees.

Once when a special lot of these had arrived she dispatched Lafaele to Apia to bring them up on the pack-horse. She cautioned him to be very careful of the printed tags on the plants, so that she would know what they were. Returning, he proudly handed her a little packet wrapped in a banana leaf. It contained all the labels.

Fanny's vegetables, flowers and fruits became legendary – in a place where even the limes from the hedges were so overabundant that they were used in scrubbing the kitchen floor. One of her rare failures was an attempt to make beer out of bananas. After the brew was bottled it blew up with a big explosion, and a nasty fermented odour spread for acres.

She tried to paint some oil portraits of her handsome Samoan servants and acquaintances, but there were many difficulties. 'In the first place the paints become liquid in the heat, and run like water. . . . I mean to try to learn something about watercolours. . . .'

Belle praised her prowess as an engineer. She directed the boys in putting a culvert in the new lane – the old jungle track – before the rainy season. She and Joe had them build a bridge over the river from two fine trees with 'salmon-pink bark and a mixed scent of sassafras and wintergreen'. With a spirit-level, strings and pegs, she laid out an excellent tennis court and croquet ground on the couch-grass of the front lawn. She later built a carriage house with large sliding doors. The times to start and to stop work were signalled to the gangs with an echoing blast on a conch-shell, as used in Samoan warfare.

She found a spring on the mountainside and devised a small reservoir and a system of pipes which brought the water down to the house. She worked with the Samoan boys, and many years later Austin remembered how once, laughing, 'she asked me to rub and unlock her fingers made stiff by cementing the retaining wall of the reservoir'.

She finally had a showdown with Mary, Mrs Stevenson's maid. On top of everything else, late one night Mary had ridden back from Apia on a horse with its leg badly hurt, apparently due to careless tethering. Her impertinence to the angry Fanny led to a quarrel with Maggie Stevenson, and the girl became the elder lady's personal maid, ostentatiously refusing orders from anyone else.

When Mary's year of service was up she joyfully returned to Australia. This left Vailima with a staff of all islanders – known with some suspicion on 'the beach' as nearly all 'popies' or Catholics and supporters of High Chief Mata'afa.

Louis sent off his vivid beachcombing story, *The Beach at Falesà*, which was to appear serially in *The Illustrated London News*. Often criticized for side-stepping the relations of men and women, he was now accused of immorality. He sighed to Sidney Colvin, 'This is a poison bad world for the romancer, this Anglo-Saxon world; I usually get out of it by not having any women in it at all; but when I remember I had "The Treasure of Franchard" refused as unfit for a family magazine, I feel despair weigh upon my wrists.' Those who have charged Fanny with prudish censorship might have noted the sordid sex which she allowed to pass in *The Beach at Falesà*.

While ill with dysentery in March 1892, Louis had announced to Colvin that he had slid into *David Balfour*, the sequel to *Kidnapped*. (For British publication the new title was changed to *Catriona*, but it remained *David Balfour* in America.) 'Really I think it is spirited,' he wrote; 'and there's a heroine that (up to now) seems to have attractions: *absit omen!* . . . And the tale interferes with my eating and sleeping. . . .'

One day when Fanny was planting coffee, with Lafaele helping, their Fijian boy came to her on an errand. He was made up with a blackened nose and black stripes under his eyes: war paint. Lafaele told her that the war was now really going to start, and the first battle would be very near. 'Now Tamaitai – *please*, Tamaitai – you look out. Samoan man fight, he allee same devil – now *please*, you look out.'

Louis and Fanny were finding that the great hazard of running an establishment in Samoa was the dread of war, when the owners might find that all their servants had been ordered out to fight for the chiefs. Through Louis's influence the household staff were usually allowed to stay at home, but several times the outdoor workers disappeared until peace was resumed.

The Stevensons were surprised to have a courtesy visit from King Malietoa Laupepa, dressed in a white uniform with long knee-high leggings of yellow leather, and escorted by three white-clad soldiers with rifles. He stayed to lunch and drank *kava* with Louis, the traditional sign of good will. The couple promptly returned his call at his shabby native 'palace' on a point in the lagoon. 'Louis wishes very much', wrote Fanny, 'to get Malietoa and Mata'afa to work together; in no other way can there be peace in Samoa.'

Though gratified by these civil exchanges the Stevensons were slightly embarrassed, for they had arranged to go to Malie for a courtesy visit to Mata'afa. As he was the 'pretender', they often raised their wineglasses at the table to drink to him with a toast of 'Charlie-over-the-water'.

Early on 2nd May, Louis, Fanny and Belle started out for Malie in a boat manned by Mata'afa's boys. As they approached Malie they saw a handsome thatched house rising 'like a church spire'. Mata'afa was a 'sweet old man', and from him and his seat they had an impression of 'dignity, plenty and peace. . . '. When all were seated on elegant mats, *kava* was served to the king and Louis simultaneously – a rare honour; then to several aides, and then, wrote Fanny, by the royal order, 'to the two "backs of the house" (Belle and me, whom he evidently supposed to be both wives). He was much puzzled as to which was the superior in station. He first gave me the seat of honour after Louis, and then . . . placed Belle where I had been. Instead of being served singly, two bowls were offered us at the same moment, so there could be no jealousy. . .'.

The Stevensons presented their host with a hundred-pound keg of beef, a gift which the town crier announced from the doorstep to all the village. They heard a distant sound of singing, and a procession of young men in wreaths, two by two, marched up and each deposited a present before the guests: roots of taro, young fowls, and an immense root of fresh *kava*. 'We returned by moonlight in the boat, ardent admirers of Mata'afa.'

On 17th May the Stevensons were surprised to receive a call from Chief Justice Cedercrantz for the first time in five months. He wished to see Louis, who had just completed his book on the Samoan situation. Fanny told him that her husband was not well enough to see anyone. '. . . I offered the C.J. wine, beer, lemonade, chocolate, and finally, when he refused even water and a cigarette, I was goaded into saying, "Then you will not break bread with us?" to which he smiled sweetly and silently. . . .'

The Stevensons suspected that, since Louis had warned Cedercrantz in a letter when he meant to attack him, the C.J. was returning the courtesy by coming to let Louis know that he was in danger of deportation. They wondered if the threat against Louis came from his three visits to Chief Mata'afa. 'I am suspicious of something', wrote Fanny, 'I know not what, and want Louis to be very careful what he is about, or he may find himself a cat's-paw. . . .'

President von Pilsach and Cedercrantz – Louis called them 'the Twins' – bought the island's only newspaper in order to oppose him. They tried to catch him in a libel suit. A half-caste Englishman whom he had sometimes employed as an interpreter was charged with conspiring with Mata'afa, and Louis hurried anxiously to consult his solicitor friend Carruthers.

Carruthers outwitted 'the Twins' by promptly briefing advocate Stevenson as a lawyer in the threatened case, so that he could not be called to give evidence.

'. . . We are expecting an invasion of Kiplings', Louis wrote in March to Mrs Fairchild; 'very glad we shall be to see them; but two of the party are ladies. . . . You European ladies are so particular; with all of mine, sleeping has long become a public function. . . .'

Louis went to stay at the hotel in Apia to be on hand when the steamer arrived, but Kipling and his bride had changed their minds and were not on board.

'The twelfth anniversary of our marriage', noted Fanny on 19th May 1892. 'It seems impossible. Also impossible that two years ago (or a little more) we came up to live in the bush. Everything looks settled and as though we had been here for many years. . . .'

'Never got a word set down', sighed Louis to Colvin after the celebrations on the anniversary day.

Of *Catriona* he admitted: 'I am afraid my touch is a little broad in a love story. I can't mean one thing and write another. As for women, age makes me less afraid of a petticoat, but I am a little in fear of grossness. However, this David Balfour's love affair might be read out to a mothers' meeting – or a daughters' meeting . . . but with all my romance, I am a realist and a prosaist, and a most fanatical lover of plain physical sensations plainly and expressly rendered; hence my perils. To do love in the same spirit as I did (for instance) D. Balfour's fatigue in the heather; my dear sir, there were grossness –

ready made! And hence, how to sugar? . . . Anyway, the first pro-
loguial episode is done, and Fanny likes it . . . (I have been forced
to blather to Fanny on the subject of my heroine).'

'It came over me the other day suddenly', Louis wrote to Colvin in
June, 'that this diary of mine to you would make good pickings after
I am dead, and a man could make some kind of book out of it without
much trouble. So, for God's sake, don't lose them, and they will
prove a piece of provision for "my poor old family", as Simile calls
it.'

Moors later wrote to the Rev. Farren that Stevenson, 'a sick man,
was indeed the Work Horse supporting with difficulty, and in a
trembling way, the whole expense of a large household of idling
adults – Human Sponges'.

Work was easier in the dry season between April and October,
when a fresh south-east trade wind blew all day. '. . . the climate',
Louis told Colvin, 'is either gold or poison', but 'it suits all our
family. . . '.

Fanny was anxious to start plantations of coffee and vanilla, and
especially of cacao, which had already succeeded experimentally on
the island. She hoped by the sale of such crops to make Vailima self-
supporting and thus to free her husband from some of his financial
pressure.

One day she handed Lafaele a quantity of vanilla seedlings with
careful instructions on how to plant them. The next morning she
found that they had all been put into the ground upside down.
Lafaele was 'terribly mortified' and wanted to replant them, but
he had to go to town with the pack-horses. So Fanny and Belle
worked hard all day, turning every plant right side up. The following
morning they went to look at their handiwork. To their horror
they found that in the night the penitent Lafaele had got up and
replanted every seedling wrong side up again – 'to give my mother a
surprise, which he certainly did', said Belle. They had another try at
planting the vanilla, but the exhausted seedlings did not survive.

'Joe went down to the dentist . . .' reported Fanny's diary,
'coming home by moonlight.' This was only one of many references
to her Pan-like son-in-law's visits to the dentist.

Then in midsummer 1892 she wrote tersely, '. . . we found Joe

Strong out in various misdeeds, robbing the cellar and store-room at night with false keys. In revenge, when he found that he was discovered, he went round to all our friends in Apia and spread slanders about Belle. We turned him away and applied for a divorce for Belle, which was got with no difficulty, as he had been living with a native woman of Apia as his wife ever since he came here – an old affair begun when he was here before. . . . He came up here late one night to beg forgiveness and asked to be taken back. I was so shocked at seeing him that I had an attack of angina, which seems to remain with me. Louis was made sole guardian of the child. . . .'

When the decree was signed Joe returned to California. Belle and Austin now moved into the main house, leaving Pineapple Cottage as bachelor quarters for Lloyd and occasional male guests. With a stinging relief because 'my sparrow-hawk and I are off', as she put it to Aunt Maggie, she settled down to be 'truly the daughter of this interesting household'. Her mother was much more upset after the years of anger with Joe and the shameful climax, and was overwrought in mind and body.

The beach was sibilant with gossip. Previously Fanny had praised Mr and Mrs Moors' delightful parties with both Samoan and European entertainment. But now she wrote of Moors: '. . . for some reason, only explainable by Joe Strong, he is our bitter enemy; more particularly Lloyd's and mine, we two being Joe's pet aversion. . . .'

Moor's memoirs are touched with acid references. 'Many a day and night, when Stevenson felt played out or written out . . . he would come down to be cheered up. . . . I fancy the women folk were given to coddling him too much at home. . . .'

Remarking that the upkeep of the completed establishment at Vailima cost R.L.S. about $6,500 a year, Moors wrote, 'Mrs Stevenson and Mrs Strong were not the most economical women in the world. The parties they gave were elaborate affairs, and there were plenty of them.'

In spite of an author's need for quiet, Louis was ambivalent about it and the continual entertaining seems to have been more his impulse than Fanny's. 'We never knew', wrote Belle, 'when he rode into town, how many he would bring home for dinner. . . .'

'Never', Fanny recalled of *Catriona* (*David Balfour*), 'was a novel written in more distracting circumstances . . . with natives on the verge of war – political changes – uncertain of his personal liberty – his every action misconstrued and resented by the white inhabitants . . . fatigue and excitement. . . . But he also . . . accepted every invitation he received to attend public functions or private entertainments, in accordance with his theory that social intercourse was necessary in so small a community. . . .'

Stevenson, often afflicted by 'scrivener's cramp', was now so plagued that he had to copy the final draft of *David Balfour* with his left hand. Fanny had tried to write for him, but he felt that she was much needed elsewhere for supervisory work. And as he put it, 'The intolerable click of a typewriter removes from me all that makes it valuable to a man'. One morning Belle found him anxiously wagging a limp hand over a high stack of letters to be answered before the next week's steamer. 'Couldn't you dictate to me?' she suggested.

The experiment was a success, and she was fascinated by his huge correspondence – with famous authors, naïve admirers and cadgers. Soon he began to dictate his literary work to her also, and paid her a small wage. They worked from early breakfast to lunch time. While he dictated, walking up and down, he unconsciously acted the roles of his characters. One day, seeing her smile, he explained that if he once discovered they were only ink on paper he would be unable to go on with them.

Opponents have stressed the occasional discord between the two Mrs Stevensons under the Vailima roof. Colvin later used a Jamesian flash of insight about the elder Mrs Stevenson when he wrote to Lloyd of her 'peculiar gift of disguising all facts at all unpleasant, whether from others or from herself . . .'.

'My three ladies', as Louis called them, founded the Vine-ula Club, a social organization for Apia's half-castes and the Samoan wives of white men, meeting once a week at Vailima. Fanny was president, assisted by Belle, but it was really a major project of Margaret Stevenson. The members were to be shown how to participate in the 'nice' ways of European society, and to dance in ballroom style in Vailima's best room. At every meeting their appearance and deportment were criticized by the hostesses. Sometimes the Vailima ladies would spend an hour or two at the main half-caste village, giving instruction in 'various arts and sciences'. Soon, however, the Club petered out. The half-castes were snobbishly offended because the Stevensons' cook was made a member.

The social notes in *The Samoa Times* often mentioned the functions 'on the hill':

> The private ball given by Mr and Mrs Stevenson at their residence, Vailima, on Wednesday evening was a most successful one. The weather being fine, the guests derived great pleasure from their journey to and fro, independent of their entertainment. About forty couples engaged in dancing, which was kept up with great spirit until three o'clock in the morning. The music was exceptionally good, which partly accounts for the late hour mentioned. We have not heard of a single guest who did not enjoy himself or herself, and it therefore must be said that the hospitable entertainers cannot be otherwise than gratified at the result of their ball.

Said Moors of the Stevensons, 'They were a great dancing people.' Sometimes the music was provided by Belle or others on the out-of-tune piano, sometimes by a hand-organ cranked by an enthusiastic servant.

At the Apia balls, as biographer Graham Balfour wrote, almost everyone was invited 'without regard for social station: diplomatists and naval officers, traders and bar-keepers, clerks and mechanics . . . and . . . their wives and daughters, white, half-caste or wholly Polynesian'. The only rule was that no Samoan man could be invited, 'unless some elderly and august chief were introduced as spectator'. This rule was based not on prejudice but on the fact that there were far more white men than women. Partisan families met at the balls and in the sets they had to dance together even though they might not choose to speak.

White jealousy of the Vailima family took petty forms, and the doings on 'the hill' were the subject of the most impassioned gossip on 'the beach' – sometimes mischievous, now and then malicious. One of the wildest legends, inspired by Belle's darkness, was that she was Louis's daughter by a native woman. (It was not noticed that she was only eight years younger than her stepfather.) The Stevensons were vastly amused, especially Louis, who made up great tales about the old love, who he said was a Moroccan – 'black, but a damned fine woman'. When Fanny scolded him for not wearing his cloak in the rain, he pouted, 'Moroccy never spoke to me like that!'

Chapter VI
'Tiger and tiger lily'

In August 1892 the family prepared for a visit from young Graham Balfour, the second cousin who, having read law at Oxford, was on a slow trip around the world. Even Aunt Maggie had not seen him since his boyhood.

When the steamer came in, Louis told Colvin, he and Fanny and Belle 'were out at the anchorage in the hotel boat as she came up, spotting rather anxiously for our guest, whom none of us had ever seen. We chose out some rather awful cads and tried to make up our mind to them'.

The newcomer turned out to be a very tall, fair, handsome young man with a moustache. 'You can never mistake a Balfour', Aunt Maggie said proudly.

The first afternoon, having found all the family going barefoot about the house and woods, he appeared the same way.

'Why, he's the same kind of fool we are!' exclaimed Louis.

Balfour had come for a month, but in all he stayed more than a year, making several interim voyages in the South Pacific. For Stevenson he was a godsend because, though much younger, he shared the family background and provided conversation about literature, art and the European world for which his cousin hankered. He took a strong interest in Samoan affairs and even learned the language. Both Louis and Fanny were delighted to have an educated companion for Lloyd, whose bachelor cottage he shared. The two young men made trips to native villages, and the newcomer was soon called 'Palema', the transliteration of Graham. He played chess and piquet with Louis, and helped Fanny with her garden and her engineering of the new waterworks.

'. . . within a single day', he was to write of her, 'we established a firm friendship that only grew closer until her death . . . "steel-true and blade-straight. . . . Honour, anger, valour, fire. . . ." ' He praised her devotion to her husband and children and her loyalty to her friends. 'Her integrity and her directness were such that one could, and frequently did, differ from her . . . in the strongest terms without leaving a trace of bitterness.

'To her enemies, of course,' he added, 'she showed another side. Opposition she did not mind, but dishonesty and deceit were unforgivable.'

For Belle, Graham's presence at Vailima was a mixed blessing. She fell in love with him. Her lot was not easy as an attractive divorcee of thirty-four in that outpost with few eligible men. After her years of humiliation with Joe Strong, the handsome and upright young Scot represented a dazzling contrast in character and way of life.

Fanny would have been far from averse to such a new son-in-law. She wrote to Mrs Sitwell, 'It will be a wrench when he goes. He says he will come back, but I know what will happen; he will marry somebody, & we'll hate his wife, & there'll be the end of it; for of course, if we hate his wife he must hate us. . . .'

Balfour had arrived in time for a wave of giddy social gaiety in Apia. This marked the visit of the Countess of Jersey, wife of the Governor-General of New South Wales, Australia, with her brother Captain Rupert Leigh, and her young daughter. She stayed with Bazett Haggard – the British Land Commissioner – whom she described as 'a great character. When he visited Sydney he was known as "Samoa", for he never talked of anything else. . .'.

'On the evening following our arrival', Lady Jersey wrote in her memoirs, 'he invited Robert Louis Stevenson and Mrs Stevenson to dinner. . . . I shall never forget the moment when I first saw him and his wife standing at the door of the long, wood-panelled room in Ruge's Building. A slim, dark-haired, bright-eyed figure in a loose black velvet jacket over his white vest and trousers, and a scarlet silk sash. By his side the short, dark woman with cropped curly hair and the strange piercing glance which had won for her the name in native tongue, "The Witch Woman of the Mountain".'

The Governor's wife was the guest of honour at dinners, balls, picnics and polo matches on the beach. She was entertained several times at Vailima, where she was much diverted by the vivid ménage. Louis's work suffered. Fanny, much unnerved by the final dismissal of Joe, was in no mood for the celebrations. She took an instant dislike to the titled rival. Perhaps it was the more galling since the visitor was as unconventional and adventurous as herself. She fumed at Louis because he, like everyone else, made a fuss over Lady Jersey. He admitted later that his wife turned the time of the visit into a 'wretched period' at home. Though she swallowed her criticism in public, in her diary she pronounced the Governor's lady 'too much like [Kipling's] Mrs Hawksbee.... They were a selfish "champagne Charley" set, with the exception of the daughter. . . . Lady Jersey tall and leggy and awkward, with bold black eyes and selfish mouth; very selfish and greedy of admiration, a touch of vulgarity, courageous as a man, and reckless as a woman.'

Louis, on the other hand, believed that 'Lady Jersey is in all ways admirable, so unfussy, so plucky, so very kind and gracious', while her brother was 'a nice sort of glass-in-the-eye chap'.

Lady Jersey had got it into her head that she wanted Stevenson to take her on a *malaga* to visit the rebel Chief Mata'afa. It was unbelievably indiscreet for a Governor-General's wife – 'the Queen of Sydney' – to mix in Samoan revolutionary politics. But she persuaded Louis, equally rash and at even more risk, to take her along incognita. 'The lark is certainly huge,' he wrote to Colvin. 'It is all nonsense that it can be concealed; . . . and I would not in the least wonder if the visit proved the signal of war. . . .'

One notes the pointed absence of Fanny, who violently disapproved of the expedition – with reason. The party included Captain Leigh, Belle, Lloyd and Graham Balfour, with Henry Simile as interpreter, and a couple of servants. It was secretively agreed that Her Ladyship should pose as Louis's cousin.

As the cavalcade approached Malie, Louis recorded, 'we found the guard making a music of bugles and conches. Then I knew the game was up and the secret out. . .'. No further proof was needed when, after the feast, Lady Jersey was served first with *kava*.

After the party's return from the *malaga* there was much shaking of heads – including Fanny's – in Apia, Sydney and London. Stevenson's position was more precarious than ever for having embarrassed his own government as well as the local *status quo*. British Consul Cusack-Smith was furious, and for once Fanny was on his side.

'Stevenson', reminisced Lady Jersey in her memoirs, 'was not only a writer of romance, but a hero of romance.'

Emotionally Fanny had had a devastating summer. Louis later admitted that the rage and shame in getting rid of Joe had done her 'no end of harm'. Then before she could have a rest without unwelcome stimulus, Lady Jersey and party had arrived. It was not consolation enough to call the Governor-General's wife 'vulgar' and to say 'I told you so' when Louis got into difficulties. She kept on nagging with such wild unreason as never before. It was almost more than he could bear. Any woman must be going out of her mind to make such a mountain out of a molehill.

It was then, he confessed later to Colvin, that he 'began to have a suspicion of the truth'. Naturally he drew back and tried to convince himself that he was mistaken. But the moods, tantrums and illusions of the last year had piled up into a cloud of foreboding like the sinister light before a hurricane. There was 'nothing you can say is *wrong*', but it wasn't '*right*'. Fanny still sat at her end of the dining-table and worked in the garden. But subtly she had become, for days or weeks at a time, a stranger.

Where before he had felt exasperated and misused, now he was alarmed and compassionate. What could he do? He did not mention his apprehension even in his most intimate letters home. Apia seemed appallingly far from the help of doctors and friends in Britain and America. There was only the fat little German Dr Funk. Louis took hope from Fanny's old resilience, the way she had often re-bounded with surprising *élan* from a low level of body or spirit.

It may have struck him with a shock in those early months of her 'neurasthenia' that his own wife was the embodiment of a female *Jekyll and Hyde*. His success emphasized her own failure as a creative artist. Her coin of love-hate had admiration on one side, subconscious envy on the other.

Just as Joe had kept the household 'by the ears', as Louis said, now it was the frequent oddity and irritability of Fanny. Most of the painful burden fell on her husband, though Belle and Lloyd rallied from their self-absorption and tried to help him smooth over the scenes and cover up for outsiders. '. . . these children are so good to me', he said with touching incredulity.

As for Fanny, after the years of struggle against tuberculosis and poverty, why should she break down just when she had attained most of the things she wanted? One might guess that – in part – she collapsed after she found that she was no longer indispensable to Louis. When he had lacked health and success, she had fought to help to give them to him – to work miracles of will and love. But now his health was better and he had other props besides herself. His mature work had outgrown her and he did not need her advice on potential masterpieces. In his exile he was dwelling more and more on his Scottishness, where she could not fully follow him either in life or in books. True, he could never have managed Vailima without her, and she was still a great deal to him, but her ego could not bear being less than the unique, the top. Share they must, if not happiness, then unhappiness.

Rising above this challenge, as man and writer, was to be Stevenson's grim test in his latter years. His wife was indeed his 'tiger and tiger lily'.

Chapter VII
The threat of deportation

Louis wrote tenderly about his step-grandson to Miss Boodle. Sometimes Austin wandered in the weird shadowy bush, afraid, but talking. He 'found strange seeds, like lollipops or precious stones', and collected little shells of many shapes and colours. He caught eels and small bright fish in the streams, and watched various beautiful birds which lived off nutmegs, one a 'neat little bronze bird with a tail like a scallop shell. . . .' Yet Austin dreamed of the romance of Europe and America.

'Once the child was sent on errands to Apia. He set off on horse-back with hand on hip and pockets full of letters and orders, at the head of a procession of huge white cart-horses with pack saddles, and big brown native men with nothing but gaudy kilts. He ordered his luncheon alone in a queer little Chinese restaurant on the beach – as if he owned the archipelago.' He wore 'a dirty white cap, a faded purple shirt, little brown breeks that do not reach his knees, bare shanks, bare feet stuck in the stirrup leathers, for he is not quite long enough to reach the irons'.

At a family conference they decided to send him to school at Monterey in the care of his Great-Aunt Nellie Sanchez. She had just lost her husband Adolfo through quick consumption; and her small son 'Louie' was near Austin's age.

All the family and the flower-wreathed servants went down to see off 'our young adventurer', as Louis called him. In a 'dark, deadly hot' afternoon a drizzle started, and when Fanny put up her umbrella her horse reared, cannoned into the others and bolted for home, nearly wrecking the cavalcade and the champagne bottles which Louis carried. Her back was wrenched but she went on. At length Austin was safely conveyed in a small boat to the *Mariposa*, and put aboard with feasting, 'tips', and five baskets of fruit for the captain. Louis 'did the affable celebrity life-sized', as he said. While the boat drew off, three handsome ladies supported the child on deck, 'looking very engaging himself, between smiles and tears. Not that he cried in public. . . . But there is always something in a mite's first launch'.

'When we rowed back to shore and I saw that big ship disappearing over the horizon', wrote Belle, 'I thought my heart would break.'

She almost lived for the monthly letters from her schoolboy. Then one mail day, while she was working hard with Christmas preparations, the big bag was emptied as usual, but there was no letter from Austin. She went up to her room and Fanny came to sympathize with her. Suddenly they heard a shout, and saw Louis riding across the lawn, waving a letter. He had galloped to town and made the postmaster 'turn the post office inside out', finally finding the missing envelope wedged in a drawer.

Moors wondered in his memoirs whether Stevenson as an author would have done better unmarried, away from the influence of his wife and stepchildren. 'True, his marriage was a happy one; but I make bold to say that neither was his character bettered by it, nor his art benefited. He was very fond of his wife and easily led by her; "Fanny" was like a king; she could do no wrong. Mrs Strong, too, was headstrong and talkative, and generally got her way with him.'

He quoted Carruthers' mention of the 'swaying of his better judgment by other people'. And 'in justice to Stevenson', Moors said, 'I felt compelled to say my opinion is those slippings from his own nature were due to the women folk of Vailima. . . .' It became 'quite evident' to Moors that 'if Stevenson was to give us of the best that was in him, he must get away from the restraints and annoyances that he was subject to at Vailima'.

The Wrecker had not long been published and, though it was selling well, Moors and his friends in America thought R.L.S. could do much better if he were free of '. . . that collaboration [which] was destroying his reputation'. He had received $5,000 for the serial rights of his own fine Master of Ballantrae and $6,500 for The Wrecker, shared with Lloyd.

Neither Fanny nor Louis had ever forgotten the charming little Nassau Island, with which they had fallen in love during their cruise in the Janet Nicholl. Moors opened negotiations to buy it on their behalf, but then one of Louis's fits of depression overtook him and he lost interest. About a year later the island came into the open market and Moors himself bought it. 'Stevenson said if he could get away somewhere to work undisturbed he might accomplish something worth attempting.' So, according to Moors, he and Louis schemed to make visits to Nassau Island together. 'The important question was how to keep the ladies away from our island retreat, but he said he could manage it somehow.'

Though much has been made of this prejudiced account, Fanny herself had recorded on 29th May 1892 that Moors had bought Nassau without seeing it, 'entirely on my recommendation'.

Despite the harassed author's need of peace, if he, a 'handless man', had gone stag with Moors to the isolated island, Fanny would probably have had to pull herself together and go to rescue him. He was no camper. Moreover he nearly always fell ill when he was away from her care for any length of time.

Louis himself was loyally mindful of the fact that the pain she occasionally caused him was not characteristic: 'It ain't her.' Her 'real self' he did not cease to love and find absorbing, perhaps the more poignantly because it was in danger, and she needed him as he with his haemorrhages had often needed her. In her mental illnesses he felt a sort of anguished homesickness for her.

The Stevensons had become friendly with the American Land Commissioner, Henry C. Ide, whose wife and three young daughters were still at home in Vermont. Learning that the second daughter,

Annie, had had the social misfortune of being born on Christmas Day, Louis sent her a mock-deed of his own birthday, drawn up in formal legal terminology with a big seal. In asking her to take the name Louisa he made her his name-daughter in the Samoan way.

'I, Robert Louis Stevenson, Advocate . . . author . . . sole owner and patentee of the Palace and Plantation known as Vailima . . . a British Subject, being in sound mind, and pretty well, I thank you, in body:

'In consideration that Miss Annie H. Ide . . . was born, out of all reason, upon Christmas Day, and is therefore out of all justice denied the consolation and profit of a proper birthday;

'And considering that I, the said Robert Louis Stevenson, have attained an age when O, we never mention it and that I have now no further use for a birthday of any description; . . .

'*Have transferred* . . . to the said Annie H. Ide, *all and whole* my rights and privileges in the thirteenth day of November . . . to have, hold, exercise, and enjoy the same . . . by the sporting of fine raiment, eating of rich meats, and receipt of gifts, compliments, and copies of verse. . . .

'*And I direct* the said Annie H. Ide to add . . . the name Louisa – at least in private; and I charge her to use my said birthday with moderation and humanity . . . the said birthday not being so young as it once was. . . .

'And in case the said Annie H. Ide shall neglect or contravene . . . I hereby revoke the donation and transfer my rights in the said birthday to the President of the United States of America for the time being:

'In witness whereof I have hereto set my hand and seal . . .

SEAL

Signed Robert Louis Stevenson.'

Witness Lloyd Osbourne
Witness Harold Watts

The deed was duly registered in the Court at Apia and a copy was sent to Annie Ide in America. She continued to celebrate the birthday all her life.

In October 1892, wrote Graham Balfour, '*Weir of Hermiston* was begun, and for three or four days Stevenson was in . . . a seventh heaven . . .; he worked all day and all evening, writing or talking, debating points, devising characters and incidents, ablaze with enthusiasm, and abounding with energy. . . . Then he settled down, and a few [evenings] later read aloud to the family . . . the first draft of the opening chapters.'

More than ever R.L.S. was at his best in a novel of Scotland, and not even his toughest critics could deny that *Hermiston* would potentially have been his masterpiece.

About this time, to the annoyance of his friends in Britain, he felt compelled to withdraw a short story from the publisher's hands because Fanny did not like it. He added a postscript to Colvin on 4th December: 'My wife protests against "The Waif Woman" and I am instructed to report the same to you. . . .' As a result the story did not appear in the volume of *Island Nights' Entertainments*. Heavily based on a Scandinavian saga, it was a tale of a possessive wife whose sexual fascination gave her mastery over her husband, and whose greed was punished by fate. Louis's friends thought Fanny objected because she felt that the weird female character suggested herself. It has often been assumed that her displeasure was the sole reason why 'The Waif Woman' was unpublished until after her death. But Belle wrote that, when she and her mother were finally packing to leave Vailima, she found Louis's manuscript tucked behind some books in the library, with a rejection slip – 'the first, I imagine, he had received in many years'.

'I am at daggers drawn with the government', Stevenson informed Miss Una Taylor, a Bournemouth friend, in October 1892; 'have had my correspondence stopped and opened by the Chief Justice – it was correspondence with the so-called rebel king – and have had boys examined and threatened with deportation to betray my relations with the same person. . . .'

When H.M.S. *Ringarooma* arrived to collect sealed orders, it was rumoured on the beach that it had come to deport Stevenson. He took the precaution of hurrying out to call and make friends with the commander and officer in case he was to be placed under their arrest.

Once he took the chair at a public meeting of protest against the regime. Fanny backed him up, and more. Always passionately prejudiced in favour of an underdog, she was a fanatic champion of Mata'afa, that 'sweet old man'.

She had been behind the scheme when Louis persuaded several of the high chiefs to grow cacao and had given them the seed for their plantations – 'to cultivate their lands instead of wasting their energies in useless warfare', as she later explained in a Preface. To Mata'afa he proposed the erection of a mill to manufacture fibre. He himself meant to provide the money to buy the machinery and materials, and was already negotiating with British firms when the war broke out. 'As this . . . [was] a large expenditure, he tried to push on the two novels. . . .'

A rumour was spread that Stevenson was aiding Mata'afa – which seemed to all but a few white foreigners to mean that he was helping to smuggle in a large quantity of arms and ammunition. 'A veranda lantern, a present from my mother-in-law', recalled Fanny, 'was supposed to be used for signalling a mysterious vessel that had been hovering near the coast.' There were 'rumours of a concealed road to Mata'afa's village, or that three thousand Mata'afa warriors were encamped in our woods. I remember our amusement when a high white official, taking tea on our veranda, nearly swooned with fright when he heard the *pu* (a war conch we used for calling our working men together), believing that he was to be treacherously attacked. . . .'

Louis was trying hard to reconcile Mata'afa and 'the amiable, broken Laupepa, a mere puppet in the hands of a few white men . . . whose interest lay in the sale of certain commodities'. '. . . They now started a regular system of persecution against [my husband]. Several new labourers at Vailima confessed to being spies sent to watch Tusitala's movements. Open threats of deportation were made. Long after, the captain of a passenger ship told me he had been approached on the possibility of luring my husband on board the ship and deporting him. . . . Futile attempts were made to induce the Laupepa warriors to attack Vailima. . . . Innuendoes and covert slanders pointing to Tusitala appeared in our only newspaper. . . .'

'This is a strange life I live,' wrote Louis to Colvin on 30th November 1892; 'always on the brink of deportation.'

In early December his enemies acquired a single advance copy of *Footnote to History*, his book on Samoa. From Fiji Sir John Thurston, the High Commissioner for the Western Pacific, issued a regulation for peace and order in Samoa, threatening fine and imprisonment for any British subject guilty of sedition towards the Samoan government.

Louis and Fanny seriously considered other places in the South Seas where they might settle if they were expelled from Vailima. The fear of loss was increased by the fact that they had started to build the 'second half' of the house, which was being constructed by the 'German Firm'. The threat seemed a heartbreaking waste of Louis's great expense and his wife's imaginative toil; she was doomed to create wonderful gardens only to leave them. He wrote post-haste to ask Colvin to use his influence in Whitehall.

Time was long in sea-miles, but perhaps as a result of Colvin's efforts, in March the Foreign Secretary wrote to reassure Stevenson, and in April the Colonial Office rebuked Thurston for issuing such a prejudiced regulation without the approval of London.

Louis's debunkers have said that he had only fancied the possibility of his deportation, but though he doubtless dramatized himself, as a man who still loved to play soldier, correspondence on file at the Foreign Office and the Colonial Office has proved that the hazard was real.

Nonetheless an official in Whitehall scrawled dryly on a document that Mr Stevenson would do better to attend to his novel-writing.

Chapter VIII
'The indiscreeter petticoat'

By the end of November the new addition to the house was triumphantly roofed, to be occupied in time for Christmas. Stevenson was greatly relieved to find that he could pay for it. He had made – and spent – nearly four thousand pounds in that year, he told Colvin, '. . . but I live here so entirely on credit, that I am determined to hang on'.

Now the house, as described by Graham Balfour, was 'of two

blocks of equal size, placed . . . in échelon' – the second slightly behind the front level of the original house, with the wide verandas joining. 'After December 1892, the downstairs accommodation consisted of three rooms, a bath, a storeroom and cellars below, with five bedrooms and the library upstairs. On the ground floor, a veranda, twelve feet deep, ran in front of the whole house and along one side of it. . . . The chief feature within was the large hall that occupied the whole of the ground floor of the newer portion of the house – a room about sixty feet long and perhaps forty wide, lined and ceiled with varnished redwood from California. . . .' Here were installed the bust of Grandfather Robert Stevenson, the two gilded Burmese gods flanking the great staircase ('Are they alive?' asked a chief), the piano, the Rodin group, some carved heirloom cabinets dated 1642, the Sargent portrait of Louis with Fanny, the St Gaudens medallion, various other family pictures and treasures, and the big built-in safe believed to contain the Bottle Imp of Louis's story.

Fanny summed up the estate in one of her Prefaces to Louis's works: 'The house at Vailima has been contradictorily described as a palace where the master sat enthroned amid hordes of obsequious vassals, and as a sordid, poor place in the jungle, where food was scant, and poverty sat at the elbow of the jaded novelist spurring him on to continual, feverish exertions. Neither was true. . . . To a man just off a cruise among the islands, no doubt an evening spent at the house in Vailima, with its waxed floors and antique rugs, its rooms blazing with lamps, the glitter of glass and silver, and the flower-bedecked noiseless house-boys, would seem like a glimpse into paradise. On the other hand, a tourist fresh from the colonies or San Francisco would accept all this as a matter of course, but would note with disapproval the bare feet of our butler, and be much annoyed when the shoes, put out overnight to be blacked, showed by their sodden condition in the morning that they had been washed, inside as well as out, under the garden hose. . . .'

The expenditure was, however, an unending burden on Stevenson's pen. The second wing of the house, like the first, cost about $7,500. Moors, as his local man of business, figured the total cost of the various buildings at some $20,000. Stevenson found that the maintenance of the whole establishment required about $6,500 a year. Fanny's arduous plantations of cacao, vanilla, coffee and pineapples were not a commercial success, for several reasons: the climate, the unskilled labour, and not least the fact that the Stevensons were too fair with their hands to compete with the regular planters, paying the men in cash rather than in trade, and extending feudal hospitality to their families.

Baxter often chided Louis about his worrying financial situation. 'My rate of expenditure is hellish', he replied. '. . . Lloyd and I grow grey over the monthly returns; but every damned month there is a new extra.' However, as Lloyd was to point out, had his stepfather survived longer after the early investments in the estate, he could probably have lived indefinitely on his annual royalties and interest with much less strain on his work.

The truth is probably that the Stevensons' extravagant establishment was like a runaway horse which, having started, they could not stop. At first – after years of poverty – it was fun to play Lord and Lady Bountiful. But later, though they would both have preferred a simpler existence, they could not drop the heavy weight – and habit – of responsibility and hospitality expected of them.

'We don't live for the necessities of life', Stevenson told Lloyd. 'In reality no one cares a damn for them; what we live for are its superfluities.' Certainly his wife was a whole-hearted partner in this outlook.

Belle and Fanny were full of ingenious plans for the celebration of Christmas in the new baronial hall. White folk from Apia and the warships were invited to stay overnight for a house party, with feasting, games and dancing on the waxed floor of the great hall. On Christmas Eve the family and house guests all helped to trim the tall ironwood tree, the feathery mock-conifer of the tropics, in the new hall, supposedly as a surprise for the staff. At the top was a good-sized pink Cupid; the branches were laden with ornaments, candles and presents, with many more parcels piled at the foot.

When the quick darkness fell the tree was lighted, the doors opened, and the Vailima servants and their relations trooped in and sat cross-legged around the tree for the distribution of the gifts.

The New Year of 1893 began with an epidemic of influenza brought, like most 'civilized' diseases, by a passing ship. The contagion 'ran like quicksilver over the island', affecting the Samoans more than the whites. Fanny isolated Louis upstairs in the hope that he might escape. He had temporarily put aside *Weir of Hermiston*, and was working on a Scottish historical romance called *St Ives*, the name of the flirtatious hero.

But one morning at breakfast Belle found her mother 'white-faced and anxious'. Louis had a cold, which always meant the threat of blood-spitting. Fanny had been up all night. 'He mustn't talk at all, or make the slightest effort', she said. Nevertheless he had two small haemorrhages. One notes that in the tropical climate he had been almost free of these when he had been able to live a more casual outdoor life without so much worry.

Aunt Maggie and Lloyd took turns in entertaining the patient in the morning, and Belle in the afternoon. They played draughts and halma, and he wrote on a pad, '*Talk!*' Belle, often teased as a chatter-box, obliged. But this too palled. She knew that he was longing to get back to *St Ives*. Suddenly she was inspired. In her schooldays she had learned to talk on her fingers with a sort of deaf-and-dumb alphabet. 'Louis brightened with interest,' she recollected. He mastered the alphabet quickly and, though it was slow work, in time he actually dictated fifteen pages of the manuscript.

Moors said that there was disharmony, even rivalry, between Fanny and Belle, not only over the housekeeping at Vailima, but also because Fanny was jealous of Stevenson's growing dependence on her daughter as his confidential amanuensis. Louis himself confided to Colvin that he had 'bad times' over their continual petty quarrels. Fanny would offend Belle, who then cried all day, whereupon Fanny would unburden her usual warm remorse upon her husband, until the two women nearly drove him out of his wits. But Fanny seems to have been gratified by his acceptance of Belle's literary services, which she remembered with pride in the Prefaces. Since Louis had a perma-nent financial burden from his wife's relations, her clan instinct – like his – loomed much larger than any passing vexation.

While he was ill he scribbled a little verse:

MOTHER AND DAUGHTER

High as my heart! – the quip be mine
That draws their stature to a line,
My pair of fairies plump and dark,

The dryads of my cattle park.
Here by my window close I sit,
And watch (and my heart laughs at it)
How these my dragon-lilies are
Alike and yet dissimilar.

From European womankind
They are divided and defined
By the free limb and the plain mind,
The nobler gait, the naked foot,
The indiscreeter petticoat. . . .

Buxom and free, flowing and fine,
In every limb, in every line,
Inimitably feminine. . . .
So far the same they seem, and yet
One apes the shrew, one the coquette –
A sibyl or a truant child.
One runs, with a crop-halo, wild;
And one, more sedulous to please,
Her long dark hair, deep as her knees
And thrid with living silver, sees. . . .

               . . . so, for ever go
And come upon your small brown feet:
Twin honours to my country seat
And its too happy master lent:
My solace and its ornament!

Chapter IX
Fanny's secret illness

Now Fanny herself became gravely ill. Stevensonians have known
that she had some unnamed illness in the later winter and spring of
1893. But a few 'censored' letters written afterwards have recently

revealed that what ailed her was a relapse of her psychosis – much the worst.

For a while she was wildly wandering, despite the helpless efforts of her husband, aided by Belle and Lloyd. There was a dreadful scene which went on all night. For the first time she was physically obstreperous. She wanted to run away, and for about two hours Louis and Belle held onto her bodily to keep her from rushing out of the house.

She was subdued at length, and recovered enough for her husband and daughter to decide that she was ready for a tonic change of scene. Maggie Stevenson had left on a visit to Scotland. After mid February Louis, Fanny and Belle sailed in the American steamer *Mariposa* for Sydney on what Stevenson, whistling in the dark, misled his friends by defining to Colvin as 'a month's lark'.

The first few weeks in Sydney he described as 'delightful'. Fanny was free of her shrill haranguing – quiet and calm. The party loyally stayed at the old Oxford Hotel where, said Belle, 'the head waiter reserved all the hearts of celery for our table'. Fanny wrote home that her husband was taking a holiday and was in high spirits, even making speeches and answering toasts. They enjoyed going to theatres and restaurants. 'We gave parties in our rooms at the hotel, went to other people's parties, took long drives, and walked about through the Domain.' Louis was now so famous that people stared at him in the streets.

The late summer days were oppressive and the nights humid. The Australian doctors repeated the verdict of their European colleagues – that Louis might live to a normal old age if he kept free from strain. But as usual he was unwell in Sydney and spent some of his time in bed, writing.

There he once received an interviewer who asked him his own favourite among his books, so far. He named *Kidnapped*. As a piece of literature he gave first place to the story 'Thrawn Janet'. 'Mrs Stevenson, who had just entered the room, said she liked best his *Life of Fleeming Jenkin*. "I cried over that book, and never over anything else of his", she added.'

One day Louis came back to the trio's suite with three topaz rings – his birth stone – one for each of them. Inside his own were engraved the initials *F* and *B*, and in theirs, *R.L.S.* He presented them to Fanny and Belle with a poem which began:

These rings, oh, my beloved pair
For me on your brown fingers wear
Each a perpetual caress
To tell you of my tenderness. . . .

Another time he and Belle slipped out and, 'on the sly', as he said, bought for Fanny 'a gown of gaudy black velvet and Duchesse lace'. Belle described its debut when they sailed into the large dining-room, Louis in evening clothes made by the best tailor in Sydney, herself in a new yellow silk dress. 'Both dames', he told Colvin, 'are royally outfitted in silk stockings, etc.'

'But alas!' he added. Fanny was able to wear her handsome new gown only once before they left. For then, as he admitted later, 'she got bad again'. She had her old fixations and hallucinations. 'Fanny saw you twice today', he once confided to Baxter. Belle's friend, Dr Fairfax Ross, took charge.

A few months later Dr Ross visited London and had a long talk with Sidney Colvin. 'He says', Colvin reported to Baxter, 'L's weak lung is doing its best to recover, & would almost certainly do so, if he gave it any chance; by freedom, that is, from exposure, malaria, worry, & over-work; all of which things, he says, are doing him harm, so as to make the issue doubtful: but under good conditions he might get quite well and live as long as any of us.

'Of *her* condition he thinks ill – both as to body and mind.'

As for Louis, Fanny recalled, '. . . It fell to a London "lady journalist" to undo all he had gained in health and strength. . . . On the return voyage . . . she waylaid him for an interview in a draughty part of the ship, holding him with a monologue until he caught a heavy cold that kept him confined to his cabin until we reached the tropics.'

'An amusing but tragic holiday . . .' he summed up jauntily to Colvin on 1st March as they neared Apia. '. . . Fanny quite sick, but I think slowly and steadily mending; Belle in a terrific state of dentistry troubles . . . and myself . . . a fine pleurisy. . . .

'. . . We return, as from a raid, with our spoils and our wounded. I am now very dandy: I announced two years ago that I should change. Slovenly youth, all right – not slovenly age. So really now I am pretty spruce; always a white shirt, white necktie, fresh shave, silk socks, oh, a great sight!'

At Vailima there followed many weeks of 'heartbreaking anxiety over Fanny'. Dr Ross had warned Louis that she might have a relapse, so he and Belle and Lloyd were prepared. The children were 'good as gold' and all three worked well as a team. The quarrelsome phase of Fanny's psychosis seemed to have passed; since her return she had been 'kind . . . querulously kind'. She complained about the food and would hardly touch it.

'Well, there's no disguise possible', Louis finally wrote more frankly to Colvin in early April, '. . . we are miserably anxious. . . .' They were in a quandary. Dr Funk had given her an alarmingly strong medicine, and she alternated between stupors and 'deathbed scenes'.

She had her most 'insane fit' of all, but this time she was gentle, with wistful hallucinations. Dr Funk assured her husband that her life was not in danger. But when Louis asked if the same was true of her mind, the little German would not deny the possibility of risk. Hardly had he left when she relapsed again with another frightening scene. Then she calmed down and appeared to be without delusions.

As if the domestic situation was not difficult enough, the family were expecting the arrival in the next few days of a house guest, Mr Isla Sitwell, a relation by marriage of the 'other' Fanny. They could not receive a stranger with the hostess out of her mind. There was still hope that she might have one of her swift reversals and be better by tomorrow. But if not, Lloyd was to entertain the visitor at the hotel and politely send him off in the same steamer.

By a godsend, the miracle occurred. 'I am thankful to say the new medicine quieted her at once . . .' Stevenson wrote two days later. She had been reasonable and pleasant. Belle slept with her at night in her own room, and shared stints of duty with Louis all day so that the patient was never unattended. He pronounced the reformed Belle 'a blessed friend' to him. '. . . A crape has been removed from the day for all of us . . .' he told Colvin of Fanny. 'You can't conceive what a relief this is; it seems a new world. She has such extraordinary recuperative power that I do hope for the best. I am as tired as a man can be. . . .'

After a few days Fanny began to stop taking the powerful drug but was normal and quiet, so Louis was encouraged and lay down to rest.

The weather was stormy and the rain and sea roared together with a sinister menace, but he did not mind anything except the 'horror of madness'.

The gale delayed the steamer, and when it came the family ventured to risk entertaining Isla Sitwell at Vailima. 'Isla is the pure unadulterated Briton,' Louis informed his mother in Scotland; 'he won't drink *kava*, he won't touch any native foods. . . .' Graham Balfour had also returned from a cruise – again to fill the weary Belle with longing.

'Fanny was devilish ill. . . . No doubt but [she] had an alarming illness', Louis admitted to Mrs Stevenson in a letter of half-truths dictated to Belle on 17th April. 'Old Funk did better than I could have hoped. The bother didn't exactly help my cold and for a long time I did a brisk business in spasmodic cough that's over now. In the midst of all this Belle kind of bust up – I think it was only worry and overwork. I was mortal glad you weren't here. Now we are all recovered or recovering – Belle protests against this and says to tell the truth that Fanny is not recovering. But though it is true she seems to have taken a cast back, she is far indeed from being so dreadfully ill as she was before.' (The amanuensis interrupted to write: 'She lies in bed, does not smoke, doesn't want to eat, or speak; Louis does not want to alarm you but I think you should know what a really anxious time we are going through. . . . I would like to see her take an interest in something. *Belle*.') 'Well, perhaps Belle is right,' Louis's dictation continued, 'but I indulge myself in a little better hope. . . .

'. . . In the interval we have had lunch, and I personally, as totally distinguished from the amanuensis, think Fanny emphatically better than yesterday. (She ate no lunch and she ate no breakfast, if you call that better. B.)'

However, a few days later Louis reported to Colvin: 'Well, Fanny *is* really better, nothing to the contrary, and I shall get Belle to sign the same and show this to be neither deception nor self illusion.' (She is really. Belle.). . . .'

'Last night, the cats woke both her and me about 10, Belle was not yet in bed; so we all three sat in my room and had some grog and a cigarette, and were as jolly as sand boys. It was delightful: Fanny as nice as possible, and did not seem ill one particle. Yesterday, too, she went all round her garden with an umbrella, and quite tired me out following her. . . .'

A month later he exulted that she appeared 'to be all right again'. She seemed quite sensible, except for some old illusions which he supposed she might never lose. But those were trifles if she was 'really all right'.

With her lifelong flair for the macabre, her own situation had been like some exotic and sinister tale which she herself might have devised: the tropical estate with its luxurious hospitality, and indoors the famous author's wife struggling with madness.

Though in the earlier stages Louis had often lost patience with her carping aberrations, it is moving to see that he poured out love and attention to woo back her mind – almost as if he were courting her.

Some have assumed that he was disenchanted with his wife because of her temporary dementia. But on the contrary – except in dispirited moods – he seemed to feel the more tenderness for her, in the way that parents may cherish an abnormal child. After all, the process worked both ways: she had not ceased to love him because she had nursed him at his physical worst in the gruelling squalor of his haemorrhages. Each had a soft spot for the lame dog. If she was jealous of his success it was subconsciously. Habit or no, the marriage stood the test of mutual care under harrowing conditions. And with naïve sincerity both partners always regarded it as 'romantic' and a great love. Perhaps, with ups and downs, it was.

Behind the secretiveness of Victorian modesty, Fanny's several spells of ill humour and delusions during those two years or so in her early fifties may have derived from the menopause. Since her whole life was on an exaggerated scale, possibly this condition may have had a similar effect.

It would be understandable that her subconscious mind was burdened by the fact that she had not borne children to Louis. Though the couple had apparently agreed that their circumstances made it unwise to have a family, she may have been sensitive about the reflection on her age, and certainly pained by her husband's inevitable disappointment at being childless. What he had called the 'false alarm' of parenthood at Hyères in 1884 had been repeated by her claim – more likely imagined than real – that she had again been pregnant at the age of about fifty during the South Sea cruising, as she wrote to Mrs Low. The finality of the menopause, stressed like most symptoms by the Victorians, may well have given her a depressing sense of guilt and failure which led unconsciously to abnormal brooding and thence to periodic disturbance of the mind.

In the same trying spring Louis had resumed the half-finished *Ebb Tide* which he and Lloyd had begun in Honolulu. But at that moment several acres behind the house were being cleared of forest and planted with pineapples for export, in the hope of making the plantation pay, and for a while this project took up Lloyd's time.

Perhaps the book was the better for more work from the senior collaborator, since his solos were always superior to anything he did with Lloyd or Fanny or Henley. Most painstaking with his adult fiction, it took him twenty-one days to write twenty-four pages of *The Ebb Tide*, which was completed in mid year.

'If Stevenson were in a hot fit of work . . .' recollected Balfour, 'he could do nothing and think of nothing else, and toiled all day long. . . . On the other hand, if he were ailing or disinclined for writing, he would stop work some time before luncheon. But almost at any time he was at the mercy of visitors, white or brown. . . .'

As soon as Fanny was better she was back at doctoring and nursing others. A businesslike note from Louis survives, sent downhill to her when she was caring for some sick child in Apia.

'Dear Fellow, – What I feared somehow! This goes down with the bed-pan; the soup will follow in course. I shall likely ride down in the afternoon. The nurse is a good idea. Miss Skelton it should be, I fancy. – Yours ever, R.L.S.'

The reliable Graham Balfour was at Vailima during part of Fanny's mental illness, and he seems, without mentioning it, to have put it in perspective as only a small portion of the Stevensons' whole relationship.

'The mistress', he remembered, 'was in vividness and character and warmth of heart the equal of the master – and with full and perfect affection and loyalty they held their own paths. Once a controversy on some line of policy or conduct had run high between them; either of the two in turn appealed subsequently to my judgment, and I was young enough to express my agreement with certain points on either side. The inevitable followed and both fell upon me with indignation. . . . But next morning at dawn Stevenson appeared at my bedside with a very generous apology.'

Many of the couple's friends at home were bored with hearing of 'politics and natives', but Henry James rejoiced to tell Louis that Mrs Sitwell passed on every savoury scrap of news about Vailima. 'I know what you all magnificently eat, and what dear Mrs Louis splendidly (but not somewhat transparently – no?) wears. Please assure that intensely-remembered lady of my dumb fidelity. . . .'

Touched, Stevenson replied in June that Fanny was now quite well again, and promised James a photograph of her taken in Sydney 'in her customary island habit as she walks and gardens and shrilly drills her brown assistants'.

Doubtless not unaided by her husband's prestige with *McClure's* magazine, she had sold its editor a short story called 'Under Sentence of the Law (The Story of a Dog)', which appeared in June 1893. This was her last published fiction.

Sad news came from Edinburgh that Baxter's wife had died. With grief and financial troubles, he was taking to drink. Bob too had been bereaved the year before with the loss of a child.

Louis's sense of Scotland was so powerful that one rainy morning as he stood on the veranda he felt the actual presence of '. . . highland huts, and peat smoke, and brown swirling rivers, and wet clothes, and whisky, and the romance of the past, and that indescribable bite of the whole thing at a man's heart, which is – or rather lies at the bottom of – a story'.

He and Fanny often dreamed aloud together of a trip home. In an eager dialogue they described their disembarkation at Southampton, their arrival in the boat train at Waterloo Station in London, and then their clip-clopping in a hansom cab to stay a while with Colvin.

They were always hoping at least to meet the old friends – especially Colvin – at midway points: Egypt, Ceylon, San Francisco, Honolulu. Like Kipling, James Barrie was definitely planning a visit to Vailima in a year or so – if his host had lived long enough. But Stevenson was destined never to meet either writer except by correspondence. 'There was some waterfall', recalled Barrie, 'at the top of which I was to sit, let go, and in a second or two come to my senses in a glossy pool. I was warned that the natives would not think much of my work until I had done that.'

In a long letter to Barrie on 2nd April, 1893 – the very period when Fanny had been, in secret, most ill – the brave Louis had sent him a set of pen portraits of the family whom he would meet:

FANNY V. de G. STEVENSON
The weird woman
Native name: Tamaitai
This is what you will have to look out for, Mr Barrie. If you don't get on with her, it's a pity about your visit. She runs the show.

Infinitely little, extraordinary wig of grey curls, handsome waxen face like Napoleon's, insane black eyes, boy's hands, tiny bare feet, a cigarette, wild blue native dress usually spotted with garden mould. In company manners presents the appearance of a little timid and precise old maid of the days of prunes and prisms – you look for the reticule. Hellish energy, relieved by fortnights of entire hibernation. Can make anything from a house to a row, all fine and large of their kind. My uncle, after seeing her for the first time: 'Yes, Louis, you have done well. I married a besom myself and have never regretted it.' . . . Doctors everybody, will doctor you, cannot be doctored herself. . . . A violent friend, a brimstone enemy. Imaginary conversation after your visit: 'I like Mr Barrie. I don't like anybody else. I don't like anybody that don't like him. When he took me in to dinner he made the wittiest remark I ever heard. "Don't you think," he said, "the old-fashioned way," etc.' Is always either loathed or slavishly adored; indifference impossible. The natives think her uncanny and that devils serve her. Dreams dreams, and sees visions.

ROBERT LOUIS STEVENSON
The tame celebrity
Native name: Tusitala
Exceedingly lean . . . general appearance of a blasted boy – or blighted youth. . . . Past eccentric – obscure and oh no we never mention it – present industrious, respectable and fatuously contented. Used to be fond of talking about Art, don't talk about it any more. . . . Really knows a good deal but has lived so long with aforesaid family and foremast hands, that you might talk a week to him and never guess it.

Friendly grocer in Sydney: 'It has been a most agreeable surprise to meet you, Mr Stevenson. I would never have guessed you were a literary man!' Name in family, The Tame Celebrity. Cigarettes without intermission except when coughing or kissing. Hopelessly entangled in apron strings. Drinks plenty. Curses some. Temper unstable. Manners purple in an emergency, but liable to trances. . . . Given to explaining the Universe – Scotch, sir, Scotch.

BELLE
Native name: Teuila

Runs me like a baby in a perambulator, sees I'm properly dressed, bought me silk socks, and made me wear them, takes care of me when I'm well, from writing my books to trimming my nails . . . manages the house and the boys, who are very fond of her. Does all the hair-cutting of the family. Will cut yours and doubtless object to the way you part it. Mine has been re-organized twice.

LLOYD
Native name: Loia

Six foot, blond, eye-glasses – British eye-glasses, too. Address varying from elaborate civility to a freezing haughtiness. Decidedly witty. Has seen an enormous amount of the world. Keeps nothing of youth, but some of its intolerance. Unexpected soft streak for the forlorn. When he is good he is very, very good, but when he is cross he is horrid. Of Dutch ancestry, and has spells known in the family as 'cold blasts from Holland'. Exacting with the boys, and yet they like him. Rather stiff with his equals, but apt to be very kindly with his inferiors – the only undemonstrative member of the family, which otherwise wears its heart upon both sleeves; and except for my purple patches the only mannered one.

Chapter X
Meddling in the Samoan war

That summer there were continual warlike interruptions to Louis's work. 'Sometimes a party of warriors with embarrassing presents – one was a large white bull – would stop for *kava* and a chat, firing a parting salute that endangered not only our livestock but ourselves,' recalled Fanny in a Preface. Occasionally, even at family prayers, 'a passing band of hostile warriors, with blackened faces, would peer in at us through the open windows, and often we were forced to pause until the strange, savage, monotonous noise of the native drums had ceased. . .'.

One morning when Louis was dictating *St Ives*, Belle looked out anxiously and asked, 'Louis, have we a pistol or gun in the house that will shoot?'

'No,' he answered calmly, 'but we have friends on both sides.' And he went on with the story.

'One of the petty persecutions . . .' continued Fanny, 'was an order restraining him from the purchase of firearms . . . we were living . . . on an historic battlefield just at the border between the opposing forces. At any moment a collision might take place at our very doors. . . . We had no reason to fear either side, except in one case; in Samoa no prisoners were taken. Even a wounded prisoner would be instantly decapitated. . . . Tusitala knew that wounded men from either side would look to him for protection. . . . He therefore asked permission to import half a dozen rifles. This request was insolently refused. Not long after my son saw his opportunity and forced the hands of the authorites then in power, who themselves unwillingly imported the six rifles that we afterwards kept in the study.'

At the end of June Stevenson and Balfour rode down to Apia for news, but found only rumours. On a sudden temptation they galloped over to the rebel outposts to reconnoitre. Near Chief Mata'afa's villages they passed among armed warriors enthusiastically drilling and thrilling with preparations for war.

'They came back quite wild with excitement, burning to join in the fray', Fanny sighed in her diary. 'It is going, I see, to be a difficult task to keep Louis from losing his head altogether.'

A day or two later she and Belle accompanied him over the same road, so that Belle might make sketches of the warlike scene to send abroad to the newspapers. As the trio neared a village which was potentially hostile, Louis directed that they should ride very fast to avoid being stopped. Fanny told the others to go ahead and she would follow at a more dignified pace.

However, at a small bridge in the middle of the village her horse stopped and began to shiver – whether from fear or a fit, she did not know, but she could not budge it. People watched curiously from the huts, and then a man and boy came and began to lead or drag the horse forward. Louis, who was far ahead, came back to find out why she was so slow, and was alarmed.

A little farther they paused for Belle to make a sketch of a guarded ford and of a flag of truce, a white rag hung with sticks on a coconut tree. She had apparently dropped her whip while she was drawing, and Louis galloped back to find it. As the two women waited, the Chief Justice passed, and some Samoans in his escort stopped to talk to Belle in their own language.

'Who is that woman?' one asked rudely, pointing to Fanny.

Belle told him that he should say, 'Who is that lady?'

'She is a pig-face', replied the man. 'Pig-face' was an insulting idiom.

Belle scolded him with Victorian decorum for his cowardice in being impolite to ladies, and made him repeat after her, 'You are a beautiful lady, and your mother is a beautiful lady.' '. . . his friends laughed at him with much enjoyment.' But she and Fanny did not tell Louis what had happened.

'In conjunction with the Three Great Powers', Louis exulted to Barrie, 'I have succeeded in getting rid of My President and My Chief Justice. They've gone home. . . .'

But as Balfour wrote in retrospect, 'the evil had been done', the consuls were weak and interfering, and outrages 'went on under the very noses of the consuls and the guns of the warships', as the indignant Stevenson pointed out in three more letters to *The Times*.

He and his stepdaughter went down to a ball in Apia, where a woman confided to Belle that she was gravely alarmed: there was almost certainly going to be an attack upon the whites. Someone told Louis that a royalist chief had said that he, Stevenson, was the source of all the trouble, and not only he but his family should be punished. 'One good job,' he wrote to Colvin; 'these threats to my home and family take away all my childish temptation to go out and fight. . . .' He told Secretary of State Maben that he intended to protect himself and his property as best he could.

At Vailima there were tentative preparations for a possible state of siege, and in Apia there was great fear of atrocities if Mata'afa captured the town. The Stevensons ate their fat pig to remove it from the temptation of foragers. They laid in a supply of food and of *kava*. Vailima now flew Lloyd's American flag as well as Louis's Union Jack. The family were relieved because Mother Stevenson and Austin were both away.

'In these exciting times', remarked Fanny, 'it is really dreadful to find oneself in the position of the British female. . . . I suppose if our house should be attacked, Belle and I must retire to a back apartment with some crochet work and not ask what is going on. A strange thing that would be for a person of my spirit. . . .'

On 4th July the men forbade the two women to go to the American Consul's ball in honour of Independence Day. But 'Belle and I had made up our minds to strike for freedom', though Louis was 'in deep sulks at our attitude'. They were then told to dress plainly and they gave in, though they had meant to go in their grandest gowns – as all the other American women did.

The next morning the mother and daughter rode into Apia to devote the day to Belle's sketching of the war preparations. Armed warriors marched to and fro with blacked faces and red kerchiefs around their brows. Boats kept coming in, sometimes fifty strong, with drums and bugles which the wielders did not know how to play, a jester cavorting in the prow and the crew uttering 'menacing ululations'. Fanny and Belle determined to walk to Mulinuu, the royal village on the point, to find more picturesque material, though it made their feet sore to walk in shoes after being so long barefoot, 'but I would have gone if I had had to walk on my head', wrote Fanny. They were politely received by the villagers and drank *kava* in a grass house where Belle sketched further powerful warriors.

Returning to the hotel in Apia, they met Louis – still sulking – and Mr Haggard, the British Land Commissioner, who was intoxicated not only with drink but with 'excitement and romantic feeling.'

He declared that he had several weapons, and if the town were rushed he would hold the small building which housed his office. 'He bitterly wanted women to protect, and besought Belle and me to ... lie under a table (on the upper floor) and hand cartridges out to him.

' "No," I said, "I do not wish to be found dead, lying under a table, shot through the stomach." '

South Sea fashion, the consuls told the government troops that they might take their positions but must not start the war until after the mail steamer had called. When it came there was a letter from Mrs Stevenson in Scotland. She had given up the old house in Heriot Row and said that she had arranged to send off the furniture to Samoa. Fanny wondered if they would have a house to contain it. Meanwhile some of the government warriors left their bivouacs in the bush and went home at night to sleep. 'They said it was not comfortable, poor children,' commented Fanny.

The next day most of the Vailima boys were allowed to go to the races. But in the evening as the family sat around the table after dinner, a message came to say that there had been desperate fighting at an outlying village, and the many wounded had been brought in to the Mission House in Apia. Louis leapt up and said he would ride down at once.

'I will go too', said Fanny. Whereupon Louis, who had agreed the night before to 'bury the hatchet', said then he wouldn't go. However, he did. He, Fanny and Lloyd rode downhill by lantern in the dark but starry night.

At the long frame Mission House they saw lights shining from every window and people running about the lawn. The Rev. W. E. Clarke told them that many wounded and three dead men had been brought in, while eleven heads had been presented to the government and were hanging in baskets on a tree near the King's hut in Mulinuu. One was the head of a 'village maid', or local maid of honour, incredible in Samoa.

Fanny wrote that from their very arrival at the mission 'I was convinced that we were "intruders", and it seems we were. I never could have gone myself, but Louis was in such a frantic state of excitement that I was determined to keep him in sight. I have never personally meddled with the missionaries, though always good friends enough without any intimacy . . .'.

Stevenson forecast 'a long and bloody war'. But on 10th July it was reported that Mata'afa was routed. He had set fire to his village and fled to the island of Savaii. His nephew – and heir – had been decapitated with a hatchet. The nephew's faithful wife – the maid of the village – with whom he had eloped, refused to leave him. She was killed in the same fight, and her head was brought in to the government – one of three women's. Louis saw the Secretary of State and demanded that the takers of the three women's heads should be punished. 'Well,' grimly wrote Fanny, 'there was a woman's head for each great power, or, if one likes better, for each consul.'

Henry Simile told her that on the first woman's head to be brought in, the hair was 'short in the woman's fashion, with a fringe cut across the forehead and curling thick around the neck, "six inches long, just like yours, madam" '.

Meanwhile Lafaele, who had gone to work for Carruthers for sixteen shillings a week, came up and begged to return to Vailima for his old wage of thirteen shillings. 'Never mind money', he said. 'I no care for that. I like come back because I love Madam too much.'

On 17th July Fanny was furious because Louis had gone to town and come home 'filled with the *tala* that Mata'afa is an intriguing coward. . . . Now, when they are afraid of their own men, and Mata'afa is a childless fugitive, all the stones are thrown at him. To begin with, my sympathies are always with the "underdog in the fight". But, besides, I remember, when Mata'afa was the man before whom all trembled, we offered our friendship and broke bread with him. If I gave him loyalty then, fifty thousand times more do I give it now. They say they have found compromising letters from Louis addressed to Mata'afa. That is not true. . . . But this diary of mine I now make a compromising document: . . . to one purpose, and I intend to do everything in my power to save Mata'afa: doubtless very little, but it shall be my utmost. And if Louis turns his face from him by the fraction of an inch, I shall wear black in public if they murder him, or if he is brought in to Apia a prisoner I shall go down alone and kiss his hand as my king. Louis says this is errant mad quixoticism. I suppose it is; but when I look at the white men at the head of the government and cannot make up my mind which is the greater coward, my woman's heart burns with shame and fury and I am ready for any madness.'

In town that day, as the Vailima family sat on Haggard's veranda, his half-caste interpreter Yandall appeared with a wound in his head and a bruise on his jaw. He had been attacked while he was a passenger in a boat under the American flag and with a safe-conduct from King Laupepa. 'Haggard was very meek on the subject', wrote Fanny. 'Suddenly I rose up and said vehemently that all the white men in Samoa were cowards, and left the party. I am afraid I behaved very badly. At luncheon healths were being drunk, and I drank the health of "H. J. Moors, my worst enemy and the only white man clinging to Samoa who is not a coward".' (Moors, in fact, was away in Chicago at the World's Fair.)

It was proposed to disarm Mata'afa's thousands of followers on the island of Manono, and the Stevensons feared that this might mean a massacre. Louis was ready to go with the British warship to Manono. But it was first necessary for him to ask Consul Cusack-Smith's permission to send his letter to Mata'afa – though it seemed 'very undignified' in Fanny's opinion.

On the following day the several Allied men-o'-war left port to track down the rebels. The royalists had won a battle, and in the late afternoon two German ships returned with word that Mata'afa had surrendered and was on board the British vessel with twenty-eight of his chiefs.

Early the next morning Louis and Lloyd rode down to Apia to meet the rebel party. 'Mata'afa looked old and broken . . .' and his villages had been burned, despite a promise – to the fury of Fanny. The following day the Vailima servants were busy cooking Samoan food for the imprisoned chiefs – fine large taros, a hundred *polisamis*, young coconuts and bananas. Lloyd and Graham delivered the meal to the ship.

'I wish', said Fanny, in an entry partly over-inked by her heirs, 'I were able to write a little tale that I might save some money of my own . . . for there is such a blessing and pleasure in sharing any-thing. . . . Of the last I got twenty-five dollars out of a hundred and fifty, which I sent to my dying brother-in-law. I wonder what would become of a man, and to what he would degenerate, if his life was that of a woman's: to get the "run of her teeth" and presents of her clothes, and supposed to be always under bonds of the deepest gratitude for any further sums. I would work very hard to earn a couple of pounds a month, and I could easily earn much more, but there is my position as Louis's wife, therefore I cannot.'

Slowly Vailima began to creak back towards normal. A stream of visitors, white and brown, brought more political rumours and gruesome stories of head-taking, the captors cavorting along in primitive gore.

On 24th July Fanny reported that Louis looked much better, after the strain of the war was over, 'and certainly my savage attack concerning our conduct to Mata'afa could not have been good for him. He called me an "idiotic Enthusiast". Well he's another, and I insist on his being consistent; at least to his own ideals. It is not in him to be either a philosopher or a cynic.'

Lloyd went to Apia the next day with some *kava* and tobacco for Mata'afa on the warship, only to hear that he and the high chiefs were to be deported at once to the Tokelau Islands, while the lower chiefs were to be imprisoned in Apia. Lloyd hurried home and found his mother and stepfather on the point of riding down to see Mata'afa. 'I felt very badly that I was not allowed to go before', regretted Fanny. 'It was thought to be "not convenable" that ladies should show any sympathy with their broken friends *until the captain had called*! What sort of a devil from hell is the British matron, and why should I, of all people in the world, take her for my pattern in conduct? . . .'

Balfour remembered a scheme by which Fanny later proposed to release Mata'afa and the other high chiefs from their exile – they had been moved to the German island of Jaluit – and carry them off to Australia. 'The project was a wild one and would only have led to their return and disgrace, and in these terms and much stronger expressions we discussed it, without ever abating one jot from our personal friendship.'

Chapter XI
'A violent friend, a brimstone enemy'

Mr Gurr, a neighbour of the Stevensons, described how, in the long shadows of a late afternoon in August 1893, his pretty Samoan wife Fanua had been playing tennis with Louis on the grass court. Suddenly they saw him halt and stagger, and Fanny rushed up to him as a haemorrhage started. Fortunately the flow soon stopped. 'Mrs Stevenson', wrote Gurr, 'then insisted he should not play tennis any more. . . .' Lloyd remembered how afterwards at the tennis parties they could see his 'wistful face' watching them as he paced the veranda, often glancing up at the evening star in the sunset glow over Mount Vaea.

In that last year he confided to his stepson the 'physical dishonour', the 'degradation' of his invalidism. Lloyd wrote, 'To me his heroism took on new proportions, and I was thankful I had refused an important post to stay with him.'

Louis was the only member of the household who had ever climbed to the top of the mountain, and several times he expressed a wish to be buried there – if indeed he could not die in Scotland as he longed to do. Lloyd meant to clear a path to the summit, but procrastinated about a task with such depressing implications.

In the summer Louis again took up *Weir of Hermiston* for a while, interrupted by bristling letters on Samoan politics to *The Times*. In September *Catriona* was released in London. It was a great success, praised as 'blending the novel of manners with the adventure romance'. 'Mr Stevenson', announced Andrew Lang, 'has drawn a good petticoat at last.'

'. . . Women seemed to him the victims alike of man and nature', Lloyd explained in a Preface a generation later. 'He often spoke of the chastity forced on them under pain of starvation; he often said there would be no children had men been destined to bear them and that marriage itself would disappear. What man, he asked besides, would ever have the courage of a woman of the streets? In those days of large families the accepted right of men to breed their wives till they died filled him with loathing. . . . Yet very little, if anything, of this ever got into his books.'

'. . . It has been said he was unable to draw real live women', wrote the Scottish biographer, Rosaline Masson. 'It has been alleged that Mrs Louis Stevenson held this opinion, and that she interfered in the drawing of women characters, and dominated Louis's work in that respect. The answer is clear. Take the last three novels. [*Catriona* (*David Balfour*), *St Ives* and *Weir of Hermiston*.] In them the women are drawn with true insight, with delicacy and firmness; they are vivid and convincing. . . . And they are all, like the plots and backgrounds of the three novels, drawn entirely from his own Scotland, where none could follow him to help him. . . . Young women and old women, Highland and Lowland – but all Scotswomen; the women of his *memory*, the women of his *youth*.'

He told Fanny that he meant soon to begin an entirely different sort of book, to be called *Sophia Scarlett*, with all the principal characters women. . . . ' "There was a time", he said, "when I didn't dare to really draw a woman; but I have no fear now. I shall show a little of what I can do in the two Kirsties [in *Weir of Hermiston*]; but in *Sophia Scarlett* the main interest shall be centred in the women." He did not tell me the plan of the story any further than that it was to be laid in Tahiti, Sophia Scarlett owning a large plantation, which she managed herself.'

Of *Catriona* he had admitted, 'Catriona costs anxiety – she is as virginal as billy'. But now he wrote to Colvin that he was planning a novel in which a woman of questionable morals would be the chief character. Henry James was 'delighted to learn of this. . .'.

In September the archipelago was ravaged by an epidemic of measles, often made fatal by the islanders' ignorance of treatment. The Vailima hall became an impromptu hospital where Fanny and Belle nursed twenty-two Samoan men. When their faithful butler was taken ill in Apia the mother and daughter went down to see him. Finding him very sick, they had him carried home in a native sling on a pole.

Meanwhile Graham Balfour was about to go up to Honolulu to take a schooner for a South Sea cruise in his hosts' footsteps. As a change after the strain of politics and illness, Louis decided to accompany him on the steamer to Honolulu. Fanny did not fancy the sea voyage, but suggested that he should take Talolo, the cook, who spoke fluent English and was thrilled to visit the Polynesian metropolis.

Before they disembarked Talolo developed measles, and they were quarantined at the quiet Sans Souci Hotel on Waikiki Beach, which still contained panels painted by the Strongs during their residence there. Louis rested under the palms, but wrote an indignant letter to *The Honolulu Advertiser* about the newfangled telephone, 'bleating like a deserted infant from the dining-room'.

When the quarantine ended he became, according to the writer Arthur Johnstone, 'a familiar figure again seen as he rode through the streets of Honolulu, or loitered at the Hawaiian Hotel or Pacific Club'.

He delivered a witty lecture on Scottish history ('one long brawl') to the local Thistle Club. He was made an Honorary Chieftain, and was given the club's small bronze thistle. Ever afterwards he wore it on the lapel of his velvet jacket. He was wearing it when he died.

The day before he was to return to Samoa he caught a cold which turned into pneumonia. Graham had sailed, but Talolo nursed him until Fanny arrived by the next steamer.

During his convalescence the Stevensons sat for hours each day on the broad front *lanai* with its view of the sea and the Waianae Mountains – 'discussing various subjects', wrote the hotelier. 'It was most interesting to watch them; no two people could have been more suited to each other, or more devoted. . . .' They were also 'very untidy'.

Their old friend King Kalakaua had died. His sister, Queen Liliuokalani, had sat briefly on the throne and then been deposed by the missionary party, and Hawaii was now a territory of the U.S.A. Rallying as usual to the underdog, Louis and Fanny called on the large dignified ex-queen.

The Honolulu visit was destined to be R.L.S.'s last glimpse of the world beyond Samoa.

Austin was back at Vailima. Belle had been eating her heart out for her distant son until 'the family took pity on me' and sent for him. Louis wrote to the cousin whom his mother had visited in New Zealand, and suggested that the boy should be sent to school under his care in Wellington, from whence he could spend the long vacations at Vailima. Austin, explained Louis, was 'not very forward in his schooling' and 'not very brilliant at understanding'.

Meanwhile in Edinburgh the elder Mrs Stevenson was preparing to leave for Apia, having sent off a cargo of furniture after the sale of the old home. Vailima was soon grander than ever with the gleaming mahogany, silver, family portraits and vintage wines from Heriot Row. Yet even with the tropical background and the antiques, somehow the clutter of ornaments on the chimney-piece and elsewhere made it seem indelibly Late Victorian.

On 15th November the Stevensons made another militant gesture on behalf of their Samoan rebel friends. The twenty-three minor chiefs were housed in the Apia jail, 'a wretched little building', inside a corrugated iron fence beside a mangrove swamp. Their quarters were thatched lean-tos in the courtyard. Food was sent in – which they shared with their jailers – and they were courteously treated by the prison officer, a friendly, cultured Austrian soldier of fortune named Count Wurmbrand. But the chiefs' mean situation was a great loss of face, and the Stevensons realized what this meant to Samoans. Though it was an affront to white officialdom, Louis, Fanny, Belle and Lloyd hired a carriage and drove ostentatiously to the jail, to deliver gifts of *kava* and tobacco.

'I am a sort of father of the political prisoners', Louis added, '. . . in that riotously absurd establishment.'

On Boxing Day – after another rich Christmas festival at Vailima – the imprisoned chiefs reciprocated by inviting the Stevenson family to a native feast inside the jail courtyard. There were rumours that an uprising was being plotted, and Louis and Fanny realized that they would be gravely compromised if this proved true. 'Tusitala and his family would be good hostages', Louis wrote of himself. But they backed their own belief in their friends and accepted the invitation.

The chiefs had arranged for their relatives to bring in the ceremonial pigs, chickens, fish, fruit, *kava* and gifts. The Austrian captain received the Vailima party at the gate, where their boy was waiting to take the horses. Belle was seated at the right of the highest chief, Fanny was called first for *kava* drinking, while Louis was hailed with tributes as 'our only friend', and begged to accept gifts as 'a present from the poor prisoners to the Rich Man'. The offerings included fine *tapa* cloth, dozens of fans and baskets, a pig, eight pineapples and – as the *pièce de résistance* – *ulas*, valuable necklaces of scarlet seeds, which the chiefs took off and draped over the guests' shoulders. The Stevensons protested at this sacrifice, but the reply showed that it had a political significance. They were told that King Malietoa Laupepa had wanted to borrow the *ulas*, and they were to wear them past the king's palace.

Here was more risky intrigue, but the family were all willing to take a chance. They paraded on foot along the whole Apia street and past the ramshackle thatched palace with their scarlet *ulas* and loads of gifts, amid local cries of 'Beautiful!' which Louis interpreted as 'O my! ain't they dandy'. '. . . no such feast', he assured Colvin, 'was ever made for a single family, and no such present was ever given to a single white man.'

A little later Fanny's 'violent friendship' made her the heroine of another jail adventure. Talolo's father-in-law, one of the imprisoned chiefs, fell ill, and she went down to nurse him. Louis called the local doctor, who recommended that the sick man be moved to more comfortable quarters. Fanny induced Count Wurmbrand to pretend ignorance while she smuggled the patient out of the jail. However, the white government was indignant and Wurmbrand lost his job, to the dismay of the Stevensons. Louis posted bond for the return of the escaped prisoner on his recovery – a promise which was honourably kept.

Count Wurmbrand was compensated by being asked to live free at Vailima. A guest described him as 'chief cow-herd', but he made an amusing and cultivated companion. He and Belle led 'the German', the fashionable dance, when the Stevensons gave a grand ball on 22nd February for George Washington's birthday. The maids had twined garlands around all the portraits and statues in the great hall, even the dignified bust of Grandfather Robert Stevenson. Rows of candlenut torches flared near the gate where hitching-posts had been set up, and a swarm of boys waited to help the guests dismount and to take their horses. The dancing was said to include the first cotillion ever seen in Samoa.

Chapter XII
The stormy petrel

Early in 1894 a third small war broke out. The newly appointed
Chief Justice Ide acted 'very wisely and mildly', and accepted
some of Stevenson's advice in making up 'a plan which has proved
successful – so far'. However, the faults of officialdom in the background moved Louis to write more indignant letters to *The Times*.

Again Vailima boys were conscripted, with war-blackened faces
and oddly mixed weapons. War drums thumped in the woods and
sometimes troops of warriors pranced across the lawn in front of the
house. Adelaide Ide noted that several times the 'nervous romantic'
Mr Stevenson 'caused his house to be barricaded with mattresses and
he retained permission to import ammunition . . .'. At one scare he
galloped down to the Ides' bungalow to beg them to take shelter at
Vailima.

There was fighting along the coast, the royalists being aided by
several Allied warships – including Vailima's favourite, the *Curaçoa*
– which were dispatched to shell the rebels.

'Part of *St Ives*', Fanny recalled in a Preface, 'was written to the
booming of the guns rolling over the hills, as the men-of-war attacked
Luatuanu'u. At each report a wail arose from our native people,
most of whom had friends or relatives at the front. This was very
trying for the amanuensis, but she kept bravely at work, making only
an involuntary pause at the detonation of a big gun. . . .'

Fanny heard Louis tell Belle that he meant to dedicate *St Ives* to
her, adding, 'It shall be the best thing in the book, my dear.'

It is possible that her sympathetic role played a small part in the
powerful growth of his last books – not only in saving his strength,
but because her passive admiration may have encouraged him more
than his wife's vigorous sharing. True, he invited the participation
of others by his insistent habit of reading aloud his new chapters to
the household and guests. Almost anyone would do if Fanny was not
there, though she was the most responsive sounding-board for his
ideas. If he did not want his wife to express her opinion he need not
have laid himself open to it.

Nevertheless after several years of living mentally with the Stevensons, one grows to feel convinced that it would have been preferable if he had not allowed her to advise him so much in his work. Sometimes, as in *Jekyll and Hyde*, she was right. She was wrong in opposing his boys' books – like *Treasure Island;* but it is important to note that he went ahead regardless. Though he did not let her criticisms dominate his writing they made his craft drag its anchor more or less. He might have made other mistakes, but they would have been his own.

Fanny's famous intuition was a godsend one evening. The Stevensons noticed a dusty figure coming up the path in front of the house. To their surprise it was the puppet King Malietoa Laupepa, accompanied by an interpreter. He had arrived to pay a visit of reconciliation to Tusitala. He was received by Louis and Fanny in the great hall, where his host offered him a gift. He said he would like to have a pistol. This disconcerted the Stevensons, for the only pistol available was a beautiful one mounted in mother-of-pearl, which had been presented to Louis by Sir Percy Shelley. By Samoan custom, however, it would have been inexcusable to refuse, so Louis went to the big safe in the corner and took out the keepsake.

He emptied it of its cartridges and handed it to Fanny. She found that something was wrong with the trigger, and tried it four times. King Malietoa leaned over in front to watch. Then some lucky instinct made her examine it again. In the fifth chamber the last cartridge still lay; if she had clicked it one more time, it would undoubtedly have killed the king.

He started with alarm, then handsomely dismissed their concern with a smile and a wave of the hand. But in those troubled days, if the bullet had been fired the Stevensons could no longer have lived in Samoa. After the royal visitor left they spent the evening in harrowing speculations about what might have happened.

The family circle became seven again, with Aunt Maggie returning from Scotland, Lloyd back from a brief trip abroad, and Graham Balfour from his South Sea cruise.

In the spring Stevenson had learned that Henley's little daughter Margaret had died. An only child, she was not quite six, golden haired, and her father's idol. Barrie had just used her as the model for Wendy in *Peter Pan*. Now, deeply moved, the childless Stevenson wrote a warm letter, saying, 'There is one thing I have always envied you, *and envy you still.*'

In the early summer Henley's reply arrived, 'in good taste and rather touching', Louis told Baxter. Fanny, however, with 'that appalling instinct of the injured female to see mischief', suspected that Henley was hinting for a loan. Louis was doubtful but wanted to err on the side of generosity. He authorized Baxter to pay, when necessary, a very small allowance to Henley, adding with embarrassed lightness, 'if I gave him more, it would only lead to his starting a gig and a Pomeranian dog'.

Though Fanny's own dark-eyed resentment was more conspicuous, once in a conversation at Vailima she said shrewdly, 'Louis thinks he forgives, but he only lays the bundle on the shelf and long after takes it down and quarrels with it'. He admitted storing the bundle, but insisted, 'I would let it stay there; but if anyone else pulled it down I would tear it with fury'.

To help relieve his continuing financial strain, Baxter and Colvin arranged to issue the handsome Edinburgh Edition of his collected works. He was delighted and grateful. He paid Fanny the greatest compliment in his power: the series was dedicated to her.

'Fanny has had a most distressing bronchitis for some time', wrote Stevenson to Miss Boodle on 14th July. 'I have just been to see her; she is lying . . . in her big, cool, mosquito-proof room, ingloriously asleep.'

Nevertheless in that fateful year both husband and wife were unusually well physically, though he went through a stale period, feeling work-weary and even life-weary. Prophetic as his own Cassandra, he had told Mrs Sitwell in April, 'I was meant to die young, and the gods do not love me.' And to Gosse: '. . . where I have to go down is a precipice'.

Though he showed rare fortitude in doing his best work in those last years under the strain of his wife's intermittent psychosis, it may be that the work was itself his painful recompense. The depths of his suffering, and of searching into her desperation, may have taken him out of the self-consciousness which he had shown in writing about the relationships of men and women. Illness and pain were old stories to him, but they were his own, which required less imagination than those of another person – and that person a woman, a wife and mother. After his years of inhibition and Victorian self-censorship, Fanny's affliction had shocked and pounded him into forgetting his technique for its own sake, and seeing womankind – all mankind – as human beings.

It was much later revealed that Stevenson and his stepson had a prolonged quarrel during that autumn. Probably the foremost reason was the one mentioned by Moors and others – that Lloyd had made a beautiful Samoan girl his mistress. Louis was hardly one to throw stones out of the glass house of his Edinburgh youth, but – as his father had done before him – he was said to feel that if the young man had seduced a respectable girl he should marry her. Louis, with his hot chivalry, championed her and showed her kindness. Fanny, however, was so outraged by the open scandal that she faced the girl and put an end to the affair.

In September a number of the formerly imprisoned chiefs came to call on Louis. They announced that, in gratitude for all he had done for them, they would build a road to connect Vailima with the main road. Even yet, no wheeled vehicles could move over the forest track and this seemed almost too good to be true. The chiefs brought the young men from their villages, and daily supplies of food were sent from home; the Stevensons merely lent tools. This amazing and unique gesture was completed in October. It was called The Road of the Loving Heart.

Powerfully touched, Louis and Fanny arranged a splendid feast of acceptance in the new native house which they had built for Samoan ceremonies. Since all the guests of honour were Mata'afa men, few white Apians were venturesome enough to come. Louis delivered a speech with full Samoan etiquette. He urged the chiefs to 'make roads and gardens, and care for your trees, and sell your produce wisely'.

'In the end of September,' recalled Balfour, 'he wearied of St Ives, within sight of its conclusion, and fortunately turned again to Weir of Hermiston. It was the third time he had taken it in hand, for he would not work at it when he felt uncertain of himself.' Belle wrote in her diary on 24th September: 'He generally makes notes in the early morning, which he elaborates as he reads them aloud. In Hermiston he has hardly more than a line or two to keep him on the track, but he never falters for a word, but gives me the sentences with capital letters and all the stops, as clearly and steadily as though he were reading from an unseen book.'

Outgrowing or rather having ingested his early preoccupation with style, his whole force was building up to the greatness beyond self which was to emerge in the unfinished *Weir of Hermiston*.

Lloyd noticed that in those last months Stevenson had a 'strange serenity', as if in premonition. He said to his stepson, 'I am not a man of any unusual talent, Lloyd; I started out with very moderate abilities. . . . What genius I had was for *work*!'

Critics who charged Fanny with a prudish influence thought that she could not have approved of the fate in store for young Kirstie in *Weir of Hermiston*. But later, among the unfinished manuscript, she found a poem which indicated that Louis planned to dedicate this masterpiece also to her:

> . . . Take thou the writing; thine it is. For who
> Burnished the sword, blew on the drowsy coal,
> Held still the target higher; chary of praise
> And prodigal of counsel – who but thou?
> So now in the end; if this the least be good,
> If any deed be done, if any fire
> Burn in the imperfect page, the praise be thine.

'If I had to begin again . . .' he wrote to Bob in November, 'I believe I should try to honour Sex more religiously. The worst of our education is that Christianity does not recognize and hallow Sex. . . . Well, it is so; I cannot be wiser than my generation.'

Bob too was having troubles – expecting another child and still very short of money, having squandered his patrimony in the debonair youth of 'the Two Stevensons'. But Bob, at any rate, was a father.

In a letter to Edmund Gosse – who also had a young family growing up – Louis wrote of himself a little later as 'a childless, rather bitter, very clear-eyed, blighted youth'.

One can only wonder how much Fanny was aware of her husband's frustrated longing for parenthood, and how far she felt herself lacking. As a mature guess, it may in part explain her insistence on being a 'mother' to his writings – to help create and rear the brood of books and stories which were almost as close as his flesh and blood to him, and therefore to her. It may also have influenced her resolve to be adequate in backing him up in whatever he wanted to do – an effort which makes her breakdowns seem all the more poignant for them both. Childbearing, she could hardly have squatted on a mine dump, lived seasick in a stormy schooner, and gouged a Garden of Eden out of the jungle. The Stevenson saga would have been very different if she had been an inexperienced girl with several children playing around her husband's desk.

Balfour, who alone of the intimates lived with the couple near the end, absolutely agreed with Lloyd that, for all her hypochondria and her disturbing burdens, it was she whose watchful care and resourcefulness kept the invalid afloat for many years.

In November the oppressive wet season began, but Samoa was at peace, and Louis had not been so well for years. H.M.S. *Curaçoa* was finally ordered home, and on the Saturday night before she sailed the Stevensons gave a big dinner party for the captain and officers.

At long last a close friend was *en route* to visit Samoa: Charles Baxter, bringing the first two volumes of the Edinburgh Edition, of which the advance subscription had saved the latest threat of insolvency.

Thanksgiving Dinner was the year's last entertainment at Vailima. Again the Stevensons had a long table of Americans in the great hall with its stately staircase – 'the novelist's pride', as Adelaide Ide had described it. 'It was a gay dinner,' wrote Belle, 'the big swinging lamps throwing their light over shining silver and glass. . . .' There was roast turkey, and a red sauce made from a native berry which Fanny had found in the woods, and 'pumpkin pies' concocted with sweet potatoes. The Heriot Row glasses held sherry, bordeaux, madeira and port. 'At dessert, Talolo brought in champagne that to everyone's surprise was cold, for it was steamer day and we had been able to get ice.'

When the glasses were filled, Louis rose and proposed a toast of Thanksgiving. He was in his best squire mood. He proclaimed, wrote Belle, 'how thankful he was for the wife who made this occasion possible. He owed her not only his happiest years, he said, but, through her tender care, his very life as well. He was thankful that his mother was with him . . . who . . . had forsaken all other ties. . . .'. (Belle did not report that he said he loved his mother best of all – as Aunt Maggie gloated to her sister.) 'He was thankful for the two he looked on as son and daughter, who graced his home. Smiling at Austin, he said: "Vailima is blessed – there's a child in the house." '

Chapter XIII
'Under the wide and starry sky – '

Happily there was another sunny interlude in the rains during the first few days of December. Louis was in fine fettle over the powerful progress of *Weir of Hermiston*. But not so Fanny. Aunt Maggie wrote to her sister: '. . . For a day or two Fanny had been telling us that she knew – that she felt – something dreadful was going to happen to someone we cared for; as she put it, to one of our friends. On Monday she was very low and upset about it and dear Lou tried to cheer her. Strangely enough, both of them had agreed that it could not be to either of *them* that the dreadful thing was to happen.'

Fanny's gloomy premonitions often came to nothing, though like most prophets she was more likely to remember the hunches that had been right. This time she feared that the victim of fate might be Graham Balfour, who had recently left Vailima for another schooner voyage in Micronesia. She herself wrote soon afterwards to Mrs Sitwell: '. . . For three days I had known that something terrible was going to happen in the house. That last day I was almost insane with terror and Louis had just been laughing at my childishness and teasing me about it.'

The last evening – 2nd December – was a Sunday, with family prayers. Louis read a new prayer which he had written: 'Go with each of us to rest . . . and when the day returns . . . call us up with morning faces and morning hearts, eager to labour, happy, if happiness shall be our portion – and if the day be marked for sorrow, strong to endure it.'

After dinner, in high spirits, he proposed that the family should play charades. They all stayed up late, miming and giggling.

The next day he dictated to Belle a strong beginning of Chapter IX of *Weir of Hermiston*. He felt certain that it was his best book, which, said Lloyd, 'made him buoyant and happy as nothing else could'. ('How can I keep up this pitch?' he wondered.) When he read aloud the day's stint to Fanny she agreed with his verdict.

A mail had just arrived, and in the afternoon he dictated his replies to his friends' long letters. Some said his last was to Gosse; more likely it was an unfinished one to Adelaide Ide.

On that afternoon of 3rd December, Lloyd recalled that he rode home from Apia, stopped to chat with the family on the veranda, and went off to his cottage to change and take a swim in the pool.

Towards sunset – around six o'clock – Louis came downstairs, and rallied Fanny about her dark forebodings. To divert her mood, he talked of a possible lecture tour to earn money in the United States. Then he played a game of patience to soothe her. He said he was hungry. He brought up a bottle of fine old burgundy from the wine cellar, and suggested that they make a special mayonnaise which he had devised – 'one of the famous Vailima salad dressings', in the words of Adelaide Ide.

He was chatting gaily while he helped his wife to stir up the oil and lime juice on the veranda. Then suddenly he put his long thin hands to his head. 'What's that?' he exclaimed. 'Oh, what a pain!' And he added, 'Do I look strange?'

Fanny quickly lied, 'No'. But he fell on his knees beside her. She and his devoted butler-valet, Sosimo, helped him up and guided him through the door of the great hall into his grandfather's armchair. He instantly lost consciousness. She ordered brandy, fanned him, and cried his name to try to rouse him. She called to his mother and Belle, and they came hurrying.

From Pineapple Cottage, Lloyd heard an odd stir in the big house and someone shouting his name. He ran over. He found his step-father lying back, breathing harshly, his eyes wide open. His mother was kneeling beside the chair with Aunt Maggie and Belle, all very pale. Fanny had the servants bring a bed downstairs into the hall, and Lloyd lifted him and carried him to it; he was very light, with a red face. Lloyd's tears rolled down as he unlaced and took off his stepfather's boots, remembering how he had said he 'wanted to die with his boots on'. Fanny rolled up her husband's shirt sleeves and she and his mother rubbed with brandy the pitifully thin sticks of his arms.

Then Lloyd had the fastest mare saddled – she had won several races – and rode downhill at breakneck speed to fetch Dr Funk. At Lloyd's insistence the plump little German mounted the swift horse, handing the younger man the small black bag he dared not carry. Lloyd 'helped himself' to a tethered horse – and galloped off just as 'the astonished owner emerged from a bar . . . and stared.' Word was also sent to H.M.S. *Wallaroo* for Dr Anderson, who followed quickly.

The Rev. Clarke had meanwhile been summoned to Vailima. Lloyd found him kneeling in prayer beside the unconscious man, 'his family about him frenzied with grief, as they realized all hope was past. The dozen and more Samoans that formed part of the little clan of which he was chief sat in a wide semi-circle on the floor. . . . Some knelt on one knee, to be instantly ready for any command. . .'.

Dr Funk muttered, 'Ach, ach!' He told the family that Stevenson had had an apoplectic stroke from a blood clot on the brain. Dr Anderson concurred. He murmured, 'How can anybody write books with arms like these?' To which Margaret Stevenson burst out, 'He has written *all* his books with arms like these!'

Nothing more could be done. In half an hour – at ten minutes past eight – Louis's breathing faded away.

Mr Clarke wrote that while Stevenson lay dying, he saw Fanny's small figure standing alone and apart by the foot of the great red-wood staircase, rigid with shock. As she had once said, 'Without Louis, I am nothing'.

When all was over, Stevenson's body was covered with the big Union Jack which flew over Vailima. There was no wailing or keening among the servants. Lloyd whispered instructions and they hurried off with messages. 'My mother and Aunt Maggie sat motionless,' wrote Belle, 'white-faced, and stricken.' Soon chiefs began to arrive with fine mats and flowers which they laid over the bed, bowing and saying, '*Talofa*, Tusitala'. 'After that,' Margaret Stevenson told her sister, 'our Roman Catholic boys asked if they might "make a church", and they chanted prayers and hymns for a long time, very sweetly. . . .' Sosimo crouched in vigil besides his master all through the night, while chiefs arrived from afar.

The doctor had said that Louis must be buried before three o'clock the next afternoon. But how to convey him up the wooded peak to his chosen resting-place on top of Mount Vaea? Lloyd sent several nearby chiefs to get men and tools to cut a path in the short time available. Long before dawn scores of young men arrived with axes and knives, and Maggie Stevenson dressed them in mourning hastily collected from the trading stores: black cotton *lavalavas* and white singlets.

'The only sounds we heard through the night', Belle remembered, 'were the chopping of trees on the hillside, the low murmur of native voices responding, and Sosimo reciting the Catholic prayers for the dead', in mingled Latin and Samoan.

The new day was beautiful, sunny and cool, rare at that season. All morning Samoans came with flowers, until the great hall glowed with an un-Presbyterian brilliance. So many handsome mats were brought that they hid the Union Jack over the body. Fanny, stunned but moving automatically, helped to dress her husband in a white linen shirt, dark trousers and a blue sash in the tropical custom, as he lay in his quickly carpentered coffin. His plain silver wedding ring was on his finger – the mate of the one which she always wore, from the days of their marriage when they could not afford gold.

The superhuman task of clearing a path to the peak was completed by early afternoon. Lloyd had climbed up with a party of 'outside' men from the Vailima clan to dig the grave, 1,300 feet above sea level. 'Nothing more picturesque can be imagined than the narrow ledge that forms the summit of Vaea, a place no wider than a room, and as flat as a table.'

At about one o'clock the first relay of strong Samoan pallbearers began the steep and rugged ascent – made the more difficult as they carried shoulder-high the coffin with its pitifully light burden. 'They have just gone up the mountain now', wrote Mrs Stevenson to her sister. '. . . None of us has realized yet what has happened, and we shall only feel it all the more as days go by . . . I feel desolate indeed, and don't know what I shall do. . . .'

Half an hour later the family and friends, nineteen white people and sixty Samoans, toiled up the rocky slope; some were forced to drop out. At the top the coffin waited under the frayed British flag which, said Aunt Maggie, 'used to fly over us in those happy days upon the *Casco* . . .' The coffin was lowered into place and almost hidden with wreaths and crosses of flowers, and then the Vailima 'inside' men grasped the spades for the final covering of earth. Mr Clarke read parts of the Church of England burial service and the new prayer written by Louis, which he had read at family worship on the evening before his death:

'. . . suffer us a while longer to endure, and (if it may be) help us to do better . . . if the day come when these must be taken, have us play the man under affliction. Be with our friends; be with ourselves. . . .'

Eventually, a large tomb was built of big blocks of cement over the grave in Samoan style. In 1897 a plinth was added, flanked by two bronze plaques designed by Gelett Burgess. One, in Samoan, bore the words, 'The Tomb of Tusitala', followed by the biblical speech of Ruth to Naomi: '. . . thy people shall be my people, and thy God my God: where thou diest, will I die. . .'. At right and left were portrayed a thistle and a hibiscus flower.

On the other side, in English, was the 'Requiem' which R.L.S. had first drafted for himself years before, when he had nearly died after travelling across half the world to join Fanny:

A   Ω
1850   *ROBERT LOUIS STEVENSON*   1894

> Under the wide and starry sky,
> Dig the grave and let me lie.
> Glad did I live and gladly die,
>   And I laid me down with a will.
>
> This be the verse you grave for me;
> *Here he lies where he longed to be;*
> *Home is the sailor, home from sea,*
>   *And the hunter home from the hill.*

As Fanny knew with bitter comfort, the whole Anglo-Samoan pageant of the funeral would have been after Louis's own heart.

'. . . he went as he wished to go', she later wrote to Colvin, 'leaping from the highest pinnacle with the great drums beating behind him. . . .'

Her biographer Nellie said that her sister was sustained by her belief in after-life and reunion. Nellie ascribed her 'silent fortitude' to an inheritance from their mother, who was never known to give way in a crisis.

The shock, almost the treachery, of the end outraged Fanny: after all her years of combating tuberculosis – on guard against every draught, every cough – it was not the old enemy which had killed her husband but a new and unforeseen one, a stroke. Mercifully she cannot have realized how much his worry over herself may have contributed. It is significant to note too that with a real and great trouble she did not break down. '. . . After all these years of preparation', she was still mourning two years later to Colvin, 'I was not ready when the time came. That very day, I had said to him, "I am not a coward; for a woman I am brave". Vain words; where is my courage now? . . .'

'Life seems to have stood still with us since Tuesday,' her mother-in-law wrote home five days after the funeral, 'and none of us can do anything but think over our loss, which only grows greater as we begin dimly to realize it. . . .

'Sosimo, Lou's special boy, is quite unconsolable; he keeps Tusitala's room in exquisite order, and when Fanny and I were there this morning, we were touched to find two glasses filled with beautiful fresh white flowers on the table beside his bed.'

Though the widow and her children planned to remain at Vailima, they could not expect to keep up the 'plantation' on the same scale without the breadwinner. 'Yesterday,' wrote Margaret Stevenson on 16th December, 'we had another sad scene to go through, the paying-off of the outside boys. . . . In the afternoon we all assembled in the hall, the first time that it had been used since the funeral; and Lloyd made a speech, explaining how sorry we were. . . . One of them replied. . . . Then they sang a couple of songs of farewell to Tusitala . . . and we drank *kava* together and shook hands with them all.'

Of the outside boys, the family kept only Lafaele to take care of the horses, cows and pigs; Leuelo, Fanny's garden boy; and a frail one-eyed Tongan boy who was of little use but was unlikely to find work elsewhere.

On Mount Vaea the chiefs declared a taboo against firearms, so that the birds could sing in peace around the tomb of Tusitala.

By chance a mail had gone out to New Zealand on the night after the funeral, and Fanny and her mother-in-law and the others had to drive themselves to write tragic letters home to Britain and America. A few days later Fanny asked Mrs Sitwell to insert an advertisement in the appropriate papers, requesting that letters written by R.L.S. should be sent on for her to edit. With her pitiful megalomania for Louis she even begged Mrs Sitwell to get the London literary clique to agitate for the annexation of Samoa by Britain, so that his grave might lie upon British soil.

The news of the death was cabled abroad from Auckland, but the newspapers questioned its authenticity. Henry James wrote to Fanny of how at the first word he had rushed around to Mrs Sitwell, crying, 'It isn't true, it isn't true; say it isn't true!' For ten days there was 'a flicker of hope', but then he received a cable from Fanny, sent on her behalf from San Francisco.

Of the countless letters she received, his – a long one – was the masterpiece. As always, it was he who was able to enter most creatively into her life and experience and now her loss.

'My dear Fanny Stevenson,' he began, 'What can I say to you that will not seem cruelly irrelevant or vain? . . . You are such a visible picture of desolation that I need to remind myself, that courage, and patience, and fortitude are also abundantly with you. . . . To have lived in the light of that splendid life, that beautiful, bountiful being – only to see it, from one moment to the other, converted into a fable as strange and romantic as one of his own, a thing that *has* been and has ended, is an anguish into which no one can enter with you fully and of which no one can drain the cup for you. You are nearest to the pain, because you were nearest the joy and the pride. . . . He lighted up one whole side of the globe, and was in himself a whole province of one's imagination. . . . He has gone in time not to be old, early enough to be generously young and late enough to have drunk deep of the cup. . . . When I think of your own situation I fall into a mere confusion of pity and wonder, with the sole sense of your being as brave a spirit as he was (all of whose bravery you shared) to hold on by. . . . More than I can say, I hope your first prostration and bewilderment are over, and that you are feeling your way in feeling all sorts of encompassing arms – all sorts of out-stretched hands of friendship. Don't, my dear Fanny Stevenson, be unconscious of *mine*, and believe me more than ever faithfully yours,

Henry James.'

Fanny infinitely valued this heartfelt memorial. But when she and the other heirs invited James to be her husband's literary executor, he bowed out with utmost courtesy from the complicated and involving task. He was always first and fully the artist – the spectator rather than the participant – unlike Louis, who had recently written of himself that he was '·06 per cent artist and ·04 per cent adventurer'.

One other letter she treasured equally. It came from Hawaii, pencilled on a scrap of paper, and unsigned.

'Mrs. Stevenson.

Dear Madam: – All over the world people will be sorry for the death of Robert Louis Stevenson, but none will mourn him more than the blind white leper of Molokai.'

Part II

The matriarch 1894 - 1914

Chapter I
The purple shadow of glory

'Mrs Stevenson', the Scots lawyer Lord Guthrie recalled of Fanny, 'never used the word "widow".'

When Sir Percy Shelley had died in Bournemouth she had written to Lady Shelley: 'No matter who is left, a widow is alone. . . . That is what always, as much as anything can, reconciles me to the thought that I shall probably outlive Louis. . . . I suppose we [women] are stronger and tougher than men, else we never could have been mothers.'

In the early weeks after her husband's funeral Fanny, in consultation with his mother and Lloyd, planned to give to each of Louis's intimate friends some memento which he had used. With incredible magnanimity in terms of Victorian sentiment, she offered to Henley the Union Jack which had been taken down and laid over the body in the hall. Whatever it cost her, she knew how much her husband would have approved of the gesture.

Henley declined to accept the great gift. Here was another way for him to affront her – even though it also meant rebuffing Lloyd, who had always hero-worshipped him. Years later in California Gelett Burgess wrote that she was still intensely bitter about this.

Aunt Maggie returned to her old sister in Scotland. There, in the Stevenson family Bible, she wrote under the birth and marriage entries for Robert Lewis Balfour: '. . . Died suddenly of apoplexy at Vailima, Samoa . . ., and I am left alone and desolate.'

'I believe, for Louis,' Fanny wrote to Colvin, 'all is for the best; he went as he wished to go. . . . It is hard to believe that I am to go on and on indefinitely and always alone. . . . After all the years of preparations I was not ready when the time came. . . .'

Charles Baxter had travelled as far as Suez when his old friend died, and went on to pay a muted visit to Vailima, bringing the first two volumes of the Edinburgh Edition. He had been named co-executor of the estate. Soon after his return he incurred the wrath of his late hostess and her son by making good Louis's promise to Longmans to include the *Fables* in a new edition of *Dr Jekyll and Mr Hyde* without thinking it necessary to ask Fanny's permission. These wry philosophical tales – including the unflattering *Waif Woman* – were outside the boundaries of either her practical realism or her less sophisticated fancies.

McClure and Scribner in turn were wrangling over the rights in the uncompleted *Weir of Hermiston*, which Colvin was preparing for the press with an Epilogue suggesting the probable ending, using notes provided by Belle as amanuensis. '. . . Hermiston I *know* to be a masterpiece', Fanny told him. 'And, a thought hardly to be borne, I know, too, that Louis had not yet arrived at the maturity of his powers. He was very near the true beginning of his work. Of that I must not speak – I cannot bear it.'

Graham Balfour, on his South Sea cruise, had not learned of his cousin's death until March, when he was ashore in the Carolines. He rejoined the family later at Vailima and took charge of a trunkful of manuscripts and other papers to convey back to Britain.

Lloyd went for a sea voyage to convalesce from dengue fever, and Austin was sent, as Louis had planned, to Wellington College in New Zealand, within reach of Vailima for the long vacations.

So for some time Fanny and Belle were alone in the big empty house in the isolated forest. They sewed, read, learned chess and gardened. In the evenings they walked a mile through the woods to visit Mr Carruthers and his Samoan wife. They went barefoot, with 'the feel of the soft, mossy grass under our feet'. When Carruthers saw the flicker of their lantern through the palms he wound up his little tinkling musical box to welcome them.

One might have expected Fanny's mind to collapse again from the shock. But curiously, for all her desperate gloom, there seems to have been a certain lessening of her tension. Stationary in death, Louis was more wholly hers than he had been for the years in which he had been outgrowing her. She no longer had to keep up with him.

She continued to live as a sort of Dowager Queen of Samoa, ceremoniously entertained at island feasts.

Stevenson's will, apart from the Samoan property, left personal estate in Britain of £15,525. Half was held by his mother until her death. A third of his estate without death duties was bequeathed to Uncle Alan's children – Bob, Katharine and Dora. Austin received a legacy with a life interest to Belle. The residue, including manuscripts, books, furniture, etc., went ultimately to Lloyd after a life interest to Fanny. If Lloyd died without heirs Colvin and Henry James were to have his share.

Louis need not have feared for his wife's provision. The continuing royalties gave her an adequate income, though with no new works there was not the same scale, and for several years she felt hard up – until further volumes of the Edinburgh Edition came out and the *Letters* and the *Life* began to appear with many reprintings. Moreover, since Louis had been a member of the Bar in Scotland, she also drew an annual widow's pension of sixty pounds.

As second choice after the evasive Henry James, Colvin was made literary executor. He began to edit the *Vailima Letters* which Louis had written to him personally, as the dead man had requested for the profit of his heirs, and the collection was first published in 1895.

The arrangements for writing the biography were to involve several years of controversy, intrigue and riddles which have only gradually come to light.

At Bournemouth in October 1885, while Louis was still intimate with Henley, he added a codicil to his will: '. . . If my wife shall find herself able and willing to undertake my life with her own hand, I desire that this shall be left to her, and I should so have arranged it from the first if I had not understood her to refuse: at the same time I request her to allow my formerly designated biographer, W. E. Henley to give his own account . . . and to share emoluments with him in proportion. . . . I beg Henley to carry along with him in the work the counsel of my wife and Sidney Colvin; . . . I would rather

be misunderstood than cause any pang to anyone whom I have
known, far less whom I have loved. . . .'

The quarrel with Henley naturally eliminated him as a potential
biographer. The subject had again been raised in Tahiti in December
1888, when Louis thought he was dying and handed Lloyd a sealed
letter to be opened after his death. Having advised his stepson to
consult Charles Baxter, he went on about the biography: . . .
'This should be edited (if he will) by Colvin . . . some money should
be forthcoming. You must beg Colvin not to run away with all the
profits by incessant alteration and delay: that is the danger of
S.C.

'. . . Colvin and my heirs might share 1/3 to 2/3; but this again
must depend on the scale. See that Colvin has justice.'

Now Colvin started work, very slowly indeed, on the story of his
friend.

With Fanny's power of feeling and the current idealization of prolonged grief – an example set by the widowed Queen Victoria
herself – her depression and weakness grew worse. Lloyd and Belle
too were unwell. The doctors urged a change, and in April 1895 the
party sailed for San Francisco.

They stopped at Honolulu, where Fanny was distressed to find her
old friend, the deposed Queen Liliuokalani, imprisoned in Iolani
Palace under close guard. Because of the tropical laxness, however,
the Vandegrifter was able to get in through the kitchen door.

Short of cash, she found life expensive in San Francisco, where the
family first took the three-room 'downstairs flat' of Dora Williams's
house on Russian Hill. They acquired, however, a manservant. Fanny
wrote to Colvin about a Samoan boy who had stowed away on a ship
to San Francisco. 'Naturally he was thrown out on the wharf like
spoiled fruit. The poor wretch wandered about shivering in the cold,
sleeping in doorways, and eating what refuse he could pick up. . . .
"I walked seven miles, one day, and there was not a coconut", he
said. At last, when he had taken a cold and felt dreadfully ill, Belle
passed him, and his quick eyes caught sight of her South Sea
earrings. . . . He began to sing a Samoan song. Naturally, Belle
turned at once . . . he cried out her Samoan name, "Teuila". Of
course, he is with us, sleeping in a camp bed in the kitchen, and acting

as our servant, until we can persuade some ship to take him home. . . .'

Graham Balfour stopped in San Francisco *en route* back to England from his wanderings. Belle and Lloyd met him at the dock, and the wistful Belle must have hoped in vain that he would have a change of heart.

Fanny went to spiritualist seances – 'some pretty curious places', said Gelett Burgess in a memoir – with Dora Williams and the poet Bruce Porter. Once Dora claimed that a medium brought her a message from Louis. But for all Fanny's own psychic bent she disapproved of Mrs Williams's gullibility over sham spirit lights made with matches, and the two women quarrelled. Except for Henry James, to be a friend of Fanny's was to quarrel with her, it seemed. But the quarrels rarely lasted.

John Lloyd re-entered her life as man of business. He was now a bank president married to a genteel lady who disapproved of his old flame and her daughter. Judge Rearden, alas, had died.

Wanting income for themselves and honour for R.L.S., Fanny and her son were intent on the production of the unpublished manuscripts, the biography and letters. They spent weeks at a big table, going over Louis's papers. Still hankering for her own recognition as an author, she urged Sidney Colvin to help to get a production of *The Hanging Judge*, the play which she had taken over from Louis and Henley. Despite her frequent scourging of publicity, she also replied to Colvin's discreet query 'about adding the poem addressed to me, "Dusky, trusty, etc." to the new edition. Do just what you think well to do. It is a very beautiful thing and I do not think it would be bad taste to publish it. . . .'

Her health improved. But Nellie, herself unwell and 'very nervous', found her sister 'subtly changed . . . not exactly old, yet . . . she only yearned to go back and be near the grave on Mt Vaea'.

It was a momentous summer for Lloyd – and his mother too. Now aged twenty-seven, he had fallen in love with a young school teacher named Katharine Durham. She was a large handsome brunette with a soft voice. (Ever since Antwerp, as Belle pointed out, all Lloyd's girl friends were pretty.) '. . . From the time I first saw the girl', Fanny confided with fateful optimism to Mrs Sitwell a few months later, 'I have been hoping that she impressed Lloyd as she did me; as it turned out our taste was the same.'

But at the end of October she was alarmed about her son's health which, she told Colvin, 'has suddenly broken down under, I really do believe – the strain that Charles [Baxter] has put upon him'. While he was still 'very weak and nervous', the family resolved to spend the winter in Honolulu, *en route* back to Samoa.

Nostalgically she wrote to her mother-in-law in Scotland: '. . . Everything here reminds me of Louis. . . . People say: "What a comfort his great name must be to you!" It is a pride to me, but not a comfort . . . It gives me a sharp shock when I hear him spoken of as dead. . . . He is only waiting, I seem to feel, somewhere at hand.'

She learned that the busy and deliberate Colvin expected to take three or four years in writing the biography – as Stevenson had feared. She protested, yet she added, 'You are the only one fit for the work.' She also told him, '. . . I see your difficulty about the *Life*. I should say go ahead as frankly as possible, and then, if necessary, we can tone down. I should like to be honest, but at the same time not to hurt anyone's feelings. That always troubled Louis. . . .'

Chapter II
The mother-in-law

In February 1896 great news was announced: Lloyd's engagement to Katharine Durham. She was soon to sail from San Francisco for the wedding in Honolulu.

'It is a very nice, quiet, sensible girl that he is going to marry', Colvin and Mrs Sitwell were assured by Fanny. 'She has no money, but in many ways that is an advantage; there will be no harassing relations looking out for her interests. That will be left for Lloyd and me. . . .'

The fiancée was a mid-Westerner from Springfield, Missouri. Her father's people had been Quakers, and her mother was a descendant of Puritan Vermonters, many of them Congregational missionaries. Katharine herself had been teaching in a mission school in New Mexico.

'Her life', Fanny told Colvin, 'has been very grey and filled with self-sacrifice of which she was not conscious. Samoa will not, therefore, be a dull place for her as it would be for so many girls, and I believe she will be quite happy there.'

The prospective mother-in-law and many in the Stevenson circle regarded Katharine as an earnest pedantic young woman. Apparently her intellectual aspirations appealed to Lloyd and his mother. Perhaps they made the mistake of kindly patronizing her. Two years later Gosse was to find her a talkative bore without tact or humour – a bluestocking *manquée*. Yet her will to be admired was as potent as Fanny's.

'Looking back on my own life – ' she wrote twenty-four years later to Robert Catton, a Scotsman living in Honolulu, 'why, Fanny Van de Grift's experience couldn't hold a candle to all the adventure and romance of an order that could shame no one, that my life has given me. . . . The country where I taught in a missionary school was as wild as could be imagined. One of our schoolboys was once murdered at our door – political opponents shot each other – I remember crouching one night behind a big trunk while there was shooting outside. . . . But there were native festas [*sic*] – dances – cowboys – sheep camps, picturesque wild Indians . . . crystal airs. I loved it all – it was a bit of old Spain – intense passions, courteliness [*sic*] – great hospitality – gentleness . . . color in everything.' There had even been, she added dreamily, a virtuous Spanish admirer, pure, platonic – and married.

Fanny, however – all unaware – wrote to Colvin: 'I have still to see whether my new daughter-in-law is able to take my place and leave me free to go when I like. She is a very good, sensible, capable girl, and not too young, so I am hoping more, perhaps, than I should, from her. She will arrive here on the ninth of April, and they will be married at once.'

Years later Robert Catton wrote to his fellow Scot, Lord Guthrie: '. . . I was one of the few guests at their wedding here and it seemed to me that the grey mare was decidedly the better horse in that team'.

On 7th May 1896 Fanny and party sailed for Samoa in the *Mariposa*.

Fanny and Belle's homecoming, 'being unexpected, was rather forlorn', Belle remembered. The travellers reached Vailima in the evening and went to bed 'rather drearily in the empty house'. Belle meant to get breakfast as best she could and then send out word to their former servants. She woke late and ran guiltily to the window. To her surprise she saw smoke rising from the cook-house chimney, Talolo at the door, and Iopu, the yard man, carrying a pail of water. She hurried to her mother's room and found her sitting up in bed with a breakfast tray served by Sosimo. The news of their return had gone out overnight by the 'bush telegraph'.

News came from Britain that Graham Balfour was engaged. 'It is a terrible blow to us to lose him', Fanny admitted to Colvin. 'I had counted on his being with us for the building of the tomb which we shall begin very soon. . . .'

In time Balfour became a distinguished administrator in public education – he was eventually knighted – and his wife was destined to be, like himself, an ardent devotee of Fanny. Rhoda Balfour recalled later: 'When Mrs Stevenson heard of my engagement . . . she wrote me the kindest and tenderest of letters. . . . She had hoped that Palema would continue to make his home with them, and she had great confidence in and love for him. . . . Yet . . . she gave generous sympathy to a stranger, who caused her fresh loss. . . .'

Belle's reaction was not described.

As for the advent of the new Mrs Lloyd Osbourne, all went well at first in that paradise where she saw herself as a brilliant bride while Fanny had in mind a nice dutiful daughter-in-law. Living in a famous author's house with many servants and an exotic garden was a dream of luxury for a poor girl to describe in her letters home.

Apia society was agog to meet her. Long afterwards she told Robert Catton that Mrs Newell, the missionary's wife, 'whispered in my ear when I first came to Samoa, "If you ever need a friend come to me". It seemed strange at the time . . . but the day came when I understood. . .'.

One might sympathize with any young wife married to a man with a powerfully dominating mother, and Fanny's deranged spells had been devastating even to her experienced family. Only slowly was it apparent that under the girl's outward amenity she was a neurotic too. From her own letters and sayings she sounds not unlike a caricature of Fanny's darker side, but more muddled.

'. . . once she said to me', Katharine later wrote of her mother-in-law to the American writer Hellman, ' "Louis's favourite flower was the carnation." . . . but if she said it was the carnation I knew it was some other flower. . . .'

She quickly began, like the rest of the family, to feel herself a vital part of the Stevenson legend. With girlish hero-worship she picked up everything she could learn about the man and his works. Soon it seemed irrelevant that she had never met him.

'Of course [Fanny] fascinated Stevenson in the first place . . .' Katharine later admitted grudgingly to Hellman – as if she had ever seen the couple together. 'Colourful as she was – she was fascinating if one didn't have to live with her.

'About her eyes: they were striking, but cattish, cruel, shifting, always moving in little quick jerks sideways. . . . Altogether her face was pretty like a gypsy's . . . but her figure was squat. She had no neck at all and her head sat down on big square mannish shoulders. Though I am a rather large woman neither Fanny nor Belle could put on one of the waists to my dresses. Their low height came of too short legs. Stevenson called Fanny's hands "boy's hands". Her fingers were always pressed close together and straight out and her thumbs bent backwards. They were rather small and so were her feet – but still the right size for her body. She wore, even on the street, dancing slippers which looked more inappropriate then than they would now. Her feet were pretty, bare – a little like a child's.

'She never outgrew childhood,' Katharine decided, 'and it seemed to me that she belonged to the childhood of the race . . . in some dark-skinned peoples. But she was not feminine, she was more a man. Her one great service to Stevenson was the pleasure she took in listening to his tales – and he always wanted a listener. . . .

'She never talked or joined in the general conversation in a company but sat and watched everyone out of the corners of her eyes – but when she had a small audience she would tell in a most plausible way the most thrilling adventures, a patchwork of many tales she had read, as her own experiences – or of a ghost and spirits she had encountered. I do not think she was mad, but of the year 10,000 B.C. and a pure romancer.'

Fortunately Lloyd was gaining weight and strength at last. Fanny herself had cured him, she told Dora, when the doctors had failed. In October 1896 she wrote jubilantly to Colvin that her son had been appointed American vice-Consul in Apia.

She apologized to Colvin for her impatience about the biography. 'I had meant to begin by asking you never to read my letters when they begin in a peevish or fretful way. Just burn them. . . . When I feel ill my first thought is "I cannot die and not have seen the *Life*". And to be perfectly frank, when I hear that you are not well, my first thought is still for the same thing. . . . If you want to annihilate me, threaten to throw it over. It is for that that I live from day to day. That first, and then Lloyd. . . .'

Meanwhile the young couple were expecting a baby at the end of the winter.

'Lloyd's existence', Fanny confided to Colvin, 'has for so long been surrounded, as one might say, by Louis and me that it seems impossible for him to stand alone. Louis's death very nearly destroyed him altogether. Katharine told me, with some amusement, that Lloyd had been asking her if she had felt no compunction at leaving her home, her family, and country for him, seeming quite pleased with her natural answers. But she turned to him and said, "Would you have done as much for me? Would you leave your mother for me?" She said she felt a perceptible chill in the air as he replied in a distant sort of voice, "I could never leave my mother under any circumstances." . . . I want to be near you while you are at work, and yet if I went to England I should have to trail my whole family after me. . . .'

Did she like to exaggerate the dependence of Lloyd, or was it his idea as much as hers to turn the marriage into a *ménage à trois*? There he stood, unenviably – not a very strong character himself – between the two brown-skinned woman of titanic will, his large wife and his tiny mother.

Fanny mentioned to Dora Williams that '. . . somebody had the bad taste to send a newspaper cutting about Sam Osbourne being in Africa. I take no interest in his whereabouts'.

Her major project was to build the tomb which Gelett Burgess had designed in California. Louis's birthday on 13th November was marked by a celebration both at Vailima and at the grave. On top of

Mount Vaea the company banked the grave with flowers and a wreath of heather which Mrs Stevenson had sent.

In March Katharine had her baby, a boy. '. . . I am awfully tired, as you must see by my writing', Fanny told Dora. 'First the baby; a splendid big boy who had just missed weighing 10 pounds. We think he is *very* beautiful. . . . He howled for three days and nights, but since has been docile as a lamb. His name is to be Alan after an old friend of Lloyd's and ours, Alan Herbert. Katharine wanted to call him Louis, but I couldn't; not to live in the same house, and hear it continually. I really could not, even to please my dear, good Katharine who was much disappointed and a good deal hurt, I fear. . . .'

'. . . my dear, good Katharine', echoed Fanny's voice, so far. Apparently she did not realize how much her daughter-in-law was already beginning to seethe inside.

Like Fanny, the bride was drawn to the occult, and she believed herself to be in communion with Stevenson. Once, she later told Hellman, when she was walking alone in the garden at Vailima, 'almost frenzied with anxiety and grief, a voice said, "Louis is here"'. Then she felt happy.

'Another time at Vailima a letter Stevenson had written to be opened after his death, as I went through the medicine room, lay on the floor open and oh, the tragedy of that letter . . . wherein he wrote of himself as the goose with the golden egg, and wherein he followed this ironic phrase with instructions as to how, after the golden-egged goose had died, some of his old publications should be used to bring forth money for his heirs. . . .' She said that she had picked up the letter as a scrap of paper 'to see if it should go in the waste-paper basket. . . . How came it before me? . . . [these] things have not been accidental. . . .

'I do know Stevenson has often come to me, helped me when broken-hearted, urged me to write. . . .' She felt that he was 'begging for justice to be done him, through an honest revelation of his life.'

After Hellman had published his debunking article, 'The Stevenson Myth,' in the *Century* magazine of New York for December 1922, Katharine started a correspondence with him from California.

'... For twenty-five years I have carried the burden of this secret on my heart. ... But friends have urged me to publish my notes. ...' Hellman quoted from her material in his subsequent book, though he suppressed the most violent accusations as 'family animosity'. In the intervening years she had been pouring out her grievances in long letters and conversations addressed to Robert Catton and numerous others – enough to cause some doubts and damage to the Stevenson marriage. Her letters overflowed with charges against the faults and sins of Fanny, Lloyd, Belle and the Colvins. Gradually she allied herself with Moors, with Sam's sister and other enemies of her mother-in-law in Samoa and abroad, enlarging every unflattering tale.

Her major theme was that R.L.S. had been martyred by his wife and stepchildren. She blamed Fanny for his fatal stroke, saying it was she who, on the last afternoon, had upset him by urging him against his will to undertake a lecture tour in America to earn money. 'Stevenson ... need not have died', she assured Hellman.

'There was no mourning at Vailima when Stevenson went', she maintained to Gosse, explaining that the heirs cared for nothing but the money. 'Fanny, that primitive woman', she added to Catton, 'told me her reason for marrying Stevenson. She thought he was going to die and she married him to get money.' ... As for Louis, he 'married Fanny because of the affair', from a sense of honour, saying, 'I am not a cad'. 'She was very seductive, you know, and got her way sometimes with men.' Gosse labelled her long diatribe to him '... a perfidious and dangerous document'.

Moors was probably the one who 'gave her to know' about Lloyd's past. 'Alan was the excuse', she told Catton, 'as I long afterwards learned for deserting a Samoan wife Stevenson befriended and was insisting at the time of his death should be legally married. No half cast [sic] children was his excuse; the poor girl had to submit and died after he took me, unknowing, to Samoa, of her humiliation and grief.'

But in the early summer of 1897 Fanny, enjoying her role of doting grandmother, reported to Colvin that they were waiting for Bishop Willis's arrival from Honolulu to christen 'our wonderful baby'.

Soon Lloyd and his wife took a trip home with their new son. Fanny was expecting them back when a cable came from Edinburgh saying that Margaret Stevenson had died of pneumonia, aged sixty-eight.

A relation wrote of how, delirious, she thought she saw her son at the foot of the bed. 'There is Louis! I must go', she exclaimed, and fell back unconscious. She died the next day.

Fanny brooded at losing this closest tie with her husband. But she was asked to come to Scotland to help to settle the Thomas Stevenson estate, in which hers was to be the main interest for life.

She told Nellie that if she could have chosen, she would have preferred to end her own days at Vailima, but it 'now became clear' that she would have to leave. Her health was worse again. Belle and Lloyd had children to educate. Austin was sixteen, and horticulturally a disciple of his grandmother. He wanted to be a landscape architect.

She could not stay at Vailima alone, and keeping the place meant employing a gang of men constantly at work to 'fight the forest'. She told Gosse in London the next year that 'when she was out of sorts she used to be driven almost mad by seeing the monstrous rapidity with which vegetation grew in Samoa, how a thing that began to come up one day would be three feet high the next. . .'.

So with anguished regret she put the place on the market. It was bought – for only £1,750, after all Louis's hard earnings and expense – by a retired German fur merchant from Vladivostok. She reserved the mountain top with the tomb and the land around it, with a right of way.[1]

---

[1] When the Germans annexed Samoa in 1900, Vailima was used as their Governor's residence. In the First World War the New Zealand occupation turned the place into the British Government House. Later, with the island of Upolu under the mandate of the United States, the estate was the residence of the American Administrator. Knocking noises were attributed to the ghost of R.L.S.; but – unless made by rats – they might equally have been the echo of Fanny's hammer.

In 1961 Western Samoa became the first republic in Polynesia, as the Stevensons would surely have wished; and their old home, the presidential mansion, remained a sight for tourists. It was partly wrecked by a hurricane in February 1966, but was rebuilt as a permanent home for the Head of State.

Chapter III
The squabble over the biography

'She had always been a woman of unflinching will and great courage', admitted the critic Hellman of Fanny. This comment referred
to her exploit in May 1898, when she was in New York on her way
to Britain with Belle and Lloyd and his family. She was very unwell
with her old persistent gall-bladder trouble. Her doctor in New York
had told her that if she insisted on leaving her sick-bed to sail, she
'would make the homeward journey in a coffin'. On the way to the
steamer she lay in agony on the floor of the carriage, but when her
alarmed son wanted to get an ambulance to take her back to the hotel,
she ordered the cabman to go on.

'One afternoon . . .', recalled McClure, 'I went with Sidney
Colvin and Mrs Sitwell . . . to Paddington Station to meet Mrs
Stevenson when, after Stevenson's death, she at last returned to
Europe. . . . When she alighted from the boat train I felt Stevenson's
death as if it had happened only the day before, and I have no doubt
that she did. As she came up the platform in black, with so much
that was strange and wonderful behind her, his companion of so
many years . . . I could only say to myself: "Hector's Andro-
mache!" '

The young Mrs Graham Balfour had not been long married when
Fanny arrived in London. '. . . I remember the trepidation with
which I followed the parlourmaid upstairs in Oxford Terrace, and
was ushered into the room where a lady of infinite dignity was lying
on a sofa . . .; after one steady look from those searching "eyes of
gold and bramble dew" (which had rather the effect of a sort of
spiritual X-ray), I lost my feeling of being on approval, and in ten
minutes I was sitting on the floor beside the sofa, pouring out my own
past history . . . and feeling as if I had known Tamaitai for years. . . .
She was curiously detached, and yet you always wanted her sympathy, and if she loved you it never failed you. . . .'

Fanny still kept her great gift as a listener.

The British friends flocked to call on her. After seeing her and her
family Henry James wrote to Mrs Sitwell: 'I want to talk with you of
those people – who are very touching and interesting to me: Fanny S.

so fine, in her way, and so almost putting – dimly – the other there between. She is like an old grizzled lioness – or resigned captive South Sea Chieftainess.'

Lloyd's wife said that Mr James 'always made me think of the Family Physician. . . . He was a splendid talker but kept silent if someone else would do the talking. . .'. Her baby was then 'only a little more than a year old. James loved him and wanted to hold and hug him which I am sorry to say Alan didn't like. . . .'

Charles Baxter had been having grave financial worries of his own and was trying to recoup by investing in a dyeing business. He had two more children by his second wife, a Dutch girl. Katharine Osbourne wrote to Catton that 'Baxter tried to get Lloyd and Fanny to save him from business failure but they wouldn't. . . .'.

Fanny later wrote to Gosse: '. . . I do owe Charles Baxter much gratitude for the Edinburgh Edition for which he was responsible . . . as his idea. . . . It brought me in five thousand pounds when I bitterly needed money. . . .'

As for Henley, neither he nor Fanny made any move towards a meeting. He referred to the family as 'the Samoan crowd' or 'the South Sea Islanders'. Lloyd, however, still had a soft spot for his boyhood hero. He wrote to him, but the elder man did not answer his letters. So he went down to Worthing, where the Henleys were staying; he had previously sent a note to say that he was coming. Henley dispatched his brother Anthony to the station to warn the visitor that 'in no circumstances' would he be received. Lloyd returned to London on the next train.

Gosse, calling on Fanny one morning, found that she was 'dreadfully ill, and suffers a great deal'. But it was then that he gave Edward Marsh his classic description of her – as strange, lovable, extraordinarily passionate, violent, and gay – with unique 'ways of feeling' which 'R.L.S. must have caught from her'.

The daughter-in-law did not fare so flatteringly. Marsh was a guest at a dinner party at Gosse's home in Delamere Terrace, Bayswater, when Mr and Mrs Lloyd Osbourne were present, as was the novelist George Moore. 'The wife is by far the most *rasoir* woman I ever met', wrote Marsh in his diary; 'she is a highly trained American girl who has studied zoology and said the battle of Omdurman reminded her of Xenophon's *Anabasis*. I discovered even before dinner that her favourite subject was New Mexico, and I was not surprised at Edmund [Gosse] beginning the table conversation with trying to keep her off it by saying, "Mrs Osbourne, let me entreat you to instruct Mr Moore on the subject of New Mexico. . .". She at once began a lecture on the subject. Later on Edmund's fury got beyond his control, and when she said the French had as much right to Fashoda as we had he said, "My dear lady, that is nonsense. I can't entertain the idea for a moment, and I'm sure you haven't studied the subject!" '

In Scotland the family visited the eighty-six-year-old Aunt Jane Balfour and Louis's old nurse Cummy. Katharine formed an alliance with Auntie, who professed to like her and have confidence in her. She even gave Katharine some of the Stevenson furniture and mementoes which her sister Maggie had left.

When the party returned to London, Fanny was interviewed in Oxford Terrace by her American friend Gelett Burgess for the September 1898 issue of the *Bookman* of New York. Questioned, she replied that her favourite likeness of her husband was the St Gaudens medallion, and she valued *Weir of Hermiston* most among his books. Burgess continued:

' "What have you written yourself?"
' "Please don't ask me that!" she exclaimed.
' "But you used to paint?"
' "No! But Louis once tried. . . ."
' "How do you like London?"
'Mrs Stevenson looked at me, and I remembered the description of her glance in "An Object of Pity" – Lady Jersey's privately printed *pot-pourri* of Ouida-esque nonsense – "a glance as of one sighting a loaded pistol", – and I escaped.'

The family rented a country house at Dorking in Surrey, within easy reach of London. Fanny's old trouble with her gall bladder was worse, and Belle wrote on her behalf to Henry James, who replied from his Georgian red-brick house near the sea at Rye, Sussex.

He told her 'how much, in these days, I am with you in thought. . . . I rejoice, too, that you have, like myself, an old house in a pretty old town and an old garden with pleasant old flowers. . . . I deeply regret the turn your mother's health has taken. . . . Give her, please,

my tender love, and say to her that if London were actually at all
accessible to me, I should dash down to her thence without delay. . . .
I am extremely busy trying to get on with a belated serial – an effort
in which each hour has its hideous value. . . .; to you all it will mean
much, for you too have lived in Arcadia! . . .'

Meanwhile, ill or well, Fanny had been determined to speed the
biography. On arriving in London she and Lloyd had naturally
expressed disappointment and impatience to Colvin on learning that
he had only begun to collate the material and had written nothing.
'. . . I had been misled', she later confided to Gosse. '. . . It was a
great shock to me when I found out the truth; but I got so many
shocks in the electric atmosphere of London that this one in time
grew small by comparison.'

Writing in June to Colvin as 'My dear friend', she assured him,
'Between you and me there must be – there can be – no quarrel.'
She begged him to remember that they were acting in accord with
Louis's wish – a 'sacred command'.

In reply Colvin told her that if she would trust him the work
would be most worthily done, but he could not do his best if he were
pressed, and he must give up the assignment if she did not care to
rely on him. With this rhetorical offer he assured her of the
permanence of his affectionate friendship.

Colvin was meanwhile editing, with a preface, the further collect-
ion of Stevenson's letters which were to be published in 1899 in
London and New York: *Letters from Robert Louis Stevenson to His
Family and Friends.*

While they were being prepared for publication Fanny wrote to
Charles Scribner for advice: 'Some of the letters that are intended
to go into the book should not, in my judgment, appear at all. When
my husband was a boy in his late 'teens' and early twenties he and his
father – a rigid old Calvinist – quarrelled on the subject of religion. . . . Mr Thomas Stevenson loved me and was as kind to me
as though I were his own daughter. I cannot, for the sake of an extra
volume that would produce a certain amount of money, do anything
that in my heart would seem disloyal to the dear old man's
memory. . . .'

In September a critical operation for gallstones was performed upon Fanny by Sir Frederick Treves, surgeon to royalty. He asked no fee, saying that he considered it a privilege to give this service to the widow of Stevenson. She sent him the hundred-dollar special printing of the Edinburgh Edition with a grateful inscription. Her recovery was slow – even uncertain for a time. Her detractors did not make enough allowance for her illness in the handling of the row over the biography, and blamed her for discourtesies which were mainly Lloyd's.

Her progress was not hastened when she learned that Eve Blantyre Simpson, sister of Sir Walter, had written a book called *Robert Louis Stevenson's Edinburgh Days*, which mentioned the black-sheep experiences of Louis's youth. Fanny called the book 'most malicious'. Colvin said it should be boycotted.

Several other delicate considerations probably made Colvin procrastinate with the *Life*. There was the embarrassment of Louis's early but important love letters to Mrs Sitwell. There was the need to tell of his generosity to his friends, among whom Colvin himself had been a chief recipient. And there was the difficulty of how to treat the scandal leading to the Stevenson's marriage. Apparently Fanny had earlier had the courage to be more candid, but later Lloyd wrote from Edinburgh to Colvin, asking his permission to make deletions regarding 'my mother's divorce and the reasons that led to Louis's going out to California'. (When in 1915 Clayton Hamilton wrote – inaccurately – of the meeting of Stevenson and Fanny at Grez that 'their affinity was instant and their union immediate and complete', the first edition of his book was withdrawn on the outraged protest of her heirs and the passage was deleted from the second printing. In Balfour's official biography the subject of the divorce was smoothed over with a few tactful lines.)

After the glow of Samoa Fanny was shrivelling in the English autumn, and decided that her convalescence would move faster in Madeira – where Louis had wanted to go. Belle had left for New York City to be with Austin, who was a student there. ('Beg him, from me,' his grandmother wrote to his mother, 'not to pick up vulgar expressions in New York'.) In November Lloyd and his family accompanied Fanny in travelling by easy stages through France, Spain and Portugal. In early December they sailed from

Lisbon in 'a filthy little Portuguese steamer', with 'horrible food', as she wrote to Nellie. Its cargo was hay and kerosene, and the passengers scattered cigarette butts and smouldering matches all over the ship.

After forty-eight hours they anchored in the beautiful crescent bay of Funchal, where they rented a house. The tiled roofs of the old Portuguese town curved up the mountains to the *quintas* set among terraced gardens and vineyards with wine-carts drawn by bullocks. Fanny – after all the scenery of Europe and America and the Pacific – exclaimed characteristically that the island was 'the most picturesque place' she had ever seen. 'The people are very gentle and well bred, like Samoans.'

'My plans are vague', Fanny wrote to Belle. 'The years ahead of me seem like large empty rooms, with high ceilings and echoes. Not gay, say you, but I was never one for gaiety much – and I may discover a certain grandeur in the emptiness.'

Relations between Fanny and her daughter-in-law were gradually going downhill. 'She was a strong colorful character', Katharine afterwards informed Hellman, 'with a will which could have conquered provinces, but all her ambition was turned to subjugating the individuals about her. She was clairvoyant, uncannily so, she watched and studied everyone to turn anything her way or to thwart any of their plans and ambitions that were aside her use. . . .'

The growing dislike between his womenfolk must have strained the nerves of the highly strung Lloyd. Fanny was 'much concerned' to learn that Belle was to do some lecturing about her cosmopolitan experiences. She gave her a little advice – having obviously practised as she preached. 'Now remember what I tell you, always strike a personal note in your dress, and the way you do your hair; don't look like other people. If you succeed in that you are nowhere; only a plain, little pudgy dark woman. Keep to the slightly oriental, the rather unusual, and you are a houri. Looks go a long way in lectures, too. Look out for your voice . . . and *always* look out for the *twang*. . . .'

In March 1899 Colvin wrote to Fanny in Madeira and regretfully informed her that with pressure of work and fatigue 'my head has quite broken down again and I cannot go on with the biography for the present'. As she was still weak from her surgery Lloyd aggressively took over the new spurt of business correspondence. 'Dear Mr Colvin,' he wrote back on 15th April, 'Your letter came as a great shock to my mother and myself. . . .' He firmly suggested that rather than let the work drag on indefinitely Colvin should give it up.

Support came from Sir Algernon Methuen, the publisher, who told Baxter, '. . . The postponement of publication has to some extent endangered the prospects of the book.'

Lloyd had written with prompt alacrity to Baxter that 'Colvin has at last thrown up the sponge, thus cancelling all former contracts for the *Life*'. He went on to say that Colvin had been overpaid for editing the *Letters* and suggested that he should receive a final sum of only a hundred pounds.

Colvin himself told Baxter that he thought he ought to have a share in the royalties of the *Letters*, 'perhaps something less than a third'. A third was, in fact, the tentative proportion suggested by Stevenson in the Tahiti letter of 1888 about Colvin's remuneration for the *Life*. Louis's directive had ended, 'See that Colvin has justice'.

On 22nd April, by the next steamer, Colvin confirmed to Lloyd that he would indeed agree to bow out as biographer, 'though naturally cast down at what had been the great hope and interest of my life'. Lloyd exulted to Baxter, 'Last mail I received a sad, smooth letter from Colvin, acquiescing in the inevitable, and resigning the *Life*. . . . He seemed very crushed in his letter, and it would be well to keep him in that condition. There's no more fight in him. It's pleading now.'

Baxter hastened to write to Colvin that he hoped his decision was not final. 'I think Louis would have wished me to intervene.' He expressed the same views in an urgent letter to Fanny. He told Colvin, '. . . I don't care whether you like my onslaught on Fanny or not! She deserves it.'

One might suspect that Fanny was hiding behind Lloyd, and Colvin behind Baxter, to get someone else to be louder and tougher in bargaining over the memorial to their beloved Louis. With the popular curiosity which famous authors attracted in those decades before film and television stars, the squabble over the R.L.S. biography gave rise to literary gossip for many years.

Fanny and her party returned to London in May and took rooms in

Porchester Terrace, Bayswater. Apparently she and Colvin exerted
themselves to be gracious. '. . . It has been an inexpressible relief
to me', he wrote Baxter, 'to find myself on the old affectionate terms
with the family. . . .'

Lloyd had offended his stepfather's circle by the disrespect with
which he had treated Louis's old friend. He referred to him as 'the
dog in the manger'. As Colvin shortly told Graham Balfour, the
young man 'has an unlucky way of putting things in writing at least,
that puts my back up and makes concession impossible'.

'I am afraid this means war – open war', fumed Colvin to the
hard-pressed Baxter. But later he said that he had written 'on the
spur of the moment'. He submitted an account for his time and
expenses on the *Letters*.

Baxter rebuked Lloyd on 7th June: 'My dear Lloyd, I *cannot*
treat Colvin as a sharp. His letter is really perfectly explicit, and it
means what it says – viz., that £483 6s 8d is his whole claim.'

Lloyd was apparently ashamed of his cockiness; he prided himself
on his manners. He wrote Colvin in a more friendly way in July –
from Grez, where 'Katharine and I are here living among the ghosts
of the past'.

(In March 1960 Lloyd's son Mr Alan Osbourne, in a letter to
The Times Literary Supplement of London, belatedly surprised
Stevenson readers with the revelation that Fanny and Lloyd had
never wanted Colvin to write the *Life*. Lloyd especially had thought
that the tactful if devious way out was to let him delay until he might
'hang himself', with the fussy procrastination of which R.L.S. had
warned his heirs.)

But by now Fanny had already approached Graham Balfour to
undertake the *Life*, according to his son Michael, writing in *The
Times Literary Supplement* in January 1960. '. . . Mr Balfour
could be a rival to no accepted man of letters', she explained later to
Gosse, 'and yet I believed him capable of doing the work . . .
adequately, honestly and well. Besides, he was a member of Louis's
family and held in the deepest affection by him. . . .'

At first Graham Balfour 'absolutely refused'. Yet as Michael
Balfour put it, '. . . life at Vailima clearly constituted a vivid
personal experience which left a permanent mark on members of the
household . . . a special bond . . . [Fanny] wished attention directed

to the developed man rather than the development. And not only
was she a person whose views were clearly entitled to consideration,
but she was also one accustomed to pursue any cause she considered
just without remorse or reserve.

'. . . the bond . . . was strengthened by [Graham's] having
inherited, along with a devotion to her husband, that husband's
valuation of her. He never ceased to insist that, but for her care,
Louis would have died long before 1894. Without being blind to her
weaknesses, he would never allow them to distract attention from
her merit or tolerate the criticisms in which many who encountered
her superficially were apt to indulge. He therefore regarded her
request as an obligation to be shouldered and set to work.'

When Graham Balfour submitted his completed manuscript of
the *Life* to Fanny, she approved it at once. 'If I had fault to find,
nothing would or could keep my cat's claws out of the fur', she
assured him.

Henry James read one of the first copies and on the evening he
had finished it he wrote generously to Balfour to congratulate him.
He pointed out, however – with truth – that Louis's personality had
been so vivid and his life so adventurous that the 'exhibition' of
them made his work '*pay* somewhat'. '. . . You may say that the
work was, or *is*, the man and the life as well; still, the books are
jealous and a certain supremacy and mystery (above all) has, as it
were, gone from them. . . . He had of course only to be then himself
less picturesque, and none of us would have had him so by an inch.
But . . . he is thus an artist and creator in some degree the victim of
himself. . . .'

Chapter IV
Fanny, loved or hated

When Fanny felt strong enough she decided to return to San
Francisco. She had not long been back when she received 'a great
shock' in a telegram from Austin in New York. His mother had had

an operation for appendicitis with grave complications. 'It was thoughtful of you to wait till she was safe before letting me know.' Austin was to become the most satisfactory and certainly the most successful of the step-in-laws whom Louis had lived to meet. The next year, aged twenty, he stayed with his grandmother on his way back to New Zealand to lay out Cornwall Park in Auckland in his new profession of landscape architect. He 'has grown up a fine, manly fellow', Fanny wrote to Robert Catton, 'in every way the opposite of his unfortunate father'.

She wanted to live in sight of the Pacific, rolling on to the South Seas. So she built a house on the hill top of Hyde and Lombard Streets, near the home of John Lloyd and his disapproving wife. As she remarked, 'It is awfully exciting to build a house.' The architect followed the design she had made by constructing a miniature house out of matchboxes on the corner of a table.

While her new home was being built Fanny went for a camping trip, accompanied only by her faithful Irish maid Mary, among the redwoods in the Santa Cruz mountains ten miles from Gilroy. She was so charmed by the shady valley that she determined to buy a small ranch and later build a permanent summer home. 'At the ranch I have one tent with a curtain in the middle', she told Belle. 'We sleep on one side of the curtain and sit on the other. I have only the most primitive facilities for cooking, and the butcher is twelve miles away over a mountain road. . . . I am dependent on the boarding-house for my bread. . . .'

Here again was the old Fanny reawakened. Her family often called her 'Mrs Robinson Crusoe'.

Late in the year the house in San Francisco was ready. Flat-roofed and somewhat 'on the Mexican order', it fitted into the landscape and was, she said, 'like a fort on a cliff'. A high wall and vine-draped colonnade hid a garden soon rich with geraniums, fuchsias and rare plants from all over the world, with low-growing trees to yield the wide view to the windows. She could look down on the climbing city, glittering with lights after dark, and on the bay lively with ocean liners, ferries and fishing boats. Here again were the much-travelled Stevenson portraits, the silver and Chippendale, the big Burmese gods at the door, the St Gaudens plaque of Louis, the Tokelau buckets, and a 'thousand objects gathered in her wanderings'.

'At night', her daughter-in-law wrote to Hellman, 'she would . . .
watch people standing on the corner of the street under her window
and imagine all sorts of wicked intentions of theirs when they were
only waiting for the street cars. She would come in my room and try
to get in to telephone to the police headquarters and it was sometimes
pretty hard to escape making her angry with me. She had small low
openings in the walls between rooms that she might scoot through
down on her knees if a burglar or a murderer forced himself in – and
there was a steel plate between panels of the outside doors – and
secret panels for hiding things in for she loved to frighten herself –
or tell herself all sorts of weird tales. . . .'

Before leaving Apia, Fanny had heard of a little half-caste girl, an
orphan, who had been left a fortune in lands and money by her
American father. When the child was five her guardian had sent her
to San Francisco to be educated. Somehow she had disappeared and
her property in Samoa was unclaimed, while others used the rents.
When Fanny was settled in San Francisco she searched for her,
first in private schools and seminaries and then in orphan asylums.
In a Catholic orphanage was a young girl with a similar name. Fanny
went to see her, taking a Samoan basket and some shells. As soon as
the child saw the basket she gave a joyful cry. She was found. The
problem now was to prove her claim and secure her property. Fanny
made a special trip across the continent to Washington, where she
talked to senators, Catholic priests and other influential persons. She
finally succeeded in the restoration of the girl's lands and some of
the back rents. Meanwhile she had the little Cinderella stay at her
house, bought her a new wardrobe, gave a party for her, and saw her
off on the steamer to Samoa.
The R. L. Stevenson Society honoured Fanny at its annual
meetings on Louis's birthday. She always insisted on inviting the
ageing Jules Simoneau from Monterey to stay with her for these
occasions, though he apologized for his shabby clothes. Once the
dinner was given at the old restaurant which the poor young Louis
had frequented, and she took Simoneau in her carriage. '. . . when a
fashionable young lady in the party objected', wrote Nellie, 'she was
rebuked by being sent home in a street-car'.
Bob Stevenson died in April 1900, leaving an impoverished

widow and two children. Here was another blow for Fanny, still trying to preserve, like a court in exile, the enchantment of the Stevenson world.

More and more she hankered for her little camp in the mountains. She gave the place the Samoan name of Vanumanutagi, 'Vale of the Singing Birds'. Soon she again designed a model house with matchboxes, glued and painted, and with pebbles for the foundation wall. Then she hired a country carpenter to build the low bungalow with a veranda on two sides and a big brick fireplace. Boulders from the stream were used for the foundation, and she was thrilled to find many bearing clear imprints of fossil ferns and birds and snakes. But in her absence – shades of her struggles at Vailima – the stones were all cemented in place 'with the nice smooth sides outward and the fossils turned inward'.

In the long dry summers there was always the danger of forest fires. One occurred when she was at the ranch with only her maid Mary and Mary's sister. At first they thought a sea fog was rolling in over the hill tops, but soon its choking smoke poured down into the valley. Horsemen came galloping to warn the ranchers and report the progress of the fire-fighting. At one time the only escape – the road to Gilroy – was threatened. Fanny planned that the three women should save their lives by wrapping themselves in wet blankets and crouching in a hollow in an open field.

At the ranch she began 'with the greatest reluctance' to write the prefaces to the biographical edition of her husband's works. 'It appals me', she told Charles Scribner, 'to think of my temerity in writing these introductions'.

The brilliant young American novelist Frank Norris brought his wife and child to live in a cabin up the slope. Fanny, more than ever inclined towards protégés, spent time and money to help him with the place. Then suddenly he died. She built a large stone 'memorial seat' at a roadside spot with a splendid view. 'I have helped lay the stones', she wrote to Scribner in 1902, 'and have dabbled in mortar until I can hardly use my hands to write. This sort of work is so much more interesting than scratching with a pen. . . .'

A second son was born to Lloyd and his wife in 1900. This time Katharine held out against her mother-in-law's sentiment and named the baby Louis. Many people called the sturdy child Lou, and

Fanny herself ostentatiously preferred the middle name of Wolfert.

'Louis was most unwelcomed', Katharine later informed Robert Catton. 'Mrs Stevenson actively and L.O. passively were so inhuman in their persecution because of the coming event that I at that time often prayed that he would die at birth. . . .'

'L.O. did not like having children. They were an expense, they took care and attention he wanted the monopoly of. They entailed responsibility he refused. . . .'

For some years the young family shared Fanny's home in San Francisco, and under its roof the discord mounted again and again to the breaking-point. It was hard on the charming little boys, pulled to and fro between the two possessive women. Fanny fondly painted their portraits. From Lloyd's treatment of Colvin one can guess how tactless he may have been to a young woman with an abnormal appetite for praise. As for Katharine, a 'holier than thou' attitude, shown throughout her letters, must have nauseated the mother and son and driven them to a habit of perverseness. 'Think of Lloyd deserting his children when they were age one and four, and never doing anything for them. . . .'

This alleged break in relations was in 1901, but it actually continued by stages while the family went on living with Fanny. The reason why Lloyd left her, Katharine assured Catton, was 'unbelievable'. '. . . Fanny, Lloyd and Belle had primitive natures . . . love of cruelty, egotism and perverseness. . . . Tamaitai for a year was doing everything she could to spoil our lives. . . . Tamaitai made Lloyd leave his family as he was dependent on her. . . . She deliberately set to work to make me as unhappy as possible, to wean him from us. And that is what Lloyd said to me. "Her hellish inquisition of you has left an ineffaceable impression on me and you will have to go." Another time he said, "What is the matter with my mother is that she cannot bear to see us happy.". . .

'Belle came', Katharine went on, 'and she was only too happy to stir up Tamaitai's evil heart still farther.' Belle, as her sister-in-law recorded at length, was always a trouble-maker. '. . . Lloyd, it was seen, could not be induced to leave us so Belle goes [sic] up a plan to send him to New York to try to get a play on the stage and not let me go. Then when Lloyd was gone, Tamaitai and Belle started in trying to make something appear as if I were untrue to Lloyd in his absence. . . . Then they got Lloyd not to come back. And Tamaitai would give him money to stay away but not if he lived with his family and Lloyd was unwilling to take me and the children and earn a living for us . . . such terrible heartbreaking memories . . . the injustice, the cruelty. . . .'

In 1919, five years after Fanny's death, Robert Catton wrote to Lord Guthrie about a visit he and his wife had paid to Katharine Osbourne in California. '. . . she gets rather tiresome about her mother-in-law's shortcomings which may have been many, but I did not see them and I still maintain she was the one woman for R.L.S.'

Three years later Mrs Helen Purdy, an ardent Stevensonian in Berkeley, California, wrote further to Catton about Katharine: '. . . Her hatred of Mrs Stevenson is appalling. . . . She does not talk with excitement nor passion. In a perfectly level, soft, pleasing voice she makes the most astonishing assertions which I cannot fit in with what I have previously read, heard, and known myself. . . . Sidney Colvin comes in for his share of the things Mrs Osbourne told me – and *I do not believe them.*' Then Mrs Purdy added a puzzling remark. 'Notwithstanding my disbelief, in some ways I was more attracted to Mrs Osbourne than I had been before. . . .'

What could she mean? Perhaps it was the same rather touching quality which, one guesses, may have drawn Lloyd and Fanny to the brooding young woman in the first place: aspiration.

Chapter V
'This Seraph in Chocolate'

An unforeseen storm awaited Fanny after Graham Balfour's official *Life of Robert Louis Stevenson* in two volumes was published in London in October 1901. The editor of *Pall Mall* magazine asked Henley to review it, and at first he declined. But somehow he could not resist, and after all this time – thirteen years after the quarrel and seven after the death of Stevenson – the old bitterness was poured like acid over the grave. He headed the review 'The Two Stevensons'.

'To me there were two Stevensons: the Stevenson who went to America in 1887; and the Stevenson who never came back. . . . At bottom Stevenson was an excellent fellow. But he was . . . incessantly and passionately interested in Stevenson. . . and the smallest of his discoveries, his most trivial apprehensions, were all by way of being revelations . . . he was never so well pleased, never so irresistible, as when he wrote about himself. Withal, if he wanted a thing, he went after it with an entire contempt for the consequences. . . .

'. . . Not, if I can help it, shall this faultless, or very nearly faultless, monster go down to after years as the Lewis I knew, and loved, and laboured with and for . . . this Seraph in Chocolate, this barley-sugar effigy of a real man . . . is not my old, riotous, intrepid, scornful Stevenson at all. . . .

'. . . a wit? I do not think he was. . . . On occasion he would play the fool . . . a buffoon to whom you could not show the door. . . .

'I remember, rather, the unmarried and irresponsible Lewis: the friend, the comrade, the *charmeur*. . . .'

Balfour's biography had mentioned, as an example of Stevenson's generosity, the allowance made to a hard-up friend – a small sum, Louis had added lightly, lest he squander it 'on a gig and a Pomeranian dog'. Henley must have recognized the anonymous reference to himself, for he jeered that this negligible donation 'scarce becomes the lips of a man who had several kennels of Pomeranians and gigs innumerable'.

The review ended, '. . . and for ourselves, let us live and die uninsulted, as we lived and died before his books began to sell and his personality was a marketable thing.'

The editor asked Henley to tone down his long hymn of hate, but he refused. The *Life* had cautiously omitted any mention of the quarrel. Why, readers wondered, should the old friend thus personally flay the dead? Henley's own sympathetic biographer, the late John Connell, voiced the motive of this 'brutal unguarded performance'. 'There was one person on whom, at last, he was going to be avenged. He wanted to savage Fanny, and he wanted to wound her in her love for R.L.S., as harshly as he believed she had wounded him in his love. . . . Parts were clever; the intention throughout was mercilessly cruel.'

In the years since Stevenson's death Henley must have been breathing fire while he watched Fanny's enshrinement as the relict of an acclaimed genius.

For her there was again a painful upheaval in this desecration of shroud and widow's veil. She told the poetess Alice Meynell that Henley must have been drunk when he wrote the review. But with her usual recanting of her own rages, she said that she believed Henley was embittered by his lameness, his misfortunes and the passing of his youth, and yet again quoted her favourite adage, 'To know all is to understand all'. The ailing man died in 1903, and some years later when his widow wrote to ask her for letters to be published in his *Life*, she sent them with a gracious note, commenting that 'some of them are very good reading indeed. . .'.

Henry James was drawn into the argument – as far as that masterly spectator could be dragged into any real-life drama. With heavy dignity he spoke for many people when he wrote that the outburst was rather 'a striking and lurid – and so far interesting – case of long discomfortable jealousy and ranklement turned at last to posthumous (as it were!) malignity'.

The blasting of a famous reputation made a great sensation in Britain. Several indignant rebuttals were printed, but the phrases 'Seraph in Chocolate' and 'barley-sugar effigy' became war whoops for a generation. In America the attack was little noticed. In any case Henley and his clique still considered it not in the best taste that Stevenson's first recognition on a large popular scale had come in his wife's country – a sign, to them, of the second-rate. Thus, despite the protests of many loyal readers, R.L.S. became neglected for a while as a 'precious' minor author, dated and overrated. It was in any case a time when most late Victorian writing, like Victorian furniture, was in a revulsion of unpopularity. The irony was that Louis, particularly in matters of romantic love and sex, had chafed at much in his own era which was now held against him.

Where Fanny had formerly been heralded as a noble guardian of genius, for decades many writers tended to picture her as a mischief-making tyrant. Most of her husband's reticence about physical love was attributed to this passionate woman who had accepted scandal for his sake.

Chapter VI
Mexico and a new protégé

In 1902 Henry James was asked by a friend who was touring California for a letter of introduction to Mrs Stevenson. The Master
complied, but warned him: '. . . I must tell you that I feel myself to
be launching it rather into the dark. That is, I have a fear that she is
rather changed – or rather exaggerated – with time, illness, etc., and
that you may find her somewhat aged, queer, eccentric, etc. . . .
Only remember this – that *she* (with all deference to her) was never
the person to have seen, it was R.L.S. himself.'

Fanny's vaunted apron strings had apparently loosened enough for
Lloyd to be much away in New York and London with his writing.
His wife was left to live grimly in his mother's home with her boys.
Katharine was a conscientious mother, adoring her sons with the
same blind possessiveness which she found so intolerable in her
mother-in-law. She was obsessed by the feud, though Fanny as
always had many other strong interests. 'I was doing so much for
Tamaitai as I had to,' Katharine later fumed to Catton, 'and with
never the least word or look of appreciation.' This silence seems self-
evident, for the two women were hardly on speaking terms.
    With her neurotic need to feel afflicted, Katharine vowed that her
husband had ignored his children. But again she recorded that 'Lloyd
always wrote me as long as I would let him. After four years I told him
to write us no more, and when he continued to do so I sent his
letters back unopened'. If so she must have had X-ray eyes, for she
added, 'One of his last letters said, "My respect and admiration for
you has increased with the years. . . ."'
    Lloyd was now a professional writer of books, plays, stories and
articles – undistinguished but workmanly entertainment. Nothing
equalled in quality or profits his collaborations with Louis, but his
name appeared in leading popular markets. His best pieces were a
few humorous stories with South Sea backgrounds. In 1902 he and
Belle were co-authors of a book called *Memories of Vailima*.
    Austin, too, though still practising as a landscape architect, had
begun his career of playwriting. He and his Uncle Lloyd collaborated

on a play called *The Exile*, which was produced in London in 1903. They were also working on a stage adaptation entitled *Treasure Island, A Melodrama in Five Acts*. Fanny was enthralled. To have a reincarnation of her husband's talent in her son and grandson, even though not of Stevenson's blood, would be a gratification beyond words.

Protégés played a strong part in Fanny's twenty years alone – nephews and nieces and other young aspirants. Perhaps their adoption helped to compensate for the fact that she had not been a mother to those children for whom Louis had longed.

Now in her twilight there came an astonishing afterglow which her enemies regarded with raised eyebrows. A new object of her 'violent friendship' had turned up in San Francisco. Edward Salisbury Field was a young *bon vivant* aged about twenty-five, hardly older than Austin. He was the son of an old schoolgirl friend from Indianapolis, where he had been born. His father had gone into book-publishing there under the firm name of Merrill & Field, now Bobbs-Merrill, but in 1883 Field *père* entered the real estate business in Los Angeles, where his son had been sent to public schools and Occidental College. Ned had travelled much abroad and spoke idiomatic French.

Naturally the young man called on his mother's old chum, and the meeting struck the sparks of prompt affinity to which Fanny was prone. 'I can never forget', an admirer reminisced in *The Los Angeles Times*, 'his gayety, his quick wit, his delightful humor, his drollery as a raconteur'.

Best of all he was something of what Louis had called 'a literary man'. He had got a job as a feature writer and artist with the Hearst chain of newspapers in California. He produced light verse and cartoons, especially a series of fantastic drawings for children, signed 'Childe Harolde'. He was so much noted for his wit and charm that he became a friend of his employer, the legendary William Randolph Hearst, and his fellow tycoon Templeton Crocker.

In personality he was an original too, debonair in the early (not the mature) Stevenson tradition – so much that when he died suddenly nearly thirty years later, 'he was buried in a colored shirt and blue tie, as he didn't wish to depress anyone with solemnity even in death'.

'For several years, beginning in 1905,' primly states *The National Cyclopedia of American Biography*, 'he was secretary to Mrs Robert Louis Stevenson.' 'Secretary' was hardly the word. The terms 'protégé' and 'companion' were generally used. Nellie wrote in her sister's *Life* that he had become 'a member of her household'.

Inevitably there was gossip in California and abroad about Mrs Stevenson's great new friend, some forty years younger. He got on well with Belle and Lloyd, but Katharine wrote that he was a sponge on the Stevenson fortune. Even when he left the Hearst syndicate for the uncertain returns of free-lance writing, he had his father's real estate business in the background. Katharine advertised his presence in her mother-in-law's house as a scandal, probably without foundation. '. . . She was much of a siren, you know,' she told Catton. 'Very vain and loved always the attentions of young men and was not happy without someone in her grasp. . . .'

Though Ned Field could never be a substitute for the unique figure of R.L.S., he spoke Fanny's language – midwestern-cum-cosmopolitan; he too liked art, literature, the casual outdoor world and good living. He was a middlebrow – and so was she, without Louis's circle to aspire to. Her gift for listening needed a clever man at her table, and for a conversationalist like Ned, as for Louis, her powerful interest must have been a secret of her appeal. For nine or ten years – until her death – he was to be her continual companion and escort.

His own family, however, apparently became uneasy. With a pastiche of the Thomas Stevensons' sentiments a generation earlier, they were anxious for their son to settle down with a nice girl rather than to be monopolized by an ageing *bohémienne*. After a couple of years, while she and Ned were wintering in rural Mexico, the naughty Fanny schemed in a letter to Belle: 'I wonder if you have forgotten that I once asked you to send me a photograph of a pretty girl for reasons of state? Please do so; no one will see it outside of a small circle. It doesn't make any difference whose likeness it is. You could buy one in a shop, and I would send you the money for it. A blonde is preferred. I really think the young man ought to have it. He will only show it once to his family, and then it will be locked up in his trunk. If you send it just direct it to Ned F. and I will understand.'

In November 1904 the San Francisco fogs, plaguing Fanny's bronchitis, drove her south to Mexico, accompanied by her maid Mary and Ned Field. On the return journey the trio stopped at Ensenada, not far below the California border, and she bought a ranch. The Rancho El Sausal lay on a magnificent Pacific beach in dry sunny air. A little stream was banked with the scarlet 'Christmas berry', and birds sang in the willow woods which gave the name of Sausal to the 'sweet lost spot', as Fanny described it to Mr Scribner.

The same party came back the next winter. The ranch-house was only a humble cottage and supplies were hard to get, but '. . . If I had no family I should stop here forever'.

One day, she reported to Belle, 'excited cries from Ned called [us] to the back verandah; there was a coyote trotting past . . .'. One morning she put on her long boots and found them pebbly with peas and peppermints 'laid away by a provident rat. Last evening we trapped 9 rats! . . . I hate to catch them, but we just *have* to. . . .'.

She cultivated the few foreign mining people for the sake of her nephew Louis Sanchez, who was studying to be a mining engineer. She also got on well with the Mexican officials. When a Christmas box from Belle in New York arrived at Ensenada, the *comandante* made sure that the Señora Stevenson received it in time by sending it to El Sausal by three mounted policemen.

Though the *rancho* was isolated she was not afraid. The penalties for any crime were incredibly hard; housebreaking was punished by death. Several times the party were surprised by hoofbeats and a tired dusty man dashing up on a foamy horse and begging for something to eat. Still a champion of the underdog – like Louis – she always gave him food and drink. When the police came galloping up and asked if she had seen an escaped prisoner, she said 'No'.

Chapter VII
The San Francisco earthquake

Leaving the Rancho El Sausal in mid April 1906, Fanny, Ned and the maid headed homeward by rail up the California coast. In the motion of the train they had not felt the repercussion of the vast earthquake which had just devastated San Francisco. At length they saw tumbled buildings, and were stopped by a wrecked bridge.

They spent the night on the train, and the next day hired a team and drove roundabout to the small town of Gilroy, near Fanny's ranch, Vanumanutagi, in the Santa Cruz mountains. There they heard that San Francisco was burning. Belle was in Italy, Lloyd in New York, and his estranged wife staying elsewhere with the children. But Fanny was extremely alarmed not only about her house but about a maid who was living in it, and about her relatives and friends in the San Francisco Bay area.

Ned Field made his way as best he could to the flaming city while she stayed in the small hotel at Gilroy, awaiting news. 'I could have got to my house on Thursday night,' she wrote afterwards to Dora Williams, 'and indeed I wanted to be there to look after things, but I have such a horror of being a burden on men in a time of danger that I reluctantly stayed where I was. . . .' The telegraph wires were down and no mails were going out; for three days she was at the mercy of her lurid imagination. 'One man told me that he had watched my house burn, and that Della was burned with it. I did believe my house was gone, but was sure that someone had saved Della. . . .'

Then the flames were checked, after a loss of fifteen hundred lives and most of the city, and Ned Field got back to Gilroy with the news that Fanny's relatives and Della and the property were safe. Troops had been hastily mustered to clear the threatened buildings and control the fire-fighting and the mass exodus. Many women and children and unneeded men had been bundled off to stay across the Bay or on the Peninsula, including the John Lloyds and Mrs Williams.

During those three days and nights Ned and Fanny's nephews had looked down from the hill top on the crackling city below, and watched the blaze as it 'leaped from street to street in its mad race up the hill', as she wrote to Dora. People fled like wild animals from a forest fire. Her house was in the path of the flames and was nearly lost. 'It was made all ready to dynamite when the men found they had forgotten to bring their explosive. . . . Then my house rescuers were allowed to get on my roof and look after my place. . . .' A small puddle remained in the pool, the only water left. Field and the nephews dipped rugs and sacks and, climbing to the flat roof, took turns in dashing through the scorching heat to beat the cornices as they began to smoke. The fire was so close that they gave up and dug a hole in the garden, in which they buried Fanny's chief treasures, including the Stevenson silverware and the St Gaudens medallion of Louis.

By a miracle a strong sea-wind halted the flames. Exhausted, the sooty fire-fighters found the house and contents intact, except for a huge hole in the roof where the earthquake had thrown down a heavy brick chimney on a spare-room bed.

'After the fire', Fanny told Dora, 'there was an attempt to rush the house by roughs who had been helping to throw over the movable parts of the roof – or at least they had got into the garden *with* the helpers. They evidently meant to loot, but were finally chased out. . . .'

The outlook was 'ghastly', for the house 'stood high on its clean-swept hill like a lonely outpost in a great waste of cinders, half-fallen chimneys, and sagging walls'. The ruins smoked for two weeks and took on a 'strangely old look . . . like . . . the excavations of an ancient city'. The wind moaned around the house through the broken maze of wires which hung in the streets. Homeless refugees surged past, and some built lean-to shacks from pieces of board against Fanny's walls. Blankets and warm garments were handed out to them, never to be returned, but she 'was glad that they should have them'.

Beyond the desperate need for water (in a city of nine hills), food, clothing and shelter, there was suspense over persons who were missing for days. There were no stamps or posts, no banks or money. From Gilroy, Fanny thoughtfully sent Mrs Williams some stamps and a ten-dollar bill, though she was uncertain whether Dora would receive them. 'I only had fifty cents', she wrote, 'for several days after I arrived here, and know that sometimes a little cash in hand is comforting to a degree. . . . Now, if you need any money you *must* tell me, and I will send it to you. Fortunately Mr Field did his banking somewhere in Southern California, and as he had plenty of money in the bank, and put it all at my disposal, I have had enough. . . .'

She inquired after the welfare of the John Lloyds. (The roof of their town house had caught fire many times, but it had been saved.) 'They have, I imagine, a fancied grievance against me – a grievance at this time!' At the end of her letter she sent 'kindest regards to the Lloyds if you see them. I can feel nothing but kindness, when it comes to the bedrock, for any living soul'.

Meanwhile, by one of the melodramatic coincidences which striped the lives of mother and daughter, in Sorrento Belle had just been in danger from the eruption of Vesuvius. 'For 13 hours they were in thick darkness', Fanny told Dora, 'almost dying from suffocation, the ground and air shaking, and a mob of frantic peasants trampling them down in their wild endeavours to escape! . . .' Belle had not long reached Rome when she was shocked to hear the newsboys crying, 'San Francisco *tutta distrutta!*' She waited for several days before a cable came: 'Mother safe.'

The calamity prevented Fanny from going east for Austin's wedding on 6th June. She wrote to him with her fond regrets, explaining that 'I do not know if the wedding present I bought for you still exists'. Now aged twenty-five, he was marrying a delightful girl named Mary Wilson in Providence, Rhode Island. They were to live in New York. After Fanny's less desirable in-laws – Joe Strong and Katharine Durham – third time was charm. The bride soon shared her husband's warmth for his Fanny-Gran, whom they nicknamed 'Foxy', for 'Foxy Grandma'. In 1905 he had given up landscape architecture and turned his full attention to playwriting, with two more plays produced in London and New York in that year and the next.

In the same turbulent year Fanny learned that Tahiti was devastated by a terrific hurricane. Hearing that Chief Ori, Louis's 'brother', had lost his grass palace and other property, she sent him money to rebuild the houses.

She also helped old Jules Simoneau and his wife, whose son had lost everything in the San Francisco fire and could no longer support them.

Even 'Mrs Robinson Crusoe' could not at present live in the ruins and disorder of the city, especially as she could get no water on her hill top. So she decided to stay at the ranch at Gilroy, where water was plentiful and she could buy provisions. She remained until the autumn, though she told Nellie that it was 'an eerie place to stay in'. The area lay close to the main earthquake fault, and for a year afterwards the ground quivered, with a roaring as of an express train and explosions like cannonading added to 'the creaking and swaying of the little wooden house'.

When she finally returned to San Francisco she still found great discomfort, and from her high windows it depressed her to look down on the chaotic city. She could not sublimate this experience as Louis would have done in a dazzling and searing description. So in November she escaped with Lloyd and Ned Field on a trip to Europe.

Chapter VIII
The obsession

Lloyd, no less fascinated by mechanisms than he had been in his printing-press days, had become a pioneer in acquiring a car. He was fanatic about motoring and wrote articles and stories on the theme. He now undertook to drive Fanny and Ned around Europe in his formidable contraption. She was game, as usual. Louis might well have been inspired to doggerel if he could have seen his Vande-grifter perched aloft in her blowing duster and veil.

The trio had by-passed London *en route*. Old pricks still smarted and Fanny knew herself to be a centre of gossip. In February 1907 Henry James replied to a letter from Bruce Porter in San Francisco. '. . . You are vividly interesting too on the subject of Fanny Steven-son and her situation – and your picture is filled out a little by my hearing of her as in a rather obscure and inaccessible town "somewhere on the Riviera"; communicating with a friend or two in London in an elusive and deprecative fashion – withholding her address so as not to be overtaken or met with (apparently).' Then he added his notable definition: 'Poor lady, poor barbarous and merely *instinctive* lady – ah, what a tangled web we weave! I probably shall fail of seeing her, and yet, with a sneaking kindness for her that I have, shall be sorry wholly to lose her. She won't, I surmise, come to England.'

She did, but not yet. 'Passing swiftly through Hyères of haunting memory', as Nellie recorded, the party rented a pretty house in the village of St Jean-sur-Mer, with a walled garden sloping to a terrace over the sea. They spent the winter motoring and reading, the two men writing.

Field helped Fanny with the compilation of the new Pentland Edition of Stevenson's works, edited by Gosse, which was being prepared for publication in 1907. This project called her to London. So in April the trio motored north again, passing through the hills of the Cévennes where Louis had made his 'Travels with a Donkey' – the petite stubborn Modestine who had reminded him of 'a certain lady'.

In London they took lodgings for a month in Chelsea, where they welcomed the familiar circle – including Mr and Mrs Sidney Colvin. Mrs Sitwell's intolerable husband had died some years before but Colvin had only recently lost his dependent mother, so the devoted couple could afford to marry at last. He was fifty-six and she sixty-two; they were like figures in a Pre-Raphaelite painting. Sir Osbert Sitwell, a distant relation of her first husband, found her elegant even in old age, with her 'fine aquiline profile'. He wrote that she had been 'an almost professional diviner of literary talent'. Oscar Wilde described her as 'a parrot with a tongue of zinc'.

In due course Colvin was to be knighted – like Stephen, Gosse, Barrie, Conan Doyle and Balfour, and as Fanny must have felt that Louis might have been if he had lived.

For the summer she and her two young men took a Georgian country house called Fairfield at Chiddingfold, in Surrey – 'a charming old house in an old-world garden'.

Now that R.L.S.'s cronies were getting on in years they were more mellow, and swore in print that Mrs Stevenson had been second only to her husband in their affections. Katharine de Mattos came to stay, and 'the beloved Graham Balfour', and other old friends. Thirteen years before, from Vailima, Stevenson had warned James Barrie that if his wife didn't like him he'd better watch out. The test was now made, for Barrie lived at nearby Farnham and the two households often exchanged visits. He was 'a dear, shy man who had so little to say to so many, so much to say to her', wrote Nellie.

Austin and his new wife joined the house party. They were in London for the production of his latest play, *The Toymaker of Nüremburg*. They were the most accepted members of the step-clan which Louis had tried with such wistful panache to establish. Over the years they corresponded cordially with the Colvins, Mrs Jenkin, Rhoda Balfour and other intimates, and the Colvins wrote to them as 'My dearest Children' and called themselves 'your English god-parents' and even 'your English parents'. Though Austin never approached greatness, his grandmother lived to watch him become one of the best known playwrights of his generation in New York and London. After the First World War 'everyone' had heard of his hits of stage and screen, *Three Wise Fools* and *Seventh Heaven.*

Like Graham Balfour, Austin always defended his Fanny-Gran in spite of her faults, and nearly half a century later he told Michael Balfour, son of Sir Graham, that he did not wish to meet a certain eminent Stevensonian 'because of what he wrote about my grandmother'.

Modest though Fanny had become regarding her own literary ambitions, she could not quite relax her hold. Edmund Gosse recorded that in London she had consulted him about what to include in the Pentland Edition, and had again suggested *The Hanging Judge*, the play on which she had collaborated with Louis in 1887. 'On reading it', wrote Gosse, 'I determined that it should not be so included; Mrs Stevenson acquiesced, but left the play with me, in case my view should change. It has not changed. . . .' But to gratify her he conceded that it might be privately printed in 1914, though R.L.S. had never wanted his inferior work to see the light.

In mid August Fanny, Lloyd and Ned became tired of the incessant rain, and gave up Fairfield to take a long motor trip in France before returning home. *En route* to the Channel they stopped at Rye to call on Henry James. Fanny was thrilled, as she told Nellie, to 'see the house he lived in, admire his garden, drink tea in his drawing-room, and talk long and pleasantly. . . '. He was sixty-four and she sixty-seven, bulky and keen-eyed in her arty clothes with her two escorts in the chaste elegance of Lamb House. James was a gentleman almost to the point of caricature, while Fanny was perhaps never quite a lady.

'When Mrs Stevenson took Ned Field to see Henry James,' Katharine Osbourne informed Catton, 'he wrote to someone in San Francisco about it, calling Mrs Stevenson "the old scamp". The heroine of his story of "The Liar" was Mrs Stevenson.'

James was to survive Fanny by two years, but they were never to meet again.

In little more than a year San Francisco had been rebuilt from its ashes with incredible courage and enterprise. But for some time Fanny had been saying that she felt the need for a warmer and more open-air climate, even though another move widened the gap from her old life with Louis.

In recent years too, spiritualism had been taking an ever stronger hold upon her. Gelett Burgess reported in a memoir that she grew 'over-excited' at the *séances* and the sessions with the *ouija* board. Malevolent spirits beset her in her own home and, she claimed, 'poked and pinched her'. The house was so much haunted by persecuting presences that, in 1908, in Burgess's words, she 'fled to another part of California'.

As Nellie remarked, 'with the curious fatality that made everything connected with her take on some romantic aspect', the house became an enclosed convent for Carmelite nuns.

At Monte Carlo she had met an American woman who had told her of an estate called Stonehedge which was for sale at Montecito, near Santa Barbara, California. Rounded hills rose at the back, and there were fine old trees – eucalyptus and date palm. The grounds had a spring of clear water, and the house was haunted by the ghost of a beautiful countess.

Belle wrote that the place was 'in rather a neglected state', so Fanny could use her zeal in developing it. Her friends pronounced it hopeless. However, she called in a carpenter from the town and set to work, stripping and altering, and adding her eccentric burglar traps and escape hatches. In the end the red-roofed white house had 'a pleasant southern look that fitted in well with the luxuriant growth of trees and flowers. . .'.

Seven acres gave scope for her experiments. At Santa Barbara, 'where north and south meet', she was able to grow both subtropical and temperate plants. Her engineering skill went into the digging of a well and the installation of an electric pump.

Indoors there were again the much-travelled furnishings, with the St Gaudens medallion reinstated over the living-room fire. On the chimneypiece was 'a curious collection' of photographs – including Ah Fu side by side with Sir Arthur Pinero. She spent much time there in a big Victorian armchair with her haughty Siamese cat in her lap. Insistent on 'peace', she had fewer visitors, but 'people of note' sought her out.

Contrarily, for all her strong-mindedness – her feminine pioneering in smoking, cutting her hair, divorcing, and wearing divided skirts at Vailima – she did not follow the militant vogue of her times: she was not a suffragette. Certainly she herself had done well enough as a power behind the throne. Once in California when Belle was a speaker at a meeting for women's votes, Fanny sat looking on with mingled pride and disapproval. 'Yet', recorded Nellie, 'after the suffrage was granted to women in California, her family was amused to see her go to the polls and vote and carefully advise the men employed on her place concerning their ballots.' Trust the Vandegrifter to advise her retainers.

Belle was often with her mother, but Lloyd spent much of his time in New York where – 'clubbable', in Gosse's word, like his stepfather – he was an habitué of the Lambs Club. Ned Field was a resident of Stonehedge. Fanny enjoyed his outdoor bent and sometimes went with him for a day's fishing.

In the last two or three years Field had been sliding from journalism into the writing of plays, short stories and novels, though he was not yet well known. In the old cherished way he discussed his scripts with Fanny. His talent remained trivial, but plainly she had high hopes and zest.

He was first noticed in 1910 as a minor playwright of light farces, under his middle name of Salisbury Field – 'as he calls himself now', sniffed Katharine Osbourne to Catton. His plays had such titles as *Good Intentions, Twin Beds, The Rented Earl* and the long-running *Wedding Bells* in 1919. '. . . a few funny lines . . . a little sweet froth to pass the time', grudgingly conceded Katharine. '. . . and so he has made some money at last; it puts him in a more dignified position than living solely on Louis Stevenson's money.'

On the other hand his influence in his father's business had extended to the chameleon Fanny. She, as Catton wrote with a Scots inflection to Lord Guthrie, had 'acquired a good deal of real estate in California and seemed to be making a hobby of "proputty, proputty".'

In 1909 a painful fracas was made public. Mrs Lloyd Osbourne sued for legal separation from her husband. She demanded three hundred dollars a month for the support of herself and the children, declaring that Lloyd earned five hundred dollars a month from his writings. He replied that with the ups and downs of authorship he had had no income for a year and had been forced to borrow money from his mother for living expenses.

In November Katharine retaliated so far as to make a statement to the press. She announced that she and her husband had been parted for many years, and it was his mother who had broken up the marriage. She had tried to live at peace with Mrs Stevenson but found it impossible. Her husband had gone to New York, and she, being penniless, had been forced to live in her mother-in-law's house, though they never spoke to each other. Mrs Stevenson was a woman 'of a dominating temper, and wanted to rule every one near her'. She had 'widened the breach' between the couple, and 'had urged me more than once to get a divorce'. At length Mrs Osbourne had gone to New York. After 'trying to awaken my husband from his indifference', she had taken her sons to live in Italy, and had finally obtained a judicial separation.

The press announcement was copied in many papers in America, Britain and elsewhere, to Fanny's stinging humiliation. 'I have never dared to say anything to Mrs Stevenson about her daughter-in-law since she and her husband parted', Catton confided to Guthrie several years later.

'. . . So I went off and lived in Italy,' Katharine was still harping to Gosse long afterwards, 'and let Belle and Tamaitai blame me, all this for the sake of Stevenson's memory. . . Sometimes I wasn't given any money at all . . .' In reciting her grievances she had not given her mother-in-law credit for eventually providing her with a house in California as well as an allowance. Later Katharine sold the house and used the capital.

Lloyd had not lost his appreciation of pretty faces and for years Katharine sneered about his philandering. But meanwhile she could not be persuaded to give him a full divorce as he and his mother wished. Fanny, not cured of her matchmaking, had already chosen Katharine's successor. She had taken to her heart a young protégée of charm and character, a girl named Ethel Head who lived at Gilroy near Fanny's ranch – which she eventually willed to her. Ethel in turn adored her and became part of the matriarchal entourage. 'She either cared for people or she didn't', Ethel explained later. Acquaintances in California said that 'Fanny "pushed" her at Lloyd at the time of his final trouble and separation from Katharine'.

'Finally as a last stroke', Katharine reminisced to Catton, 'to try to break my heart completely, Tamaitai and Belle conceived a plan to take the boys from me. Only then I got a divorce so the courts would give the boys to me. Absolutely.'

However, it was some years after the separation before she could be induced to sue for the decree *nisi*. In 1914 just after Fanny's death, Mrs Colvin wrote to Austin and Mary Strong, '. . . Lloyd was here a month or two ago with a young "wife" . . . [Is] he divorced and married?' And more than two years later she was still asking them '. . . about Lloyd's divorce, has it *really* taken place and is he married again?'

By 1916, yes. His second match, to Ethel, was much better than his first, though there were no children.

Katharine maintained to Gosse that the boys 'are mine, trained and educated by me, and I have had all the care, work and anxiety. . . . They hardly know their father. He is a stranger to them . . .', she added inaccurately. Several times her letters to Catton contained entries about getting some of 'R.L.S.'s money' out of Lloyd for them. Both boys turned out well.

As a fellow martyr of Stevenson, Katharine claimed to know more of him than anyone else. She gave a number of lectures and wrote some articles about him. In 1911 a Chicago publisher printed

Robert Louis Stevenson in California by Katharine Durham Osbourne, and began to release the book. It was so libellous towards her mother-in-law that Fanny, supported by Scribner's, managed to have the first edition suppressed. Only four copies are believed to exist.

In 1912, when Fanny was sending Henley's widow the requested packet of his letters, she warned Mrs Henley not to show any of them to Lloyd's wife, who 'says that she is going to write a scandalous life of Louis in which she means to attack me most viciously'.

In 1922 the publisher John Howell of San Francisco announced the forthcoming book, *The Marriage of Robert Louis Stevenson*, by Katharine Durham Osbourne. But then she wrote from New York to Catton: '. . . I have accepted money from Lloyd (for Alan and Louis) not to publish my book and I felt it was right. . . .'

In public Fanny had always maintained a haughty silence about the vendetta with Katharine, but she secretly waited for vengeance. On 2nd November 1912 she made what was to be her last will and testament. She named her children Isobel and Lloyd as executors and principal heirs. Other beneficiaries included Louis Sanchez, Austin Strong, Edward Salisbury Field, Ethel Head, Alan and Wolfert [Louis] Osbourne, and Katharine Durham Osbourne.

The bequest to the last-named stated: 'To Katharine Durham Osbourne, of incredible ferocity, who lived on my bounty for many years, at the same time pursuing me with malicious slander, I leave five dollars.'

When the will was made public some fifteen months later on the death of the testatrix, the 'remarkable passage' and 'bitter words' were headlined in many lands. '£1 LEGACY TO SON'S WIFE', proclaimed *The Pall Mall Gazette*, to which R.L.S. had once been an impoverished contributor. 'We have been much grieved and perplexed'. wrote Mrs Colvin to the young Strongs, 'with all that we have seen in the papers about Tamaitai's will lately & should much like to know the truth about it. . . .'

Katharine predictably went up in smoke with the assertion that her mother-in-law had 'cut the boys out of her will while leaving valuable property to Ned Field and Ethel Head'.

Fanny's estate was valued at $120,500. The bulk was bequeathed to Belle, with instructions to pay Lloyd three hundred dollars a month for life. She also left Belle her furniture, silver, pictures, clothing, furs and jewellery. It was not unnatural that the mother should will most of her own property to her daughter, since Lloyd and his family were provided for by the Thomas and Louis Stevenson estates which Lloyd inherited at the termination of Fanny's life interest. The lucrative R.L.S. royalties would be his further income and his heirs' for many decades. Fanny was also leaving him – with Ethel – the Vanumanutagi ranch at Gilroy. Her own home at Stonehedge went to Belle, who had shared it. The bequest of the nearby property to Ned Field apparently followed the real estate investments which she had made through his family firm. The small legacies to her three grandsons hardly meant that she had 'disinherited' two of them as Katharine claimed.

All the same, Helen Purdy of Berkeley spoke for many others when she said she wished Mrs Stevenson had not written that paragraph about Katharine Osbourne.

Chapter IX
'A fable as strange and romantic as one of his own'

'She looked like a witch when she was old', wrote Katharine Osbourne of her mother-in-law to George Hellman, 'and walked with a cane like a crone.'

Said Nellie: 'All who think of her, even in her last days, must have a picture in their minds of the dainty, lacy, silken prettiness in which she sat enshrined. She was pretty as a young woman, but as she grew older she was beautiful. . . . She kept her spirit young to the last, so that no one could ever think of her as an old woman, and young people always enjoyed her company.'

Mr Catton, visiting Santa Barbara, spent a day with Fanny and Belle and assured Lord Guthrie that he found them 'well and stout, the elder lady somewhat lame but as "soople" in her wits as ever'.

She had been growing more humble. 'With this note,' she had written to Scribner in 1910, 'I send the introduction to Father

Damien. . . . I know this thing is about as bad as anything can be. . . . If, however, it is beyond the pale, write and tell me, please, and I will try once again. Louis's work was so mixed up with his home life that it is hard to see just where to draw the line between telling enough and yet not too much. I dislike extremely drawing aside the veil to let the public gaze intimately where they have no right to look at all. . . .'

Insistent on being 'different' and therefore conspicuous, she was always torn between contrary desires for deference and for privacy.

An edition of more Stevenson correspondence was being compiled, and Colvin asked Henry James whether it should include Louis's letter to him about a quarrel with Fanny. 'Fanny S. will be a bigger fool than I ever took her for', replied the Master, 'if she resents the lively description of their domestic broil. It helps to commemorate her and makes her interesting – and just so, I feel sure, she will rejoice.'

Fanny still travelled – several times to New York, and sometimes to the warmth of Mexico. She always felt the old *élan* when she set out on a journey. Compared with most elderly widows she was still a dynamo.

Once at the Rancho El Sausal her party had found the cottage looted and left in 'a dreary mess' by duck hunters, and the others would have gone away in despair. But not so the Forty-niner, who marshalled them all in scrubbing, carpentering, cooking, and chasing out a swarm of bees.

In March 1910 she had her seventieth birthday and her health was beginning to crack. Nevertheless she told Nellie that she 'would rather go to the well and be broken than be preserved on a dusty shelf'. So she revisited the Mexico City region, accompanied by Belle, Ned Field and her nephew Louis Sanchez, for whom she found a good job as a mining engineer. The altitude of Mexico City was too high for her heart, but she liked to sit beside the canal with the flower-boats by day and the tinkle of guitars on moonlit nights. She and Belle haunted 'queer old shops' and loaded themselves more than ever with barbaric jewellery from the state-run pawnshop where fine ladies had left their treasures.

In contrast to this exhibitionism her hatred of newspaper gossip had become an increasing phobia. Though she had pensioned Jules Simoneau and paid for his burial and his wife's tomb, a reporter wrote that she had neglected her husband's old friend and let him wither away in want in his last years. She was too proud and prejudiced to set the record straight.

From Scotland she received word from Lord Guthrie that Louis's old nurse had had a fall which broke her hip at the age of ninety-two. Through the years Fanny had often written to Cummy and had amply added to the original pension settled on her by Thomas Stevenson. A few months earlier she had 'cordially agreed' to make a further annual payment at Lord Guthrie's suggestion. As soon as his letter told her of the accident she sent him a cable, giving him *carte blanche* for Cummy's benefit. A few weeks later Cummy died. Fanny ordered a grand wreath to be placed on the coffin, and bore the cost of the last illness, the funeral and the handsome tombstone.

She began to feel a great weariness clouding her old vitality. It was in June 1913 that she wrote to Scribner her much-derided statement that she was really a 'clinging vine' and had spent her life caring for others when she yearned to be taken care of – 'but fate still seems against me'. Even Nellie conceded, 'Nevertheless, I truly believe she enjoyed being the head of her clan, the fairy godmother, the chieftainess of her family, to whom all came for help and counsel.'

She found the days long and lonely, and often consoled herself with the game of solitaire with which she had amused Louis while he lay mute.

In her household the loyal Mary had married an Irish compatriot and left Fanny's employ, but she was now served by another devoted maid, Agnes Crowley.

She had been threatened by asthma, so in November 1913 she went with Agnes to the desert health resort of Palm Springs. The dry clear air was a tonic, and when she came home Nellie said that 'all the fears of her friends and family were lulled'.

She 'consented' to shape into book form the notes on the voyage of the *Janet Nicholl* which she had made chiefly for Louis's guidance – though he hardly used them. 'The little book, however dull it may seem to others, can boast of at least one reader', she wrote in the Preface, and – seasick landlubber though she had been – she added the Fannyish superlative, 'for I have gone over this record of perhaps the happiest period of my life with thrilling interest'. *The Cruise of the Janet Nichol* – misspelt with one *l* – was her last piece of writing.

She finished reading the proofs a few days before she died, and the book was published some months afterwards.

In mid February 1914, with golden acacia and blossoming orchards in California, a week of 'wild storm' beat upon the south-west. For Fanny there was always a dramatic stage set, even the last. On 18th February, a few weeks before her seventy-fourth birthday, Nellie received the following letter from the faithful maid Agnes:

'My dear Mrs Sanchez:

'We are a very sad little household – we are all heart-broken, to think our dear little Madam has gone away never to return. It seems too awful, and just when she was enjoying everything. We were home from Palm Springs just one week when she was taken away from us – but you can console yourself by thinking that she was surrounded by love and devotion. She was not sick and did not suffer. Tuesday evening, 17th February, she felt well and read her magazines until nine o'clock, and Mr Field played cards with her till 10.30. Then she retired. The next morning I went in to attend to her as usual, and there was my dear little Madam lying unconscious. I thought at first she was in a faint, and I quickly ran for Mr Field; he jumped up and put on his bathrobe and went to her while I called Dr Hurst. It took the doctor about seven minutes to get here, and as soon as he saw her he said it was a stroke, but he seemed to be hopeful and thought he could pull her through. He put an ice pack on her head and gave her an injection in the arm and oxygen to inhale, and she seemed to begin to breathe natural, and we all hoped, but it was in vain. She never regained consciousness, and at two o'clock she just stopped breathing, so you see she did not suffer. But oh Mrs Sanchez, we all seemed so helpless – we all loved her so and yet could do nothing. Dr Hurst worked hard from 8.30 till two o'clock, and when the end came he cried like a little child, for he loved Mrs Stevenson very much. It was an awful blow to us all – it was so sudden. The place will never seem the same to William and me, for we loved our little Madam dearly, and it was a pleasure to do anything for her – she was always so gentle and sweet. I adored her from the first time I ever saw her, and will always consider it the greatest pleasure of my life to have had the privilege of waiting upon her.

I remain very affectionately,

Agnes Crowley.'

The coincidence that would most have awed Fanny with her occult sense of destiny was the fact that she, like Louis, died suddenly from a cerebral haemorrhage.

Born in the March winds, her family considered it symbolic that she should go amid the gales – the Stormy Petrel. The rains pounded down for several days with railroad washouts for hundreds of miles, so that Lloyd was delayed in travelling from New York to the funeral.

When he arrived, his mother's coffin was removed to San Francisco, where a simple ceremony was held for her relatives and a few close friends. 'On her bier red roses, typical of her own warm nature, were heaped in masses', wrote Nellie. The family was touched when her Japanese gardener appeared with an elegant wreath of flowers from her own planting.

According to her wish, her body was cremated, the ashes later to be taken to Samoa to lie on the mountain top beside Louis's grave.

After her death even the haughty Siamese cat moped, refused food and soon died. Belle was kept busy for weeks answering the letters of condolence which piled up from all over the world.

'To say that I miss her', wrote Austin, 'means nothing. Why, it is as if an Era had passed into oblivion. She was so much the Chief of us all, the Ruling Power. God rest her soul!'

Before Fanny's burial wish could be fulfilled, there occurred an event of a Proustian complexity. On 29th August 1914, Belle married Edward Salisbury Field.

She was fifty-six and he about a score of years younger. Though she had grown dumpy like her mother, she still had her wonderful eyes, her warm smile and luxuriant hair, her vivacity, her exotic style of dress. She had had many admirers. It is interesting to speculate as to why this union, if it were to happen at all, did not take place long before – in Fanny's lifetime. The news must have set Henry James pacing up and down his Chelsea drawing-room. Still more, one longs to know what Louis – and above all, Fanny herself – would have made of it.

Even Katharine Osbourne conceded that 'the marriage was a great success. . .', so it must have been agreeable indeed. (Oddly, the first marriages of Fanny and both her children were failures, while the second round went well.) As the mother and daughter had lived so long in Louis's shadow, now Belle and Ned went on in Fanny's.

More than once in the coming years Belle's husband and son – nearly the same age – had plays running on Broadway at the same time. But Field gradually gave up writing plays and turned to film scripts in the growing sphere of Hollywood. Described as a 'playwright and real estate operator', the latter role led him to yet another Proustian turn in the triangular story of mother, daughter and posthumous son-in-law. Oil was struck on some of his land, and little Isobel Osbourne – mining-camp child, struggling artist, and poor relation of R.L.S. – became a very rich woman, the possessor of three houses and the companion of millionaires. Field died in September 1936 in his sleep after a convivial dinner party to celebrate her birthday. She lived on in an aura of memories, memoirs and interviews until 1953, her ninety-fifth year, surviving Lloyd and Austin.

Not many months after Fanny's death, great masses of Stevenson's papers, left at Stonehedge, were offered by her children at successive sales: rough notes and unfinished or rejected manuscripts which she had thought unsuitable for release, with her husband's discrimination in mind.

Colvin was a culprit too. In December 1919 Helen Purdy of Berkeley wrote to Catton: 'How *could* Sidney Colvin sell those Stevenson letters? I did not expect much better of Isobel Strong Field and Lloyd Osbourne. . . . It seems as if those most closely connected with R.L.S. hastened to make all they could from the connection. Only poor old Jules Simoneau held onto his treasures, and *he* needed the money most.'

Meanwhile, with the Great War in Europe, and Samoa latterly a German possession, it had not been until the late spring of 1915 that Belle and her new husband could sail with Fanny's ashes for Apia. ('. . . that habit of freighting the dead has something repulsive to me', murmured Catton to Guthrie.)

Early in the war the New Zealand Expeditionary Forces had occupied the island of Upolu, and the Union Jack was again flying over Vailima as Government House for the British. The Administrator, Colonel Logan, and his wife came out by boat to meet the steamer and took the Fields up the hill to stay as their guests.

'I felt like a person in a dream', wrote Belle, 'as we walked over the house – the same and yet changed out of all recognition.' Many of the great trees were gone, the redwood-panelled hall was painted white, bathrooms had been installed and the waterfall pool was functional with a dam and cement flooring.

By a queer repetition for the Stormy Petrel the day before the service was windy, rainy and foreboding. But in the night the sky cleared and 22nd June was a perfect day, sunny but cool, like that of Louis's funeral.

Only one of the Vailima household was left by 'time and wars' – Mitaele, the youngest, now the grey-haired father of nine children.

The little bronze case containing Fanny's ashes, wrapped in an exquisite mat, had been laid on a table in a room off the veranda. From stone ovens behind the scenes came the aromas of the sumptuous native dishes being prepared for the feast. Early in the morning the Samoan guests began to appear, including forty-odd chiefs. Soon the casket was hidden under masses of brilliant flowers. Half-caste and white friends arrived, including three Sacred Heart nuns who knelt to say a prayer for their old benefactor and hostess.

At nine o'clock the cortège started the steep climb to the summit. 'The procession,' wrote Belle, 'very picturesque in white clothing and wreaths of flowers, wound slowly up the mountainside in a zigzag path under the forest trees. Overhead the branches met in a leafy roof, and on each side of the narrow path the jungle closed in, thick, lush, and green. . . .'

When the cortège reached the top the casket was laid on the base of the tomb and covered with fine mats and flowers. Colonel Logan read the service and a Samoan pastor made an eloquent speech. Then the mats were removed and the small bronze case was fitted in and cemented over by the same half-caste mason who had built the tomb for Louis.

An old chief said to Belle in his own tongue, 'Tusitala is happy now. His true love has come back to him.'

Belle and her husband had brought to the flower-massed tomb a large bronze tablet for Fanny, to match the one which marked the fine slim bones of Louis Stevenson. Above the ashes which were all that was left of the intense little woman, the tablet bore the inscription:

F. V. de G. S.
Aolele

– and a quatrain from Louis's poem to her:

Teacher, tender, comrade, wife,
A fellow-farer true through life,
Heart whole and soul free,
The August Father gave to me.

Louis's tablet still showed at the upper corners the thistle for Scotland and the hibiscus for Samoa. An hibiscus had been obvious for Fanny's tablet too – but what second flower? After long hesitation, Belle had had the perfect inspiration for her mother and Stevenson's wife: the tiger lily.

So here too lay Fanny Stevenson, a score of years after her husband – here she lay where she longed to be. Like Louis, she would have been pleased with the splendid Samoan funeral and feast, and the shared resting-place 'under the wide and starry sky'. A sterile marriage, without children, but a life together which was, and is, a legend. 'A fable as strange and romantic as one of his own', in the echo of Henry James.

Should Stevenson have married Fanny? Yes and No, but on the whole, Yes. Probably it is true that her care kept him alive to write. Even her enemies have conceded her physical attraction for a highly sexed man younger than herself; but with his invalidism and her neurosis, the bodily expression must have been sublimated by a sense of vitality and continual interest. The infinite variety of Fanny was absorbing to Stevenson, keeping him most of the time curious, amused and tender. His books must owe more to her dynamic insight than we can know, far more, in fact, than to her interference. Part of his growth was Fanny's. '*Sex and x*' was the formula of the magnetism between them – the *x* standing for the originality, the individuality which made their affinity. The marriage was indeed a passionate companionship.

It is fascinating to wonder what major works might have emerged if it had been the frail Louis who had survived his wife by twenty years, and if he had been able – deeply, wryly, affectionately – to launch out and develop his women characters and their full relationships with the men in his novels.

Above all, the imagination stumbles at what could have happened if – tongue in cheek and hand on heart, in a true Stevenson gesture – he had ventured to put into fiction the most powerful and contradictory character, male or female, he can ever have known intimately in his life: his most violent friend, his wife.

Bibliography

Especially valuable:
Sanchez, Nellie Van de Grift (sister), *The Life of Mrs Robert Louis Stevenson.* Chatto & Windus, London, 1920.
Field, Isobel Osbourne Strong (daughter), *This Life I've Loved.* Michael Joseph, London, 1937.
Furnas, J. C., *Voyage to Windward* (the best biography of Robert Louis Stevenson). Faber & Faber, London, 1952.
Balfour, Graham, *The Life of Robert Louis Stevenson* (official biography). 2 vols., Methuen, London, 1901.
Stevenson, Robert Louis, *Works* (including letters), 35 vols., with Prefaces by Mrs R. L. Stevenson, Lloyd Osbourne and Sir Sidney Colvin. Tusitala Edition, Heinemann, London, 1923-4.
Stevenson, Robert Louis, *Works* (including letters), 26 vols., ed. Lloyd Osbourne, with Notes by Mrs R. L. Stevenson. Vailima Edition, Heinemann, London, 1922-3.

Adams, Henry, *Letters*, 2 vols., Constable, London, 1930.
Adcock, A. St. J., ed., *Robert Louis Stevenson – His Work and His Personality.* Hodder & Stoughton, London, 1924.
Aldington, Richard, *Portrait of a Rebel, Robert Louis Stevenson.* Evans, London, 1957.
Allen, Maryland, 'South Sea Memories of Robert Louis Stevenson',

The Bookman, New York, August, 1916.

Asquith, Margot, *Autobiography*, 2 vols. Butterworth, London, 1920.

Baildon, H. B., *Robert Louis Stevenson*. Chatto & Windus, London, 1901.

Baker, Ray Jerome, *Honolulu Then and Now*. Baker, Honolulu, 1941.

Balfour, Michael, 'How the Biography of Robert Louis Stevenson Came to Be Written', *The Times Literary Supplement*, London, 15th and 22nd January 1960.

Bay, J. C. B., *Echoes of Robert Louis Stevenson*. London, 1920.

Benson, E. F., *As We Were*. Longmans, London, 1930.

Black, Margaret Moyes, *Robert Louis Stevenson*. Famous Scots Series, Oliphant Anderson & Ferrier, Edinburgh and London, 1899.

Boodle, Adelaide A., *R.L.S. and His Sine Qua Non*. Murray, London, 1926.

Booth, Prof. Bradford A., 'The Vailima Letters of Robert Louis Stevenson', *Harvard Library Bulletin*, Cambridge, Mass., April, 1967.

Brown, George E., *A Book of Robert Louis Stevenson*. Methuen, London, n.d.

Brown, Horatio F., *John Addington Symonds*. Smith, Elder & Co., London, 1903.

Burgess, Gelett, 'An Interview with Mrs. Robert Louis Stevenson', *The Bookman*, New York, September 1898.

Burlingame, Roger, *Of Making Many Books*. Scribner, New York, 1946.

Butcher, Lady Alice Mary, *Memories of George Meredith*. London, 1919.

Charteris, Evan, *John Singer Sargent*. Heinemann, London, 1927.

Charteris, Evan, *The Life and Letters of Sir Edmund Gosse*. Heinemann, London, 1931.

Chesterton, G. K., *Robert Louis Stevenson*. Hodder & Stoughton, London, 1927.

Clare, Maurice, *A Day with Robert Louis Stevenson*. Hodder & Stoughton, London, n.d.

Colvin, Sir Sidney, *Memories and Notes of Persons and Places, 1852–1912*. Arnold, London, 1921.

Connell, John, *W. E. Henley*. Constable, London, 1949.

Cooper, Lettice, *Robert Louis Stevenson*. English Novelists Series, Home & Van Thal, London, 1947.

Daiches, David, *Robert Louis Stevenson*. Maclennan, Glasgow, 1947.

Dark, Sidney, *Robert Louis Stevenson*. Hodder, London, n.d.

Doyle, Sir Arthur Conan, *Through the Magic Door*. Smith, Elder & Co., London, 1907.

Edinburgh Public Library, *Catalogue of the Robert Louis Stevenson Collection*, Edinburgh, 1950.

Ellison, Joseph W., *Tusitala of the South Seas: The Story of Robert Louis Stevenson's Life in the South Pacific*. Hastings House, New York, 1953.

Elwin, Malcolm, *Old Gods Falling*. Collins, London, 1939.

Elwin, Malcolm, *The Strange Case of Robert Louis Stevenson*. Macdonald, London, 1950.

Fraser, Marie, *In Stevenson's Samoa*. Smith, Elder & Co., London, 1895.

Furnas, J. C., *Anatomy of Paradise*. Gollancz, London, 1950.

Gilder, Richard Watson, *Letters*. Constable, London, 1916.

Gosse, Edmund, *Critical Kitkats*. Heinemann, London, 1896.

Gosse, Edmund, *Biographical Notes on the Writings of Robert Louis Stevenson*. Privately printed, London, 1908.

Green, Roger Lancelyn, *Stevenson in Search of a Madonna*. English Associates, Essays and Studies, Murray, London, 1950.

Guthrie, C. J. (Lord), *Robert Louis Stevenson*. Green & Son, Edinburgh, 1920.

Gwynn, Stephen, *Robert Louis Stevenson*. English Men of Letters Series, Macmillan, London, 1939.

Hamilton, Clayton, *On The Trail of Stevenson*. Hodder & Stoughton, London, 1915.

Hammerton, John, *Stevensoniana*. Grant, Edinburgh, 1910.

Hart, James D., ed., *From Scotland to Silverado, Robert Louis Stevenson* (selections), with Notes and Introduction by Mr Hart. Harvard University Press, Cambridge, Mass., 1966.

Hassall, Christopher, *Edward Marsh, A Biography*. Longmans Green, London, 1959.

Hellman, George S., *The True Stevenson*. Little, Brown, Boston, 1925.

Hellman, George S., *Lanes of Memory*. Knopf, New York, 1927.

Hinkley, Laura L., *The Stevensons: Louis and Fanny*. Hastings House, New York, 1950.

Hubbard, Elbert, *Little Journeys to the Homes of English Authors*. Putnam, London, 1903.

Issler, Anne Roller, *Stevenson at Silverado*. Caxton, Caldwell, Idaho, 1939.

Issler, Anne Roller, *Happier for His Presence*. Stanford University Press, 1949.

Issler, Anne Roller, 'Robert Louis Stevenson in Monterey', *Pacific Historical Review*, Los Angeles, August 1965.

James, Alice, *Diary*, ed. Leon Edel. Hart-Davis, London, 1965.

James, Henry, *Partial Portraits*. Macmillan, London, 1888.

James, Henry, *Letters*, ed. Percy Lubbock. 2 vols., Macmillan, London, 1920.

James, Henry, and Stevenson, Robert Louis, *Letters.*, ed. Janet Adam Smith. Hart-Davis, London, 1948.

Japp, Alexander H., *Robert Louis Stevenson*. Werner Laurie, London, 1905.

Jersey, Countess of (M. E. Villiers), *Fifty-One Years of Victorian Life*. Murray, London, 1922.

Johnstone, Arthur, *Recollections of Robert Louis Stevenson in the Pacific*. Chatto & Windus, London, 1905.

Kelman, John, Jr., *The Faith of Robert Louis Stevenson*. Edinburgh, 1903.

Lang, Andrew, *Adventures Among Books*. Longmans Green, London, 1905.

Lawson, M. S., *On the Bat's Back: The Story of Stevenson*. Lutterworth, London, 1950.

Le Gallienne, Richard, *The Romantic Nineties*. Putnam, London, 1925.

Leslie, Mrs Shane (née Marjorie Ide), *Girlhood in the Pacific*. Macdonald, London, n.d.

Lockett, W. G., *Robert Louis Stevenson at Davos*. Hurst & Blackett, London, n.d.

Low, Will H., *A Chronicle of Friendships, 1873–1900*. Hodder & Stoughton, London, 1908.

Lucas, E. V., *The Colvins and Their Friends*. Methuen, London, 1928.

McKay, George L., compiler, *A Stevenson Library: Catalogue of the Edwin J. Beinecke Collection*. 6 vols. Yale University Press, 1951, et seq.

Mackay, Margaret, *Sharon (Honolulu in the 1880s)*. John Day, New York, 1948.

McClure, S. S., *Autobiography*. Murray, London, 1914.

Maitland, F. W., *Life and Letters of Leslie Stephen*. London, 1904.

Masson, Flora, *Victorians All*. Chambers, London and Edinburgh, 1931.

Masson, Rosaline, *The Life of Robert Louis Stevenson*. Chambers, London and Edinburgh, 1923.

Masson, Rosaline, *Poets, Patriots and Lovers*, Clarke, London, 1933.

Masson, Rosaline (ed.), and others, *I Can Remember R. L. Stevenson*. Chambers, London and Edinburgh, 1925.

Meredith, George, *Letters*. 2 vols., Constable, London, 1912.

Safroni-Middleton, A., 'With R.L.S. in Old Samoa', *The Journal* of The Robert Louis Stevenson Club. London, May 1950.

Moors, Harry J., *With Stevenson in Samoa*. Fisher Unwin, London, 1910.

Osbourne, Alan, A Letter to the Editor of *The Times Literary Supplement* (about the writing of the official biography of R. L. Stevenson), London, 25th March 1960.

Osbourne, Lloyd, *Some Letters of Robert Louis Stevenson*. Methuen, London, 1914.

Osbourne, Lloyd, *An Intimate Portrait of Robert Louis Stevenson*. Scribner, New York, 1924.

Osbourne, Lloyd, and Strong, Isobel, *Memories of Vailima*. Scribner, New York, 1902.

Prideaux, Col. W. F., C.S.I., *A Bibliography of the Works of Robert Louis Stevenson*. Revised edition, Hollings, London, 1917.

Prideaux, Col. W. F., C.S.I., *Stevenson at Hyères*. Privately printed, 1912.

Raleigh, Professor Sir Walter, *Robert Louis Stevenson*. Arnold, London, 1895.

Rosenbach, A. S. W., *Catalogue of the Robert Louis Stevenson Collection in the Widener Library*, Harvard University. Privately printed, 1913.

Ryan, J. Tighe, 'A Gossip about Robert Louis Stevenson', *The Antipodean*, Sydney, 1894.

Simpson, Eve Blantyre, *Robert Louis Stevenson*. Spirit of the Age Series, Luce, London, 1906.

Simpson, Eve Blantyre, *The Robert Louis Stevenson Originals*. Foulis, Edinburgh, 1912.

Simpson, Eve Blantyre, *Robert Louis Stevenson's Edinburgh Days*. Hodder & Stoughton, London, 1914.

Slocum, Captain Joshua, *Sailing Alone Around the World*. Low, 1900.

Smith, Janet Adam, *R. L. Stevenson*. Great Lives Series, Duckworth, London, 1937.

Stephen, Sir Leslie, *Studies of a Biographer*. 4 vols., Duckworth, London, 1898–1902.

Stern, G. B., *No Son of Mine*. Cassell, London, 1948.

Stern, G. B., *He Wrote Treasure Island*. Heinemann, London, 1954.

Steuart, John A., *Robert Louis Stevenson: Man and Writer*. 2 vols., Low, London, 1924.

Steuart, John A., *The Cap of Youth: The Love Romance of Robert Louis Stevenson*. Low, London, 1927.

Stevenson, Fanny Van de Grift (Mrs R. L.), *Cruise of the Janet Nichol among the South Sea Islands, A Diary*. Chatto & Windus, London, 1915.

Stevenson, Fanny Van de Grift, and Robert Louis, *Our Samoan Adventure*, ed. Charles Neider. Weidenfeld & Nicolson, London, 1956.

Stevenson, Fanny Van de Grift, 'Some Letters of Mrs R. L. Stevenson and One from Henry James', with a commentary by Sidney Colvin. *The Empire Review*, London, March–April, 1924.

Stevenson, Fanny Van de Grift, 'More Letters of Mrs. Robert Louis Stevenson', ed. Sidney Colvin. *Scribner's* magazine, New York, April, 1924.

Stevenson, Margaret Isabella Balfour, *From Saranac to the Marquesas and Beyond*. Methuen, London, 1903.

Stevenson, Margaret Isabella Balfour, *Letters from Samoa*. Methuen, London, 1906.

Stevenson, Robert Louis, *Collected Poems*, ed. Janet Adam Smith. Hart-Davis, London, 1950.

Stevenson, Robert Louis, 'In the Latin Quarter – I, A Ball at Mr Elsinare's', from *London* magazine, 10th February 1877, reprinted in *The Stevensonian*, The Journal of the Robert Louis Stevenson Club (London), ed. Ernest J. Mehew.

Stevenson, Robert Louis, *Memories and Portraits*. Methuen, London, 1898.

Stevenson, Robert Louis, *Letters from Vailima to Sidney Colvin*, ed. Sidney Colvin. Methuen, London, 1896.

Stevenson, Robert Louis, *Letters to His Family and Friends*, ed. Sidney Colvin. Methuen, London, 1899.

Stevenson, Robert Louis, *Letters to Charles Baxter*, ed. Clement Shorter. Privately printed, London, 1915.

Stevenson, Robert Louis, *Letters to Charles Baxter*, ed. De Lancey Ferguson and Marshall Waingrow. Oxford University Press, 1956.

Stevenson, Robert Louis, *Prayers at Vailima*, Introduction by Mrs Stevenson. Methuen, London, 1904.

Stevenson, Robert Louis, *Some Letters*, ed. Lloyd Osbourne. Methuen, London, 1914.

Stevenson, Robert Louis, and Fanny, *The Hanging Judge*, a play, with Introduction by Edmund Gosse. Privately printed, London, 1914.

Strong, Austin, 'His Oceanic Majesty's Goldfish', *The Atlantic Monthly*. Boston, May 1944.

Strong, Austin, 'The Most Unforgettable Character I've Met', *The Reader's Digest*, Pleasantville, N.Y. March, 1946.

Strong, Isobel, *Robert Louis Stevenson*. Little Books on Great Writers, Series, London, 1910.

Swinnerton, Frank, *Robert Louis Stevenson*, A Critical Study. Secker, London, 1914.

Symonds, John Addington, *Letters and Papers*, ed. Horatio F. Brown. Murray, London, 1923.

Symonds, John Addington, *Our Life in the Swiss Highlands*. Black, London, 1907.

Symonds, John Addington, *Recollections of a Happy Life*. Black, London, 1892.

Symonds, John Addington, *Some Further Recollections of a Happy Life*. Black, London, 1893.

Taylor, Albert P., *Under Hawaiian Skies*. Advertiser Publishing Co., Honolulu, 1926.
Taylor, Una, *Guests and Memories: Annals of a Seaside Villa*. Oxford University Press, 1924.
Thompson, Francis, *The Real Robert Louis Stevenson*, ed. Terence L. Connolly. New York University Publishers, 1959.

Index

374   Index